Language and Context
THE ACQUISITION OF PRAGMATICS

LANGUAGE, THOUGHT, AND CULTURE: *Advances in the Study of Cognition*

Under the Editorship of: E. A. HAMMEL

DEPARTMENT OF ANTHROPOLOGY
UNIVERSITY OF CALIFORNIA
BERKELEY

In preparation

Language and Context

THE ACQUISITION OF PRAGMATICS

ELIZABETH BATES

Department of Psychology
University of Colorado
Boulder, Colorado

ACADEMIC PRESS New York San Francisco London
A Subsidiary of Harcourt Brace Jovanovich, Publishers

ACADEMIC PRESS, INC.
111 Fifth Avenue, New York, New York 10003

United Kingdom Edition published by
ACADEMIC PRESS, INC. (LONDON) LTD.
24/28 Oval Road, London NW1

Library of Congress Cataloging in Publication Data

Bates, Elizabeth.
 Language and context.

 (Language, thought, and culture series)
 Bibliography: p.
 1.   Children–Language.   2.   Pragmatics.
3.   Psycholinguistics.   I.   Title.
P118.B3   401'.9   75-40605
ISBN 0–12–081550–8

PRINTED IN THE UNITED STATES OF AMERICA

81 82   9 8 7 6 5 4

*In loving memory
of my father,
Ferdinand Charles Bates*

Contents

Preface

In all revolutions a price is paid for progress. In the 1960s Chomsky's theory of transformational grammar brought about what many view as a scientific revolution in psychology. The only "price" for unquestionable advances in psycholinguistic research seemed to be the loss of a few tiresome behaviorist notions that we could do without anyway. However, in child language research in particular there was another, hidden cost. Chomsky's influence brought about a concentration on formal aspects of syntax and on language as a unique, species-specific system that bears no apparent relation to the development of perception, cognition, social interaction, or any of the other nonlinguistic capacities of the human child. Indeed, it was not altogether clear in the mid-1960s if language had very much to do with communication. In short, the study of child language was—at least temporarily—cut off in theory and method from the rest of developmental psychology.

This volume represents a growing effort in psycholinguistics to correct the imbalance of the 1960s and early 1970s and to restore the connections between language and the context in which language is acquired. The book centers on the acquisition of pragmatics or the use of language in context. For years pragmatics has been viewed as the "soft underbelly" of formal linguistic theory—the border area within which the correct use of language absolutely requires knowledge about the speaker, the listener, and the social and physical setting of an ongoing discourse. Precisely because pragmatics is a difficult area for formal linguistic theory, it is an ideal starting point for an effort to "re-psychologize" the study of child language.

Heuristics from Piaget's theory of intellectual development are used frequently throughout this work. The book is divided into three sections, investigating the development of pragmatics in the sensorimotor, the pre-

operational, and the concrete operational period. In each section the relevant developments in language and language use are related to the major
social and cognitive developments of that stage. In many instances
Piaget's concepts have been extended to describe linguistic events that
Piaget himself never treated. The result may not always please orthodox
interpreters of the theory. However, the goal of this work is an integrated
view of language as it develops in a context of cognitive and social interactions. This kind of work precludes exegesis on separate texts for linguistic,
cognitive, or social theory. Although certain details of Piaget's work may
have been stretched beyond bounds, hopefully the spirit of his theory has
been preserved.

Returning to the metaphor of revolution, this book is hardly a clarion
call to yet another paradigm shift in psycholinguistics. Much of what was
gained in the 1960s return to rationalism is respected here. Perhaps this is
best defined as a blatantly revisionist work, calling for a restoration of
balance and a return to normality in child language research. Surely it has
been true all along that the only real "language acquisition device" is the
whole child growing up in a social world.

Acknowledgments

To thank properly all the people who have helped me during my graduate years and my first years of teaching, I would have to write another volume as long as this one. To spare my readers, I must thank only a few people briefly, with love and thanks implicit for so many good friends.

My thanks go to Terry Halwes and Peter Greene, who have guided my reading in constructive metatheory across the years. Special thanks to Peter for his support and encouragement in my writing of the first version of this manuscript; to Carol Feldman, who introduced me to the interesting topic of pragmatics; to Michael Silverstein, who took over the unhappy job of dissertation chairman at the eleventh hour (I almost wish I had a few graduate years left to learn more from him); and to Robert LeVine, for his knowledge and experience in cross-cultural psychology.

To my colleagues and friends in Rome, there are not enough ways to say thank you, for their humor, their patience with my American impatience, their thoughts, criticisms, and comments at every stage of my work. I could never have completed this project without them. I will confine myself to an alphabetical list of melodic names: Francesco Antinucci, Laura Benigni, Luisa Camaioni, Cristiano Castelfranchi, Vittoria Giuliani, Domenico Parisi, Annarita Puglielli, and Virginia Volterra. All of these people have cooperated in a particularly direct fashion in one or more phases of this project, and some phases of the project have been published together elsewhere. Particular thanks go Cristiana Cremona, Eleanora Gangere, and Valeria Venza for their assistance in data collection.

Since the first version of this manuscript was circulated, I have collected a whole new round of personal and professional debts—again too many to cite in detail here. To mention just a few, my thanks go to Penny

Boyes-Braem, Virginia Volterra, and Brian MacWhinney for particularly detailed reading and criticism. Thanks also to Dan Slobin for his support and interest in this work. In two hours over expresso with his entire graduate seminar, I compiled a long list of insights and criticisms that formed a basis for the revised manuscript.

Throughout graduate study, I was supported by the National Institute of Mental Health. The dissertation research was carried out with NIMH Cultural Anthropology Field Grant No. 1-FO1-MH4294-01. Videotape equipment was provided through a National Science Foundation Dissertation Improvement Grant, through Professor Robert LeVine. During the summer of 1975, when this manuscript was revised, I was supported by a University of Colorado Summer Faculty Research Initiation Fellowship. Also, I owe a great deal to the Istituto di Psicologia, Consiglio Nazionale delle Ricerche, for placing their excellent facilities at my disposal during eighteen months and two summers as a guest researcher.

Finally, my love and endless gratitude to Diane Farris for coffee and a sense of humor on dreary Chicago days; to Anthony, for his company in Rome; to Barbara Sanders and Louise Silvern, for pulling me through the first year on the job; and to two amazing Irish women, my mother, Kathleen Bates, and my aunt, Rosemary Stone, who fueled two generations of graduate study with love and vigil candles.

Language and Context
THE ACQUISITION OF PRAGMATICS

CHAPTER I

Why Pragmatics?[1]

Language is a tool. We use it to do things. But unlike all the other instruments that we have evolved to deal with our world, only language can take itself as an object. We can talk about talking, or refer indirectly to our own acts of speech—a peculiar activity that has been described by an ancient zen metaphor as "The hand trying to grasp itself." This metasemantic property can lead us into a confusion between the USE of language and the CONTENT of language. For example, when a small child is asked *Why is a cow called a cow?* he is likely to respond with something like *Because it has horns.* This tendency to mix levels is not restricted to children alone. St. Anselm argued for the existence of God by claiming that the ability to discuss an All-Perfect Being implies His existence. And, as we shall see later, several linguistic models of language also conflate the rules for using language with its semantic content.

However, the same peculiar relationship between content and use also permits us to do many things with language, operating simultaneously at several levels. For example, I say to a man in a waiting room *Is the window open?* The content of the question is fairly simple, a proposition formed by a predicate and one argument: OPEN (window). At one level this proposition is being used in a question, to ask for information. At yet another level, in a context in which I am obviously uncomfortably cold, the question itself is being used, not as a request for information but as a polite command to close the window. This same process could be reflected in yet another mirror. For example, I have a terrible cold. My roommate

[1] Portions of this chapter have appeared previously in Elizabeth Bates, "Pragmatics and Sociolinquistics in Child Language." *In* D. Morehead and A. Morehead (Eds.), *Directions in Normal and Deficient Child Language.* Baltimore: University Park Press, 1976. © 1976 University Park Press, Baltimore.

knows that I have a cold, and yet the window is open. Using the same question, in that setting, I only pretend to be polite knowing full well that my use of a polite command will cause both my wishes and my irritation to be known. One use takes another as its argument, in a set of action embeddings folding into one another. This property is not simply an internal aspect of the grammar. It is an operation that takes place at the interface between language, thought and social motivation. To create sentences that take their meaning from the context in which they are used, one must combine linguistic, cognitive, and social rules.

This book is a study of how children learn to use language, to exploit the special relation between content and use. It is not a study of how children acquire "grammar" in the traditional sense, nor how they learn the meaning of words. Of course, to know how to use a sentence one must also control the syntactic–semantic rules of the language. To that degree, this study will overlap with more traditional research on the acquisition of language content. But the focus of the study is on use, on the child's ability to select a particular type of sentence and to "fix it up" until it will work effectively toward certain social ends. This approach to language acquisition should enable us to examine the interrelationships among linguistic, cognitive, and social development.

Within linguistic theory, the study of language use can be called "pragmatics." The most widely cited definition of **pragmatics** is that of Charles Morris (1946), who divided linguistic science into three areas:

1. SYNTACTICS—the relations holding among signs.
2. SEMANTICS—the relations between signs and their referents.
3. PRAGMATICS—the relations between signs and their human users.

There are some weaknesses in Morris's popular definition. It does include the important relation between language and context, insofar as signs are somehow related to human users. But this vague definition misses the epistemological distinction between content and use, the psychological difference between objects and procedures. The term pragmatics itself had been taken from the pragmatist philosopher Charles Peirce (1932). Peirce presented a theory of **semiotics** based on three types of signs:

1. ICONS—signs that are related to the things they stand for by virtue of some direct physical resemblance, e.g., a hieroglyph picture of a house.
2. INDICES—signs that relate to the things they stand for because they participate in or are actually part of the event or object for which they stand. For example, smoke indexes the existence of fire by virtue of the fact that the two are part of the same phenomenon.
3. SYMBOLS—signs that are related to the things they stand for by an arbitrary bond agreed upon by those who use the symbol, e.g., the word "dog" to stand for certain quadripedal mammals. A sign is classified as a symbol if it is neither (1) nor (2).

Silverstein (1973), Dewey and Bentley (1949), and others have criticized Morris's definition of pragmatics because it departs from the important philosophical distinctions established by Peirce. Silverstein stresses that symbols and icons can be described within a semantic–syntactic system, which specifies the relations between signs and the things they stand for independently of use by some speaker. There is no need for a real context of use for symbols and icons to be interpretable. Indices, however, can only be interpreted within an actual context of use. Examples are the shifting pronouns "I" and "you," which have different referents depending on who is speaking. Other examples include anaphoric utterances that can be interpreted only by referring to previous discourse, or polite phrases (e.g., *Is the window open?*) that take on their full meaning (e.g., as a command) only with respect to a given social context. A sentence such as *Cats have nine lives* is almost entirely interpretable within a syntactic–semantic system, regardless of who is using the sentence in what context. But a sentence such as *Yeah, I feel like that too* relies heavily upon use in a given context if it is to be understood.

Hence, pragmatics is not simply another kind of sign relation, equivalent to syntactics and semantics. One could not write a dictionary interpreting indices in the abstract, e.g., all the possible real-world referents for the pronoun "I." Pragmatics is the study of linguistic indices, and indices can be interpreted only when they are used. One cannot describe the meanings of indices—one can only describe rules for relating them to a context, in which the meaning can be found.

In recent semantic theory, as we shall see, there has been a tendency to describe pragmatic rules with proposition-like structures, equivalent to the descriptions for semantic–syntactic relations. Insofar as pragmatic rules are ACTION rules for FINDING relationships, this sort of description may confuse two distinct cognitive processes. In this book, the focus is on multiple epistemological levels in language use, shifting from action to mental object. Therefore, the definition of pragmatics that is adopted here will include the original distinctions intended by Peirce—the study of indexical rules for relating linguistic form to a given context. As I shall discuss shortly, these rules will be of particular interest for the study of cognitive development in children.

When I undertook the research reported here, pragmatics was a hot area in linguistic theory. This in itself might have been a tempting reason to study the development of pragmatics in children, since a broad set of heuristics from linguistic theory have been available for laboratory testing. However, the most important reason for studying pragmatics in child language is that it occupies the interface between linguistic, cognitive, and social development. This permits us to bridge psycholinguistic theory and general developmental research. During the 1960s, when psycholinguistics became a popular research area, there was a tendency for studies to be more linguistic than psychological. The field had received its impetus from

Chomskian transformational grammar, which analyzed sentences into:

1. DEEP STRUCTURE—a set of meaning-free phrase markers stating the hierarchical relations among sentence constituents. Phrase markers are semantically interpretable, but it is an essential tenet of transformational grammar that phrase markers are not in themselves semantic relations.

2. SURFACE STRUCTURE—a constituency of derived, "wordlike" entities that are the input to the phonological component (i.e., can be projected into sound).

3. TRANSFORMATIONS—which map deep structures onto surface structures.

An important point is that this entire syntactic system is interpreted by the semantic component, but does not in itself contain the meaning of individual sentences. Psychologists using Chomsky's model sought to establish the psychological reality of syntactic deep structures (e.g., phrase structure constituents such as "subject" and "object NP") and transformations (e.g., interrogative, negative, and passivization). The methods they used were psychological, but the theory was identical to Chomsky's. Order of acquisition by children was used as a measure of complexity. For example, Brown and Hanlon (1970) examined the sequence of acquisition of 1-, 2-, and 3-transformation sentences to establish that transformational complexity as defined by linguists bears an isomorphic relation to the acquisition of processing rules by children. Memory and perception tasks with adults were also used to establish the reality of transformations and deep structure constituents. For example, Mehler and Savin (1969) reported that when auditory clicks were located randomly across a sentence, subjects tended to hear them at the boundaries predicted by deep and surface structure segmentation. The problem with the research of this period is that although the methods were psychological, the theory was nothing more than a restatement of linguistic abstractions—e.g., transformations are real, and children acquire them one at a time. There was little effort to translate linguistic formulations into a more psychological theory of cognitive structures and information processing. In fact, the division between the two was rendered absolute by a theory attributing linguistic knowledge to "competence," with information processing factors appearing only in "performance." Lyons and Wales (1966) surveyed the poverty of psychological theory in psycholinguistics at a 1966 conference:

> It is now proposed that, first, children are born with a biologically-based, innate capacity for language acquisition; secondly, the best guess as to the nature of the innate capacity is that it takes the form of linguistic universals; thirdly, the best guess as to the nature of linguistic universals is that they consist of what are currently the basic notions in a Chomskian transformational grammar. Metaphorically speaking, a child is now born with a copy of *Aspects of a Theory of Syntax* tucked away somewhere inside.

Linguists cannot be held responsible for what psychologists do with their theories, but in a sense, 1960s psychologists had little choice. As long as they were working within a linguistic paradigm, using heuristics from Chomskian transformational grammar, psychologists were restricted in the number of generalizations that could be made to general cognition. According to Chomsky (1957, 1965), the syntactic component of the grammar makes the largest contribution to sentence structure. The semantic component merely interprets the syntactic structure, through the insertion of lexical items in deep structure slots. Since the most powerful component of the grammar is by definition meaning free, it is difficult for a psychologist to relate theories of sentence construction to theories of thought, logic, perception, feeling, or social function. Those psychological events, by definition, can contribute only secondarily to sentence structure.

Toward the end of the 1960s, a controversy arose within generative grammar regarding the contribution of meaning to syntactic structure. The renewed interest in meaning was NOT a sympathetic response to the plight of psycholinguists, although we have profited from it. Instead, the attempt to formalize the semantic component was a necessary extension of the syntactic theory itself. Certain kinds of meanings—e.g., quantified terms such as *All girls kiss some men*—simply did not behave in a neutral fashion under transformation. For example, the sentence

(1) *John hit the ball.*

undergoes no shift in propositional content, but rather a shift in focus or emphasis when it is passivized, as in

(2) *The ball was hit by John.*

Quantified terms, however, are subject to radically different interpretations before and after the passive transformation:

(3) *All girls kiss some men.*

(4) *Some men are kissed by all girls.*

Similar problems began to collect for pronouns, reflexives, negation, preposed adverbs, and several other structures. It became necessary to build more and more special constraints into the syntactic component to deal with different kinds of semantic content. The trend led some of Chomsky's students (e.g., Ross, 1970; McCawley, 1968; Lakoff and Ross, 1968) to propose doing away with purely syntactic "deep structure" in Chomsky's sense, substituting a logical–semantic structure that contains information such as the scope of quantifiers and negation, the internal components of complex verbs (e.g., *kill* = CAUSE(BECOME(NOT(ALIVE)))), and so forth. All the "meaning" necessary to match sentences to a sequence of sounds is described as a deep structure. The transformational component then acts directly upon such a semantic tree, without passing through a special stage of pure syntactic structure. This new school of thought within transformational grammar is referred to as "generative semantics."

Other transformationalists have adopted an extended version of Chomsky's standard theory, which preserves the simpler syntactic structure of the old theory as the input to the transformational component. The semantic component than interprets the set of phrase markers at various stages in derivation. For example, the shift in meaning due to the surface location of a quantifier term is interpreted at the surface level, whereas other constituent arrangements are interpreted at the deep structure level.

The particular issues that separate these two schools need not concern us here. However, although the revisions in generative grammar have not been designed for our benefit, it is true that the resulting proposals for semantic structure look much more like thought structures than any of the preceding versions of transformational grammar. Linguists are now attempting to account for ALL the meaning that is signalled in surface structure. This has led from an initial effort to describe quantifiers and other logical terms, to a set of structures that describe pragmatic meanings as well. There is a whole new array of special pragmatic–semantic "trees," including

1. PERFORMATIVES—which describe the intention of the speaker to use a sentence as a question, a command, etc.
2. PRESUPPOSITIONS—assumptions about the context that are necessary to make that sentence verifiable, or appropriate, or both.
3. CONVERSATIONAL POSTULATES—a particular class of presuppositions about the nature of human dialogue in general.

It would be perfectly in keeping with the psycholinguistic tradition to examine the psychological reality of these new pragmatic–semantic structures, using techniques that were once applied to transformations and syntactic phrase markers. However, we would then be no closer to a truly psychological theory of language and thought than we were in 1964. First, in attempting to formalize the pragmatic system, linguists have been forced to the border between the conventions of language and such notions as "beliefs and expectations" of speakers. Hence—whether they are willing to admit it or not—linguists working in the area of pragmatics need psychological models every bit as much as psycholinguists need heuristics from formal linguistic theory. It is, then, no longer appropriate for psychologists to apply linguistic concepts directly without first considering their fit to current knowledge about cognitive processing and social dynamics. Second, many of the new linguistic models treat the pragmatic trees as if they were on the same cognitive level as propositional content.

For example, the propositional–referential content of the sentence *John hit the ball,* as well as the speaker's intention in using the sentence and the decisions he makes regarding the listener's knowledge, are all described with the same formal machinery. I will contend in this book that pragmatic procedures and intentions may involve different levels of processing than the procedures involved in constructing propositional "objects." If we want to describe a pragmatic–semantic system that involves several levels of processing, current formal linguistic models are clearly insufficient for our purposes. I am not suggesting that the period of cooperation between linguists and psychologists is over. But the time is ripe for an intelligent synthesis between linguistics and psychology, one that will require more than a reification of trees.

Linguistic heuristics will be used in this book as a guide to the degree of complexity of a given structure, and to the cooccurrence restrictions between semantic and pragmatic rules. But an effort will be made to translate linguistic terminology into psychological terms before those structures are sought in child language. Just as children are not born clutching the latest edition of *Aspects of a Theory of Syntax,* they are also denied prenatal access to *Papers from the Texas Conference on Performatives, Presuppositions, and Conversational Implicature.*

The cognitive model that will be used in the present study is taken from Piaget's theory of genetic epistemology (e.g., Piaget, 1970). I should note here, however, that Piaget himself has written relatively little on language development in children, and virtually nothing on pragmatics. In extrapolating from his theory in this book, I have occasionally made some unorthodox uses of Piagetian terms. These points should be clear in the text. The same is often true for the way in which traditional linguistic terms are used here. In the next few pages, I will review some basic linguistic concepts necessary for a study of pragmatics, so it will be clear how some controversial terms are being used in this study.

After the section defining linguistic terms, there will be a brief digression into one more set of definitions, from artificial intelligence models of language—particularly some pragmatic concepts used in recent models. The purpose of this section is to draw attention to parallels between the Piagetian epistemology used in this book, and the working model of language–thought relations used by information scientists.

Finally, some predictions are offered about the course of pragmatic development from 0 to 6 years, based on Piaget's theory of cognitive development. This last section should serve as an outline for the data presented in the rest of the book. This book can be viewed as a starting point—a skeletal model of pragmatics that psychologists will find useful and that will at least provide a great many questions for future research.

All the data reported in the present study were collected in Italy, from children learning Italian as a native language. There are advantages to the choice of Italian as a target language, but of course, all claims concerning possible pragmatic universals should be considered as hypotheses that require testing in a variety of language communities.

Definitions of Linguistic Terms

A. *Meaning and Reference*

The philosophical issues of reference intersect with a variety of problems in epistemology and logic. It would be impossible to summarize all of these issues here. However, there is one general problem that is particularly relevant to a study of pragmatics: the distinction between meaning as OBJECT and meaning as ACT.

At one extreme in the philosophy of meaning we find the positions of Austin (1962), Wittgenstein (1958, 1972), and Quine (1960). In *Philosophical Investigations* and *The Blue and the Brown Books,* Wittgenstein presents the concept of the language game. The meaning of the word "brick," according to this analysis, is not simply a referential correspondence between the sound "brick" and a reddish rectangular object. Rather, the meaning of the word is built up through the circumstances or "games" in which the word is used—e.g., handing certain kinds of objects back and forth while building houses. Insofar as we all use the same sound in similar circumstances, there is a conventional meaning attached to that sequence of sounds. But the meaning is not restricted to a given "referent" or entity to which that name belongs. It consists of rules for using that name, in linguistic and nonlinguistic contexts. In *Word and Object,* Quine employs a similar analysis. He compares the network of meanings which different individuals may have for the same word to the arrangement of branches within garden hedges clipped to look like elephants. Viewed externally, they follow the same pattern. But we have no way of knowing what internal arrangement of action patterns have been joined to produce the conventional use of a word. This position on the nature of meaning essentially reduces all of semantics to rules of use, so that pragmatics and semantics are indistinguishable levels of meaning.

This position was a reaction against another extreme view that meaning is an object—either an entity existing in the mind (what Quine calls "the museum theory"), or a sound corresponding to an entity in the outside world. The view that names must correspond to something real was often quoted within ontological arguments such as St. Anselm's suggestion that the ability to think of an All-Perfect Being implies His existence. A more modern version of the meaning as entity theory, with completely different goals, can be found in Russell's theory of denoting (1905). According to Russell, a sentence has to refer to something—be about something—to be meaningful. Otherwise, how could we tell whether it is true or false? Russell was puzzled by certain paradoxes that seemed to arise in mathematical logic and ordinary language if one held to this view. To solve these problems and to save the reference theory of meaning, Russell invented his "theory of descriptions." The theory of descriptions is a logical device that enables propositions to refer to things even though the subject term itself (e.g., "the winged horse") refers to nothing outside of the proposition. For Russell, compound propositions could be reduced by logical analysis to simple propositions ("atomic propositions"), but, ultimately, every atomic proposition must refer to something for the compound proposition to be meaningful. The Russellian analysis has been used to criticize ontological arguments like that of St. Anselm, in which the very existence of a name is used to argue for the existence of a corresponding entity. But it is interesting that the concept of meaning as reference is assumed in both approaches. The major difference lies in the possible objects or entities to which a term may refer.

Within such entity theories of meaning, there are two ways of handling pragmatics. One is to construe rules of use as meaningless operations that need not be verified since they convey no information. For example, the operation equating *it* to *the ball* in *John hit it* adds no meaning, and hence need not be verified. The other approach is to reduce rules of use to statements or descriptions that contain the pragmatic meanings, such as a statement describing the relationship of a pronoun to its antecedent in the situation where the pronoun is used. For example, the sentence *John hit it* would be analyzed into a set of minimal propositions, one of which is the statement "It = the ball in situation X." These pragmatic propositions must then be verified according to the same principles as other propositions. As may become clear later, this is the approach that is implicit in some recent generative semantic models of pragmatics, in that the rules for relating linguistic form to context are stated as propositions equivalent in most respects to the more traditional propositional–semantic content of the sentence.

There are several mixed proposals midway between the two extremes of referent as thing and referring as activity. Frege (1952), who had influenced Russell, distinguished two types of meaning: reference (object referred to) and sense. Thus a sentence like *The winged horse flies* expresses a sense or meaning, even though there is no winged horse. In addition to sense Frege also wanted every sentence to have some kind of reference, so he invented a special referent for such phrases as *The winged horse*—namely, the null or empty class. Russell thought that Frege's second kind of meaning, his "sense," raised more problems than it solved, and that his null referents were artificial. Both Russell and Frege defined meaning in terms of entities. They disagree on the number and type of entities necessary for an analysis of meaning. Strawson (1950) agrees with

Frege that not all meaning can be reduced to reference and he believes there are mental experiences that cannot be ascribed truth values. However, Strawson's writings have a different flavor, in that he stresses the active role of speakers in the creation of meaning within different contexts, as opposed to more passive reception by sense "entities."[2]

The view that will be taken here is that meaning and referring are psychological activities, acts that speakers do rather than properties that sentences or speakers have. Words do not "have" referents—speakers use words to refer or point to something existing in an hypostasized world. It is true that speakers in a given language community have tacitly agreed to use a given word in similar ways. And of course, children must learn the conditions of that agreement. But the act of making a sound stand for something else resides in the speaker, and is not of psychological interest beyond that usage. Hence, **reference** as it will be used here describes the use of a word or phase by a speaker to stand for an entity–event in the outside world, or an entity–event in his own imagined world.

Reference is a more restricted term than "meaning." **Meaning** is defined here as the set of mental acts or operations that a speaker intends to create in his listener by using a sentence. Utterances communicate only insofar as they cause the listener to carry out mental acts similar to those used by the speaker in creating a given meaning; but whether or not it communicates efficiently, an utterance still "means" what its speaker intended it to mean.

Despite the fact that we are dealing with mental acts or intentions, this position does not exclude the possibility of describing or classifying these mental acts within a semantic–pragmatic theory. Quine is correct in that we can only infer on the basis of external behavior whether speakers and listeners carry out the same internal acts in understanding a word or sentence. However, it does not seem necessary to arrive at Quine's behaviorist conclusion that mental activities are thus irrelevant or inaccessible. They are simply difficult to observe, like many of the phenomena of "tougher" sciences, e.g., atomic physics. On the basis of our regular and predictable social interactions, our shared genetic tendencies, and regular patterns of development, we are justified in assuming that speakers and listeners carry out similar mental acts when they communicate. And as a child's linguistic behavior approaches that of adults, we can conclude that he is acquiring an internal pattern similar to the one shared by adults.

There is also a special sense in which we can continue to speak of meaning entities. The epistemological position that is adopted in this book is based on the theory of knowledge outlined by Jean Piaget (e.g., *Genetic Epistemology,* 1970). According to Piaget's theory of representation, a

[2] I am grateful to Seth Sharpless for several interesting discussions about this section.

symbol (or **sign** in Peirce's terms) is at once both an act and an object, in that all mental objects are derived from the child's actions upon the world. Real world objects do not copy themselves onto a passive organism. Rather, the organism itself interacts with the world of objects, carrying out various activities on them and with them. It tries to impose its own schemes on the world (assimilation) and changes those schemes when it meets resistance (accommodation). Through this process the organism can achieve a dynamic and balanced interaction that is the source and substance of its knowledge. The organism never knows the world itself. It only "knows" its own actions upon the world. Within this framework, a symbol or representation is the internal reenactment (re-presentation) of the activities originally carried out with objects or events. Just as the child originally KNEW a triangle by imitating its contours with movements of the eye, touch, etc., he later SYMBOLIZES a triangle by recalling or imitating the scheme (or part of the scheme) of movements that were originally used to know that pattern. Hence there are no mental templates or icons, no triangles in the mind, except as they are created at the moment of recall from an action blueprint. This view of knowledge is not unique to Piaget's developmental theory. Similar positions have been put forth with regard to adult processing by Bartlett (1932), Neisser (1967), and a number of other psychologists who have been collectively referred to as "constructivists." Furthermore, as we shall see shortly, the same epistemological position characterizes a great deal of recent work in artificial intelligence.

When the child becomes capable of such internal representation (between 12 and 18 months according to Piaget), we can discern two kinds of knowing. **Figurative knowing** refers to the internal activity of building symbols, imitating a world of objects and events. While the important cognitive work takes place internally, we can infer the presence of such a symbolic capacity when the child takes an object and makes it stand for something else—e.g., a block is used as a car, a clothespin becomes a doll. **Operative knowing** is also derived from the original action schemes carried out in the outside world, but in this case internal activities are carried out UPON the symbols themselves. Figurative knowing is at work when the child imagines a toy block in the absence of that block. Operative knowing is at work when he mentally rotates that block, or imagines a way in which that block can be placed inside something else. Although we speak of the two as if they were separate activities, of course these two types of knowing are indivisibly fused from the time the capacity for representation is established, just as actions and a world of real objects were continually intertwined at earlier stages of development. Furthermore, the distinction between figurative and operative knowing is always relative to a single moment in processing, since the figurative aspect of creating symbols is at all times built out of mental operations rather than entities.

The important point for present purposes is the following: Since symbolization is an operation,[3] a symbol or meaning is an object only insofar as it is taken by a higher internal activity—moved, transformed, talked about, or otherwise manipulated in the absence of the original real-world objects. Since internal action schemes can operate on one another, i.e., they take other schemes as "arguments," we can speak of mental entities or objects. But when we do speak of symbolic objects, we are referring to something that happens to mental acts at a given moment in processing, rather than to some stable and inalienable porperty of a symbol. The source of all knowledge is action, according to Piaget. In a Piagetian approach to language, meaning is a coordinated set of internalized action patterns which can be associated with a set of sounds in systematic ways, for the purpose of communication. Meaning is an object only insofar as these particular action patterns are taken as the arguments of a higher activity of communication, and hence mapped into sounds. Despite Quine's behaviorist disavowal of mentalism, the Quinian approach is very similar to Piaget's. A child learns to mean by learning to act (Quine, 1960).

Within this epistemological framework, **referring** is the use of a sound or complex of sounds to stand for some object or event. Whether that event–referent actually exists in the outside world, or is only imagined, is not really relevant, since all objects are known only through actions imposed on them by the speaker. **Meaning** is a set of mental operations carried out by the speaker, which the speaker intends to create in the listener by using a given sentence. Whether or not the speaker actually succeeds is a separate issue.

Like a single act of reference, a **proposition** is also defined here as an internal activity of speakers rather than an object located in sentences. A proposition is a state or change predicated of one argument, or a relationship predicated of two or more arguments. In this study, when we provide formal representation for propositions, each predicate or argument node should stand for a corresponding mental operation or recurring complex of operations. We are not interested in a concept of propositions as logical objects that are verifiable independent of the speaker's beliefs. A child or adult "has" a proposition only insofar as he can carry out some further operation on it, such as mapping it into sounds, embedding it in higher propositions, or calling it up indirectly in the form of presupposed or entailed information. When this does occur, the internal "stuff" of which propositional objects are made is still mental activity. If it is not being created or used in the service of some higher activity, the same informa-

---

[3] Piaget has used the term "operation" in two senses: first, as a general term interchangeable with "procedure" or "scheme"; and second, in a very precise mathematical sense, involving certain properties of reversibility that many procedures and schemes do not have. We will use the term operation in the more general sense of procedure or scheme.

tion structured within that proposition exists as something the organism "does." And in fact, we will suggest that the propositions that children eventually "have" as part of the meaning of sentences, are originally organized as action schemes that the child carries out, mentally or literally, at an earlier stage in development.

By extension, when a speaker uses a sentence (i.e., utters something), that sentence can be said to "have" or contain one or more propositions only insofar as the speaker has constructed the underlying propositional relations as part of his meaning. Thus an utterance may fail to encode or have a proposition in a conventional, external sense, but the speaker still "has" the proposition as part of the meaning of that utterance. He may have failed to communicate, but he still MEANS that proposition. This is often the position of small children who have not yet acquired the linguistic conventions of their community. IF WE ARE TO UNDERSTAND THE PROGRESS A CHILD MAKES IN ACQUIRING THOSE CONVENTIONS, WE MUST MAKE SOME EFFORT TO INFER WHAT HE MEANT TO SAY, HOWEVER UNSUCCESSFULLY.

At first glance it may seem that, along with Wittgenstein and Quine, we have reduced all of semantics to rules of use, so that pragmatics and semantic content are no longer distinguishable. However, it is still possible, within a Piagetian epistemology, to distinguish the rules for using and mapping propositions (operative knowing) from the rules for constructing propositions (figurative knowing). Therefore, the distinction between pragmatics and semantics is not absolute, but relative to a given moment in cognitive processing. It should be noted here that in attributing the construction of propositions to the figurative component, we have gone beyond Piaget's own, more limited use of the term "figurative." (This question will be discussed in more detail in Chapter III.) However, this division of language processing into figurative and operative components has particular advantages for describing the chameleon nature of pragmatic operations. As the terms are used here, any operative procedure can potentially be turned into figurative knowledge, when it is taken as the object of a higher operation. Hence, any pragmatic use of language can also be turned into a propositional object (see Chapter V on metapragmatics). The ability to distinguish these two kinds of mental activities, and to exploit that awareness by playing one against the other, will be the pivotal achievement in the acquisition of pragmatic competence.

B. Performatives

The first major category of pragmatic structures, or rules of use, is the speaker's goal in using a proposition. This structure has been discussed as the "speech act," "performative," or "illocutionary force" associated with a sentence. It describes the speaker's intention to issue a command, ask a question, make a promise, etc.

The concept of "speech act" was first introduced in modern language philosophy by J. Austin, in his 1962 book *How to Do Things with Words*. The speech act analysis was in part a response to philosophers like Russell who claimed that all language could be analyzed into atomic propositions with corresponding truth values. Austin proposed instead that some utterances—such as *I order you...*, *I christen you...*, or *I now pronounce you man and wife...* —are events in themselves. While one could determine whether a speech act had or had not occurred (e.g., a drunk smashing a bottle against the Queen Mary has not actually christened the Queen Mary no matter what words he uses), it would be senseless to call such a sentence true or false. In fact, not only these special sentences, but all utterances can be analyzed into three kinds of speech acts: LOCUTIONS, ILLOCUTIONS, and PERLOCUTIONS.

Locutionary acts include all the acts that are required for the making of speech, e.g., constructing propositions and uttering sounds. In an example offered by Austin (1965:100), a person who just witnessed a locutionary speech act might describe that act as follows:

> He said to me "Shoot her!" meaning by "shoot" shoot and referring by "her" to her.

By contrast, an **illocutionary** speech act is a conventional social act, recognized as such by both speaker and hearer, that takes place when a sentence is uttered, e.g., a command is issued, a child is baptized. The same man who witnessed the above LOCUTIONARY act, according to Austin, might describe the concommitant ILLOCUTIONARY act as follows:

> He urged (or advised, ordered, etc.) me to shoot her.

In other words, an illocution is the conventional social act of ordering, advising, urging, etc.

Finally, a **perlocutionary** act creates the effects, planned or unplanned, of having used a sentence, e.g., *The listener is annoyed, the married couple lives happily ever after.* Austin continues his example by suggesting that the same person who witnessed the preceding LOCUTIONARY and ILLOCUTIONARY acts might describe the resulting PERLOCUTION as follows:

> He persuaded me to shoot her.

Persuades differs from *ordering, advising,* etc. in that the persuasion might have been a byproduct, perhaps even an unintentional byproduct, of any number of locutions and illocutions. For example, the speaker might have unintentionally persuaded the listener to shoot the woman by reporting a number of unpleasant details about her behavior.

In terminology that can be applied to child language, a locution requires the uttering of sounds and construction of propositions. Hence, locution requires the onset of verbal speech. An illocution requires the intentional use of a conventional signal to carry out some socially recognized function, e.g., commanding or indicating the presence of objects or events so that illocutions might be carried out with conventional gestural signals, such as pointing. Perlocutions require simply that a signal issued by one person have some effect on the listener, intentional or unintentional. Therefore, the hunger cry of a newborn infant can at least be regarded as a perlocution. As we shall see, all three of these speech act concepts will be useful in analyzing the development of communicative intentions in children.

The sentence

(5)   *John is leaving the room.*

can be carried with a variety of illocutionary forces, yielding sentences such as

(6)   *Is John leaving the room?*

(7)   *John, leave the room!*

(8)   *If only John would leave the room!*

The illocutionary act is signalled by a series of elements: intonation, the mood of the verb, the presence of an explicit performative verb (e.g., *I order you . . .*), plus, of course, punctuation in written language or extra-linguistic context in spoken language. Furthermore, Searle underlines that not all illocutionary acts have a propositional content, and offers as examples such expressions as *Hurray!* or *Hello.* Although Austin had originally specified that all the three aspects of a sentence—illocutionary, locutionary, perlocutionary—are speech acts, the term "speech acts" has generally been reserved for the illocutionary force of an utterance. Searle's distinction between propositional content and illocutionary force contributes to this usage of the term.

Readers familiar with transformational grammar will note the strong parallels between Searle's analysis and linguistic issues pertaining to deep structure and transformations. It was perhaps inevitable that attempts would be made to incorporate the performative analysis into a generative grammar. The first such effort is Ross's "On Declarative Sentences" (1970), in which he claims that even the relatively "neutral" simple declarative sentence is dominated in deep structure by a higher sentence *I say to you . . .* , that takes as its complement the neutral proposition, e.g., LEAVE(*John*). The so-called performative analysis has been used extensively by generative semanticists since Ross's article. Evidence for the syntactic reality of a performative hypersentence has been drawn from issues such as pronominalization, reflexivization, and the behavior of certain adverbials. The procedure generally involves

1. Selecting a syntactic phenomenon that occurs in subordinate clauses

2. Demonstrating that main clauses also show this behavior under certain circumstances

3. Explaining the behavior of these main clauses as the product of the

usual subordinate clause rules operating from a higher performative main clause.

For example, reflexive pronouns are generally permissible only when the antecedent has previously been specified

(9)   *John said that the book was for Bill and himself.*

(10)   **The book was for Bill and himself.*

Yet the rules seem to differ for first and second person pronouns:

(11)   *John said that the book was for Bill and myself.*
(12)   *The book was for Bill and myself.*

These exceptions can be made to follow one general, economical rule for pronominalization if we admit the existence of a performative hypersentence (*I say to you . . .*) in deep structure. If this structure is implicit in all sentences, then the speaker and listener are already specified in the dominant, performative clause. Therefore, no special exceptions are required to the rule for pronominalizing subordinate clauses. Fraser (1971) and others have offered extensive criticisms of the syntactic arguments for a performative hypersentence. The matter is by no means settled within generative grammar. However, the performative analysis continues to be a popular solution to syntactic problems that involve information about the speaker, the listener, and the speech act itself.

Parisi and Antinucci (1973) outline a generative semantics model in which both the performative hypersentence and the propositional complement are represented as a configuration of predicates and arguments. Their model differs from the earlier approaches in that an effort is made to analyze the internal structure of the *I say to you* proposition, into a set of semantic primitives. The performative is seen as a complex of causal predicates with corresponding arguments, similar to componential analyses for other complex verbs (e.g., McCawley's analysis of *kill* as CAUSE(BECOME(NOT(ALIVE)))). For example, the imperative performative has the following structure:

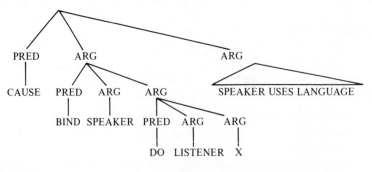

I am about to explain the notation used in this formal structure, to give the reader a better understanding of the kinds of formal models Parisi and Antinucci and others have offered to describe the performative. A word of caution is in order first. This formal model is offered purely for purposes of illustration. We will use it again later in Chapter II, to show how formal notation can be used to describe sensorimotor intentions. But at no point will we suggest that this particular formal structure, and no other, is THE psychologically real structure underlying communication. We simply want to illustrate how this KIND of componential model has been and can be used to describe the development of communicative intentions in children. If the details of this particular model are unclear below, the reader is asked to wait until Chapter II for clarification. If the details are still unclear at that point, let me assure the reader that they are not particularly important for present purposes.

Having thus disclaimed any responsibility for particular notational systems, let us look briefly at the notation used by Parisi and Antinucci in describing the performative. First, the triangle stands for an unanalyzed proposition, one that could be broken down by further analysis into more minimal or "atomic" units. Like the symbol x in algebraic notation, the triangle can stand for any proposition that the speaker cares to insert in the performative structure. The CAUSE-BIND predicates are used by Parisi and Antinucci to distinguish indirect causality, e.g., *John broke the glass,* from direct causality, e.g., *The rock broke the glass.* If the structure to be described were a case of simple efficient causality, as in the sentence with *rock* as subject, a single CAUSE predicate would suffice. CAUSE alone represents direct causality. BIND is an abstract predicate that serves a variety of functions when combined with other predicates. For example, the modal verb *must* is analyzed as BIND(event X), while *may* is analyzed as NOT(BIND(event X)). When combined with the predicate CAUSE, the combination CAUSE-BIND describes an indirect causality, acting through some intermediate agent, instrument, etc. Hence, if John picks up a rock and throws it at the window, then it is the rock that causes the window to break. John merely binds the CONDITION of the rock causing the window to break. However, if Frank were to pick John up bodily and throw him through the window, then it would be fair to say that John directly caused the window to break. In this case, it is Frank who sets the causal chain in motion, i.e., binds the event CAUSE(X,Y). Hence, Frank would be the first argument of BIND. Finally, with all causal predicates, the first argument is the cause and the second argument is the effect. In the case of intentional causality, it is the **goal** that causes the selection of **means**. Since the performative structure describes a causal intention, it is the goal—e.g., DO(Listener, X)—which is the first argument, and the means—e.g., USE(Speaker, language)—which is the second argument of the CAUSE-BIND complex.

Since there are many possible performatives, the componential structure can vary from one speech act to another. For example, the
DO(Listener, X) argument will vary in structure according to the
speaker's goal in a given situation. Parisi and Antinucci claim that the
interrogative is simply a kind of imperative in which the listener is
ordered to perform a speech act himself. Furthermore, the declarative
performative is also a type of imperative, in which a particular mental act
of "assuming" is commanded of the listener. Parisi and Antinucci give the
declarative the following representation:

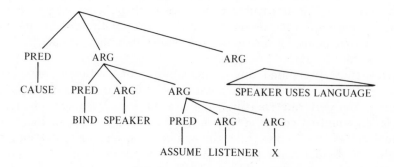

Recently, similar componential analyses of the performative have been
presented by American linguists including Sadock (1974) and McCawley
(1973). McCawley goes back to Austin's original classification of
performative verbs, into categories such as **behabitives** (speech acts
attempting to influence the behavior of the listener, such as commands,
requests, etc.) and **expositives** (speech acts offering information, such as
declarations, proclamations, etc.). McCawley suggests that the speaker's
knowledge about what makes a class of speech acts similar can be
described with a set of components shared by the verbs in that class. For
example, the behabitive class includes verbs with an internal structure
containing CAUSE(DO(Listener, X)). These same components would
underlie performative verbs when they are used descriptively (e.g., *John
ordered Bill to mow the lawn*) as well as when they appear in implicit and
explicit performatives (e.g., *Bill, mow the lawn!* and *I order you to mow
the lawn,* respectively). A similar analysis by Sadock will be described in
Chapter VIII. These analyses differ from that of Parisi and Antinucci primarily in the particular kinds of semantic primitives used to describe
performative intentions. For example, instead of CAUSE–BIND,
McCawley uses CAUSE–DO to describe indirect causality.

The question of syntactic evidence for performative hypersentences is
not entirely relevant to the present study. First, it is difficult to imagine
how psychological research could settle such details of linguistic notation

as the difference between CAUSE–BIND and CAUSE–DO. Second, the performative analysis tends to equate the performative clause with all other propositional structures, so that it obscures the important psychological distinction between pragmatic use and semantic content. However, whether or not performatives appear in linguistic deep structures, they must appear somewhere in the psychological makeup of speakers, as the speaker's goal in using a sentence. There are enough connections between illocutionary force and surface form to warrant including some sort of theory of speech acts in the grammar. For example, speakers do indeed treat "I" and "you" pronouns differently than "he" and "she" pronouns. But it may not be necessary to formulate the performative as a propositional object that supposedly belongs to the sentence itself. Rather, we can view performatives as intentions that belong to the speaker with respect to his sentence. In this study, we will continue to use some of the generative semantic analyses of performatives, particularly those analyses that break the performative into its causal components. As we shall see later, there is a structural similarity between the analysis of the causal components of the performative, and the child's analysis of causality in communication. Therefore, formal linguistic analysis can serve as a heuristic to developmental research. However, it should be clear that we consider the performative structure to be a description of the speaker's intention, rather than some property of sentences. As such, the performative is similar to an "execute" message in a computer program, with the goal written in—SPEAKER USES SENTENCE (X) SO THAT LISTENER WILL DO (Y) (command), or SPEAKER USES SENTENCE (Z) SO THAT LISTENER WILL RECOGNIZE THAT SPEAKER IS BOUND TO ACTIVITY (Y) (promise).

This solution is of course a departure from Austin's original use of the term illocution. Austin was describing a social event, an act that actually happens when a given sentence is uttered. Instead, we are describing a potential act, from the point of view of the speaker, which motivates the speaker's use of that sentence. These are two very different levels of description, and it may indeed be true that Austin himself would not have approved of our usage of his terms.

Finally, the use of propositional notation is also justified by our assumption that ALL propositions describe mental acts and intentions. Both the semantic content and the performative goal are mental operations. If we have a cognitive theory in which the speaker can take mental acts as the objects or "arguments" of higher mental acts, then the propositional format of the performative will permit it to be taken as a proposition in a metapragmatic sentence—e.g., *I told you to stop that.* It was noted earlier that figurative and operative knowing are to some degree interchangeable, insofar as an operation can be taken as the object of another operation.

Hence, the causal structure within the speaker's goal in using a sentence can in turn be taken as the propositional content of another sentence. In short, the speaker can talk about talking, embedding his own speech acts in higher speech acts. The propositional format for describing performative structures permits us to describe the speech act–goal in both of these roles, as an act and as a propositional object.

The importance of this last distinction will hopefully become clearer later on, when we describe a transition in early childhood from simply using performative procedures, to talking about or indirectly referring to past discourse or aspects of an ongoing speech act.

C. Presuppositions

Another construct that has been used extensively in pragmatic analyses is the concept of **presupposition**. There is considerable controversy regarding the nature of presuppositions (cf., Kiefer, 1973), and we must define this term with particular care to clarify its use in this study.

There are three possible definitions of presupposition:

1. Semantic or logical presupposition (P_1)
2. Pragmatic presupposition (P_2)
3. Psychological presupposition (P_3)

As in the case of reference versus referring, these definitions differ primarily on the issue of presuppositions as objects, or properties of sentences, versus presupposing as an activity of speakers. We will now examine these three types of presupposition one at a time, to arrive at the psychological definition that will be used in the present study.

1. Semantic Presupposition

Presuppositions were originally described in language philosophy with respect to the problem of verifiability. The information available in a given sentence can be divided into three types: asserted meaning, entailed meaning, and presupposed meaning. These three types of information differ insofar as they have different truth conditions.

First, the meaning ASSERTED by a sentence is true if the sentence is true, and false if the sentence is false. Take the example

(13)   *John has a sister.*

Our knowledge of the meaning of the word *sister* enables us to construct the paraphrase

(14)   *John has a female sibling.*

We know that these sentences make the same assertions because the negation of (13)

(15)   *John does not have a sister.*

requires the negation of (14)

(16)   *John does not have a female sibling.*

The truth conditions for two equivalent ASSERTIONS can be formalized as follows:

$$\left. \begin{array}{l} T(13) \Rightarrow T(14) \\ F(13) \Rightarrow F(14) \end{array} \right\} = \text{ASSERTION}$$

However, in addition to the information that is actually asserted by sentence (13), we can deduce further information such as

(17)   *John's parents had more than one child.*

Sentences (13) and (17) do not make the same assertions, since even if sentence (13) is false, sentence (17) can still be true. For example, John may have 12 brothers even though he has no sisters. In this case we say that the truth of sentence (17) is **entailed by** the truth of (13), but not asserted by (13). If a given sentence (Y) is entailed by a sentence (X), then Y is true if X is true, but Y is not necessarily affected if X is false. The **entailment** relation for the preceding sentences can be formalized as follows:

$$\left. \begin{array}{l} T(13) \Rightarrow T(17) \\ F(13) \Rightarrow \text{no conclusion} \end{array} \right\} = \text{ENTAILMENT}$$

Finally, there is one further kind of information that can be deduced from both sentence (13) and its negation, (15). Both the positive and negative forms of the statements require that, within whatever world (13) and (15) are relevant, sentence (18) must be true:

(18)   *John exists.*

If there were no entity called John, then neither (13) nor (15) could be verified. And according to Russell, a sentence that cannot be computed is by definition nonsense. Thus, the truth of sentence (18) is **presupposed by** both (13) and (15). This set of relations yields one of the definitions of **presupposition** just listed. A logical or semantic presupposition (P_1) is a condition deducible from the meaning of a sentence, which must be true for that sentence to be either a true or a false proposition. For the preceding sentences, this relation can be formalized as

$$\left. \begin{array}{l} T(13) \Rightarrow T(18) \\ F(13) \Rightarrow T(18) \end{array} \right\} = \text{PRESUPPOSITION}$$

By this definition, any information implied by a sentence, which is not affected by the negation of that sentence, is a presupposition. This relation can be used as a test to determine whether entailed information is logically presupposed by a sentence.

2. *Pragmatic Presupposition*

The definition of presupposition given on page 21 was originated for a restricted purpose—to facilitate the computation of true and false information from a given set of sentences. Theoretically, this concept completes a closed system of logical relations that can hold between sentences. But there are other types of information deducible from a given sentence, which have to do with the relationship between that sentence and the context in which it is used. This information is neither asserted, entailed, nor presupposed in the sense just outlined, because it is not a property of the sentence itself. For example, the utterance

(19)   *Mr. Smith, can I get your coat?*

usually indicates that the listener is an adult male, and may also suggest that the listener is either a social superior or a distant acquaintance of the speaker. If (19) were used with a small child, or with a close friend, it would probably be for purposes of humor, an intentional violation of expectations. Similarly, the sentence

(20)   *Do you want your din-din?*

suggests that the listener is a child or possibly a nonhuman pet. In our culture, the sentence

(21)   *I simply love your tie.*

indicates that the speaker is either female, or as R. Lakoff (1973) suggests, a male who shares the peripheral power and status of females. However, none of these conditions in any way affects the truth or falsity of the propositions contained in these sentences. Instead, they are pragmatic presuppositions, conditions necessary for a sentence to be appropriate in the context in which it is used (P_2).

These conditions were originally described by Austin (1962) with regard to speech acts, or performatives. Austin had claimed that there is a class of sentences which cannot be either truth or false, since they are events in themselves, e.g., *I now pronounce you man and wife.* However, although such sentences cannot be verified, we can determine whether they have functioned properly or not. For example, the sentence *I now pronounce you man and wife* fails to function if the speaker has no legal right to perform marriage ceremonies. Austin calls these constraints on speech acts **felicity conditions**. By definition, felicity conditions are also pragmatic presuppositions.

At first glance, pragmatic and semantic presupposition seem to be separate categories. However, there are ambiguous cases in which what seems to be a semantic presupposition will vary according to the context in which the sentence is used. This is frequently the case with lexical presuppositions. The meaning of lexical items can often be divided into presupposed meaning and asserted–referential meaning. Fillmore (1971) offers as an example the sentence

(22)   *I blamed John for burning the dinner.*

In this sentence, the speaker presupposes that John burnt the dinner, while he asserts that it was wrong to do so. By contrast the sentence

(23)   *I accused John of burning the dinner.*

presupposes that burning the dinner is wrong, while asserting that John did it. According to such an analysis, the two verbs *blame* and *accuse* contain the same information, but distributed differently between presupposed and asserted meaning. These presuppositions generally obey the logical test for presuppositions, in that they hold true for both the assertion and the negation of the same sentence. Hence

(24)   *I did not accuse John of burning the dinner.*

still presupposes that burning the dinner is wrong.

However, in some cases lexical presuppositions shift according to the context in which the lexical item is used. Take the example

(25)   *John is a bachelor.*

The meaning of bachelor includes the information that John is an unmarried adult male. Under normal circumstances the information "unmarried" is the asserted portion of the meaning, while the information "adult male" is presupposed by the use of the word *bachelor*. For example, *John is a bachelor* would be a very peculiar answer to the question *How old is John?* or *Is John your son or your dog?* By the same token, the sentence

(26)   *John is not a bachelor.*

asserts that John is not unmarried, while the speaker usually takes for granted (i.e., presupposes) that John is an adult male. However, this kind of presupposition fails the test for logical presuppositions (P_1). If John is a 2-year-old boy, and I tell my neighbor *John is not a bachelor,* my neighbor will probably assume that John is an adult, unless he knows otherwise. Should he find out later that he was wrong, he is justified in accusing me of being uncooperative, or of misleading him. But he cannot accuse me of lying. Sentence (26) is not false even though John is only 2 years old. The condition "adult male" is necessary for the assertion of (25) to be true, but not for (26) to be true. Hence, by the logical definitions oulined earlier, the condition "adult male" is semantically entailed by sentence (25), but it is not a semantic presupposition (P_1) of (25). Instead, it is a pragmatic presupposition, a condition necessary for both (25) and (26) to be APPRO-PRIATE.

The shifting nature of pragmatic presuppositions may be clearer in the following example. Suppose that I have a single girlfriend who is anxious to marry. She has been invited to visit the home of some older friends, who mention that a neighbor's son John will be present. When she explains this fact to me, we both assume that the neighbor's son John will be a little boy. When my friend comes over the next day, I ask her *How was the party?* She smiles and responds

(25a)   *John is a bachelor.*

In this instance, sentence (25) asserts not only that John is unmarried, but that he is an adult male. The usual division of the lexical meaning of *bachelor* is

> ASSERT: unmarried
> PRESUPPOSE (P_2): adult, male

In this particular context, the meaning of the predicate *bachelor* is redivided into

> ASSERT: unmarried, adult
> PRESUPPOSE (P_2): male

The problem of pragmatic presupposition reintroduces the speaker into a theory of sentences. Insofar as pragmatic presuppositions vary according to the context and the beliefs of the interlocutors, they cannot be defined by reference to the sentence alone. Semantic presuppositions are conditions that are necessary for a sentence to be true or false. Pragmatic presuppositions are conditions which are necessary for a sentence to be appropriate in a given context. Therefore, by definition, pragmatic presuppositions are the property of speakers. This is true for lexical presuppositions such as the "bachelor" example, as well as for the conditions of use for polite forms, baby talk forms, or "female" forms in examples (19) through (21). However, insofar as pragmatic presuppositions include Austin's felicity conditions, then they also include the felicity conditions of the speech act "declare." One of the felicity conditions of declaring is that the speaker believes what he is saying to be true, or at least wants to indicate that he believes it to be true. Untrue assertions are uncooperative (albeit common) and therefore inappropriate speech acts. This means that the pragmatic definition of presupposition (P_2) **subsumes** the semantic definition (P_1). The conditions necessary for a sentence to be true or false are also conditions necessary for a sentence to be appropriate in most contexts.

George Lakoff (1973) has suggested that pragmatic presuppositions can be reduced to normal semantics if we describe them as part of the structure of the performative. As such, they make up part of the semantic tree structure underlying every sentence, and can therefore trigger the application of different sentence forms. However, the same criticism that has been made of the performative analysis in general can also be lodged against this proposal. Insofar as pragmatic presuppositions are relations between a sentence and the speaker's beliefs about the context, they involve not only mental objects, but rules for sentence use. If we use propositional notation to describe presuppositions, we must be careful to define the special psychological nature of such a propositional structure. In this study, we will use the term "presupposition" in the same way that we have defined "performative"—as a description of the speaker's INTEN-TION in using a sentence.

3. *Psychological Presupposition*

Presupposing is the act of using a sentence to make a comment about some information assumed to be shared or verifiable by speaker and listener. This presupposition can be distinctly signalled by some constituent surface structure. Or it can be left locally unmarked. When the presupposed material affects the surface form of the sentence, it can be handled within a grammar of sentences. But a SPEAKER can presuppose information in using a sentence, even if his SENTENCE does not. The presup-position will carry so long as the speaker and the listener construct the same **topic–comment** relationship between the asserted information and the assumed information.

This definition differs from Lakoff's proposal in one important respect. In Lakoff's model, once the presupposition is described in the deep struc-ture, the grammar is automatically sensitive to it. If the grammar includes a transformation (e.g., a particular word order, or a kind of intonation pat-tern) that is sensitive to a given presupposition, and that transformation has not been applied within a given sentence, then according to the genera-tive semantic model we must conclude that the presupposition was never constructed as part of the meaning of the sentence. Hence, even though presupposition is defined in terms of appropriateness as well as truth, it is still defined in terms of sentence form instead of speaker intentions. In the model used in this book, a presupposition can be psychologically present regardless of its phonetic expression, as long as both the speaker and the listener share the ACT of presupposing—or as long as the speaker THINKS that the act is shared. This definition of presupposition makes the concept potentially univerifiable within a linguistic theory, since presupposing can be carried out without affecting the external form of sentences. For this reason, I have grouped psychological presuppositions as a separate class (P_3), distinct from the definitions of presupposition used in most linguistic models. However, just as pragmatic presupposition (P_2) subsumes semantic presupposition (P_1), the class of psychological acts of presuppos-ing (P_3) subsumes all cases in which the presupposing act is signalled in sentence form (P_1 and P_2).

Let us take an example of a psychological presupposition which is not necessarily signalled in surface form. My friend George and I walk into a party where we are expecting to meet Fred's new girlfriend. Fred is just back from the Orient, and has brought his girlfriend with him from there. He told us over the telephone that her name is Mai Ling. George and I assumed that she was Oriental. We walk into the room and are introduced to Mai Ling, who is a tall Swedish blond. George turns to me several moments later and says *She's blonde*. Given our shared beliefs earlier in the day, the sentence serves as a comment on the expectation that Mai Ling would be Oriental. It is possible, even likely, that George would use an intonation pattern of surprise with his comment. In that case, the psychological presupposition (P_3) would also be a linguistic–pragmatic one (P_2), in that there would be an explicit phonetic signal of surprise. But even if he does NOT use a special intonation pattern, the presupposition can still carry. There may be nothing in the surface form of the sentence itself that in any way presupposes—semantically or pragmatically—that I expected Mai Ling to be Oriental, and that Orientals are expected to have dark hair. But the sentence nonetheless bears a topic–comment relationship to the presupposition that Mai Ling would be Oriental, because George and I have created that presupposition as a psychological event. [See Rommetveit (1974), on psychological presupposing.]

There is one particularly important reason to define presuppositions as psychological operations, regardless of their grammatical expression. As in the case of the child's limited propositions discussed earlier, it is also true that young children may presuppose information that they are unable to signal in the surface form of their utterances. In order to understand the child's eventual mastery of conventions for signalling presupposed material, we must be willing to infer, if possible, the psychological presence of presuppositions prior to their syntactic expression. We can recover the child's presuppositions in the same way that we recover underlying propositional meaning, by examining the use of sentences in a given context. But once again, the emphasis is on the pragmatic INTENTION as opposed to the pragmatic CONVENTION.

Another important point in using this psychological definition of presupposing is to emphasize the difference between presupposing as a procedure, and presupposition as a mental object. We will suggest in Chapter IV that the first acts of presupposing arise automatically out of some lower level psychological processes. We cannot be certain that the child has constructed the information in a presupposition AS A SYMBOLIC OBJECT (in Piaget's sense, as internally represented information) until he can use recognizable surface signals (conventional or idiosyncratic) that demonstrate his cognitive control of the presupposition. We will see shortly that very young children seem to move from unmarked but appropriate use of presuppositions (as in the "she is blonde" example), to the explicit marking of presuppositions in speech. This ontogenetic move from P_3 presupposing to P_2 presuppositions is based on an overall increase in the amount of material a child can control in a given moment of processing, versus the amount of material that must be left at a perceptual–motor level. The child begins to control his own procedures of "taking for granted" as symbolic structures in themselves.

In the present study, then, we will use the term "presupposition" in the psychological sense (P_3), as a cognitive activity of relating sentences to contexts in a comment–topic relationship. When we are also discussing explicit linguistic devices that mark those presuppositions (P_1 and P_2), we will so indicate in the text.

D. Conversational Postulates

There is a particular class of pragmatic presuppositions that has been used extensively in recent attempts to formalize the pragmatic system. These are a set of assumptions about the nature of human discourse, referred to as conversational postulates. The concept of conversational implicature was originally introduced by Grice (1968), to describe some systematic aspects of language that cannot be reduced to true or false statements. It is assumed that normal human beings who enter into a conversation have agreed to be cooperative. This general principle of cooperation means that speakers will tell each other the truth, that they will only offer information assumed to be new and relevant to the listener, that they will only request information that they sincerely want to have, and so forth. Of course this code of conversation rarely holds constant across a given sample of real dialogue, nor has Grice suggested that it will. Rather, he claims that we will use the set of standard rules in such a way that our deviations from the code will be recognized as violations, and hence contribute additional information. Take the example of the truth principle. If I have just come home from walking through a torrential rain and my spouse says to me *You look terrific,* we both know that the utterance is not true. Because the sentence is false, and we both know it to be false, and because we assume that there is a conversational rule against blatant falsehoods, the sentence serves in this context as an ironic statement that I am soaking wet and look horrible.

The same principle of contrast operates in much of polite speech as well. For example, a woman at a bus stop says to me *Do you know what time it is?* There is a conversational rule which says that speakers do not request irrelevant information from their listeners, and I know that my own knowledge of the time is in itself irrelevant to the stranger waiting for a bus. I therefore conclude from this clear violation that the woman wants more than she has actually requested. I cannot simply answer *Yes I do know*. I must also add *It is 4:30*.

According to Grice, and to an elaboration of Grice's analysis by Gordon and Lakoff (1971), indirect speech acts are conveyed by two kinds of uses of conversational postulates: (1) by violating a conversational postulate pertaining to the surface form of the speech act (e.g., a question asking for irrelevant information), and/or (2) by referring to one of the felicity conditions of the speech act that the speaker really wishes to convey. For example, the question *Do you know what time it is?* is more than a request for irrelevant information. It is also a felicity condition for the imperative *Tell me the time*. One cannot successfully (i.e., felicitously) command an act of which the listener is incapable. And if the listener did not know the time, he would be unable to respond to the command *Tell me the time*. Hence, the question *Do you know what time it is?* sets the stage for a direct request by establishing one of the felicity conditions for that request. Under normal conversational conditions, this hint is generally enough, and the actual imperative is not necessary. Similar "softeners" or "warm ups" can be found for other speech acts, such as the declarative. For example, one conversational postulate controlling declaratives is the presumption that the listener does not already know the information about to be conveyed. Hence the question *Did you know that Gertrude was in town?*—in itself not a terribly relevant question—refers to a felicity condition for the straightforward declarative *Gertrude was in town*. By using a felicity condition rather than the direct speech act itself, the speaker avoids the impression of presuming that his listener is badly informed. And yet the information is conveyed anyway.

Gordon and Lakoff have incorporated Grice's system into a general semantic–pragmatic theory of sentences. The conversational postulates, which Grice himself left unformalized, have been formalized within the grammar as a set of semantic components such as SINCERE and RELE-VANT. These components are contained within the performative structure of a sentence, in a form something such as I SAY TO YOU (RELEVANT) (PROPOSITION X). These components can be grouped together and replaced by other components, permitting pragmatically equivalent clusters to be interchanged. Therefore, the listener can compute the overall intention of the speaker by cancelling out contradictory components. The translation of Grice's rules into semantic primitives is an interesting conflation of semantic and pragmatic analysis, but in itself adds little to a psychological theory of pragmatics. Regardless of the particular formal notation used to describe them, in our own system we must define the conversational postulates as intentions, or rules for using utterances. As with other psychological presuppositions, the speaker uses a sentence to comment upon or intentionally violate an assumed rule of conversation. This usage may or may not be marked in the surface form of the utterance. Indeed, there is a kind of humor which depends crucially upon the unmarked nature of a pragmatic violation. If a comedian laughs out loud at his own jokes, for many native speakers the joke fails. When I walk into the house bedraggled from a rainstorm, my spouse's comment *You look terrific* is much funnier if delivered with a completely sincere expression. On the other hand, the same deadpan joke is a disaster if uttered unsincerely at a time when I do not share the knowledge that not even my mother could love me now. The ability to predict whether or not the listener shares a given assumption, and to plan one's utterances accordingly, is one of the highest achievements in pragmatic development. Much of verbal art will depend upon the multilevel use of sentences to say one thing and mean another, without losing the primary goal of communicating with the listener. While it will be useful to learn linguistic conventions associated with such operations, the same playful violations of conversational rules can be carried out psychologically without invoking the usual set of syntactic contrasts. Hence, conversational postulates also divide into P_3 presuppositions and P_2 presuppositions, marked and unmarked in the surface form of sentences.

Pragmatics and Artificial Intelligence

These rather abstract statements about the epistemological status of pragmatic rules may become somewhat clearer if we examine the importance of the same distinctions in the actual construction of machine models of natural language. Artificial intelligence data are rarely cited in either psychological or linguistic research—there seems to be an assumption that such data are not relevant to the description of real systems. And yet if a given model is supposedly the most feasible explanation of a given phenomenon—language, perception, motor systems, etc.—then that model should, in principle, work in real time. If there are two competing explanations of a given event, and one can function in real time while the other cannot, then it is possible that the buildable model is also closer to the truth. Again, this is only one kind of data relevant to models of psychological systems. At this stage of our knowledge, it is never a sufficient reason for choosing one model over another. However, the knowledge that one epistemological model functions better than another in this kind of laboratory should be regarded as, at the very least, supporting evidence for that model.

In the case of artificial intelligence models of natural language, the kind of epistemological system adopted in the present study seems to be the one leading to most recent advances in modelling language. At a recent arti-

ficial intelligence conference, a number of papers were presented on
natural language, most of which employed what has become a password in
recent cybernetic theory— the use of procedures as data structures. Older
models had maintained a clear division between the symbol statements
(objects) manipulated by the system, and the manipulations (acts) that
are carried out by that program. But in more recent models, the computer's own operations can also be called up as data structures, to be
manipulated by other, higher programs. The act–object distinction is relative only to a given moment in processing, and not to the inherent nature
of individual structures.

As an illustration of how such a system works, let us take a classical
problem in visual pattern recognition. How do we teach a program to
recognize triangles? Older models used search procedures involving templates—actual models of triangles, like slides, which could be fit over the
visual array until a match was found. The difficulty with this is that for
each kind of triangle—isosceles, right triangles, small ones and large
ones—a different template was required. Such programs rapidly became
unwieldy, involving enormous amounts of storage space and search time.
More recent programs employ a completely different principle—in a sense
another kind of epistemology. The program doesn't store or "have" triangles at all. Instead, it has a rule, an operation, of the type "Scan a line that
makes three angle turns without breaking and return to the starting point.
If you can do that, then there is a triangle." This action–description can in
turn be a "feature" in a more complex description, e.g., a three–dimensional pyramid. And the "features" used within the triangle description,
e.g., "angle turns," also have an internal structure made up of lower level
procedures. The program can learn by modifying the action rules to
describe a new concept—e.g., the description of an arch is used to build
the concept of an arcade. Hence, these programs have radically changed
the distinction between act and object, insofar as symbols are all made up
of procedures, which can in turn be called up by other procedures (cf.,
Carl Hewitt, 1973, on "actor" as the basic unit in modern computer programs). The approach to the nature of knowledge illustrated by these
artificial models is strikingly similar to Piaget's action based theory of
knowing.

Winograd (1972) has built an elementary language processing system
that also uses procedures as data structures, resulting in a clear
mechanical demonstration of the role of context and pragmatics in understanding natural language. Winograd's program has "world knowledge"
about a 3-dimensional block world, which it can both perceive and
manipulate. Objects in that world are described in terms of the kind of
action descriptions described above (e.g., the Winston program based on
an earlier project by Guzman). This portion of the program permits pars-

ing of the visual array. The program accepts questions, statements or commands about its world and responds appropriately. Now, there have been a number of clever linguistic programs that seem to answer appropriately on the basis of blind manipulations. For example, the Eliza program (Weizenbaum, 1966) simulates Rogerian therapy with its "clients" by rephrasing the human input in another form—e.g., *I hate my mother—Tell me why* (*you hate your mother*). But the Winograd program actually "understands" language by assimilating it to its limited world. The following passage of dialogue with the program should give an idea of the way nonlinguistic procedures and knowledge of the context of language permit interpretation of linguistic input (Winograd, 1972):

28. *Why did you do that?*
     TO CLEAR OFF THE RED CUBE. (*That* refers to the action
                                                      mentioned in the answer.)

29. *Why did you clear off that
     cube?*
     TO PUT IT ON A LARGE GREEN CUBE.

31. *Why did you do that?*
     BECAUSE YOU ASKED ME TO. (It remembers what it did,
                                                  not how the request was
                                                  worded.)

33. *How may objects did you
     touch while you were doing it?*
     FOUR OF THEM. (Time references can refer
                                to a time span, using words
                                such as *while.*)

                              .
                              .
                              .

After this pioneer effort, many recent cybernetic models of natural language have employed similar principles, so that programs understand discourse not just through a syntax and a dictionary, but by referring to or reconstructing the nonlinguistic context and the "reasons" why events took place. This means that artificial models of language have essentially reinvented pragmatics, rules for relating speech to context. A review by Bobrow and Raphael (1973) summarizes some of the innovations in the new programs. Besides the important advance of using procedures as data statements, there are also devices like the following.

1. FRAME AND LINK. When an action (including linguistic behaviors) is carried out, the program stores some minimal descriptions that will permit

it to reconstruct the context in which that event took place. The context-description is called a **frame**. The symbols carried over into subsequent statements, which "remind" the program of the original frame-context, are called **links**. Within linguistic pragmatics, conventions that mark anaphora or presupposition could be considered "links" in that they remind the listener of where to look in current or past context. For example, *I gave him **that** one* permits the listener to call up or recreate the original setting by using the stressed pronoun ***that*** as a link to a previous context frame. These links are similar to the pragmatic conventions used to signal P_1 and P_2 presuppositions, discussed earlier in this chapter.

2. DEMONS AND OPEN FILES. When a symbol has been constructed in central processing, information entailed by that symbol, but not explicitly asserted by it, can be called up by lower level systems, so that this information is ready should it be required for subsequent problem solving. This system serves to reduce the search time necessary for analyzing ambiguous input, since high probability interpretations present themselves first, and less likely interpretations need not be considered. For example, in Chapter VI on Italian word order, we discuss an anecdote in which the ambiguous sentence

Mangiano i selvaggi.   '(They eat) the natives.'

occurs at a cocktail party with a group of anthropologists. In Italian, 'the natives' could be either the subject or the object of the verb 'eat'. Under neutral conditions the high probability interpretation would be that human beings are generally the subject rather than the object of verbs of eating. However, the context of an anthropology meeting increases the likelihood of a cannibalistic interpretation. And in fact—even though the discussion was indeed about a restaurant where the natives go to eat—the listeners mistakenly assumed that the sentence was about cannibalism. In a sense, the file drawers for cannibalism were open and ready by the very fact that the interlocutors were anthropologists. In general, however, the context decreases rather than increases the likelihood of misunderstanding.

According to Bobrow and Raphael's review, **demons** are lower order data stacks that are stimulated when a given symbol appears. The demon may never come up for actual processing, but it is ready to step out of priority and present itself first should another relevant statement come up. **Open files** are larger data areas that are called up ready for action when a particular demon has been stimulated. Hence, an open file is merely a quantitatively larger demon.

These advances in programming—lower order events that are outside the purview of central processing but are related to whatever is going on in central processing—greatly reduce amount of search time and facilitate processing when ambiguous data comes in. As such, they look much more like real human dialogue, in which the context insures against communicative misfire when incomplete or ambiguous sentences occur. This is a particularly clear example of the need for a pragmatic component in an efficient language processing system.

3. PATTERN MATCHING PROGRAMS. This is another innovation which reduces the search load in central processing. When a higher order program needs to solve a problem X, instead of examining or specifying all the procedures required to solve X, it can call up prepared subprograms merely by asking for "a solution that looks a lot like X." The search mechanism then need only look for a few identifying symbol–labels among its subprograms, choosing on the basis of that alone. Executive processing need never examine the internal procedural structure of the subprogram, as it would have had to do in older models. This new arrangement of higher and lower order programs is analogous to the Piagetian distinction between sensorimotor organization and higher thought processes. In fact, a recent book by Piaget and associates (*Prise de Conscience,* 1974) deals with the difficulty children have in subjecting well-organized subprograms, e.g., crawling on all fours, to attentive, conscious analysis. Similarly, although language is constructed originally on the basis of sensorimotor procedures—e.g., the word *triangle* is the top node or identifying symbol of a set of procedures for knowing triangles—higher processes need never reexamine the internal sensorimotor structure of lexical meanings once the pattern matching device is familiar and stable. It is sufficient to call up only the top nodes of the lexical structure, in order to interpret a wordlike sound. We will return to this concept later, in Chapter III, with regard to the construction of symbols by the child at the end of the sensorimotor period.

In sum, it looks very much as though the most recent generation of artificial intelligence models are based on a kind of Piagetian action system, with operations taking place on different cognitive levels, and with lower order procedures forming the objects for higher order procedures. Within these approaches, current machine models of language are being built with context information, implication and entailment procedures—in short a set of data structures that very much resemble the pragmatic system described in recent linguistic theory, capturing sentence external as well as sentence internal information. The old Quillian network dictionary has been superseded by models that no longer separate linguistic data from cognition, perception, and action. The fact that this approach has been fruitful in building humanlike machines does not necessarily mean that human adults are organized that way. However, if, on other psychological grounds, this kind of organization looks like a promising model of language and cognition, then the success of the same models in artificial intelligence research is at the very least supportive.

Predictions

All the definitions just presented contain a single theme: Language is defined from the point of view of the speaker, as a set of mental operations for constructing and using sentences in context. This includes the sentence internal rules for building and mapping propositional content—rules traditionally treated in syntactic and semantic theory. But it also covers some sentence external, pragmatic structures: the speaker's goal in using an utterance (performatives) and rules for relating utterances to their contexts (presuppositions and conversational postulates). Insofar as pragmatic structures affect the surface form of utterances, they are proper subject matter for a theory of grammar. And in fact, there has been a great deal of recent activity within linguistics aimed at defining pragmatic aspects of the grammar. In this brief review, and in subsequent chapters devoted to particular topics, some of these analyses have been used as aids in studying the acquisition of pragmatics. Far better reviews of linguistic pragmatics are available in works by linguists. For example, many current issues in pragmatics are presented in papers from the Texas "Performadillo" conference on Performatives, Presupposition, and Conversational Implicature (1973). However, in the present study I am less interested in a systematic description of language conventions than in a realistic description of the child's entry into that system. Pragmatics is worth studying in its own right. But the focus here is on the cognitive system that the child brings to bear on language use. In fact, I am interested in pragmatics precisely because it lies at the outskirts of the grammar in the traditional sense, at the interface between linguistic, cognitive, and cultural competence. As such, pragmatics provides us with a probe into the child's developing mental processes.

There are in fact many psycholinguists who prefer not to take this risk (cf., Fodor, 1966; McNeill, 1970). They separate out the "pure" linguistic theory as a theory of **competence**—what a child knows about his language. Psychological problems—e.g., perception and memory limits—are relegated to a theory of **performance**, events that take place when competence is used to generate utterances. However, the Piagetian model of cognition that is used in the present study is in fact a theory of cognitive competence, of the rules used by children to generate perception, memory, and other acts of knowing. There is also such a thing as cognitive performance, when these rules are used to interact with particular kinds of content in the real world. Just as the rule for embedding sentences is limited by performance factors in memory, the rules for seriating members of a class of elements or conserving weight constancy in the face of perceptual transformation can also be affected by forgetting, by the visual complexity of the array, etc. We are not confusing competence and performance in this study, but rather attempting to establish a model of competence underlying both language and the other cognitive systems. That may well prove to be impossible, but it should at least be clear from the outset that this is the goal.

Within the general approach of translating linguistic terms into psychological versions, the above definitions were also selected because of their relation to Piaget's theory of cognitive levels. It has been stressed for each construct—meaning, reference, proposition, performative, presupposition—that there is a difference between a procedure or act, and the treatment of that act as an object of a higher procedure. That distinction is an important one because of its implications for development. In Piaget's epistemological model, the child proceeds from the lower levels of sensorimotor organization, to higher levels of thought, by learning to take his own acts as the objects of higher mental acts. Thus the set of logical operations that a child eventually carries out "in his head" are initially exercised on the plane of sensorimotor action. This is not a metaphor. Piaget makes this claim quite literally. The child who learns to move around a room—e.g., that one cannot walk through objects, or that by reversing his path he can return to his starting point—is not aware of the algebraic relations holding among his actions. But those logical relations are implicit in his sensorimotor schemes, and when he begins to think about moving about the room or planning how to get back to his starting point, his mental operations will be organized in algebraic groups precisely because they were originally exercised that way at the sensorimotor level. And when still later he moves from thinking about concrete objects, to thinking about the abstract relations holding among objects, he will in fact be reflecting upon his own thought procedures as a new kind of mental object. At each stage, the operations of the preceding level become the elements upon which higher procedures can operate.

We hope to trace the same process through the acquisition of pragmatics. First we will examine the child's initial procedures for using signals, a minimal communicative system. Then we will try to capture the move from simply using speech to thinking about his own communicative procedures—changing them, modifying them, commenting upon them, "fixing them up" with whatever conventions his language may provide.

There is an assumption here that certain linguistic conventions require a more reflective control of one's communicative procedures. For example, Gricean polite forms and hedged conditional statements seem to require not just a propositional content, nor a single set of pragmatic procedures, but a complex coordination between content and function. When a child passes from declaring and commanding, to using elaborate camouflages for declaring and commanding, he must have gone up one epistemological level, to reflecting upon his own pragmatic acts as objects in themselves. It is this switch in epistemological levels that is the focus of the present study, the ability to exploit the function–content distinction and to consider one's own communicative acts as pragmatic objects.

In the ensuing chapters, a skeletal model is offered of pragmatic development in language, based on Piaget's theory of genetic epistemology. Data have been collected on several different problems in general pragmatic development, and Italian pragmatics in particular. The choice of problems for study was partially related to predictions about the general course of cognitive development from 0 to 6 years, i.e., some acquisitions were expected very early, even prior to speech, while others were expected to appear much later in development. There is an underlying assumption, common to all studies of language development, that the order of acquisition will reflect the relative difficulty or complexity of these structures. Furthermore, a systematic pattern of errors prior to the acquisition of a given structure should yield information about transitional or partial stages in the development of that structure. Longitudinal records are used to establish the relative position of a given language structure on a developmental scale and to determine what kinds of substitutions or approximations can be found before a particular device is acquired. Some cross-sectional experiments with larger samples of children are used to provide statistical evidence for the sequence of acquisition revealed by the longitudinal records.

To emphasize the parallels between pragmatics and cognitive development, the following chapters are divided into three sections. Part One deals with pragmatics in the sensorimotor period, from 0 to 18 months. There are three chapters, on performatives, propositions, and presuppositions, respectively. Part Two discusses pragmatics in the early preoperational period, from 18 months to $3\frac{1}{2}$ to 4 years. Within this section, one chapter presents longitudinal evidence for the linguistic control of performatives, and the ability to make metapragmatic statements. Another chapter in the same section presents both longitudinal and experimental findings on the acquisition of the presupposition for topicalization and emphasis. Finally, Part Three describes pragmatics at the beginning of concrete operations, from 4 to 6 years. Here both longitudinal and experimental evidence is presented on the acquisition of counterfactual conditionals, polite forms, and other implicit speech acts. The argument is made that these later structures require reversible transformations of an internal array, particularly the coordination of the speaker's and the listener's perspectives.

A. *Pragmatics in the Sensorimotor Period (0 to 18 Months)*

First, performatives are seen as nothing more or less than the intention to communicate, in order to have some effect on the listener. This means that the earliest possible appearance of performatives or intentional communication, must await certain developments in intentionality and in concepts of causation and agency. THE PREDICTION IS MADE THAT MINIMAL, GESTURAL COMMUNICATION DURING WHICH THE CHILD APPEARS TO EXPECT OR AWAIT AN ADULT RESPONSE WILL OCCUR ONLY WHEN THE COGNITIVE BASIS FOR THE USE OF TOOLS AND AGENT–INSTRUMENTS IS ESTABLISHED, AT SENSORIMOTOR STAGE 5. Data is reported from a longitudinal study of three infants to support the hypothesis, for both imperative and declarative performatives, that intentional communication is a Stage 5 development.

Second, having established that simple gestural performatives follow minimal sensorimotor requirements, we will examine the onset of propositions and referential speech, as they are used in performative sequences. THE PREDICTION IS MADE THAT WHILE ILLOCUTIONARY PROCESSES CAN TAKE PLACE AFTER CERTAIN SENSORIMOTOR DEVELOPMENTS, LOCUTIONARY PROCESSES FOR CONSTRUCTING AND PROJECTING PROPOSITIONS MUST AWAIT THE SIXTH SENSORIMOTOR STAGE, WITH THE DEVELOPMENT OF THE SYMBOLIC CAPACITY. Data is presented from the above longitudinal study to support the hypothesis that referential speech follows gestural performatives in ontogeny, and does not take place until other, nonlinguistic manifestations of a symbolic capacity (e.g., "pretend" play) have also appeared.

Third, the fact that performatives first appear at a sensorimotor level while referential speech appears at the symbolic level introduces the concept of communication as an event that can take place on two cognitive planes. This Piagetian approach to communication is used to examine a recent controversy in the study of early child language—why 1-word speech is so rich in meaning and yet so limited in expression. While no new data are presented, the results of other studies are re-examined, raising the possibility that the passage from 1- to 2- to n-word speech can be explained by the proposal that sensorimotor meanings are being slowly reconstructed at the new and limited level of internal representation. THE TOPIC–COMMENT FORM OF LATER PROPOSITIONS IS SEEN AS DERIVING FROM THE EARLIER, SPLIT-LEVEL STRUCTURE HOLDING BETWEEN WHAT IS SYMBOLIZED AND SAID (SYMBOLIC LEVEL) AND WHAT IS PERCEIVED AND UNDERSTOOD BUT NOT SAID (SENSORIMOTOR LEVEL).

Finally, the same concept of 2-level processing is then used to examine the earliest relationship between propositions and presuppositions. Just as comment and topic may be derived from the division into said and unsaid, what will later become the proposition–presupposition relationship may derive from the same cognitive division. IT IS SUGGESTED THAT "PRESUPPOS- ING" IS A VERY EARLY ACTIVITY, A PROCESS INHERENT IN THE SELECTION OF ONE ELEMENT FROM AN ORGANIZED CONTEXT, TO BE ENCODED AT THE EXCLUSION OF OTHER ELEMENTS. Some data from the above longitudinal study and data from studies by other authors are discussed in support of this hypothesis. Hence, at the earliest stages, presupposing is something that children DO, but presuppositions are not yet something that children HAVE as a symbolic object (in Piaget's sense) that can be encoded, recalled, or otherwise modified and manipulated by the child.

B. Pragmatics in the Preoperational Period
(18 months to 4 years)

According to Piaget, after the symbolic capacity appears in the first 12 to 18 months, the child must in a sense begin the whole developmental process all over again. At the sensorimotor level, he had achieved a dynamic balance between his assimilations and accommodations to a world of real and present objects. At the symbolic level the world is once again in potential chaos. Past, present and future events intrude on one another, and mental objects can slip from control in the same way that real world objects once eluded the child's efforts. The child must rebuild and reorder his world at the level of internal representation. During this preoperational period, he has not yet accommodated to the particularly flexible nature of internal symbolic objects. He operates on flexible symbol structures in inflexible and rigid ways, as if they retained the concrete form from which they were derived. Nevertheless, the child does now think about his own procedures in a limited way. Insofar as performatives and presuppositions are already established as sensorimotor procedures for communicating, the child can now begin to think about and talk about the pragmatic aspects of language use. His speech should therefore take on a different aspect, shifting from the uttering of simple or partial propositions, to utterances that encode both aspects of the proposition and aspects of its context of use. Among the pragmatic developments that we might expect in the early preoperational period are the following.

First, performatives at the sensorimotor level are seen as procedures that are not yet organized at the level of internal representation. During the preoperational period, the child should begin to control both his proposition and his performative as symbolic structures, as mental objects that can be operated upon, and encoded together in the surface form of utterances. We should expect to find references in the child's speech to various coordinates of the speech situation itself—the speaker, the listener, the place and time relative to time of utterance. At this stage, a child can begin to "talk about talking", to refer to whole speech events as propositional objects—e.g., *I said (Proposition X)*. In this section, we will examine the onset of such metapragmatic statements, using these as evidence that there is a clear cognitive control over the performative itself as a symbol structure. WE WILL ALSO EXAMINE OTHER ELEMENTS OF DISCOURSE—CONNECTING TERMS LIKE CONJUNCTIONS AND ADVERBS, TIME AND PLACE DEIXIS—TO DETERMINE WHETHER A PREOPERATIONAL CONTROL OVER PERFORMATIVES IS ACCOMPANIED BY A MORE GENERAL CONTROL OVER DISCOURSE AS A SYMBOLIC

UNIT. Again, we will use the longitudinal speech records for two Italian children, Claudia and Francesco.

Second, at the sensorimotor level presupposing is viewed as a procedure for selecting one element for encoding at the exclusion of others, yielding a topic–comment relationship between what is said and what is left unsaid. When the child gains control over his own act of presupposing, we should expect this procedure to be available for encoding in the surface form of sentences. In Italian grammar, there are several devices for signalling a new versus an old relationship among parts of a sentence. One is to provide contrastive stress on the "new" or emphatic portion of an utterance, as is also done in English. Another device, more interesting for its implications for the rest of syntactic development, is a rule for shifting the order of sentence constituents. For example, if the subject of the sentence is considered to be new information, or contrasting information, the usual SVO order is changed to a subject final word order. Since this rule goes against the standard syntactic forms for Italian grammar, its mastery by children should be clear evidence of a firm cognitive control over both the proposition and the presuppositional relationship. IT IS PROPOSED THAT ITALIAN CHILDREN WILL SHIFT FROM A SEMIAUTOMATIC TENDENCY TO STRESS WHAT IS NEW AND INTERESTING, TO A MORE DELIBERATE CONTROL OVER THE NEW–OLD RELATIONSHIP REFLECTED IN THE MASTERY OF CONTRASTING WORD ORDERS. Such an expansion in preoperational control should occur well into the preoperational period, at a time when increased cognitive control is exhibited in other areas as well. This section will be based primarily on longitudinal speech records for two Italian children.

C. Pragmatics and Concrete Operations
(4 to 6 Years)

Piaget defines concrete operations as the stage at which the child can perform certain flexible, reversible operations on a set of internal symbolic objects ("groupings"). While preoperational thought is characterized by one-way mappings and deductive "blind alleys," the concrete operational child can undo and redo operations in his head while conserving the stable qualities of the system under transformation. Now, comprehension and production of speech can be considered one-way mappings in Piaget's sense, proceeding from surface form to meaning, or vice versa. Hence, they should be within the capabilities of the preoperational child. However, the concrete operational child is capable of reversible operations. In terms of language, this means that he can both encode and decode his OWN messages prior to uttering them. He has a two-way, reversible control over his own speech acts. He can simultaneously consider both his own viewpoint and that of the decoder or listener, to predict which presuppositions are likely to misfire, and to act to correct a potential error by modifying the message. This also permits predictions about which messages are socially offensive, so that utterances can be fine tuned along a dimension of politeness or assertiveness before they are produced in speech.

In Piaget's *Language and Thought of the Child* (1926), there are a number of suggestions concerning changes that occur in communication as egocentrism declines and the child masters reversible control over varying perspectives. In this study, we have limited ourselves to two types of Italian syntactic structures that are likely to require reversible, flexible internal operations on performatives and presuppositions.

First, the use of counterfactual conditional verbs in Italian requires that the speaker assert a relationship A ENTAILS B while he warns the listener not to assume the truth of A. This ability to assert and suspend different aspects of a single message requires a complex coordination between propositional content and the performative structure. Also, such an operation is motivated only if the child can consider the viewpoint of the listener sufficiently to know that he might jump to the conclusion that A is true unless he is otherwise warned. THEREFORE, COUNTERFACTUAL CONDITIONS SHOULD NOT BE ACQUIRED UNTIL THE END OF THE PREOPERATIONAL PERIOD, AS THE CHILD ENTERS INTO THE CONCRETE OPERATIONAL STAGE. The longitudinal build up of a capacity for conditional verbs is examined in the records for Claudia and Francesco. Then, a study is presented eliciting counterfactual conditions from 74 Italian preschool children, ranging in age from 2;0 to 6;2.

Another aspect of pragmatics requiring knowledge of the listener's perspective and a complex operation within a single speech act is the Gricean issue of politeness and conversational implicature. For example, to use the sentence *Is the window open?* as a request rather than a question requires not only a propositional content, but the knowledge that performatives can and must be camouflaged in such a way that both content and goal are communicated implicitly. We will examine the onset of various explicit versus implicit request forms in the longitudinal records for Claudia and Francesco. Then, a study is presented assessing the ability of 60 Italian preschool children, ranging in age from 3;0 to 6;2, to judge and explain differences in politeness between sentences pairs in an experimental task. IT IS PREDICTED THAT POLITE FORMS REQUIRING GRICEAN MANIPULATIONS OF CONVERSATIONAL POSTULATES WILL BE AMONG THE LAST PRAGMATIC DEVICES ACQUIRED AND WILL BE DELAYED UNTIL THE END OF THE PREOPERATIONAL PERIOD WHEN COMPLEX AND REVERSIBLE OPERATIONS ARE ACQUIRED.

Each of the three major sections—pragmatics in the sensorimotor, preoperational, and concrete operational period—contains two or three chapters devoted to particular topics. In each section, we will examine the status of the tripartite system of proposition, presupposition, and performative, as it is manifested at that stage in cognitive development.

The decision to opt for breadth rather than depth means that for any given issue in pragmatics—e.g., polite forms, conditional verbs—far more questions are left asked then answered. Hence, suggestions for further research are posed at the end of each chapter and summarized again in the concluding section.

Since this study will examine some very different pragmatic structures, at different stages of development, methods will have to be dictated by the particular problem at hand. This means that instead of one overall methodology chapter, I will introduce particular techniques at the beginning of each section. Also, relevant research by other authors will be introduced within individual discussion sections. Although an overall organization into problem–method–results–discussion is not preserved across the study as a whole, the reader will find these divisions within chapters devoted to particular topics. As a result, readers who are interested in particular chapters only need not refer constantly to earlier sections.

PART ONE

Pragmatics in The Sensorimotor Period

Despite the more or less convincing arguments offered by philosophers and linguists for the existence of performative and presuppositional structures, for psycholinguists the consequent proliferation of trees may be disconcerting. Many of the pioneer works of post-Chomskian psycholinguistics had been dedicated to establishing the psychological reality of a much more limited stock of formal objects and transformations. A variety of indirect measures—perceived location of clicks, real time requirements for processing, amount of loss in recall, and order of acquisition by children—were aimed at demonstrating, for example, that an embedded sentence has two sentence trees instead of one, or that a sentence with three transformations is more difficult to process than a sentence with two. The more recent models proposed by generative semanticists present psychologists with a much more elaborate stock of tree structures, and derivations or "mapping rules." The sentence nucleus itself has an elaborated internal structure, predicate trees underlying complex lexical items (e.g., *kill* = CAUSE(BECOME(NOT(ALIVE)))). In addition, there are the trees describing presuppositions and performatives. If there is an isomorphism between (1) the number of trees and derivations, and (2) the space and time for processing, it may be that the traditional psychological measures are too crude to capture the complexities of recent proposals.

At this writing, Antinucci and Parisi (1972) are among the only psycholinguists to have applied detailed semantic analysis to early child speech. For example, the 1-word sentence *give,* used by a 15-month-old child to demand a pencil, is described with a predicate *give* and three arguments (giver, receiver, and object). The predicate is analyzed further into its semantic components CAUSE(COINCIDE(X, Y)). The entire nucleus is taken as an argument by an imperative performative clause, which is also analyzed into its semantic primitives. In a review of their paper, Schlesinger (1973, p. 12) says "The representations are, to say the least, impressive." There is a clear implication that such structures are too impressive in their complexity to be accurate representations of what children mean in 1- or 2-word speech.

Schlesinger's discomfort with such elaborate semantic structures rests in his adherence to purely linguistic definitions of terms such as performative and presupposition. As we have defined those terms here, they are essentially psychological FUNCTIONS. Stripped of their formal notation, performative and presupposition become two basic tools for speaking. Performatives describe the capacity to formulate and execute a communicative intention. Presuppositions formalize our ability to choose which aspects of a situation to encode so as to exploit maximally those aspects that a listener already shares, and to express the selected information in a form that the listener will deem appropriate. The actual encoding of meaning, and the consequent development of a syntactic system, depend heavily on these twin capacities. Viewed as functions rather than formal objects, performatives and presuppositions may be more psychologically real than the sundry syntactic objects that have occupied psychologists for 15 years.

In the following three sections, an assumption is made that when there is communication, somewhere in the nervous system three broadly conceived language structures must exist: a performative "intention to communicate," a proposition or thing to be communicated, and a presupposing procedure for placing that proposition into a contextual frame. The form these structures take, the way in which they are acquired, and the cognitive levels to which they correspond are discussed in the light of data from my own research and that of others. The purpose of the following three sections is to establish a case for the psychological validity of performative–proposition–presupposition as a system constructed in the first year of life, in preparation for language development. At this point, we are interested only in establishing the existence of PROCEDURES. The manipulation of these same procedures as symbolic objects, which can be reflected in the surface form of utterances, will be taken up in later sections.

The following three chapters are based primarily upon data collected by Bates, Camaioni, and Volterra (1973) as part of a larger project on communication prior to speech. The method adopted in this study is a variation of the quasilongitudinal method outlined in Slobin *et al.* (1967), *Field Manual for the Cross-Cultural Study of the Acquisition of Communicative Competence*. The manual recommends a variation on the now classical longitudinal study of language development (e.g., Brown,

1973) such that several children at strategic ages or developmental levels are followed until they have overlapped each other in development. This quasilongitudinal method is recommended when time limits preclude the "beginning to end" approach with individual children, and it has proven particularly workable in studying the period prior to speech.

There are three subjects, all first-born females. At the beginning of the study, Serena was 2 months of age, Carlotta 6, and Marta 12 months. The backgrounds of the three children were similar. In all three cases, both parents were middle class, university educated residents of Rome, Italy. From the birth of their daughters through the last taping sessions, the mothers of Serena and Carlotta were not working outside the home. Marta's mother had recently returned to working mornings, and in the morning Marta was cared for by her grandmother.

Home visits were made every two weeks for Carlotta and Serena, and once a month for Marta, for 6–8 months or until the subjects had overlapped in development. Visits lasted an average of two hours, during which 15 to 30 minutes of videorecordings were taken. In addition, the mothers of Serena and Carlotta maintained diaries. For Marta, there were observational records from seven months of age taken by our colleague Laura Benigni, who was also a participant in all of Marta's taping sessions. Marta was also a subject in Dr. Benigni's research on mother–child interaction, which accounts for the slight differences in method adopted in her case.

The use of video techniques introduced necessary changes in the spontaneous approach typical of longitudinal language studies. For two reasons, it was necessary to limit the length of the films per session to 15 minutes or an entire half-hour tape when indicated by particularly rich developments (in Marta's case, all tapes were 30 minutes in length). First, the cost of videotapes is prohibitive, and several hours of taping per session were beyond our financial limits. Second, the mass of data available in complete video–audio recordings renders transcription virtually impossible if too much data is collected. For example, Pittenger, Hockett, and Danehy (1960) based an entire book (*The First Five Minutes*) on detailed analyses of five minutes of a clinical interview.

The necessity of a time limit to taping precluded purely spontaneous and unplanned sessions. Instead, we adopted a method in the tradition of ethological observation, and of Piaget's clinical method, insofar as naturalistic observation was interspersed with calculated interventions by the observer. Since the home visits themselves lasted an average of two hours, only the planned moments or particularly interesting spontaneous behaviors were recorded. Almost all sessions were attended by two experimenters, and the camera was always controlled by one of the two. The Sony AV-3400 portable has a trigger control mechanism that enabled the experimenter to begin recording immediately when the child began some particularly interesting behavior (e.g., picking up a book to show to Mommy). Hence, the 15–30 minutes tapes are a composite of segments taken throughout the two hour visits.

Sessions were carried out in the child's home (including the vacation home or grandmother's home in some cases). When interventions were made, only familiar toys and household objects were used. In a few cases where novelty reactions were of interest, a new toy was brought to the session. But stimulae were always commercially available objects that are the frequent toys of middle-class children. All sessions consisted of informal elicitations of social interactions with adults (varied to include father, mother, strangers), or spontaneous reactions to pictures, objects, mirrors, hiding games or ball games, and attempts to elicit new abilities or routines noted in the mother's diaries. The choice of interventions was guided on the one hand by the developmental signposts outlined in the cognitive studies of Piaget and on the other by the theory of social development outlined by Bowlby in *Attachment and Loss* (1969). The tapes themselves were then analyzed from the more particular point of view of communicative development.

All tapes were viewed at least twice by all three raters. The transcriptions were made in two series: (1) a precise transcription of the child's behaviors in all sessions (no phonetic transcriptions were made; interesting or seemingly relevant sounds were reproduced in standard Italian spelling), and (2) a series of derived transcripts, listing those behaviors that were relevant to the build-up of the performative.

With regard to the first phase in transcription, the word "precise" is a relative term, and we certainly do not pretend to the degree of precision presented by observers of nonverbal behavior such as Birdwhistell (1970) or Duncan (1969). We refer simply to a running record of events unanalyzed in terms of the goals of the present research. The following excerpt should give some idea of the level of detail involved:

> Carlotta 7;25 (7 months, 25 days): ... The observer moves toward C., holding out a small doll and speaking for the doll simultaneously. C. looks toward the doll and stretches her arm and hand toward it, making an open-and-shut gesture with the hand. She then lowers her hand and her glance toward the ground and pronounces a sound (eh-eh). She begins to bat both hands against the floor. The observer begins talking again, C. looks up momentarily at the observer, then looks back to the floor and bats both hands against the pavement ...

For students of nonverbal communication, these qualitative judgments are no doubt quite superficial. For example, the description "looks toward the doll" is probably, as Duncan suggests, drawn from concomitant cues such as head position relative to body, etc. However, for the broad purposes of the present study, it was necessary to place our faith in observer intuitions, and in the fact that all three observers checked their viewing of the tapes against the transcriptions.

With regard to the second phase in transcription, the running records were used to construct three tables of data: (1) a table of cognitive developments, based on Piaget's analysis of sensorimotor development with particular regard to the categories of object permanency, groups, causality and means–end relationships, and imitation (for a replication of Piaget's findings, see Uzgiris and Hunt, 1966); (2) a table of social developments, based on analyses by Bowlby, Wolff (1968), and Spitz (1966), with particular regard to smiling, crying and vocalization, fear of strangers, and attachment behaviors; and (3) a table of particular signals and behaviors that seem to precede the performative of requesting, and of declaring (in particular, showing objects, giving, exhibiting or showing off, etc.). Also included were words or wordlike productions by Marta and Carlotta, and any apparent comprehension of adult words and gestures.

Running records for the first session were made by agreement among all three raters, while transcripts for later sessions were made by a single rater and checked by the others against their own viewing of the tapes. In the second phase of transcription, all interpretations were decided upon by agreement among all three raters working from the original records. When an item in the running records was either doubtful, or particularly pertinent to an interpretation in the second phase, it was rechecked in the tapes by two of the three experimenters.

Chapter II, on performatives in the sensorimotor period, is based entirely on data from the Bates, Camaioni, and Volterra study. Chapters III and IV, on propositions and presupposing respectively, are based on this data together with my own interpretations of longitudinal data by other authors. In particular, I will refer to a study of gesture and one-word speech by Greenfield and Smith (in press), to Bloom's data on one-word speech (1973), and to data by Antinucci and Parisi (1972) and Antinucci and Volterra (1973) on the very early speech of two Italian children. None of these latter studies used videotapes extensively. All are based on a combination of audiorecordings and maternal diaries, with detailed contextual notes to aid in the interpretation of semantic intentions.

CHAPTER II

Sensorimotor Performatives[1]

ELIZABETH BATES

LUIGIA CAMAIONI

VIRGINIA VOLTERRA

Studies of language development have almost universally been addressed to the question of how children learn the structure of their language. There is a more fundamental question that is generally taken for granted in these studies: Why does a child talk? Where does he get the idea of communication in the first place? And what sort of cognitive and social developments prepare such a fundamental discovery? A study of the acquisition of performatives is, basically, a study of how children arrive at the intention to communicate.

Those studies that have mentioned performatives (subsumed under the term "modality" in studies adopting case grammar models) have indicated that performatives exist at the beginning of speech. Gruber (1967) suggests that the first one-word labels used by children (e.g., *Shoe!*) have the underlying structure *I indicate to you (a shoe)*. Ingram (1971) finds that several aspects of modality in one-word speech are marked as commands or labels by accompanying gesture and intonation. Greenfield and Smith (1974) find that the first one-word utterances by their subjects are so-called "pure performatives," speech acts such as *hi* and *bye-bye* that are in themselves events rather than descriptions of events. In a cross-

[1] Portions of this chapter have appeared in Elizabeth Bates, Luigia Camaioni, and Virginia Volterra. "The Acquisition of Performatives Prior to Speech." *Merrill-Palmer Quarterly,* 1975, **21**(3). Reprinted by permission of the authors and the Merrill-Palmer Quarterly of Behavior and Development.

sectional study of 36 2-, 3- and 4-year-olds, Bates (1971) finds no developmental differences in the frequency of declarative, imperative, or interrogative intentions as judged from videotapes. Finally, in studies of semantic
development in Italian children, Antinucci and Parisi (1972) and Antinucci and Volterra (1973) have concluded that such "speech acts" as commanding, declaring, and negating are performed with the first one-word
utterances of their subjects. In short, although adult-like grammatical
marking of communicative intentions may be delayed [cf., Bowerman
(1973) on interrogatives], some performative intentions are found as far
back in language development as anyone's records go.

We therefore decided to begin our study of performatives in the period
prior to speech itself, inferring the intention to communicate from its first
manifestations in gesture, eye contact, and prelinguistic vocalizations. The
purpose of our study was twofold: (1) to generate a set of hypotheses concerning cognitive prerequisites for purposive communication, and (2) to
examine the feasibility of using a semantic analysis of the performative to
describe communicative developments in the sensorimotor period. The
class of performatives is in fact an open class, including such far-ranging
social functions as promising, christening, and pronouncing man and wife.
For this study, we chose the two performative structures that seemed most
basic to linguistic and prelinguistic communication: the imperative and
the declarative.

According to the componential analysis of the performative outlined by
Parisi and Antinucci (1973), the declarative is actually a kind of imperative, in which the speaker seeks to elicit a particular mental activity of
"attending" or "knowing" in his listener. The imperative and declarative
are identical in structure, except for the two kinds of predicates to be
caused in the listener, i.e., DO versus ASSUME. Both performatives are
described with embedded causal structures in which a proposition or
signal is used to cause some event in the listener:

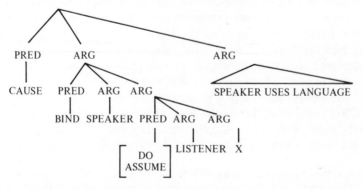

We can only infer the presence of a structure of this kind in the child on
the basis of external, nonverbal behaviors. We must establish that the

child has emitted some signal (not necessarily a convention shared by his community) with the intention of causing some behavior by the adult. There is a tradition in psychology that prefers to stop at the level of behavior, dispensing with notions like intention. Bruner (1973) has responded to this position with an approach compatible with our own:

> Intention viewed abstractly may be at issue philosophically. But it is a necessity for the biology of complex behavior, by whatever label we wish to call it [p. 2].

Bruner gives an example of evidence that a child intends the attainment of some end state in observations of infants who are still incapable of prehension. A desirable object is held before the child's eyes, and sucking and tongue movements in the mouth are immediately recorded. If the object is then given to the child, the immediate consummatory behavior is in fact to put the object in the mouth and suck it. Bruner suggests that these earlier mouth movements are "anticipatory consummatory behaviors." The desired end state is represented in this motor form within the child's system from the moment that the object is noticed. Later on, the child will be capable of selecting a means for bringing about the end state e.g., reaching out and taking the toy. When this occurs, a means–end loop has been established.

In the present study, the intention to communicate will be inferred from (1) a context indicating that a goal desired by the child is operating; (2) the emission of some movement or sound, in which eye contact is alternated between the object and the adult; (3) the persistence of behavior (2) until the inferred goal is reached; (4) consummatory behavior confirming that the child did indeed have that goal in mind.

In the first section, we will examine the development of the protoimperative, defined here as the insertion of the adult as a means to attaining objects or other goals. Then we will examine the development of the protodeclarative, defined as the use of an object—in giving, pointing, showing—as a means to obtaining attention from the adult. In both cases, we will try to determine the cognitive developments that parallel these two communicative functions.

The Imperative

In order to use adults as a means to obtaining objects, the child must (1) be capable of formulating object–goals and selecting adequate means for reaching them, and (2) be able to evoke and sustain the attention of adults. Only then can he put these schemata together into an imperative structure.

Initially, our youngest subject Serena appears incapable of formulating goals, producing only what are presumably genetically determined behaviors (e.g., crying) symptomatic of specified physiological states. The child may be totally unaware of the signal value of these behaviors, but the adult recognizes them as signals and responds as if they were produced intentionally by the child. Characteristic of such signals is the so-called "hunger cry" which many parents claim to distinguish from other cries as early as the first few weeks of life (Wolff, 1968). In a diary entry for Serena (0;17 days), her parents report a hunger cry that is distinguishable by its particular volume and insistence. A month later (1;17) the diary reports a "capricious cry" that diminishes only when Serena is picked up and held. In both cases, the cry manifests a state of need; consequently, the adult intervenes to satisfy that need—to feed her, to hold and comfort her, etc. Hence, a circle of action–reaction is established between child and adult—a first step in the development of requests. We might be tempted to conclude here, as parents often do, that the child is aware of the adult's role as agent and manipulates him intentionally. However, if this were the case we could not explain sequences occurring later in development, in which the child seems entirely unaware that the adult could intervene to help him obtain an object. At this stage, we have no evidence that imperatives are under the child's voluntary control.

The next step will be the formulation of goals, in particular those related to the objects surrounding the child, and the construction and choice of means adequate for actualizing those goals. This process has already begun in Serena with the involuntary grasping response. If the observer stimulates her palm, Serena can be made to hold an object temporarily in her hand (2;19). We could say at this point that the infant possesses a means that is not yet in the service of a goal. In the first 10 to 12 weeks, Serena passes to diffuse attempts to "approach" an object dangled before her, by gross motor movements of the entire body, movements of the head, and opening the mouth. These are similar to Bruner's anticipatory consummatory responses; the infant starts doing what she would do if she had the object, namely examining it with her mouth. We could say that at this point the child possesses a goal without an adequate set of means.

Only with the first efforts by Serena to grasp an object (without previous tactile stimulation) do we have a clear case of the realization of a goal through adequate means (4;13). This link between goal and means provides an intention structure similar to the first level of the performative. We can paraphrase this structure as

ACTOR USES MEANS TO OBTAIN GOAL

which in the concrete case of taking an object would become

$$\text{ACTOR USES} \begin{Bmatrix} \textit{reaching} \\ \textit{turning body} \\ \textit{prehension} \end{Bmatrix} \text{TO CAUSE } (\textit{Actor have } X).$$

The exact means selected to reach the goal is left unspecified in the causal structure, and will in fact change across time. In the following sessions, Serena's capacity for prehension is further refined. In the attempt to reach a doll held above her by the observer (6;10), she adjusts her entire body posture to the right and extends her right arm toward the doll, making gestures of prehension. At the same time, perhaps as a result of the muscular strain involved, the cooing vocalizations that preceded the effort are altered and intensified.

From 6 to 9 months, the second subject Carlotta pushes this sort of development even further, with the use of increasingly complex means. To reach an object, she crosses the entire room, pushes aside obstacles, and even pulls toward her the hand of the adult holding a desired toy. (Piaget notes that the adult's hand is often the first "instrument," well before the use of sticks, supports, etc. He suggests that this precocious use could be based on an analogy between the child's hand and that of the adult (see *The Construction of Reality in the Child*, 1954).

In Carlotta, the means inserted between child and goal is elaborated until, entering into what corresponds to Piaget's sensorimotor Stage 5, the child is able to create novel, intermediate means to familiar goals. Rather than just chaining the usual approach–prehension schemes, she can construct complex means–end relations in which some third element or scheme, previously unrelated to these same goal behaviors, is inserted between more familiar patterns. When the familiar means for reaching an object fails—e.g., it cannot be approached by usual locomotor means, it is out of arm's reach, etc.—the child can now create the missing link, an instrument, a tool, the use of a support, etc. For example, to take an object placed on a cloth a slight distance from her, Carlotta pulls the cloth toward her, and then takes the object (10;18).

This ability to construct complex causal chains is possible, according to Piaget, insofar as the child has "externalized" or separated portions of causal sequences from his own subjective actions. In one session around 10 months of age, Carlotta was presented with a windup toy, a baby doll in diapers which crawled across a table on all fours until the spring unwound. Carlotta's first approach, when the doll stopped, resembled her earlier schemes with interesting events—she imitated the movements of the toy herself, shaking the doll and her arms together. Piaget interprets such efforts as an attempt to extend the child's own subjective actions to make things happen—causation by imitation. The child does not yet understand that causality resides in external agents. However, later in the same sequence, Carlotta demonstrates a behavior typical of more advanced causal analysis. She watches the doll carefully until it stops again, and then pokes at it once. These pokes and slaps are alternated with pauses in which she watches the toy expectantly. There is an irresistible inference that Carlotta now understands that the source of the movement resides in the doll itself. She can only "launch" its behavior with an initial prod (cf., Michotte, 1963).

This same improved causal understanding will also permit the child to perceive the adult as a source of causality, and hence to involve him in the child's own intentional schemes as an agent or tool. A confirmation of this new understanding of agency for both Carlotta (C11;22) and Marta (all sessions) rests in the fact that both subjects, in certain situations where a need or desire can be inferred, will look at the adult and wait until that adult begins some appropriate activity. A transitional moment in this phase can be found in Carlotta's records at 11;22:

> C., unable to pull a cat out of the adult's hand, sits back up straight, looks the adult intently in the face, and then tries once again to pull the cat. The pattern is repeated three times, with the observer refusing to yield the cat, until C. finally manages to pull the object away from the adult.

This behavior is markedly different from Carlotta's reactions to the same type of situation in earlier sessions. We frequently held objects out to her, from a position in which eye contact with adult and eye contact with the object were clearly distinguishable on the videotapes. In such situations, she would reach for the object, even whimper, and finally cease altogether, without ever looking toward the adult's face. There were even occasions when she pulled the observer's hand toward her with the object, clearly aware of some physical connection between the two. But there was apparently no awareness, until between 10 to 11 months, of the causal role that the adult could play in this sequence.

The fact that adults are not invoked in object sequences until Stage 5 does not mean that the child has no schemes for interacting with adults in general. Around 6 months, both Serena and Carlotta engage in long social sequences with familiar adults—cooing, smiling, touching the other's face and hair. As the children's locomotor skills improve, they become more capable of initiating such sequences themselves, approaching the adult from across a room, climbing up to touch and be held by mother, father, or other favored adults. So the failure to involve adults in object–goals is not due to a lack of social motivation. Rather, there appears to be an inability to borrow schemes from the social repertoire for use in utilitarian sequences with objects. To do so apparently requires an improved understanding of external agency, and an ability to use novel means to familiar ends. The understanding of agency was indicated in the above examples from Carlotta (11;22). A clearer example of a situation in which social and object schemes are mixed comes in the following example (12;7):

> C. is sitting on her mother's lap, while mother shows her the telephone and pretends to talk. Mother tries to press the receiver against C.'s ear and have her *speak*, but C. passes the receiver back and presses it against her mother's ear. This is repeated several times.

When mother refuses to speak into the receiver, C. bats her hand against mother's knee, waits a moment longer, watches mother's face, and then, uttering a sharp, aspirated sound *ha,* touches her mother's mouth.

This new tendency toward causal structures involving others as agents can be paraphrased as

ACTOR USES MEANS TO CAUSE *(Adult Do* X)

in which X is expanded into

ADULT USES MEANS TO CAUSE *(Child attains goal)*

We have concluded that the sensorimotor version of the imperative is a development of Piaget's fifth sensorimotor stage. There was no evidence of using the adult as means to an object prior to this stage in Carlotta. And Serena never shows such behaviors in the period covered by the study, extending through to the kind of play with objects characteristic of Stage 4. Also, both Carlotta and Marta are capable of gestural imperatives at a time when there has been no evidence of a Stage 6 capacity for symbols. Neither child has produced her first word, and there is no symbolic or pretend play making one object stand for another.

Within this Stage 5 period, it is difficult to determine at what moment the behaviors used to insure adult compliance can actually be called "signals." The imperative signal seems to grow gradually out of more instrumental behaviors in which the child tries to reach the object himself—reaching, opening and closing the hand, cooing sounds intensified by muscular effort. As they are used more and more often to invoke adult help, these behaviors become more and more ritualized, abbreviated versions of the original action and sound patterns. Carlotta's first protoimperatives are distinguishable from other goal seeking behaviors only by the fact that eye contact with the object is broken to look toward the adult, and the adult is watched until he begins to fill the child's wishes. But by 13;2 Carlotta executives an imperative sequence which is clearly ritualized in form, similar to the imperatives exhibited by the oldest subject Marta throughout the research period:

C. is seated in a corridor in front of the kitchen door. She looks toward her mother and calls with an acute sound *ha.* Mother comes over to her, and C. looks toward the kitchen, twisting her shoulders and upper body to do so. Mother carries her into the kitchen, and C. points toward the sink. Mother gives her a glass of water, and C. drinks it eagerly.

In this sequence we see Carlotta's first clear-cut use of a pointing gesture for communicative purposes. It is precisely at this phase of development that we find Marta in the first sessions. In the examples observed for Marta, a number of gestures are used regularly, including pointing, in varied combinations of apparent imperative intention: stretching forth the arms with an open-and-shut gesture of the hand, pointing, reiterated and insistent vocalizations, and intermittent eye contact with the adult. These gestures, present to some degree in the last sessions of Carlotta, take on a clearly stereotyped form in Marta. At the same time, and probably as a consequence of the same ritualization, there is actually a decrease in the same phenomenon which we underlined in Carlotta—looking into the adult's eyes during a request. It appears that Marta is so sure of the efficacy of her signal—pointing, outstretched arms, etc.—that she often reinstates eye contact only if the initial request fails. In such cases, she not only looks at the adult, but repeats the request with greater insistence and/or variation in signals. For example, at 1:4;2 there is the following sequence:

> Marta is unable to open a small purse, and places it in front of her father's hand (which is resting on the floor). Father does nothing, so Marta puts the purse in his hand and utters a small sound, looking at father. Father still does not react, and Marta insists, pointing to the purse and whining. Father asks *What do I have to do?* Marta again points to the purse, looks at father, makes a series of sounds. Finally, father touches the purse clasp and says simultaneously *Should I open it?* Marta nods downward once and says *Si*. (Note: Marta also says *si* in the same session after a suggestion by father, but then protests when he begins to carry out his plan. Hence, it is unclear the extent to which *si* is a response to a verbal stimulus.)

The difference between the use of a simple instrument as an intermediate means and the use of an adult is that the child himself is no longer the agent. In appealing to the other as agent, the child must pass through an indirect causality, a means that is not under his direct control, and whose results may be delayed or unpredictable. The adult-tool is hence quite different from such malleable instruments as cloth supports or sticks and handles. As is clear from the above example, the indirectness and unpredictability of causal sequences involving agent-tools push the child toward an increased refinement of the rough efforts that first are used in involving adults. Those actions that were originally means for reaching a goal himself—i.e., orienting, reaching, grasping—are gradually separated from the concrete attempt to reach objects and become instead signals. They are produced in a ritualized fashion, more appropriate for communicating desire to an adult than for filling those desires himself. This includes the gesture of pointing, whose unique developmental history will be discussed further on (it is sufficient to stress here that pointing does not appear to be derived from reaching and taking). While Serena and Carlotta use reaching, vocalizations modified by muscular effort, and empty prehension gestures in efforts to reach an object just out of grasp, Marta makes abbreviated versions of the same gestures toward an adult who is across the room. The object may be so far from Marta's reach that her gestures clearly serve no utilitarian value other than communicating to the adult. And alterations in this signal behavior are contingent upon the movements of the adult toward the object, rather than the child's own proximity to it.

In Chapter III we will discuss the transition from sensorimotor signals to words with a conventional, referential use. It is sufficient to stress here that the first imperatives are sensorimotor structures, appearing prior to any manifestation of a symbolic capacity. As such, they are procedures rather than mental entities.

The Declarative

The definition that we have adopted for the declarative is somewhat more controversial than our definition of the imperative. Traditionally, declaratives have necessarily involved the speaker's commitment to the truth of some event or relationship that he describes. Obviously, for a study of preverbal development, it would be useless to define the declarative so as to require the presence of a proposition. If there is no speech, clearly there would be no propositions, and therefore, no declaratives. A more useful definition of **declaratives** for our purposes is provided by Parisi and Antinucci (1973), who define the declarative as a particular kind of imperative, which commands the unique epistemic act of "assuming" some proposition. In their model, both the imperative and the declarative are analyzed as nested causal structures, differing only with respect to the kind of "act" commanded of the listener. The speaker may also, by invoking standard presuppositions about conversation, commit himself to the truth of the information to which the listener's attention is directed. But that is not an integral part of the definition of "declarative." Larkin and O'Malley (1973) provide analyses of the declarative that would support Parisi and Antinucci's definition. These authors stress that declaratives are frequently used to remind the listener of information of which both people are perfectly aware (e.g., *Dr. Smith, you are not yet a member of the tenured faculty*), or to make jokes about issues that both people know to be false. Hence, Parisi and Antinucci's definition of the declarative as a command for the listener to attend to or assume some piece of information is a wider definition which subsumes the traditional declarative in which truth is at issue.

We have therefore defined the **protodeclarative** as a preverbal effort to direct the adult's attention to some event or object in the world. There are several reasons why we believe that this activity is the ontogenic predecessor of "true" declaratives. First, as we shall see shortly, the child's first one-word declarations or "labels" (e.g., *Doggie!*) emerge out of the same pointing, giving, and showing sequences that we are willing to accept as protodeclaratives. Now, some authors (e.g., Halliday, 1973) maintain that even linguistic labelling is a separate speech act from the true declarative. **Labelling** is connected in Halliday's analysis to a separate class of attention–seeking speech acts, while **declaratives** are still narrowly defined as sharing information for its own sake rather than for social purposes. Gruber (1973) apparently agrees, since he terms the performative of early labelling the "indicative," as distinguished from a later, more sophisticated speech act, the "reportative." We do indeed agree with these authors that at a later stage, when the child becomes more aware of truth values and the internal mental activity of others, he will add conversational rules concerning truth to the conditions for using declaratives. But as such, the **reportative** will become a subclass of a larger class of declaratives, involving the use of speech to draw the listener's attention to objects, events, and relationships. For the adult, the difference between assuming truth and attending to some event may be an important one. But for the very young child (and possibly for the adult as well), the offering of information and the demand for attention are inextricably mixed. Long before he can understand the utilitarian value of sharing information, the child will engage in declaring for primarily social reasons.

To summarize these definitions, in the case of the imperative the child formulates some event or object as goal, and inserts the adult as a means to that goal. In the construction of declaratives, on the other hand, the child formulates interaction with the adult as the goal and uses objects as a means to the adult.

The first phase in the development of the declarative involves the exercise of innate motor behaviors which have a social meaning for the species, even though the child himself does not control the signal value of these behaviors. From 2;0, Serena displayed the same sort of social predispositions noted by authors like Bowlby (1969) and Fantz (1966). For example, she stared longer at a doll with a face than the same doll without a face (4;29). And she was frequently more likely to smile at human faces and voices than at other visual and auditory stimulae. These behaviors, because of their signal value to the adult caretakers, usually result in prolonged interactions with the child. The mutual joy taken in these interactions provides the first loop in the construction of declarative communication: the formulation of social interaction as a goal.

As Serena's motor skills develop, they are immediately placed in the service of these social goals. By 4;29, Serena is no longer restricted to smiling and cooing at the adults before her. Several times in succession, when the observer moves close in front of her, Serena touches his face and grasps his hair. When the adult pulls back, Serena agitates her arms vigorously. During the entire sequence, she also continues to exhibit the social reflexes of smiling and vocalizing, as before.

In contrast with Serena's primitive efforts, Carlotta (diary note 9;6) can chain a series of approach behaviors in an effort to reach social goals. In this particular instance, her mother is stretched out on a sofa. Carlotta crosses the floor, and climbs up and across the sofa to her mother's side, where she then rubs her face against her mother's cheek. At this stage, the principle difference between "social" and inanimate goals lies not in the means for reaching them, but in the consummatory behaviors once the goal is reached. People are touched, batted at, and mouthed just like inanimate objects, but they are also clung to, rubbed against, and held close for long periods of time. There is also an apparent difference in the circumstances that are likely to activate social versus inanimate goals. According to Bowlby, the infant tends to explore the world of objects when she feels secure, while she often turns to social objects (in particular to a specific attachment figure) when this sense of security is disturbed. This was true of both Carlotta and Marta, although it was never observed in Serena by the last filming session (age 6;23). For example, during the tenth session (age 11;15), Carlotta is in the observer's arms. She begins to rub her hands against her eyes with a cranky expression, and the observer returns her to her mother's arms. At this point Carlotta turns and begins to watch the observer with renewed interest.

At the moment in which Serena and Carlotta use a set of means for obtaining physical contact with the adult, a "first draft" of the declarative has been constructed. This intentional structure could be paraphrased as:

$$\text{CHILD USES} \left\{ \begin{array}{l} \textit{approach} \\ \textit{grasp} \\ \textit{reach} \\ \textit{manipulate} \\ \textit{etc.} \end{array} \right\} \text{TO OBTAIN ADULT-AS-GOAL}$$

This structure is identical in complexity to the first phase of the imperative, and in fact covers the same developmental period in both children— Serena 4;29 through the last session; Carlotta from the first session at 6;23 through 9;6.

Up to this point the "predicate" required of the adult is simply to serve as the object of literal, physical contact. A more sophisticated version of the social means–end system is achieved when the child is able to attract the adult's attention purposively, without necessarily establishing physical contact. The child begins to work for less tangible adult behaviors—smiling, laughing, eye contact, and talking—as goals in themselves. This class of adult behaviors can be grouped under a single predicate ATTEND, which we consider to be the precursor of the ASSUME predicate of adult declarative intentions. Carlotta begins to act to obtain adult attention around 9;6, at the end of the fourth sensorimotor stage. Her first efforts at

"showing off" do not involve reference to some third element in the situation. Instead, at this point she can control adult attention only by repeating some behavior from her own repertoire which has previously been successful in evoking laughter or comment. For example, at 9;6 Carlotta is in
her mother's arms and is drinking milk from a glass. When she has
finished drinking, she looks around at the adults watching her and makes
a comical noise with her mouth (referred to in some dialects as "the
raspberries"). The adults laugh, and Carlotta repeats the activity several
times, smiling and looking around in between. Her parents explain that
this behavior had been discovered earlier in the week, and that Carlotta
now produces it regularly at eating and drinking times, always awaiting
some response from the adult.

This behavior of launching and awaiting an autonomous behavior by the
adult is similar to the poking sequence with the windup doll (10;18), in
that it seems to involve an improved understanding of external agency. It
is noteworthy that by the next session, Carlotta seems to have moved out
of Stage 4—the use of familiar means to novel ends—into Stage 5—the use
of novel means to familiar goals (i.e., the use of the cloth support). The
adult attention response is a novel goal, but Carlotta first evokes it with
some tried and true behavior from her repertoire. Shortly thereafter, she
produces the same adult response by involving a third element, an object
that is "shown off" until the adult responds. The use of a novel means,
particularly a tool or instrument, is the primary achievement of
sensorimotor Stage 5. At 10;18, we have the first recorded instance in
which Carlotta extends her arm to show an object to the adult; hence, the
object becomes a tool for obtaining adult attention.

Within this new capacity to attract attention through use of a third element, we also found a succession of substages. Initially, there is a very
subtle passage from the showing off or exhibitionism of the previous stage,
to showing. While Carlotta is playing with an object already in her hand
(10;18), she extends her arm forward with the toy for the adult to see.
Afterwards, this showing becomes a complete and autonomous activity in
itself. The child purposively seeks and takes an object in order to show it
to the adult. For example, at 1;0;7 Carlotta takes a picture book off the
table, and without hesitation lifts it high in front of her in the direction of
those present. However, when showing first appears there is apparently no
intention to give the object, as is confirmed several times when an adult
tries to take it away. Carlotta will not let go of it, and may even pull her
arm back to keep the toy. For a number of weeks, Carlotta will let the
object pass into the adult's hand only if, distracted by something else, she
loses interest in it.

The next substage occurs when giving becomes an autonomous means
for establishing contact and interacting. For the reasons just described, it
was difficult to distinguish clearly the moment when the child first intends

to give an object (watching the adult until he takes it) versus when he lets go due to loss of interest. However, at 1;1;2 we have the confirmation that the child has differentiated showing from giving. She takes a wooden mask from a chair, crosses the room smiling and looking at the observer, and drops the object in the observer's lap.

At the same moment in which Carlotta is able to give objects, she also begins to point at objects while looking back at the adult for confirmation (1;0;7–1;1;12). This is true despite the fact that a pointing gesture has been available for several weeks outside of a communicative framework, for examining objects and phenomena by herself. From around nine months, Carlotta frequently orients toward new objects or unexpected sounds and points while staring fixedly in the direction of the novelty. She also points for long periods at various detailed figures in storybooks, but never looks up from the book to notice whether someone else is watching too. Carlotta does not involve the adult in such pointing sequences until the time when she also gives objects to the same adults. In fact, when Carlotta finally does use the pointing gesture to communicate with adults, she passes through a peculiar transitional period that demonstrates how the two components are being put together (diary notes and off-camera observations after 12 months). She would first orient toward the interesting object or event, extending her arm and forefinger in the characteristic pointing gesture while uttering a breathy sound of surprise, *Ha!*, that often accompanies these sequences; then she swung around, pointed at the adult with the same gesture, and returned to look at the object and point toward it once again. This series of steps—point at object, point at adult, point at object—puts together in a chained form the components that eventually form the smooth deictic act of simultaneously pointing at an object while turning to the other for confirmation.

Werner and Kaplan (1963) have also reported a stage of pointing-for-self occurring prior to pointing for others. They suggest that pointing is an integral part of the cognitive development of "distancing," increasing the child's awareness of the distinction between the knower and the known. Acts of reference for a listener will be possible only when this primary distinction has been made by the child for himself.

This Gestalt notion of distancing also fits our data in another rather interesting way. The formation of the protodeclarative has passed across three substages—from exhibiting self, to showing objects, to giving and pointing to objects. This inclusion and progressive distancing of a third object from the child's own motor activities follows a literal movement from inside outward; giving and pointing for others are the final moments in which the object at last passes beyond the length of the child's own arm, and hence is no longer part of his own subjective motor schemes.

At the opening sessions for Marta (12 months), these developments have already been completed. She shows, gives and points to objects and awaits the appropriate adult response. If no response is forthcoming, she will repeat the behavior with greater insistence, or possibly seek another audience. At this stage she has yet to utter her first word, and shows no other signs of symbolic behavior. Hence, Marta has full control of the protodeclarative while she is still at sensorimotor Stage 5. From the other side, Carlotta begins to show objects when she has apparently entered into sensorimotor Stage 5 (i.e., when she can pull a cloth support to reach a toy on that cloth). Hence, the protodeclarative, for both subjects, is a procedural rather than a symbolic structure, beginning during the fifth sensorimotor stage. In the next chapter, we will describe the gradual insertion of propositions or words with a referential value, within the same performative frames.

It is to be expected that when the child does move from sensorimotor declaratives to the use of propositions, the effect he hopes to create in the listener will become more sophisticated. However, there is reason to believe that objects and propositions are functionally interchangeable elements for much older children as well, when they are trying to open or sustain an interaction with adults. In a study of greeting behaviors in preschool children (Farris and Bates, 1971), the following was a very frequent pattern: a child begins his approach, holding an object in his hands, and waits until the adult looks toward him. When this occurs, he deposits the object in the adult's hand, sometimes with a comment and other times in silence. There is another frequent pattern that occurs in identical circumstances. The child approaches the adult, waits until eye contact is established, and without any preliminary greeting or introductory phrase, "deposits" a proposition before the adult, such as the example *Today my daddy is coming to get me and take me to the Picklebarrel for lunch.* While this is typical of the opening phases of an interaction, the same interchangeability holds at points where an interaction is flagging. Just as Carlotta and Marta will look about the room to find various objects for pointing or giving, children in this preschool experiment would often throw out a series of propositional non sequiturs, sometimes interspersed with a sustained *and uh* ... And of course, it seems fair to add that adults can often be accused of the same thing. In both cases, the child offers a third element, either an object or a proposition, to begin an interaction with an adult, or to sustain it over time. It can be further stressed that in older children (and probably in adults as well), all the means of establishing interaction that we have examined in their developmental oₗer—physical contact, attracting attention, exchanging objects, and exchanging propositions—are interchangeable social behaviors.

To summarize, when Marta and Carlotta are at Stage 5, prior to the development of a symbolic capacity, we find three parallel behaviors:

1. The use of supports, tools, instruments in noncommunicative sequences.

2. The use of the adult as an agent-tool in obtaining objects.
3. The use of objects as tools in obtaining attention from adults.

All three cases involve the use of an extraneous, novel, third element in reaching some familiar and well-established goal. Substages have been observed within those same developments. And the behaviors involved in the communicative sequences will undergo gradual ritualization into a form that can appropriately be called signals. However, even though the communicative sequences will eventually be clearly distinguishable from other behavior systems, the structural similarities between the cognitive and communicative developments of Stage 5 indicate that they are generated from the same new causal understanding. As such, both the imperative and the declarative in the early stages are sensorimotor procedures. In the next chapter, we will examine the appearance of symbolic objects (words with referents, propositions) used within the same performative sequences. But the important point of this chapter is that performatives have been organized and exercised with literal, real world objects before the child communicates with symbols.

Sensorimotor Performatives and Formal Analysis

At the outset we stated that the purpose of this study was twofold. The first goal was to derive some hypotheses about the cognitive prerequisites for intentional communication. The data indicate that imperatives and declaratives first appear at sensorimotor Stage 5, and are parallel developments with the noncommunicative use of tools in problem solving sequences. This interesting possibility is now the basis of a cross-sectional study with a larger sample (see Bates *et al.*, 1975) to confirm the role of Stage 5 and Stage 6 cognitive developments in communication prior to speech. Hence, the first goal has been satisfied.

The second goal was to examine the feasibility of using semantic analysis to describe communicative developments in the sensorimotor period. The preceding findings yield a series of stages, in which new components are added to older means–end systems, and causal schemes are reorganized from chains of familiar approach–grasp sequences into schemes embedding novel means to familiar goals. There is a strong structural resemblance between the final form of sensorimotor performative procedures, and the componential analysis of adult performatives offered by Parisi and Antinucci (1973), Sadock (1974), and McCawley (1973). This resemblance may of course be quite coincidental. Most formal notational systems can be used to describe a variety of events and relationships; this does not necessarily mean that all events so described bear some relationship to one another. However, in the case of the sensorimotor performative, there is reason to believe that the structural parallels are no accident; the performative structure that underlies later adult speech may in fact be derived ontogenetically from the procedural flow chart underlying sensorimotor procedures for communication.

The reader will recall that the imperative and the declarative are given the following representations by Parisi and Antinucci (see page 16f. for a more precise explanation of the formal notation used in this structure):

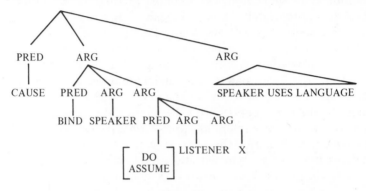

The triangle stands for an unanalyzed propositional complement, and presumably any argument or proposition could be substituted in that slot. In the present study, we have argued that performative structures are first exercised using concrete, real-world objects instead. Also, the performative described for adults involves the predicate ASSUME as the goal of the declarative. We have argued instead that children construct the protodeclarative with the more tangible goal described as ATTEND. Finally, this adult structure requires as a means SPEAKER USES LANGUAGE. In the sensorimotor period, performative intentions do not yet involve language, but rather communicative behaviors which ritualize into vocal and gestural signals. However, despite these differences, the overall set of causal constituencies are quite similar between the adult performative tree and the child's performative flow chart.

We can use the components in these two structures to describe each successive stage in the gradual build up of the imperative and declarative by children. There is, of course, nothing sacred about these particular predicates and arguments, nor do we have data to confirm that these particular predicates and arguments and no others are the ones underlying infant communication. For example, McCawley provides a slightly different analysis that we might also have used to describe the ontogeny of performatives. Instead of the USE–CAUSE–BIND system, he analyzes indirect and intentional causality with CAUSE–DO predicates. We could have used either model for the following exercise. For the moment, we will restrict ourselves to illustrating the use of the Parisi and Antinucci analysis in describing sensorimotor intentions.

The initial stage for both the declarative and the imperative involved the emission of innate motor schemes set off by specific physiological states. Serena cries because she is hungry; she smiles because she is happy. One signal serves to obtain food or relief, the other serves to prolong social interaction. Hence, for the species, these are signals generated in the service of goals. However, there is no reason to assume that these are signals from the point of view of the infant. They are not intentionally communicative, in the sense that the goal is not prefigured or represented within the child's system. Rather, there is an "on–off" system that could be described with an efficient causality statement

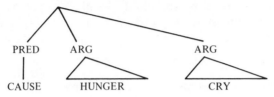

If this same structure were redrawn with the BIND predicate characteristic of intentional and indirect causality, as in

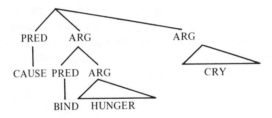

then we would have the absurd situation of crying in order to bring about hunger pangs.

When Serena is able to coordinate means and ends herself—to approach, reach, and grasp a desired object—we can use the final-causality notation to describe her intention. The same structures will describe both the social and the inanimate goal schemes—a convenient fact given that they occur simultaneously in development.

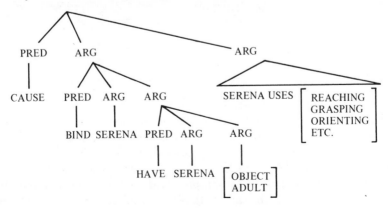

With Carlotta, the second argument of the causal predicate, or means, is elaborated until, entering into the fifth sensorimotor stage, she is able to create novel, intermediate means to familiar goals. At this point, a complex means becomes an intermediate goal, permitting an embedded means–end structure that could be paraphrased as

ACTOR USES MEANS SO THAT ACTOR USES MEANS SO THAT (*Actor has Object*)

Of course prior to this time the child already chained various familiar approach and orienting schemes in trying to reach and take an object. But these sequences seem to be not unlike a series of conjoined sentences

And X *and* Y *and* Z . . .

while the insertion of novel means requires an interruption of the chain, to embed an otherwise unrelated scheme borrowed from some other behavioral system. Just as conjoining precedes embedding in linguistic development (e.g., Slobin, 1973), the sequence of familiar means, each leading naturally into the other, apparently precedes the interruption of a familiar scheme to insert a newly created structure—a tool, instrument, a support, or an external agent. Taking the example of Carlotta's use of the cloth support at 10;18, we can formalize this new embedded causal structure using the above system of notation:

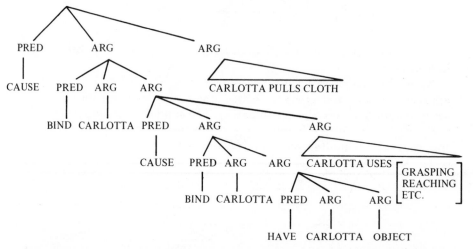

At the same level of complexity—and at the same sensorimotor stage— Carlotta begins to appeal to adults as agents in helping her obtain objects. However, there is one problem in formalizing this intention structure. While it is clear that Carlotta now knows that the adult can cause some event, it is not altogether clear that she understands the volitional aspects of the adult act. In the later samples with Marta, the alternation of ritualized signals until the adult finally complies does indicate some understanding of the capricious and undependable quality of human instruments. But for the first gestural requests, at least in Carlotta's case, it is possible that the child perceives the adult–agent in the same way that we perceive slot machines and windup ducks and other moving things that automatically act when prompted. If the child understands that she must cause the adult to WANT to do something, then we can describe Carlotta's intention with a BIND predicate in the portion of the structure describing the adult's role. Also, we can place the goal HAVE CHILD OBJECT as the first argument of the adult's causal sequence, since presumably the child understands that the adult too must share his goal. Insofar as the child does understand the difference between human agents and other moving things, we can formalize Carlotta's performative intention as follows:

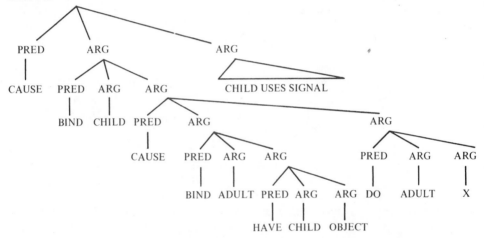

However, it is possible that the child does not yet understand the volitional aspect of adult compliance, and regards adult behaviors as a particularly inefficient kind of efficient causality. In that case the performative structure should be described without a BIND predicate in the adult sequence, and with the child's own goal as the second argument of an efficient cause. The resulting structure is as follows:

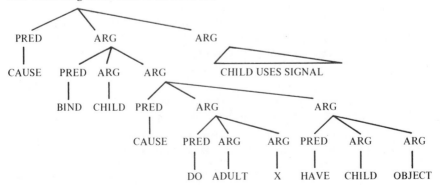

In describing the Stage 5 declarative, a somewhat similar problem arises. While we can clearly infer the child's goal in using an object to evoke adult attention, we cannot be certain of the degree to which the child understands the adult's mental activities. This means that we are limited to using the tangible predicate ATTEND—visible to the child via such behaviors as smiling, laughing, commenting, etc.—rather than the adult predicate ASSUME. Some evidence that the child has separated ASSUME from ATTEND may be obtained much later when the child can comment on events outside the immediate situation. Even at that point, we maintained earlier that declaratives can continue to serve an attention-maintaining, social function for adults as well, such that ASSUME may well contain as part of its meaning the notion ATTEND, for all speakers. However, at this stage we can approximate the later declarative structure with the following representation:

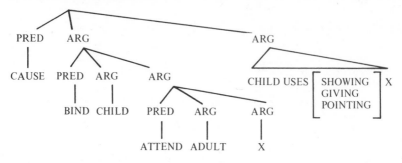

Let us repeat that the above exercise is in no way regarded as a demonstration that this particular componential analysis has a psychological reality superior to that of other models. We could have carried out the same gradual construction of components, stage by stage, using McCawley's model, or Sadock's, or any other adequate causal analysis. In other longitudinal studies, e.g., Brown (1973), developmental data were analyzed with two or more competing grammars, and one of the formal models was chosen as preferable. That is emphatically NOT what we are trying to do here. We are not suggesting that formal semantic structure underlies sensorimotor behavior. In fact, we are suggesting the opposite: If the adult speaker does have a formal componential structure underlying his utterances, then he derived that structure by reflecting on an earlier one, namely the organization underlying intentional sensorimotor communication.

We have, of course, not proven that this is the case. But by pointing out the strong structural parallels between the sensorimotor organization of communication and the formal analysis of performatives, we have at least rendered more plausible the suggestion that one is derived from the other. At the sensorimotor stage, the child is probably not at all capable of reflecting on the organization of his own communication, as a symbolic object in itself. Later on, he will be capable of such metapragmatic reflection (see Chapter V in this book), long after the performative is efficiently organized as a sensorimotor system. What we are suggesting here is compatible with a major tenet of Piaget's theory: the notion of **vertical decalage,** by which higher stages are constructed by recreating at a higher level the structures of a preceding level. Hence, concrete thought involves a mental reenactment of concrete action. And formal thought involves acting on the products and relations of concrete thought, with schemes that are ultimately derivable from sensorimotor schemata (e.g., reversals, displacements, etc.). By the same analysis, the construction of formal linguistic structures can be viewed as a vertical decalage of constructions that were first carried out at the sensorimotor level. By using the same componential notation to describe both levels, we are trying to underline structural parallels that may be crucial in the transition from one stage to another. This point will come up again in later chapters.

Conclusion

We are currently undertaking a cross-sectional project with infants between 9 and 13 months, to test the hypotheses derived here concerning the relations between illocutionary and locutionary development and cognitive Stages 5 and 6. Pilot observations of 20 infants in the Rome area indicate thus far that the findings reported here are generalizable to a larger sample. However, the current project involves a much greater refinement of eliciting techniques, including systematic administration of the Uzgiris and Hunt scales for sensorimotor development (based on Piaget), checklist time samples of behaviors in the home, and structured videotape situations eliciting reactions to novel objects, to having objects taken away, etc.

Since this project is still in progress, it might be useful at this point to note several recent articles by other authors that do lend support to our longitudinal findings. First, Dore (1973) and Carter (1974) have also demonstrated that performatives like the declarative and imperative are present at the beginning of speech, and seem to have a previous development in gesture. However, Dore apparently feels that the crucial cognitive prerequisite to general performatives involves Stage 4 object permanence (i.e., removing the screen from an object hidden before the child's eyes). He does not carry out the kinds of cognitive analyses used in our study and rests his conclusions primarily on age norms when gestural communication begins in his subjects. It is noteworthy that the age range he cites is similar to the range in which our subject Carlotta demonstrated entry into sensorimotor Stage 5 and also began using gestural performatives.

With regard to the relation between Stage 5 cognition and gestural performatives, Sugarman (1973) has studied the cognitive prerequisites for the kinds of communicative behaviors described here as the protoimperative. She also reports that children invoke adult aid in object schemes only after they have entered Piaget's Stage 5. In support of our findings regarding the protodeclarative, Escalona (1973) reports that giving and showing of objects occur in her subjects between 9 to 11 months, around the same time that these behaviors began for Carlotta and Marta. Escalona also stresses the primarily social nature of these particular behaviors.

The three types of causal intentions noted in this study—noncommunicative tool use, imperatives, and declaratives—all appeared together within a 4 to 5 week period. All three can be analyzed as manifestations of the same Stage 5 understanding of causality. However, we have no particular reason to predict a single order of development for these three structures. Piaget has used the term **horizontal decalage** to refer to different manifestations of the same operative scheme, appearing at different moments of development. For example, conservation of liquid may appear before conservation of volume, and so forth. In some cases, it is inherently more difficult to apply the new scheme to one material than it is to another, perhaps because one material is more difficult to manipulate and/or observe than another. In other cases, the order between two decalages of the same scheme may be determined by the experience of an individual child. For example, Price–Williams (1970) has demonstrated that conservation of clay appears earlier in the children of potters than in children without that experience. Since the three manifestations of Stage 5 causality discussed in this chapter are theoretically decalages of a single operative structure, it may be possible to predict the order of development on the basis of the experience of individual children. Bell (1970) has found that securely attached children will first achieve object permanence with their mothers (seeking mother when she is hidden behind a screen), a few weeks prior to displaying the same ability with inanimate objects. But other children who do not have the same secure attachment relationship attained object permanence first with inanimate objects, and only later with social objects. It is possible that children will split along similar lines with regard to Stage 5 communicative development: Some will develop the more utilitarian imperative structure first, while others will develop the socially motivated protodeclarative first. In our cross-sectional study, we have included measures of the mother–child attachment relationship, to determine whether this relationship correlates with the kinds of communicative schemes that the child develops first.

We will now go on to examine the development of propositions within performative frames, and the development of presupposing procedures for placing these propositions in appropriate relation to their context. The issue of performatives will be addressed again in Chapter V, when we examine evidence that the performative procedure has been reconstructed at the representational level, as a symbol structure that can be manipulated and encoded directly into the surface form of utterances.

CHAPTER III

The Development
of Propositions
in Performative Frames

The language system can be said to begin when performative or "illocu-tionary" structures are used to carry propositions with a referential or "locutionary" value. We have contended, however, that while the performative structure is being constructed, the eventual commerce of propositions is first carried out with an exchange of concrete objects or an indication of visible events. Words as symbolic vehicles with correspond-ing referents are then inserted into the prepared performative structures.

The last development has been the starting point for most studies of lan-guage acquisition. In the study just described, we had planned instead to conclude with that same event. There was, however, no single moment when the performative structures could be said to "sprout" propositions. Lock (in press), drawing in part from Ingram (1971) has underlined the uncertainty of the boundary between activities and representations of activities. He summarizes the situation with a statement that holds true for our own data as well:

> Anthropology recognizes that man has no birthday; zoology recognizes that life has no birthday; physics recognizes that matter has no birthday. The murky line between life and non-life, man and non-man, matter and non-matter stems from the fact . . . that while we can recognise what, for example, is definitely at either end of a conceptual con-tinuum . . . the transition from one to the other is continuous and not discrete. Such is also the case with cognitive variables—we can say that the neonate does not possess the ability X whereas the adult does, but we are unsure when it is fair to say any individual comes to possess X. In this case, for X read sentence.

In the very first uses of words by our subjects, we found a gradual passage from vocalization, to vocalization as signal, to word as signal, to word as a proposition with a referential value. Part of this process rests in the construction of the performative itself, as we have seen, while part of it rests with an independent development of the symbolic capacity. This latter development in itself deserves a separate study. We shall examine the development of symbols quite briefly here with a few relevant examples from Carlotta and Marta, and then proceed to a discussion of the holophrastic period in terms of the pragmatic system proposed here. Our discussion of the development of the symbolic capacity deals with the more general problem of the growth of reference. The second part of this chapter, regarding the meanings underlying holophrastic speech, deals with the problem of the psychological basis for propositions.

There were three types of wordlike signals in our data, reflecting different degrees of locutionary value, or referentiality. First, in both Carlotta and Marta we found examples of wordlike signals that had no discernible referential value; they were used solely as part of a performative procedure. The earliest imperative vocalization in Marta was an insistent *Mm,* relatively long in duration and high in pitch. If the adult responded with something such as *Is this what you want?* while reaching for the requested object, Marta would then grunt *Mm* at a lower pitch, of brief duration, often with a sharp nod of the head and jerk of the upper body. If, however, the adult was mistaken in interpreting Marta's needs, she would repeat the long *Mm* request with increased pointing and other gestures. Later, the *Mm* request was occasionally substituted by a more clearly wordlike creation of her own, the sound *Ayi,* which was also used deictically in pointing out novel objects or events.

For Carlotta there was a similar progression from a relatively natural sound to a somewhat more arbitrary or ritualized signal. Her first requests and declaratives were both accompanied by a sharp, aspirated sound *Ha.* Later, she developed the two-syllable sound *na-na* in any situation of need, from wanting an object to calling an adult from another room. This *na-na* is similar in usage to the first word of Piaget's daughter Jacqueline, who used *Panama* ('grandpa') to express any desire or need regardless of the presence or absence of the grandfather himself (Piaget, 1962).

One could choose to interpret these early words as mappings of an underlying proposition such as *I want X* or *Look at X.* In that case, these words would have both reference and propositionality. However, since this same information is also conveyed at the sensorimotor level with purely gestural performatives, there is no more reason to attribute a referential/propositional value to these sounds than to any of the other, nonverbal gestures that precede speech by weeks or even months. The organization of performative intentions described in Chapter II would be sufficient to generate any of these wordlike performances. The referent of sounds such as *mm* and *ayi* has no more of a symbolic base than the referent for all perceptual–motor acts of looking, touching and playing with objects.

A second type of early production is much harder to interpret, bearing a strong resemblance to referential speech but occurring in a more restricted usage than the subsequent naming behaviors. For Marta, there are the utterances *Da* ('give') and *Tieni* ('take'), and for Carlotta there are the utterances *Bam* and *Brr*.

Marta produces *DA* or *TIENI* in session 3 (14 months), and diary notes indicate that she has been doing so for at least 2 to 3 weeks. She always produces the sound in a context of exchanging an object with an adult (regardless of whether she is giving or taking). One is tempted to conclude immediately that *DA* refers to the act of giving, with all its components, exactly as does the adult word *DA*. However, Marta never uses these two sounds to describe an act of giving in which she does not participate, and more important, she never uses *DA* as a command when she wants an object from an adult. Furthermore, in the innumerable acts of giving and taking, the adults frequently intone either *DA* or *TIENI* as many as five times while stretching forth a hand. Hence an alternative interpretation, at this stage, would be that *DA* does not yet REPRESENT the activity of giving, but is PART of the activity of giving, a ritual vocal act performed when passing objects. This interpretation is supported by the fact that *DA* and *TIENI* and *AYI* are Marta's only wordlike sounds for several weeks. Also, as we shall discuss shortly, they occur prior to the period in which Marta otherwise demonstrates the capacity for symbolic behaviors.

Similarly, Carlotta uses *Bam* when knocking over towers or further messing up arrangements of toys (around 12 months). It is a sound which adults have used regularly to accompany these knocking down games. *Brr* is a sound that grandmother used on one occasion with Carlotta while helping her ride a small tricycle. Carlotta often uses the sound to accompany activities of riding or dragging things that make noise. In a particularly interesting example, observed around 12;6, Carlotta started approaching her toy piano, orienting for the position of banging on the keys. Before she reached the piano, she said *Bam* two or three times. There are two possible interpretations of this sequence: either the word is a mapping of an underlying proposition such as *I will bam the piano,* or it is an integral part of banging activities, a consummatory behavior set in motion by the intention to play the piano.

Svachkin (in Ferguson and Slobin, 1973) provides a similar example, even closer to referential naming, of a naming act used only as part of a single game. An infant discovered that when she threw her toy kitty out of her crib, the adult used the word *kitty* in bringing the toy back to her crib. She began to utter the word herself in the kitty game to make the toy come back, but did not name the toy in any other context.

Piaget (1962) also suggests that the first use of names by the child are not so much representation of some external referent, but rather are part of some subjective activity of the child. He gives the example of Jacqueline's first use of the word for *dog*. The first time she uttered the word, it was in a correct context (from the adult point of view) while viewing a dog in the street below as she stood on the balcony. But subsequent uses of the same word were not so much descriptions of dogs in various contexts, but utterances made for almost anything that Jacqueline watched from her balcony. In short, the word named her own position and activity rather than some external referent.

Greenfield and Smith, as mentioned earlier, also suggest that the first words of their subjects (a request *Mm* and the words *hi* and *bye bye*) are pure performatives, speech acts without a propositional content (as in Searle's example of the word *Hurray!*). This is in keeping with Piaget's contention that the first words are not true symbols, standing for some represented entity, but rather are subjective actions by the child in the presence of certain kinds of objects or events. Hence, symbols emerge gradually out of the sensorimotor behaviors of the infant, until they at least attain a sort of separate reality for the child distinguishable from his other activities with objects.

A third type of early production comes much closer to the requirements of referential speech, in that it is used to depict an object or event in a variety of contexts. Thus the expression seems to relate the word to its referent rather than to the subjective activities of the child. The clearest example in Marta's records is the word *Pu* (from *Non c'e piu* or 'allgone'), used to remark on the absence of an object or person (16 months). As we shall see presently, this ability confirms the development of the symbolic capacity in Marta. In Carlotta (12 months) we find a series of onomatopoeic expressions appearing at the same time, to name the animals in her story books or among her toys. In Carlotta's case, the naming of dogs and cats and ducks, etc. has a great deal of environmental support, developing through imitation in the context of a game played frequently with both parents. In this session, Mother points to a picture of a dog and says *Come fa il cane?* ('How does a dog go?'). Carlotta looks intently, points to the figure, says *woo-woo*, looks up and smiles at Mother. The same occurs with ducks (*qua-qua*), cats (*mao-mao*), and several other animals whose "sounds" the observers themselves had difficulty imitating. Included is a nonverbal "name" to identify fish, requiring an open-and-close movement of the lips. The conclusion that these behaviors constitute a true act of reference rather than a particularly clever imitation is supported by the fact that Carlotta generalizes them to recognize other dogs, cats, etc. outside the context of the game objects. For example, Carlotta is in the bathtub, and her father hands her a rubber duck. As she reaches to take it, she says *qua-qua*. Two weeks later in an observation session, Carlotta takes her plastic fish off the sofa to carry it across the room, and immediately begins making the identifying mouth movement to herself. Werner and Kaplan (1963) have discussed the first onomatopoeic child-forms at some length, and suggest that the active, physiognomic nature of such words makes them the easiest vehicles for the child's first referential speech. Nevertheless, these identifications are referential in nature, and as such they mark the passage from protoperformatives that are carried out with wordlike signals to performatives that convey a locutionary value—albeit still supported by the presence of the concrete objects and events that are reported.

Not only is the passage into referential speech a gradual one, but it seems to be paralleled by cognitive achievements that may be prerequisite to it. In Marta's case, although the sensorimotor performative was established by the first session, evidence of Stage 6 symbolic behaviors did not begin until around 16 months of age, four months after the first session. In this session, there is the first evidence of symbolic play when Marta takes a small silver duck from the coffee table and holds it to the rim of a silver dish to make it "eat." Immediately afterward, she treats the same silver duck as a spoon and uses it to "feed" the observer from the silver dish. In the same session, her aunt asks her *Dov'e il micione?* ('Where is the kitty?'), and Marta drags the adult all the way to a bedroom where she apparently remembered having left her cat. Hence, just when symbolic play is first observed, Marta also demonstrates a memory for unseen places and objects located there. In the next session, Marta is asked the whereabouts of various absent people or objects. She responds either by looking up and saying *Pu* ('allgone') or by pointing accurately toward one of the doors where the person was last seen. According to Piaget (1962), this ability to respond correctly regarding the whereabouts of absent objects confirms entry into the stage of internal representation.

In Carlotta there is a much narrower gap between completion of the performative (Stage 5) and the beginning of the symbolic capacity (Stage 6). By 13;6, Carlotta has practically caught up to Marta at 16 months. For example, prior to 13 months, word comprehension elicited either a prac-ticed routine or a rather random search for the named object. Instead, by this session Carlotta goes directly to her bookshelf when asked for a book. She has also begun systematically building towers and placing a series of rings on a stick, one of Piaget's signs of Stage 6 capacities. In diary notes for the two weeks prior to this session, Carlotta also showed a capacity to entertain for an extended period of time a goal not immediately visible to her. She had earlier become fond of dropping objects off the terrace onto the lawn below. On more than one occasion, playing in her bedroom, she has taken an object (including a large and cumbersome duck), travelled through two rooms and a hall to the terrace, and immediately dropped the object off the edge. In the same two week period, the diary notes show two separate instances of symbolic play. In one, Carlotta takes a spoon, holds it against her ear like a telephone, and begins to "talk"; in another, she does the same with a pack of cigarettes. Within two months, this same capacity for symbolic play is observed in a still more complex performance. Carlotta holds one of her toy animals over a cylindrical container and makes a series of noises that indicate an effort to toilet train the doll. This is particularly interesting given that the parents had not yet made similar efforts with Carlotta herself.

Hence, while Carlotta begins referential use of words earlier than Marta, she also demonstrates other Stage 6 symbolic behaviors earlier than Marta. And for both children, the referential use of words was preceded by the construction of the performative without words. We are led to the tentative conclusion that the sensorimotor performative is based on the cognitive developments of Stage 5, while the use of words with referents in such sequences is dependent upon the capacity for internal representation characteristic of Stage 6. Between these two levels, gestural and vocal signals gradually give way to increasingly wordlike sounds, so that it is difficult to specify the exact moment at which sounds are used to map an underlying symbol structure. This notion of separate origins for performatives and the use of symbols in those performatives may explain reports that some children have a well-developed gestural communication system (pointing to an object, making requests) for many months prior to inserting words in the same communicative sequences. The construction of communicative intentions at the sensorimotor level is essential for the development of speech, but apparently it is not enough.

There are some discrepancies between our findings regarding the child's first words and findings reported by other authors. First, many researchers have reported that the first words by children are imperatives. Piaget suggests that this is the case for his own daughters—"The first use of language is mainly in the form of orders and expressions of desire" (1962, p. 222). Then there is the folk wisdom that the first words by children are vocatives—daddy or mommy. In our own records, the first words with clear-cut referents are in fact declaratives or labels—Carlotta's animal sounds and Marta's comment *Pu* ("allgone"). It may be that the reports regarding both imperatives and vocatives result from a failure to distinguish words with referents from wordlike signals without referents, used to serve performative functions (e.g., Carlotta's *na-na*). Greenfield suggests that Piaget's own data do not support the above quotation, since the first words he reports are almost always naming behaviors, such as the "dog" example. Piaget has probably made that statement on the basis of the first wordlike sound *panama,* which he describes as an all purpose request with no particular referent.

There is another possibility for resolving the above discrepancies. With regard to the development of gestural imperatives and declaratives, we suggested earlier that children may vary in which kind of performative they construct first. As such, these performatives are horizontal decalages of an underlying causal structure. Perhaps the same thing is occurring with respect to the use of words in performative sequences. Some children may be more oriented toward utilitarian goals, so that they first exercise the Stage 6 symbolic capacity to symbolize and refer to objects that they want. Other children—such as Carlotta and Marta—may be more oriented toward social interactions, so that the symbolic capacity is more likely to be observed in the declarative sequences that serve to invoke adult attention. We see no particular structural reason, other than individual preference as to why imperatives or declaratives should be the first performatives in which words are used.

One final discrepancy might be mentioned between our data and findings by other authors. For both Carlotta and Marta, the first clearly referential words appeared concurrently with a variety of behaviors characteristic of Stage 6 symbolic representation. This includes the phenomenon of symbolic play, in which one object is used to stand for or represent another. Ingram (1974) has reviewed several studies of one-word speech, all of which report something resembling symbolic play weeks after one-word speech has begun (Greenfield and Smith, 1976; Ingram, 1971; Halliday, in press; Scollon, 1973). On the basis of these reports, Ingram concludes that the symbolic capacity as defined by Piaget is not a prerequisite for early one-word speech. The same authors do mention the onset of symbolic play later on in the one-word stage, in a period in which vocabulary increases markedly. This leads Ingram to conclude further that the symbolic capacity, while not a prerequisite for speech, does change radically the nature and use of reference by the child. This interpretation is at odds with our own observations that early reference and early symbolic play (as well as other manifestations of sensorimotor Stage 6) appear together. First, Ingram's interpretations are second hand, drawn from studies that did not deal directly with relations between speech and play. It is possible that these authors did not observe the actual onset of symbolic play, but simply reported particularly obvious or interesting instances that were relevant to some other issue. Hence first appearances, like Carlotta's spoon-telephone or Marta's feeding game, may have been omitted from their reports. Also, Ingram states that these play behaviors tend to coincide with a marked increase in vocabulary, and a higher frequency of utterance tokens. If the symbolic capacity is becoming more stable across all its manifestations, then it is likely that increased vocabulary would also be accompanied by a similar increase in the number of instances of symbolic play. This would increase the likelihood that, in studies not directed precisely toward the onset of nonverbal symbols, such play behaviors have simply become more noticeable. Finally, Ingram does not distinguish degrees of referentiality as we have in this study. He does state, however, that the earliest examples of one-word speech (i.e., before the appearance of symbolic play) are primarily "functional" in nature. Therefore, many of the instances of speech before symbols may be pure performatives, without referents, like Marta's *Ayi* or Carlotta's *na-na,* or at the very least transitional, semireferential procedures like Marta's *Da* and Carlotta's *Bam.* We also found such words in Stage 5, before the onset of symbols. If this is the case, then Ingram has not necessarily found referential speech prior to the onset of the symbolic capacity, but rather speechlike sounds in the service of sensorimotor performatives.

Given the fact that so many Stage 6 behaviors were observed simultaneously in Carlotta and Marta, even though both children were developing at different rates, we still maintain that Stage 6 representation is indeed a cognitive prerequisite for early referential speech. However, this question will require further empirical work. Bates et al. (1975), in a preliminary report on the cross-sectional study mentioned earlier, observe that well over half of their 25 subjects had shown at least two manifestations of Stage 6 by 12 months of age. In almost all of these, early forms of symbolic play coincided with early and infrequent uses of referential speech (e.g., naming animals in books). Furthermore, they suggest that the NATURE of this early symbolic play changes together with the NATURE of referential speech. In other words, the symbolic capacity, as it gradually becomes more stable and sophisticated, passes through a series of substages. We will return to this point later, with regard to the construction of propositions and the shift from one- to two- to three-word speech in children.

So far, we have established that performatives begin to carry locutionary as well as illocutionary force around 12 to 16 months, with the onset of the symbolic capacity (Stage 6) and the appearance of referential speech. This discussion has been restricted, however, to the child's capacity to refer to one referent with one symbol. As we shall see, many studies indicate that far more complex meanings can be conveyed with one-word speech, meanings combining several elements into a relational structure that deserves the term "proposition." If we define a **proposition** as a relation predicated of one or more arguments, then on the surface one-word utterances are not in themselves propositions. Yet from the way a child uses his utterances in context, we are able to recover what seems to be the intention to convey combinatorial meanings.

By examining one-word speech in context, several recent studies have convincingly established that holophrastic or one-word speech does communicate more structural meaning than is contained explicitly in its limited surface form. The method is essentially the same one that parents have used with their children for centuries: The child's meaning is inferred from the appropriate use of a single word in an organized context.

Evidence accepted by these authors includes parental interpretations, the child's acceptance or rejection of those interpretations, appropriate response to parental dialogue, and the ongoing activities of the child and those around him when a sentence is used. Bloom (1970) and Bowerman (1973) first used the so-called "rich interpretation" method to study two- and three-word speech in English and Finnish children. A famous example in Bloom (1970) is the sentence *Mommy sock,* used twice by the child Katherine to convey two clearly separate meanings—one in which the sock belongs to Mommy and the other in which Mommy is requested to help Katherine dress. While earlier efforts at grammar writing for child speech (e.g., Brown, 1973) were limited to rules for generating surface combinations only, Bloom's grammar described the different grammatical relations intended by the child in these two sentence types: a generative construction (*Mommy has sock*) and an agent–object construction with a deleted verb (*Mommy put sock*). The same technique can be used in the one-word period to derive several different meanings for a given holophrase—e.g., *Daddy* as object of action, *Daddy* as owner of object, etc. Through this technique, researchers can also examine the sequence in which different kinds of meanings are acquired throughout the one-word stage. Studies using the method of rich interpretation in one-word speech include Ingram (1971), Greenfield and Smith (1976), Bloom (1973), Nelson (1973), Schlesinger (1973), Scollon (1973), and Antinucci and Parisi (1973).

A point of general agreement in all these studies is that one-word utterances (like two-word utterances) mean more than they express phonetically. But is the complex meaning structure inside the child or in the situation interpreted by the adult? If it is in the child, in what form does he have it—can it be called syntactic structure, or semantic structure, or cognitive structure? And if he has all this structure, why is he limited to one word at a time?

With regard to the question of where the organization exists, Greenfield and Smith stress that there is a distinction between referential meaning, which the child indicates explicitly with his one-word utterance, and **combinatorial** meanings, in which the child combines his utterance with elements in the nonverbal situation to yield a relational meaning. At first glance, this position could be interpreted as a claim that the child does not "have" the locative, agentive, or dative structure of his utterances. When the child says *give* while handing over an object, the agent, object, and receiver of *give* exist in the situation while the child merely constructs the word describing the activity. However, the child does not just fortuitously say *give* in a situation that happens to correspond to giving. He himself controls the several aspects of the situation that define giving, and uses his single word inside that framework. When Greenfield and Smith say that the structure of child holophrases rests in the situation, they clearly mean situation in the phenomenal sense, as present to and contemplated by the child, and not in the noumenal sense of events out there. The child organizes himself within a structured world, and it is he who relates one aspect of the world to another through his activities. When the child says *give* while handing a block to Mommy, he is in some sense "wired in" to the block and to Mommy as perceptual objects with complementary properties, and in that sense the entire meaning structure is organized somewhere in his nervous system.

Regarding the second question, the form in which this information exists, three positions emerge regarding the appropriate linguistic representation for "rich" meanings:

1. All the information conveyed or implied by a one-word utterance is described in the semantic deep structure for that utterance (e.g., Antinucci and Parisi, 1973).

2. A linguistic representation is offered only for the element actually encoded by the child. The rest is presumably organized at a cognitive level not relevant to formal linguistic structure (e.g., Bloom, 1973; Schlesinger, 1973).

3. The linguistic representation itself is organized at two levels, one to describe the portion of the meaning actually encoded, the other to describe the implied portion of the meaning (e.g., Parisi, 1974).

Each of the positions also has different implications for a third question—the reason why these rich meanings can only be expressed with one word at a time.

The first approach, exemplified by the first publications of Antinucci and Parisi, can be found at the two-word stage in Lois Bloom's 1969 study. Bloom tried to write orthodox transformational grammars for the speech of three children, with deep structures formalized in syntactic rather than semantic terms. The two rich interpretations of *Mommy sock—Mommy has sock* and *Mommy put sock*—are described with the familiar deep structure constituents of subject noun phrase, verb phrase, and object noun phrase, at their respective hierarchical levels:

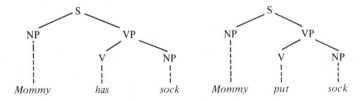

To account for the fact that only two of those elements are expressed, Bloom invokes a transformational mechanism called the **deletion rule**, which works to cancel one or more of the elements, usually the verb, in the creation of surface strings. The intended verb can in fact be inferred from the way that the sentence is used. But the different hierarchical levels are justified only by the fact that traditional grammars (i.e., transformational grammars) always have them. Bowerman (1973) and others have criticized Bloom for attributing these adult-like deep structure to children without independent evidence of their existence. Bowerman has proposed instead that these sentences can be described with semantically based deep structures with no more information in them than is actually required to explain the meanings expressed by the child. So that *Mommy sock* in a Fillmore type case grammar used by Bowerman, would have two elements in a genitive case relation for the first meaning, and in an agent–object relation in the other. There are no unnecessary hierarchical levels, and a minimum of deletion rules.

Although Antinucci and Parisi have analyzed one-word speech, using a semantic rather than a syntactic model, their first publications reflect an approach similar to Bloom's. They write in a tremendous amount of deep structure using another kind of deletion rule. Antinucci and Parisi have applied a generative semantic model to early speech—a much more elaborate and articulated linguistic model than Fillmore's list of case relations (Fillmore, 1968). Their analyses of one-word sentences such as the imperative *Da* ('give') contain a predicate with three arguments—agent (Mommy), object (pencil), and receiver (Francesco)—plus a performative hypersentence with the imperative broken into the same components outlined in Chapter I. In these first publications, all of these structures were called semantic structure and were presumed to exist on a homogeneous level of "mental operations." Antinucci and Parisi could account for the limited expression of complex meanings only by invoking an arbitrary performance limit (as in Bloom's deletion rule) on the mapping of complex meanings into sound. Partially because of a misunderstanding over this liberal use of the term "semantic" (which actually means no more than "communicated cognition" as it is used by these authors), their proposals have met with some skepticism. A written critique by Schlesinger is forthcoming. The critique is already somewhat outdated, in that Antinucci and Parisi are now also moving toward a position in which different aspects of semantic structure are ascribed to different cognitive levels (e.g., Parisi, 1974; Antinucci and Miller, 1975).

The second position with regard to linguistic representation of one-word speech involves describing only the encoded element at the level of deep structure. The rest of the meaning implied by one-word speech is relegated to "cognition," and is unformalized. Bloom's analysis of one-word speech is similar to her earlier studies of two- and three-word speech, in that she still recommends the use of traditional transformational syntax. Therefore, given that one-word speech contains only one expressed element, Bloom concludes that there is no syntax. The limit on expressing meaning is due to the fact that children have, as yet, no grammatical system for organizing meanings at the level of deep structure. Schlesinger (1973) prefers a semantic model of language, but agrees with Bloom that the organization implied by holophrastic speech is not contained in the linguistic deep structure of those utterances. Schlesinger describes the expressed portion of a complex meaning with an I-marker, or semantic intention marker. Hence the one-word utterance *Mommy* in a situation of Mommy handing baby a pencil is described with a single semantic role "agent." The rest of the situation—the receiver, the object received, the activity of giving—are excluded from semantic representation. Both Schlesinger and Bloom, while differing on the type of deep structure being built, would agree that one-word speech is limited because there is a deep structure level, independent of cognitive structure, that is still limited in size. This position has the advantage of removing the need for an ad hoc performance limit, since the deep structure contains only one element to be encoded. But there is still no independent psychological motivation for the limited level of linguistic deep structure. For example, there is no reason to suspect that similar limits are operating in other areas of information processing, since the proposed limits are strictly linguistic. In essence, the ad hoc performance limit has been exchanged for an ad hoc deep structure limit.

An alternative version of this split-level approach would be that the second level being constructed by the child is NOT a language specific deep structure level existing solely for the purpose of communication. Rather, there are two levels of cognitive processing, corresponding to Piaget's symbolic versus sensorimotor levels of organization. With the onset of the symbolic capacity, the child must slowly rebuild at the level of internal representation all that he had previously constructed at the sensorimotor level. This cannot take place suddenly, and the length of the holophrastic period would reflect the child's ability to construct only one aspect of a sensorimotor structure at a time, until he can finally internally represent and operate on an entire group of related symbolic objects. A pleasant coincidence for this proposal is that two- and three-word speech tends to appear at 18 months, precisely the point where Piaget concludes on the basis of other evidence that the capacity for internal representation is clearly established. If deep structure is a cognitively real level of organization, and mapping rules are internal operations applied to this structure, then it is advantageous that two- and three-word speech with some syntax appears when minimal internal operations on a symbolic array are established.

I have no evidence of any kind to buttress this interpretation over the other two positions on the nature of one-word speech. But this proposal does have the advantage of being potentially testable. The limitations on very early language development, according to this model, are directly related to all mental development in this period. Performance limits are not the product of the different genetic rhythms of separate systems. Rather, they are produced by the application of very general, underlying cognitive principles to different kinds of problems and experiences—in this case, communication across the linear acoustic–articulatory channel. IF THE LIMITS ON ONE-WORD SPEECH REFLECT GENERAL LIMITS ON THE NEW LEVEL OF SYMBOLIC REPRESENTATION, THEN WE SHOULD EXPECT TO FIND PARALLEL LIMITS OPERATING IN NONVERBAL PROCESSING OF SYMBOL STRUCTURES. The problem, of course, is to come up with appropriate measures of non-verbal symbolic representation (e.g., imagery, mental displacements) during the age range covered by early speech. Greenfield, Nelson, and Saltzman (1972) and Sinclair (personal communication) are currently involved in research on nonverbal representation from 12 to 36 months. But to date the parallels to linguistic development are poorly defined.

There have been some recent converts to the position that very early speech is limited by general cognitive development. In his 1974 response to Schlesinger, Parisi suggests that only part of the elaborate semantic structure underlying child speech is organized at the symbolic level. The rest can presumably be organized at a lower, perceptual–motor level. He is cautious about ascribing this difference entirely to limits on the symbolic capacity, and insists that there may also be purely linguistic performance limits on the mechanism for mapping thought into sound. Greenfield (personal communication) apparently feels that her data fit this split-level model of cognition, although the division into symbolic and sensorimotor levels is not made explicit in her 1974 analysis of combinatorial meaning. Perhaps the most surprising convert to the cognitivist position is McNeill (1974), who recently presented a paper in which the major events in the transition from gesture to one-word to n-word speech are ascribed to the gradual "interiorization" of the sensorimotor action schemes described by Piaget. Given McNeill's earlier emphasis on strong linguistic universals (1970), this new cognitive analysis of language development marks an important theoretical shift.

Can we be more specific about the nature of such a cognitive transition, from the sensorimotor to the symbolic level, with a gradual increase in the capacity of the symbolic level? This will lead us into two rather abstract questions regarding (1) the nature of symbols, and (2) the distinction between figurative and operative knowing in the processing of symbols. It is here that our Chapter I digression into artificial intelligence models will be most useful—to add some comforting metallic reality to philosophical issues that may seem occasionally to go beyond empirically testable theory into the realm where angels dance on the heads of pins.

First, let us examine in more detail the nature of symbols in cognitive development. A good many introductory anthropology texts begin with the "definition of man" as the possessor of at least two unique abilities: the use of tools and the use of symbols in speech. However, laboratory research by Kohler (1927) and field research by Goodall (1968) have demonstrated that chimpanzees are also capable of tool use. And the successful mastery of portions of American Sign Language by the chimpanzee Washoe (Gardner and Gardner, 1969) suggests that the capacity for linguistic symbols is not unique to man either. It should of course not surprise us if any and all human abilities exist in at least an attenuated form in some phylogenetic neighbor. But is there something special about the relationship between tool use and symbols that causes them to be found together in full-fledged form in man, in a more minimal form in chimpanzees? Note also that in ontogeny, tool use characterizes Stage 5, and the discovery of symbols in Stage 6 follows soon thereafter. Piaget suggests that there is a direct link between the two, that "the invention of novel means to familiar ends" prepares the organism for symbolic representation.

There is another capacity, also shared by man and chimpanzee, which is also involved in the preparation of symbols. This is the ability to analyze reality through imitation. Together, practice in imitation and in tool use at the sensorimotor level will give the human infant a flexibility in his operations on reality that will eventually enable him to represent objects to himself and operate on them in their absence. In this sense, the symbolic capacity is NOT just an amazing species-specific ability that appears from out of nowhere around 12 to 16 months of age (perhaps induced by hormones ...). Rather, it is the natural end point of earlier constructions. A closer examination of the developments leading up to the symbolic capacity—in particular imitation and tool use—may also help us understand the fundamental relationship linking linguistic symbols to other kinds of symbols in the development of mental representation.

Piaget defines a symbol as the use of one scheme to "stand for" another or the use of part of one scheme to "stand for" the whole. As such, the full-fledged symbolic capacity in mental representation—using one scheme to stand for or refer to another in the complete absence of that referent—is a vertical decalage of earlier sensorimotor exercises in part–whole relations. For example, a Stage 3 child (4 to 8 months) watches a doll disappear behind a screen, with only the doll's arm or leg left visible. From the leg or arm, the child is able to "reconstruct" the rest of the doll, i.e., he "knows" that when the visible arm or leg is present, the invisible rest is somewhere nearby. He then lifts the screen and obtains the whole doll. In a sense, then, the child used his perceptual schemes for interacting with the doll's leg (e.g., scanning its contours, feeling it, recognitory operations of the type discussed earlier) to "stand for" or recall the more complete set of perceptual–motor schemes that make up his knowledge of the whole doll. Hence, the child's doll scheme has become so well organized and stable that given a part, he can reconstruct the whole. By Stage 4, this capacity is still more stable. If the doll is now completely covered, the child can still keep his doll scheme "called up and present" in central processing long enough to remove the obstacle. If he is kept from removing the screen for several minutes, he will, however, forget. The ability to construct and keep the doll scheme in mind is still dependent on recent perceptual support. The child cannot "call up" his doll scheme in the total absence of dolls in space and time.

The ability to call up complex perceptual–motor schemes in the absence of direct perceptual input is the definition of the Stage 6 capacity for representation (literally re-presentation). When the child can call up his doll schemes, he can also operate further on his mental representation of the doll, e.g., planning to go and get it to drop it off the terrace. When the representation of the doll in itself becomes the subpart of such a larger mental scheme, we say that the mental doll scheme has served as a symbol in a representative process. That symbol may be a mental image of the doll—e.g., a reenactment of all or part of the visual schemes for interacting with dolls. Or it may be a linguistic symbol. The internal recall of the word "doll" may be sufficient to stand for dolls in a series of mental displacements, without constructing other mental images as well. Just how an acoustic–articulatory procedure, e.g., the word *doll,* comes to serve the same mental functions as an internal visual image, is a question that we will turn to shortly.

How do we know that the child is carrying on mental reenactments of his activities in the world? Obviously we can only infer such a process on the basis of external evidence. One of Piaget's examples of evidence for mental representation is the following. His daughter has come to the door with a handful of flowers. She sets the flowers down in front of the door and reaches up toward the knob. Suddenly she stops, bends down and picks the flowers up, and moves them out of the way of the door. She then opens the door, picks the flowers up, and goes in. Piaget infers that she has mentally represented what would happen if the door opened with the flowers in front of it. In fact, they would have been smashed. So she changes the location of the flowers and opens the door without incident.

Further evidence, as we saw earlier, comes from symbolic play. Piaget's daughter Jacqueline sees a bit of cloth that resembles the fringe on her bed pillow. With eyes open, laughing, she lies down and carries out the act of sleeping. Similarly, our subject Carlotta sees a cigarette package, picks it up, and holds it to her ear in the act of talking on the telephone. Now in the case of the symbols for telephones or pillows, the stimulus bears a certain literal resemblance to the thing for which it stands. In that sense, symbolic play stands midway between the earlier part–whole construction of recovering a whole doll from part of a doll, and the more sophisticated mental act of reconstructing a doll in the complete and total absence of dolls. Clearly, however, the cue setting off the schemes of sleeping or talking on the phone bears so little resemblance to the original that we must admit the child has called up and executed a rather complex whole from minimal parts.

How did the child move from the lower level part–whole analysis of a doll from a doll's leg, to the capacity to take minimal reminders of dolls, telephones, etc. and use them to reenact elaborate, almost autonomous schemes? Piaget stresses the role of imitation and tool use in advancing the nature of the part–whole capacity into a capacity to use symbols in mental representation.

In *Play, Dreams and Imitation* (1962), Piaget lays particular stress on the importance of imitation in developing representation. First, every act of accommodating to or "knowing" reality contains a certain amount of imitation. Take the artificial intelligence example of a triangle recognizing program. This program does not HAVE triangles, but rather DOES triangles, carrying out scan patterns that are in themselves procedures. Let us stress that these procedures are not copies—they are actions that bear an isomorphic, imitative relationship to triangles. The machine does not copy triangles. In fact, given the two arrays, the machine can recognize a triangle in both, because it can carry out the same scanning procedure with both.

We know reality by the procedures and transformation we can carry out with or on that reality. Imitation, as we witness it in children and chimpanzees, is a particularly clear manifestation of accommodation to reality, "knowing" or analyzing reality by carrying out procedures that are highly dependent on the exact space–time outlines of a particular aspect of reality. The child's subsequent knowledge of dolls, bottles, balls, tables, and chairs involves calling up accommodative schemes that were originally organized in imitating and acting (visually and motorically) on dolls, bottles, etc. The ultimate advance in imitation is what Piaget calls **deferred imitation**, in which a child can reenact an entire sequence hours or days after that sequence was originally presented.

Imitation, then, is the activity that prepares the accommodative aspect of representation, the ability to reenact the original conditions for knowing an object or event, even in the absence of that event. But if representation consisted solely of deferred imitation, there would be nothing creative about it, no novel transformations of reality. Mental activity would consist solely of remembering, reconstructing things past. But mental activity is also assimilative. It transforms reality, or remembrances of reality, to new uses and forms. Piaget suggests that the assimilative aspect of representation, particularly our flexibility in selecting or creating symbols to undergo mental transformation, derives from the Stage 5 capacity for tool use.

To examine how this occurs, let us first make sure we have clarified the distinction between assimilation and accommodation. These are not separate functions. They are two aspects of any given act. To the extent that the child can successfully impose a prepared scheme—e.g., sucking, grasping—to an object, he has assimilated that object. But to the degree that he must change his scheme to conform to the demands of the object— e.g., widening his grasp for a larger cup, changing the shape of his mouth to drink from a cup as opposed to a nipple—he has accommodated to that object. All acts contain a proportion of both assimilation and accommodation. But in pure imitation and exploration, the child's activity with an object or event is primarily accommodative. In playing with objects, from Stage 4 banging and swinging through to Stage 6 pretending, the child's activity is primarily assimilative, forcing reality to submit to his own plans. Of course no interaction is purely assimilative. Note that Carlotta chose a spoon and a cigarette package to serve as telephones. She did not try to pretend that the living room carpet was a telephone. Even in very sophisticated assimilations, the child must at least insure that the chosen tool or symbol follows certain minimal requirements permitting it to stand for the intended referent or serve the intended purpose. In fact, the more sophisticated the child's assimilative scheme, the more time he may have to spend choosing the proper object to serve the required function. Earlier we saw the link between imitation and mental imagery. Here we see the link between symbolic play and tool use.

As we said, Stage 5 is the "invention of new means to familiar ends." Prior to Stage 5, a child who wants to reach an object gradually hits upon a repertoire of familiar and generally applicable means, such as locomotion, reaching, etc. In part, it is in understanding the generalizability of these means that the child comes to understand that means are detachable from ends—e.g., "If reaching doesn't work, try crawling closer to the object." When familiar means fail, the Stage 4 child is stymied. He cannot invent new links on the spot. However, increased experience with using his old means, combining them in different ways, as well as a great deal of accommodative exploration of the nature of things, will gradually increase his understanding of the more general aspects of means–end, and hence causal relations.

A particularly clear example is the support relation. The Stage 4 child has a fairly good understanding of the usefulness of his own hand and his own movements as tools. He knows that unless hand and object are in contact, he must move to obtain contact before he can act on the object. He must now also learn that the same support and contact relation required for hands is also generalizable to object and object. When he understands this, at least in a more passive way, he can use a support that is already there to pull a toy toward him. When the scheme for acting on prepared supports is mastered, the next step is to invent supports when none are automatically provided. Hence, the child who pulled a cloth toward him to take a toy, learns to create the missing support by picking up a stick and using it to pull the object nearer. In the construction of dynamic cause–effect wholes, the Stage 5 child learns how to invent or otherwise provide the missing part. Tool use is, then, an active, assimilative manifestation of the same part–whole relation that was discussed above as the more imitative, accommodative reconstruction of an invisible doll from a visible part. Stage 5 is not really a totally new ability, but rather an elaboration or vertical decalage of an earlier capacity.

At the end of Stage 5, then, the human child has such a well-organized sensorimotor knowledge of the world (both assimilative and accommodative) that he can execute portions of his knowledge with only minimal contextual support. On the accommodative side, he can reenact his imitations of reality in the absence of that reality, to create mental images. On the assimilative side, he can interrupt a complex scheme long enough to find or form the missing link that impedes completion of that scheme. This ability to abstract a property of some object—e.g., length, weight, substance—and because of that property use the object as a tool, is clearly related to the ability to abstract some property of an object or portion of a scheme to serve as a symbol in play or in problem solving. This ability to select symbols-tools and subject them to some manipulation is originally exercised on the plane of action, on supports, sticks, spoons, and cigarette packs. But once the capacity for deferred imitation and representation is established, a portion of these MENTAL schemes can also be chosen to serve as the symbolic object or tool in some MENTAL manipulation. Therefore imitation and tool use, in their respective accommodative and assimilative roles, lead directly to the symbolic capacity and mental representation. These are in turn derived from the differentiation and reintegration of parts and wholes at earlier stages.

At the risk of digressing too much, one brief anecdote may illustrate just how sophisticated an 11-month-old child can be at part–whole analyses involving tool use and symbols. In our cross-sectional study (Bates et al., 1975), we administered the Hunt and Uzgiris scales of sensorimotor development at each session. One of the items investigating causal analysis and foresight involves rings on a stick, in which one of the rings is blocked with some substance that makes it impossible to place the ring on the stick. The purpose is to determine from the child's reaction to the blocked ring his understanding of the relationship involved. One of our subjects, at 11 months of age, investigated the blocked ring with her finger, scratching at the styrofoam filling and trying to push it on the stick. Finally, with a puzzled look, she grasped an empty ring, picked up a piece of cotton sitting nearby, and filled the empty ring with the cotton. Then she took her new creation and put it successfully on the stick, causing the cotton to pop out in the process. This spontaneous experiment clearly demonstrates the conceptual links between accommodative part–whole analysis, an elaborate imitation involving invention of new means (e.g., assimilating the cotton as a ring stuffer), and reenactment of the entire sequence with the new symbol for the old stuffed ring.

Granted that this system is quite sophisticated, how does it feed into the acquisition of language? How does a word get to be used as a symbol in sundry mental transformations, as well as in communication? This is a thorny problem and in speculating about it one risks doing a great deal of hand waving. However, the key seems to lie in the transitional stage in which words, or quasiwords, are equivalent to all the other procedures for acting on objects. Svachkin's child says *kitty* as a procedure for bringing back the kitty. Carlotta says *bam* as part of the process of banging on things. Marta says *da* as a sort of vocal ritual that accompanies the equally arbitrary ritual of handing objects back and forth. Piaget's Jacqueline says *dog* not to name dogs but to accompany the activity of watching things from her balcony. It seems that, initially, the child does not understand or objectify the special vehicle–referent relationship with which adults link words and things. Rather, words are merely a subset of schemes for operating on objects. As he becomes capable of using ANY of his schemes to stand for the complex to which they originally belonged— including visual, motor and other schemes—he can also use the naming procedures as symbols or parts in some larger whole. Support for the notion of word as procedure comes also from the common observation that children use words to themselves, in noncommunicative contexts, apparently in the process of otherwide exploring, recognizing, "knowing" objects (e.g., recall Carlotta making the mouth movement for fish as she recognized her fish lying on the sofa).

Nor should we be too misled by the philosophical commonplace that words bear an arbitrary relationship to their referents while other symbols do not. First, recall that the human child uses imitation widely in the process of analyzing and trying to understand events and objects. As such, he often imitates arbitrary movements of adults, games that can have no prior meaning or interpretation for him beyond the fact that they are part of something new he is trying to master. A child who imitates his mother stirring in a mixing bowl probably has little understanding of the function of that act, and yet he can still use it to remind himself or reenact kitchen activities. Given the amount of speech in his environment (plus perhaps an innately based interest in just those sounds for their own sake) it is perhaps less than miraculous that he discovered wordlike procedures together with these others. Furthermore, it is the adult who clearly perceives the difference between iconic and arbitrary symbols. There is reason to believe that the child doesn't see the word–referent relationship as arbitrary for years to come. Numerous studies have confirmed Piaget's observation of word realism in children—e.g., *Why is a cow called a cow? Because it is brown and has horns.* For the child, the word–symbol seems as much a part of the cow scheme as imagistic properties like color and horns, which can also be used as symbols (e.g., in early drawings). Recall Peirce's division of sign–referent relations into **icons,** which bear a direct physical resemblance to the things for which they stand, true **symbols,** which are related to their referents only by an arbitrary bond imposed by the symbol users, and **indices,** which stand for their referents by virtue of participating in them, as smoke indexes fire. We might suggest that for the child, at least at the beginning, ALL sign relations are indices, procedures for acting on and participating in a given event. All symbols are derived from portions of procedures for interacting with the world. Only later will the child be able to objectify his own acts of reference sufficiently to recognize the distinction between iconic, arbitrary, and indexical sign–referent bonds.

There is an important difference, however, between word symbols and other symbols, in that whereas the child can invent private symbols of other sorts for himself, word symbols tend to be derived from the social environment (although there are numerous recorded instances of children inventing their own words as well). As such, linguistic symbols will play a more important part in socializing the child's internal knowledge of the world, packaging reality in ways similar to the adult packages presented to him daily. Nevertheless, as Quine has earlier stressed, we can never be sure that we know what network of internal operations make up a given individual's knowledge of a word. We only know that he uses the word in the same way we do and hence is pragmatically socialized.

An advantage of all symbols, including linguistic ones, is, of course, the amount of processing time that they save during mental representation. Just as it was advantageous for the child to be able to recognize a whole doll by seeing only the doll's arm, it is also useful and economical to be able to think about dolls without having to reenact the entire set of schemes available for interacting with dolls. Just a part will do, serving as a symbol within some further transformation. This definition of symbols recalls the pattern matching devices described in the section on computer models. Central processing need only call up the top node of a subprogram, manipulating this symbol alone without analyzing the internal details of the subprogram each time. Thinking in symbols increases our overall efficiency. This does not mean that the "stuff" on which word meanings are made has changed its sensorimotor, procedural nature. The meaning of the symbol–word *bottle* still contains all the schemes for interacting with bottles that the child has derived across 12 to 18 months.

But in thinking with a word or image symbol for bottles, the child need attend only to this top node of the complete sensorimotor subprogram, rather than analyzing the lexical program anew each time.

However, this mature system presumes that the organism already has aspects of reality fairly well subprogrammed or chunked into lexical units, and is efficient at chunking and combining chunks into more complex propositional packages. For the very young child, this is not the case. He knows a lot about reality. And he at last has the capacity to take a part of reality and let it stand for a larger whole in such a way that he can retrieve the whole. But that capacity is fairly new, and his chunking system is quite inefficient. This brings us beyond the question of individual symbols, into the problem posed originally: Why does a child who has such a complex sensorimotor understanding of relations, objects and events, have such a hard time expressing those relations at the one and two-word stage?

The problem of lexical chunking, and the relationship between symbols and central processing, requires an examination of the distinction between figurative and operative knowing in representational thought. We said earlier that figurative knowing refers to the static, accommodative aspect of thought, the reconstruction of what is known through internal imitation of the original procedures for knowing a given object or event. Figurative procedures are indeed ACTS, but they are used in the service of creating objects for some other, higher act. Operative knowing refers to the dynamic, transforming aspect of thought, derived from the more assimilative aspects of earlier interactions with the world. At the level of mental representation, mental images are unquestionably figurative constructions. Mental rotations, reversals, displacements, etc. of such images are operative procedures on figurative structures. So far we are in complete accordance with orthodox Piagetian theory. But what is linguistic communication? What are linguistic symbols and the combination of meanings into propositions? Piaget's own use of the term "figurative"—although it varies from one work to another—refers generally to images and other mental acts linked more to perceptual accommodations.In fact,in *Memory and Intelligence* (1972), Piaget states explicitly that

> Next, there are the figurative cum semiotic mechanisms, for instance mental images, symbolic games, deferred imitation, gestural languages, etc. Lastly, there are the semiotic instruments which are not figurative in themselves, namely, the system of signs. Natural languages belong in this category ... [p. 12].

This is a rather clear statement of what language isn't. And yet Piaget never really says what language IS. He does not insist that linguistic meaning is entirely operative either. He has stated that words begin as subjective acts, or procedures. But then, so do mental images. Where does the crucial difference lie between these two types of symbols?

We want to suggest that, insofar as meanings are mental operations organized into propositional arrays for purposes of communication, meanings are the figurative input into the operations of a communicative system. We are, then, defining **figurative** as the creation of mental objects for some higher system, while **operative** refers to transformations on figurative products. Therefore, the two terms are relative to a given moment in processing, and what is operative at one level, becomes figurative when it is held in some statis form and operated on as the object of a higher procedure. Sinclair (1974) has suggested that syntactic transformations like conjoining, interrupting, embedding, deleting, etc. are all ultimately derivable from activities that the child carried out on real objects in the real world—moving, chaining, stacking, combining toys, etc. As such, syntactic transformations would be operative, like the activities from which they were derived. It follows from Sinclair's analysis that, if these deep structures (or propositional structures) have any psychological reality at all, they must serve as the figurative input to this operative system of linguistic transformations. In fact, the problems of interrupting propositional units in embedding, breaking up units to attach new morphemes, combining propositions into higher propositions, all seem very much related to problems with other arrays having a static, figurative aspect.

Feldman et al. (1974) also recognize the similarity between Piaget's figurative/operative distinction, and the actor/acted-upon distinction as it is applied to more abstract, nonperceptual mental activities. They have gotten around Piaget's limited use of the term "figurative" by borrowing Chomsky's distinction into formal (e.g., dynamic, operative) and substantive (static, object-like) to describe these two aspects of thought. This solution is similar in usage to ours, insofar as the formal structures of one stage become the substantive structures of another. But in insisting on using Piaget's term "figurative" to describe the static, object-like meaning structures of language, we also call attention to the vertical decalages that may exist when the child tries to understand and transform his new propositional objects in the same way that he once transformed tables, chairs, dolls, etc. As each new level of abstraction is mastered, the child makes the same old mistakes and the same old discoveries that he once made with lower order figurative arrays.

Furthermore, we are suggesting that the child's figurative limits in organizing his thoughts into lexical chunks and propositions (e.g., selecting and constructing symbolic parts from a larger, meaningful whole) are systematically related to figurative limits on the organization and the chunking of relationships in other types of mental processing as well. As such, it is not language specific. Also, operative problems in mapping one, two or more figurative chunks may apply equally in communicative processing as well as in other types of problem solving.

In fact, it may be the gradual growth and reciprocal interaction between figurative and operative capacities that explains the transition from one to two to three-word speech. When a child merely observes and understands that a dog is on a chair, and that he wants it off, he is employing both figurative and operative aspects of knowing that array. However, once he decides to communicate that relationship, or something about that relationship, he has objectified his act of knowing the situation, turning it into the object of his higher, communicative schemes. This means that instead of just knowing, he must reconstruct or regroup some section of the knowledge, reflecting on it and preparing it for mapping into sounds. It is here that his difficulty in speaking lays, grouping his knowledge into a figurative, propositional array and operating on it to turn it into one sound or a concatenation of sounds. The limits of this chunk-and-transfer capacity would be observed in speech as a one-word limit, a two-word limit, and so forth. But we are suggesting that a similar chunk-and-transfer limit should be observable in other aspects of thought as well. The problem as stated earlier is to find empirical measures of processing limits in nonlinguistic representation. [See Greenfield et al. (1972) for an example of such research.]

In the analysis just presented, we have ignored a number of serious questions pertaining to mental representation, symbolic processing, and linguistic meaning. For example, we have barely mentioned the distinction between comprehension and production of language and the reasons why comprehension precedes production in development. This is probably not a language specific problem. As Huttenlocher (1974) suggests, it may be related to the more general distinction between recall and recognition memory, in which recognition (like comprehension) precedes reconstruction and recall. Of course, this does not answer the question. It merely places it in the framework of a larger problem. But there are limits to the amount of speculation permitted a given author, and the problem of the relationship between comprehension and production will have to be left for future work.

Given the nature of the limits of processing outlined here, how does a child decide what to encode and what to exclude? And how does he go about organizing the relational aspects of meaning into topics, comments, and so forth? This brings us to presupposing, the third aspect of the pragmatic system of performative–proposition–presupposition. In the next chapter, we will discuss the development of procedures for presupposing. In addition, we will return to the question of formal representation treated at the end of the last chapter, examining the proper way to represent a linguistic system that is operating at several cognitive levels, even within a given proposition. For now, we conclude that reference and propositionality—the sine qua non of semantic analysis—are ultimately derivable from procedures and hence from a primarily pragmatic system. Limits on encoding knowledge into propositions and expressing that knowledge may be related to general limits in mental representation, having to do with growth of both the figurative and the operative aspects of symbolic processing.

CHAPTER IV

Presupposing as
a Sensorimotor Procedure

How does a child know what NOT to say? Are his first uses of language capricious, or does he know from the beginning what needs to be said and what can be assumed? We have suggested that one important aspect of pragmatics, the performative, is developed prior to speech itself. Another important aspect of pragmatics is the ability to exploit the context of language use so as to convey information against a background of shared assumptions.

In adult language, this ability covers a range of related phenomena. Deixis is the use of "empty" or partially defined terms such as pronouns to "point to" referents available in the speech situation. Anaphora is a kind of discourse deixis in which abbreviated speech forms are used to discuss further or refer to things that have already been said. A still broader concept, presupposition, is defined somewhat differently by various semantic theorists, but can be defined so as to subsume both deixis and anaphora.

Three possible definitions have been offered for the term **presupposition** (see pages 20–27). Semantic or logical presupposition (P_1) refers to information that must be true for a given sentence to be either true or false. Pragmatic presupposition (P_2) was defined as conditions necessary for a sentence to be used appropriately in a given context. Since a commitment by the speaker to the truth of a proposition is a necessary condition for speech acts of declaring, we concluded that the P_1 truth conditions for presuppositions are subsumed under the broader pragmatic (P_2) definition. Finally, we offered a psychological definition of presupposition (P_3)

96

as the use of an utterance to comment upon information assumed to be shared by speaker and listener. This last definition subsumes both the semantic and pragmatic definitions of presupposition, as well as operations of deixis and anaphora. But it also includes presupposing ACTS that may not necessarily be signalled in the surface form of the utterance. If the speaker uses his utterance as a comment upon some contextually available information and assumes that his listener can reconstruct the same relationship, then a psychological presupposition is present even if the sentence itself contains no explicit references to that presupposition. Hence, a decision essential to every act of speaking—the choice of which elements to encode and which elements to take for granted—requires the psychological act of presupposing. In this chapter, we will argue that some kind of presuppositional capacity, as defined here, is operating from the time that children first begin to encode their experience in speech.

First, we will demonstrate that a limited presuppositional capacity is already present in the earliest uses of language. Evidence will be offered from several studies by other authors, in particular Greenfield and Smith (1976) and Antinucci and Volterra (1973).

Second, evidence from the study by Bates, Camaioni, and Volterra (1973), together with items cited by Werner and Kaplan (1963), will be used to suggest that this presuppositional capacity is rooted in a broad, nonlinguistic operation that is present from the beginning of cognitive development.

Third, it will be argued that this same set of developments accompanies and characterizes the development of the proposition itself, giving rise to the semantic division of topic–comment. The topic–comment relation will then be used to generate the relation of presupposition to proposition. The proposal again involves the question of sensorimotor versus symbolic levels of organization, as outlined in the previous chapter.

In the last chapter, we reviewed a number of studies of holophrastic or one-word speech, all of which indicate that single word utterances communicate more combinatorial meaning than seems to be signalled in their surface form. All of these studies have dealt with the content of early propositions. Of the major studies of the holophrastic period, only Greenfield and Smith (1976) have gone on from the question of situational meanings to the matter of situational appropriateness. After much lengthier analyses of the development of content, Greenfield and Smith devote two chapters to language use: one to dialogue development (in particular question answering) and the other to the question of informativeness.

With regard to dialogue, Greenfield and Smith report the following sequence. For any given meaning category, the child first expresses that relationship himself with a supporting action–object context. Then he later expresses the same meaning in the verbal context of question answering. Finally, the same meaning appears spontaneously in two-word sequences, without necessarily requiring verbal or nonverbal support. Greenfield and Smith suggest that question answering and dialogue in general present a vital link between the expression of meanings that are highly dependent on external context, and the ability to express the same meanings in a verbal context—hence, to master syntax. In dialogue, the adult provides situationally interpretable verbal material with an open slot into which the child can insert a verbal response.

This means that the child builds his comments onto externally supplied topics. He does this first with topics available in immediate space and time. Then, he builds the system in the same order within discourse space and time, using the adult verbal frames as topics to support his comments. Presumably, this last effort will enable him to discover syntax and later to express both topic and comment himself against a background situation. On both the perceptual level and the discourse level, the child's propositions PRESUPPOSE another, richer structure. In fact, they absolutely require a presupposed structure if they are to be built at all.

The next Greenfield and Smith chapter deals with the informativeness of spontaneous utterances. **Informative** is defined here in information theory terms, as that aspect of a given situation undergoing or subject to greatest change or uncertainty. The authors examined the hypothesis that the child will use his limited expressive capacity to encode precisely that aspect of the situation containing the most information. An ideal test for this hypothesis would be a situation in which the child is applying the same action to a number of different objects—eating a cookie, then a piece of cheese, then a piece of bread. In this case, the most informative element would be the object being eaten. Similarly, if the child were applying different activities to a single object—first putting it in his mouth, then throwing it in the air—the most informative element would be the action. If the child were engaged in a dispute over who can play with a toy, the most informative element would be the agent-owner. Unfortunately, in the spontaneous interactions that make up most free speech data, the situation rarely presents itself along such neat divisions of informativeness. Where such situations do occur (drawn from their own data as well as an analysis of Lois Bloom's data), Greenfield and Smith report that children do indeed encode the most informative element in the situation. There are other kinds of data that also support the informativeness hypothesis. For example, self as agent and the verb "want" are among the last concepts to be encoded explicitly by the children in the Greenfield and Smith study. The authors suggest that these concepts are not encoded because, from the child's point of view, they are entirely obvious and certain aspects of the situation. In several analyses across dialogues, Greenfield and Smith illustrate how the next element for encoding by the child is determined by what went before, shifting his attention and interest from one element to another.

Influenced by Greenfield's findings, Veneziano (1973) examined her data for one-word speech with Italian children, and found that the same criterion of informativeness applied to most of the one-word utterances in her sample. Both of these studies in turn lend support to observations made much earlier by DeLaguna (1927), Sechehaye (1926), and Vygotsky (1962) that the child's **monorhemes** or one-word sentences tend to express comments rather than topics (cited in MacWhinney, 1975). Greenfield (1975) notes that, although the free speech data do support the informativeness hypothesis, a clearcut demonstration requires experimental manipulation of the situation, setting up the kinds of change and stability relationships described above (e.g., the same action is applied to several different objects, different actions are applied to the same object, etc.). Snyder (1975) has attempted just such experimental manipulations with children between 12 and 18 months of age. She reports that children do indeed tend to encode the appropriate, shifting element in the situation.

Both the Greenfield and Smith chapters, as well as the other studies of early comment–topic relationships, demonstrate that the child has an ability to build an utterance onto a given frame in such a way that the utterance presupposes that frame (in the P_3 sense outlined earlier). At this writing, the only other study I am aware of that directly applies a presuppositional analysis to very early speech is Antinucci and Volterra's "The Development of Negation in Child Language: A Pragmatic Study" (1973). Antinucci and Volterra contend that negation is NOT the philosophically impossible act of asserting a nonevent—e.g., *I assert that it is not raining*. As Bergson (1970) explains, there is no such thing as a nonevent. Rather, negation is a separate kind of performative in which the speaker denies a given presupposition attributed to the listener—e.g., the listener thinks, or might think, that it is raining, and the speaker instructs him not to sustain that belief. Otherwise, if the speaker were merely describing truth in the world, he would positively assert *The sun is shining* or *There are clouds in the sky*.

Assuming that every act of negation operates on a corresponding presupposition, Antinucci and Volterra analyze early negation in the longitudinal data for two Italian and two American children. The data fall into four types of negation, each with a different denial–presupposition relationship. All four types are found in the earliest transcripts.

In Type A, the presupposition is "The speaker believes that the listener is doing or about to do P." The assertion is that the speaker doesn't want the listener to do P. For example, the visitor says (in Italian) *And if we take out the cork, what happens?* Francesco sees what is about to happen and says *No-no*.

In Type B, the presupposition is "The speaker believes that the listener believes P." The assertion is that the speaker doesn't want the listener to believe P. For example, Francesco is looking at the empty candy wrapper after eating the candy, and says *No c'e pu* ('There isn't anymore').

In Type C, the presupposition is that the speaker believes that the listener wants the speaker to do P. The assertion is that the speaker does not want the listener to believe that the speaker will do P. For example, the visitor tries to make Francesco give her a toy car. Francesco does not want to give it to her and says *No*.

In Type D, the speaker believes that the listener wants him to confirm or disconfirm a statement. The assertion is a confirmation or disconfirmation of the speaker's question. For example, the mother asks Francesco *E cattiva questa bambina?* ('Is this baby bad?'), and Francesco answers *No-no*.

Antinucci and Volterra conclude that the earliest negations do occur as operations on presuppositions, and in fact can already operate on four varieties of presupposition. One might argue with the complex formulation that the authors give to these four types of negation. The authors do not distinguish between the complexity of the presuppositional structure in comparison with the severe limits in expressive capacity at the one-word stage. However, they provide further data which indicate that the child does not have the same kind of control over his presuppositions that he has over the semantic structure of the one-word utterance itself. First of all, in the four types of negation present from the beginning of the transcripts, each presupposition is at first immediately available in ongoing events in the situation, or in immediately preceding utterances by the adult. And in the earliest cases, the adult utterances themselves are always well-supported with nonverbal situational evidence. Hence, the information which the child presupposes and then negates is available at a sensorimotor level. It need not be reconstructed internally for the negation to function. Much later, the children begin to base their negations on normative presuppositions that have been violated. For example, Francesco sees a tower on a large hospital. He points to it and says *no bells*. Apparently his experience with bells has been restricted to church towers, and this hospital tower violates the norm that all towers have bells.

Which brings us to the second development, the ability to pull one's own presuppositions—normative or situational—in line with the listener's. In the earliest negations, which involve an immediate, shared context, there is little likelihood of pragmatic misfire. The situationally available presuppositions are inevitably shared by child and adult. But both negations involving norms and negations involving situations removed in time and space from the immediate context can provide the possibility of presupposition failure. The adult, for example, does not share the norm that all towers have bells: He is able to reconstruct Francesco's presupposition only because of a detailed knowledge of how negation should work in adult speech. The development of negation, according to Antinucci and Volterra, is not merely a development of the logical capacity to deny a presupposition. That ability is apparently present from the beginning of speech development. Rather, it is essentially a pragmatic development—the construction of shared norms and the development of a distinction between the speaker's and the listener's presuppositions.

If, as the above evidence indicates, it is true that the first uses of language are coordinated with presuppositions, the next question is how and when did that ability develop. Here I shall contend first that this ability need not imply that the child constructs the presuppositions of his first speech acts as symbolic objects. Second, I will suggest that this ability is, instead, the natural product of the workings of the attentional system applied within the development of communication.

In his article, "The Best Theory" (1972), Postal suggests that the weight of evidence in linguistics lies with who would add structures to syntactic or semantic analysis. Following this standard, the first contention is resolved simply. There is no evidence in early speech that the child can reflect upon presupposing, even though it is clear that he does presuppose. In the analysis of negation described above, the children are helpless in the face of presupposition failure. They cannot back up and make a presupposition explicit when it does not carry—e.g., there are supposed to be bells in towers, or *I thought you were going to take the cork out of the bottle.* For example, until the age of 1;11 (Mean Length of Utterance 2.15), Claudia's NO + Comment sentences are all NO + a positive alternative (e.g., *No, me!*) instead of NO + reiteration (e.g., *No, not you.*) At a recent Stanford Child Language Conference (1974), this same question was raised in the discussion of a paper on negation in English. Several researchers reported during the discussion that early negations in their data took the form NO + alternative rather than NO + reiteration. By adding a further, positive comment to their negations, children do not make their presupposition explicit. Instead, they add new information that makes the same presupposition. Unless there is evidence that the child is reflecting upon or modifying his presupposition as a mental object, we can conclude that presupposing at this stage is simply a procedure, a means of building and selecting encodable items from a background. Because the item chosen is informative and appropriate to its context of use, the proposition also communicates its presupposition. But the presuppositions themselves need not, at this point, be explicitly or internally formulated as symbol structures. We will return to this question again with regard to the problem of formal representation for early propositions and presuppositions.

If presupposing is a procedure for appropriate selection of items, where did this procedure come from and why does it work so well? To answer this question, let us first return for a moment to the build up of the performative outlined in Chapter II.

We stated that the capacity for declaratives involved the insertion of an object or an exhibitionistic action scheme as a means within a scheme for obtaining contact with adults. The sequence of developments leading to the first pointing and labelling (e.g., *Doggie!*) appears to follow two paths, which converge when the child first points out a distant object to the adult.

The performative is first expressed in exhibition, e.g., Carlotta learns to "give the raspberries" repeatedly to prolong adult laughter, looking about for approval after each performance. Soon thereafter the child, who is holding an object, extends it forward for the adult to see, without letting go of it. Then he begins not only to extend the object, but to deposit it in the adult's hand. After this, the protodeclarative blends with an already developed scheme of pointing for self, and the child begins to indicate to the adult objects that are out of his reach (for imperative as well as declarative purposes). Words are later inserted into this communicative sequence. Hence, the item to be communicated moves from the child outward in development—showing off own activities, through involving objects, to showing off distant objects. The point of greatest interest to us in this chapter is that when this scheme extends beyond the length of the child's arm, a pointing scheme is already available for use, having first been perfected outside of a communicative framework.

Where does the pointing scheme come from if it has not been explicitly developed for communicating? A number of authors have speculated that pointing is a derivation of reaching to grasp objects. Werner and Kaplan (1963) dispute this interpretation, for reasons that are supported by our own evidence as well. These authors cite two diary studies to support a contention that pointing develops separately from reaching to grasp. Shinn's child, at 18 months, was reported to have a well established pointing for self gesture in examining objects and pictures and in attending to novel sounds and events. The gesture, with extended index finger and closed palm, was not used for reaching. The Scupin's child had a particular arm extended gesture accompanied by the sound *da,* which was used to indicate interesting stimulae. The gesture was also distinct in form and in usage from an open and shut prehension gesture used in trying to obtain objects. Our data on Carlotta supports the Shinn and Scupin interpretations; Carlotta demonstrated a pointing for self gesture clearly used in attention sequences versus an open handed prehension gesture used in reaching to take objects. Observers viewing Carlotta's videotapes have found the pointing gesture startling in its clarity, frequency, and apparent usage outside of a communicative framework.

Werner and Kaplan place this development within their analysis of the development of reference, indicating not a desire to "take in" an object, but rather to clarify the separation between the knower and the known. It is primarily an attentional mechanism, part of what Werner and Kaplan called "the development of objects-of-contemplation." They further underline this development of reference with evidence by other authors of an inverse relation from 10 to 18 months between touching (decreasing) and looking (increasing). The object becomes increasingly distinct from the child's own activities, a thing unto itself that can, then, be referred to. This interpretation of pointing as a delineation of reference by the child is further supported by our longitudinal finding that the pointing for self merged with the scheme for transfering object referents to the adult. In Carlotta's records, giving and pointing for others emerge at the same time.

In addition to the developments after pointing appeared, we also have evidence from developments leading to the pointing gesture, evidence that further supports Werner and Kaplan's emphasis on the role of attention and contemplation. The first recorded pointing for self viewed by the experimenters was the following: A dog barked outside, and Carlotta turned wide eyed toward the window, hesitated a moment in a fixed listening posture, and then quite suddenly and clearly extended her arm toward the window, index finger extended and palm closed. Uttering a small and breathy sound *Ha!,* she held the position for several seconds. She did not at any time before, during, or after the sequence turn and look at the adults for confirmation or feedback. In the ensuing sessions, for several weeks, she used the pointing gesture in close examination of pictures (including remarkably small black and white newspaper pictures) as well as the fixed orientation sequences like the one described.

What makes this first sequence important for us is that every aspect of it except the pointing gesture was already established in orienting patterns. In a previous session, almost identical events took place: A dog barked, Carlotta turned toward the window wide eyed and held a fixed staring posture for several seconds, with a small open mouthed breathy sound *Ha!.* It chould not be more clear that the pointing gesture was inserted directly into the established orienting pattern.

We traced the orienting pattern further back to Serena, the youngest infant. Prior to prehension of objects at 4;29, Serena had developed a similar, though motorically primitive, orienting pattern. When a new object was held or shaken in front of her, she ceased gross body activity, held a fixed position with stare, and then went back to gross body activity.

The point of the above excursion is the following: The very first acts of reference, even prior to speech, grow out of a pattern of fixed orientation to a novel stimulus. It is an improvement on the simple orienting reflex, in that the attention directed to the stimulus is held momentarily, thus fostering a contemplative distinction between "me" and "it." This attentional capacity is certainly present in lower species and is present very early in humans. In fact, the preferred technique for inferring whether a neonate has perceived a stimulus difference in laboratory experiments is to habituate his orienting reflex to a similar stimulus and then introduce a new one to see if he orients again. If he does, then he has perceived the difference, along whatever parameter has been determined by the experimenters. This attentional response has been the focus of years of American and Soviet research. According to Sokolov's model of the orienting reflex (1958), the organism has a "summing device" with which he constructs a sort of model of the level of ongoing stimulation from various sensory channels. When a stimulus departs significantly from the ongoing sum of local activity, it triggers the orienting or "what is it?" response. The reflex itself has a number of components, such as the behavioral component of turning the body to "center" the stimulus, and the physiological indices such as brief depression in heart rate, change in galvanic skin response, and a characteristic EEG pattern. This "what is it" response, coupled with broad perceptual mechanisms that permit figure–ground analysis, enable the organism to classify the stimulus and decide on an appropriate behavior.

To return to an earlier question, why should it be surprising that early utterances encode the most informative aspect of a situation drawn from a structured and related background? If, as our evidence indicates, the first speech acts build on the child's solitary attentional responses, then he will naturally encode what has drawn his attention. **Informative** means that aspect of a situation undergoing greatest change. In a stable situation, **figure** is defined as that aspect of a configuration which is most likely to draw attention. The orienting system is built to discern the changing from the stable, and figure–ground mechanisms enable the organism to further isolate and analyze the novel event. Hence, the child who has learned to encode will encode the most informative elements from a structured situation precisely because those are the elements that keep his attention. Considered in this light, it is no longer surprising that children make appropriate presuppositions from the beginning of speech. It would, in fact, be far more difficult to do the opposite, encoding what is taken for granted or presupposed. The real accomplishment in pragmatic development will involve learning when NOT to presuppose in order to help a listener who does not have the same assumptions as the speaker. In short, the course of pragmatic development involves learning not to take information for granted and learning how to make presuppositions as well as propositions explicit in the surface form of an utterance.

A final question naturally follows for psycholinguists, who have dealt for years with the question of the psychological reality of deep structure. If the appropriate presuppositions for child speech exist, but the child does not know that he has them, where are they? This carries us back to the current debate among students of very early speech, a question that has been addressed more to the internal structure of utterances but is equally relevant to the relationship between utterances and presuppositions. We have suggested that, due to limits in the capacity for symbolic representation, the child must select only one element from a structured sensorimotor scheme for encoding into speech. The environment, organized at the perceptual–motor level, serves as the "topic," while the child furnishes the "comment." Later, when the child has a larger capacity for symbolic processing, he may incorporate both the topic and comment into his utterance. But the original topic–comment distinction in speech is based on a distinction between what is said and what is not said. Both the division of propositions into topic–comment and the use of said propositions as assertions against a background of presuppositions are the products of early speech caught between two levels of organization—what is symbolized and said and what is perceived and not said. This relationship in turn is derived from lower level attention and figure–ground mechanisms. In ontogeny, the same root relation is repeated at increasingly higher levels: figure–ground creates said–unsaid; said–unsaid creates the sentence internal comment–topic format; topic–comment continues to hold between a complete utterance and the material it presupposes.

There may also be a phylogenetic precedent in this sequence. McNeill (1970), classifying animal communicative systems, concludes that only man has predicative, topic–comment speech. However, if animal signals are viewed as procedures that comment on situational topics, then human propositions are not a new breed, but rather the same topic–comment relation by an animal that can simultaneously consider and encode both aspects of his signal. The great qualitative leap is cognitive rather than language specific, albeit with heavy consequences for the further development of the signal system. The human one-year-old can be viewed as halfway between animal and human adult signal systems. Due to the incomplete state of his cognitive development, he too leaves his topics out of his signals, to be expressed instead by the environment.

A proposal related to this one, though more conservative in its goals, has been offered by Antinucci (1973b) to account for the phenomenon of deixis. Antinucci observes that deixis is easier and ontogenetically prior to full expression of propositional arguments. Yet many linguistic theories of pronominalization spell out the full proposition in deep structure and then add special transformations to arrive at the pronominalized form. Hence, *He hit the ball* has a more complex derivational history than *The man hit the ball*. Antinucci resolves this anomaly with a proposal for the structure of deixis that is psychologically easier than spelling out full propositions. When a child (or adult) says *Throw it!*, he never actually represents *the ball* at the symbolic level, with all its lexical features. Rather, he constructs the symbolic structure THROW X together with an instruction to the listener to look for X in the situation. The instruction takes the surface form of a deictic element, in this case *it*. An advantage of the proposal is that the X element can be empty or partially defined in deep structure, yielding degrees of meaningful deixis from "that" to the specific inanimate "it" to modified deictics like "that round thing there."

Antinucci then takes this proposal for pronominalization a step further: He suggests that one-word speech by children already has the same deictic structure of the predicate–argument complex that later yields explicit surface markings for pronouns. The child symbolizes, or spells out in semantic structure, both branches of a presumably innate, given predicate–argument tree, but to save cognitive space and time, he sends one of the branches BACK (RIMANDARE) to the sensorimotor level, resting his proposition on the situation. Antinucci attributes this concept in part to the comparative grammarian Bopp, who proposed that all language is generated from two deictic roots: an empty pronoun and a radical "being" verb. From these two root divisions, pure predicate and empty argument node, the other objects of language are generated in a series of nested relations bearing the same essentially deictic relation to one another, a "this about that" relation.

To Antinucci's interesting proposal we must add one criticism: He does not carry its implications far enough. He stops short in ontogeny saying that the original divisions of predicate and argument are givens. The child starts out with a predicate–argument tree and sends one piece back to a lower level of organization. It would suggest instead that the branched organization of predicative speech—at the various levels of topic–comment, presupposition–proposition—is originally DERIVED from the initial effort to coordinate two levels of mind. Aspects of an integrated sensorimotor structure are selected (through the informativeness requisites of orienting and attention mechanisms) and "pulled up" to the new level of internal representation. At least at the one-word stage, nothing is "sent back to a lower level," because the child cannot yet construct that many branches at the symbolic level in the first place. The process is in a sense the reverse of Antinucci's proposal. One-word speech is not a kind of deixis. Rather, deixis mirrors the relationships that initially existed in one-word speech. Adult pronominalization may well involve "sending back" partially defined terms in a complex structure. In fact, the only way to explain the difference between one-word speech and deixis with explicit verbal signals for the X component is if one is cognitively richer than the other. Antinucci leaves no clear way of explaining the difference between one-word sentences (e.g., *Throw*) and two-word deictic sentences (*Throw it*). In a sense, we are proposing that Bopp's "root verb," pure act, exists at first by itself and creates its own objects. The sensorimotor level, according to Piaget, was built this way, in that the child came into the world with a series of procedures or activities, and gradually built a phenomenal world of objects out of those acts. Perhaps the symbolic level is created in the same way. The child actively selects an aspect of the world for encoding, thereby creating comment, and the excluded but present phenomena world automatically exists as topic. When the representational capacity expands, the differentiated comment–topic relations can both be constructed internally, at which point we are justified in calling the child's completed construction a branched proposition. If, at this point, one of the two branches is only partially defined, THEN that term is sent back to the sensorimotor level to complete its meaning.

If presupposing exists as the automatic product of a procedure for selecting things to encode, then we can make a strong prediction about the later course of pragmatic development. Again, the most interesting aspect of presuppositional development will involve learning when not to presuppose, and acquiring a set of signals that make presuppositions explicit in the surface form of speech, in order to insure their recovery by the listener. Hence we are not studying the acquisition of presuppositions so much as the improved cognitive (and hence, linguistic) control over already existing procedures for presupposing.

In the next chapter, we will examine the process by which children reflect upon and reconstruct presuppositions and other pragmatic procedures at the symbolic level. First, however, let us return to the question of formal representation for sensorimotor knowledge, presented at the end of Chapter II, and apply it to the transition from sensorimotor to symbolic representation of the performative–proposition–presupposition system.

Let us take as an example the one-word utterance *Give,* used in a context in which a child wants his mother to give him the ball. Regardless of where or how the whole array is represented, we can definitely specify several kinds of information that are somehow involved in this communicative act. First, there is a performative intention, an imperative, which could be described as we have described imperatives earlier. Second, the child in some sense has in mind a relationship of physical transfer involving three elements: Mommy, the ball, and himself. We could describe this relationship in propositional format as the tree structure underlying GIVE(Mommy, child, ball). Finally, the act of transfer in itself presumes (i.e., presupposes) another prior relationship between Mommy and the ball, which might also be described in propositional format as a presupposition HAVE(Mommy, ball). If we were to apply the full formal machinery that Antinucci and Parisi (1973) use for such utterances, we could formalize the complete deep structure of this utterance as the following (in which PRED = predicate, and ARG = argument):

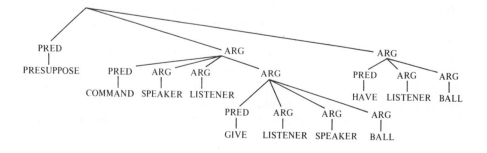

This elaborate tree would be larger still if we completed a componential analysis of certain individual predicates. For example, COMMAND could be analyzed into its subparts, as on page 16. The predicate GIVE could be subdivided into the underlying components CAUSE(X,(COIN-CIDE(Y,Z))). The predicate PRESUPPOSE could doubtless be subjected to further analysis. And so forth. All of this hierarchically arranged information can be said to underlie, in some still unspecified sense, the appropriately used monosyllable *GIVE*. But if all this articulated performative/proposition/presupposition structure is already there, why should the child be limited to one such pitiful monosyllabic squeak to express it? And how do we explain the transition in express from this squeak, to the adult request

> *Say, seeing that you have that ball, would you*
> *mind terribly giving it to me?*

which presumably has a highly similar deep structure?

This is essentially the question we posed in Chapter III on the growth of propositions. After reviewing various models for the representation of one-word speech, we proposed that all of this deep structure information was indeed present within the child, but at the sensorimotor level. Due to limits in both figurative and operative aspects of symbolic representation, the child could reconstruct (figurative) and hold for mapping (operative) only one section or chunk of his meaning at a time. This means that the performative, the presupposition, and the topic portion of the proposition all remain at the sensorimotor level. They are all psychologically present, but the unexpressed information lies at the periphery of central processing. Focal attention is applied only to the section underlying *Give*, as it is reconstructed for mapping.

We might even suggest an analogue model, with DEGREES of proximity to focal attention within the tree structure outlined above. The uncoded portions of the proposition (Mommy, child, ball), while still organized at the perceptual–motor level alone, are by virtue of their relation to the selected predicate "closer to the work area" where symbolic reconstruction is underway. Support for this proposal lies in the fact that the child may, in a series of utterances, shift the communicative mechanism from one element (e.g., *give*) to another (e.g., *ball*) when it becomes clear that the second deserves comment as well. (See Chapter VI for a more detailed discussion of the competition between novel and interesting comments and the need to specify the topic for uninformed listeners.) The performative and the presupposition, although connected to the propositional center in their respective ways, are in some sense psychologically "deeper," less accessible to the new reflection and mapping mechanism. But as we shall see in subsequent chapters, within one or two years the child will be able to focus on these aspects of meaning as well, mapping them as propositions, or building the original proposition to contain explicit links (in the sense outlined earlier) to its performative or its presupposition.

Perhaps an appropriate metaphor for an attention and symbolization mechanism that works on such an array is a spotlight, one that can at first shine on only one restricted area at a time, until it gradually grows in capacity to permit the entire array to be reconstructed and communicated. Slobin (1975) has used such a metaphor in another sense to describe linguistic development across time. He suggests that, although the child is gradually acquiring many aspects of language simultaneously, he seems to "spotlight" one or two areas at a time—for example, certain aspects of verb morphology. During that period, he devotes an intensive amount of attention, imitation, hypothesis testing, etc. to that area until it is temporarily resolved. At that point, the spotlight shifts to another area. As Slobin intended it, this metaphor describes a process that takes several years. As it is used here, the same metaphor is applied to limits in attention and processing across a much shorter time period, the time in which one full meaning is enacted at the sensorimotor level, while only one aspect of that meaning is processed for communication.

A somewhat similar analysis has been put forward by Bowerman (1974) with regard to the development of causal verbs. Bowerman reports a period in which her daughter tried to express "cause to happen" complexes by mapping only the "happen" portion of the semantic configuration. For example, she would say *eat the baby* instead of *feed the baby* (in which *feed* = 'cause to eat') and *see me the book* instead of *show me the book* (in which *show* = 'cause to see'). Bowerman is not suggesting that the child does not MEAN the full causative. But the device for reconstructing and mapping full configurations of meaning is still limited in capacity, so that the child reconstructs only the event portion of her meaning, leaving the cause portion unexpressed. In this case, according to the analysis put forth in the last chapters, the central processor "spotlights" and works on only one portion of a whole structure that will later be packaged into single words like *feed* and *show*. As a result, only part of the CAUSE-EAT and CAUSE-SEE structures are rebuilt by the figurative component, e.g., the portions EAT and SEE. Given this situation, the operations of the existing mapping system apply automatically to EAT and SEE to produce the sounds *eat* and *see*.

Note that we have expanded our terminology somewhat, equating the sensorimotor-symbolic division introduced in the last chapter with the notion of peripheral and central processing. For the young child, the two are probably yoked. The severe limits on his capacity for representation are in part due to limits in his attentional system. As a result, only the objects of focal attention will present themselves for the hard work of reconstruction at the symbolic level. The adult, however, has a much broader capacity for symbolic representation. And yet the adult too has limits to his attentional capacity. In fact, when possible—usually in informal conversations with intimates, so that the ultimate communicative goal is not lost—the adult tends to attenuate his speech as much as he can, reconstructing only what is minimally necessary to communicate and leaving the rest of his meaning implicit in the shared verbal and nonverbal context. As a result, informal adult speech approximates certain aspects of child speech. In an extreme situation like the operating room, utterances such as *Scalpel!* go all the way back to holophrastic speech. For the adult, as for the child, the central processing capacity is limited. While he can reconstruct a great deal of material at the symbolic level, the adult too is restricted in the amount of focal attention he can spare for any given communicative act. The child progresses developmentally from an ability to express comments only, to propositions with full topic–comment structure, to the expression of a complete performative–proposition–presupposition relation. The adult, under conditions of increasing economy, cuts his utterances back often in precisely that order, leaving out more and more peripheral material and moving into the focal center of his meaning. There is, then, a parallel between the development of symbolic representation in children and the use of symbolic representation by adults. In children, the development of representation is related to developmental increases in attention and memory (cf., Olson, 1973). In adults, the demands of the attentional system continue to influence the amount of material that will be constructed at the symbolic level and communicated explicitly in speech.

To represent such a dynamic system, we need formal machinery that expresses continuous field and figure–ground relationships as well as discrete hierarchical arrangements of constituents. We will turn to the problem of continuous meanings and analogue systems of representation again in the last chapter. Working with what we have so far, however, certain tree structures, such as the one on page 107, might be distributed vertically as well as horizontally as a series of superimposed horizontal planes. The highest planes would contain aspects of meaning pulled up to serve as the input to a mapping mechanism. This material would nevertheless maintain vertically its hierarchical connections to the horizontally arranged, implicit meaning on the planes below. When only part of a propositional relationship is selected for mapping, the remainder might occupy a plane between the mapping space and a lower area occupied by deeper and less focal presuppositional and performative configurations. In each case, the higher and lower planes are connected vertically to maintain their hierarchical relations. I will spare the reader pages of diagrams with planes hovering over one another, since the point should be obvious. As is always the case with formal notation, we are in the realm of metaphor. Nevertheless, insofar as any system of formal representation seeks to convey a meaningful set of relationships, the notion of dividing meanings into levels that correspond to their priority in cognitive processing (and in cognitive development) seems to be a crucial addition to a system for describing pragmatic–semantic communication. Nor is there any reason to restrict such a multilevel formal model to children alone. Many problems in notation for implicit and indirect meaning in adult speech might best be resolved by attributing these configurations to deeper, more peripheral levels that are less accessible to reflection and encoding.

For the rest of this book we will be concerned with the way that children learn to manage the cognitive levels that make up an adult pragmatic–semantic system, arriving finally at a capacity to play among these levels, softening, camouflaging, and artfully recombining his own communicative procedures.

PART TWO

Pragmatics in the Preoperational Period

In the preceding three chapters, we examined the formation of the pragmatic system during the sensorimotor period, in preparation for late speech development. At this stage (0 to 18 months), the three major aspects of pragmatics—performatives, propositions, and presuppositions—are organized almost entirely at the procedural level. The term **performative** describes the organization of the child's communicative goal, e.g., to obtain an object through use of an adult, or to obtain adult attention through the use of an object. The term **proposition**, at this early stage, describes the thing to be communicated. Propositions emerge gradually in development, from the literal use of an object in performative sequences, through meanings that are still organized mainly at a perceptual–motor level with only one or two elements constructed at the level of symbolic representation. Finally, **presupposing** is initially viewed as a procedure for selecting which element to encode, so that this element bears an appropriate and informative relation to its context.

At several points in the last three chapters we used propositional notation to describe sensorimotor pragmatics. This was done primarily to demonstrate that the components used by generative semanticists to describe linguistic deep structure can also be used to describe the intention structure of sensorimotor communication. This does NOT mean that sensorimotor organization and linguistic deep structure exist at the same cognitive level. On the contrary, by pointing out structural parallels we hoped to demonstrate that sensorimotor pragmatics is, in Piaget's terms, a vertical decalage of the linguistic system that will develop later. During the preoperational period, according to Piaget, the child reconstructs his sensorimotor knowledge of the world at a level of internal, symbolic representation. With regard to pragmatics, this means that the preoperational child will reflect upon his earlier communicative procedures, turning them into symbolic objects that can be signalled in the surface form of utterances.

In the next two chapters, we will examine the early speech records of two Italian children, to establish the point at which performatives and presuppositions are controlled as symbolic objects. These chapters depend on one important assumption: IF THE CHILD CAN EXPLICITLY SIGNAL THE PRESENCE OF A GIVEN PERFORMATIVE OR PRESUPPOSITION BY MARKING IT IN THE SURFACE FORM OF HIS UTTERANCE, THEN WE CAN CONCLUDE THAT HE CONTROLS THE PERFORMATIVE OR PRESUPPOSITION AS A SYMBOL STRUCTURE. We are using "symbol structure" in the Piagetian sense, as a scheme that is represented internally by the child and can be manipulated by other, higher schemes. Hence, we are tracing the transition from pragmatic procedures that the child "does," to pragmatic structures that the child "has." In this case, the higher scheme that takes a pragmatic procedure as a data structure is the communicative procedure of mapping meanings into sound.

In the earlier section on pragmatics in the sensorimotor period, we were able to use Piaget's outline of the six sensorimotor substages to examine substages in communicative development. In the following section, we will examine developments taking place in the next stage, the preoperational period, from approximately 12 to 18 months to about 4 to 5 years. Although Piaget provides explicit guidelines for both the sensorimotor period and the concrete operational stage that follows later, he has provided no such detailed analyses for the preoperational period. No substages or transitional phases are presented; we are left mainly with the general statement that the child is reconstructing sensorimotor schemes at the representational level. Hence, as we try to discern successive developments in linguistic control of pragmatics during the preoperational stage, we can only guess at the kinds of cognitive developments that accompany this process. Hopefully, the observations we make here may provide material for an elaborated theory of preoperational development, both linguistic and nonlinguistic.

The first chapter (Chapter V) will deal with linguistic control of performatives—the ability to "talk about talking," to refer explicitly to the coordinates of a speech act (e.g., speaker, hearer, time and place of utterance) or to the speech act itself (e.g., metapragmatic statements such as *He said "Go"*.). The second chapter (Chapter VI) will examine the acquisition of conventions signalling the presence of one kind of presupposition, in this case the presupposition concerning which information is new and which information is old in a given utterance.

To my knowledge this is the first study that has examined the child's acquisition of performative and presuppositional signals from the point of view of preoperational thought. There are, however, several recent studies of individual formal structures that encode presuppositional and performative information or both.

With regard to the explicit encoding of performatives, there have been several papers on the acquisition of conjunctions and other structures that link an utterance explicitly to preceding discourse. Among these are studies by Clancy (1974) and Jacobsen (1974). There has also been a surge of interest in time deixis as it relates to the time of utterance. Such studies include two recent articles on the imperfect past tense (Antinucci and Miller, 1975; Bronckardt and Sinclair, 1974) and several studies of temporal conjunctions (e.g., Clark, 1973; Amidon, 1972).

With regard to the explicit encoding of presuppositional links, Gordon (1974) has examined children's understanding of the presuppositions for various factive and belief verbs. Maratsos has studied the development of definite and indefinite articles (1974) and stress and pronominal coreference (1973b). Finally, Lyons (1974) is currently examining a large set of both presuppositional and performative devices in the speech of English-speaking preschool children.

Given the amount of material that we will have to cover in the following two chapters, we will not have time to discuss the above papers as they relate to preoperational cognition. They are mentioned here for the convenience of readers who would like to pursue in more detail those questions raised in this section.

Finally, both of the following chapters are related to an important area of pragmatic and semantic research, the question of structured, rule-governed discourse. Throughout the 1950s and 1960s, linguistic theory seemed to stop at the level of the sentence (cf., Harris, 1957). Recently, however, both linguists and psychologists have turned their attention to larger units of speech, including dialogue (e.g., E. Keenan, 1974, 1976; Sinclair and Coulthard, 1974) and texts (van Dijk, 1973). There has been a great deal of recent interest in memory for passages of discourse, including work by Kintsch (1974), J. Keenan (1975), Sachs (1967), and Bransford, Barclay, and Franks (1972). Discourse memory in children has been investigated by Barclay and Reid (1974), A. Brown (1975), Paris (1975), and Poulsen (1976).

A variety of studies have demonstrated that very young children operate adequately WITHIN discourse, in the sense of attending and responding appropriately to preceding speech (e.g., Greenfield and Smith, 1976; Scollon, 1973; E. Keenan, 1974, 1976; Mueller, 1972; Bloom, Rocissano, and Hood, 1975). There is much less evidence regarding the child's ability to reflect upon, control, and otherwise operate ON discourse. The next two chapters will examine the child's ability to symbolize and encode performatives and presuppositions as well as propositions. As we shall see, this ability will affect both monologue and dialogue aspects of discourse, permitting the child to connect a series of utterances into narrative units, to comment on the appropriateness as well as the content of his partner's speech, and to link his utterances explicitly to their correct point of reference in preceding discourse.

These chapters are based primarily upon longitudinal records for two Italian children, Claudia and Francesco. The data were collected by Antinucci, Volterra, and Tieri at the Institute of Psychology, National Council of Research (CNR) in Rome. Papers based on this longitudinal data include two studies of semantic structure by Antinucci and Parisi (1972, 1973) and a developmental study of negation by Antinucci and Volterra (1973). Parisi and Gianelli (1974) have compared the data of Claudia and Francesco with similar data for two lower-class Italian children. And several undergraduate theses at the University of Rome have been based on various analyses of the CNR transcripts.

During my research period in Rome, I was a guest researcher at CNR. Since the longitudinal records had not yet been examined for the pragmatic developments that interested me, Antinucci, Parisi, and Volterra placed the data at my disposal, and they were also extremely helpful in clarifying any ambiguities in the transcripts of misinterpretations in my own analyses. The availability of this excellent data freed much of my own research time for further, experimental studies of the same pragmatic phenomena, with a larger sample. As a result, I was able to obtain the optimal combination of (1) natural history of a given structure within a small number of subjects, and (2) experimental study of the same structure with a larger, statistically interpretable sample.

Both Claudia and Francesco were bright, healthy children, from somewhat similar environments. Their parents were middle-class, university educated Italians living in the Rome area. Claudia's mother was not working outside the home during the period covered by the longitudinal records. Francesco's mother had returned to working part-time as a biochemist. During her absence, he was cared for by a working-class maid. Since the maid speaks the lower-class Roman version of Italian, this must be considered as a possible influence on Francesco's speech. Francesco attended a preschool during the morning in the period from 2;6 (2 years, 6 months) through his fourth birthday. Both children are first-born. Claudia's younger brother was born very early in the research period. Francesco's sister was born slightly before his third birthday. The mother's pregnancy is an issue that clearly concerned him and is discussed several times in the records from about 2;6 to 3 years of age.

The records for Claudia extend from 1;3 to 2;9. Francesco was studied from 1;4 to his fourth birthday. Both children were visited in their homes approximately every two weeks, and two-hour audiorecordings were made at each visit. The observers were well known to the families, and the children were accustomed to the recording equipment. Sessions were for the most part spontaneous and unplanned, although the adults present tended to initiate games or other activities that encouraged the children to talk. Since both were highly verbal children, such encouragement was rarely necessary.

Transcriptions of the recording sessions include all child speech, all adult speech relevant to the child's utterances (e.g., no record is kept of adult–adult conversations ignored by the child), and information concerning the nonverbal context. The latter includes descriptions of the child's play activities, actions by the adult which prompt comment by the child, and any contextual or background information clarifying the child's communicative intentions. In Francesco's case, observer Virginia Volterra was also a family friend present on many occasions outside the research periods. Hence, her background notes and interpretations are a particularly rich and accurate source.

All transcription is made with standard Italian spelling. While there is no phonetic transcription, punctuation is used to indicate pauses, interrogative intonation, and exclamation. Also, characteristic "errors" in pronunciation by the children are indicated with Italian spelling. For example, in early sessions Francesco leaves out "r's," so that the word *perche* is spelled *pecche*. Since Italian spelling bears a one-to-one correspondence to pronunciation, these records give a fairly clear idea of the child's level of phonemic development.

Table 1 presents session number, ages, and mean length of utterance in morphemes (MLU) for Claudia and Francesco respectively. MLU was calculated with a version of Roger Brown's rules (in Slobin *et al.*, 1967) modified to make the MLU measure as comparable as possible to English measures during the same developmental stages. For example, Italian always inflects the article to agree with number and gender of the noun, while English does not. By Brown's rules, the word for 'doll'—*la bambola*—would count as two morphemes, and the plural—*le bambole*—would count as four morphemes. In English, by contrast, the plural "the dolls" counts as only three morphemes. To bring Italian figures in line with English measures, I counted each added semantic inflection, e.g., pluralization, only once across a given NP. Hence, *le bambole* counts as three morphemes instead of four. Since the children immediately extended plural to both the article and the noun as soon as pluralization emerged, this did not seem to violate the original purpose of the measure. Without these modifications, the MLU measure would have multiplied in the Italian records to a point where comparability to English longitudinal records would be imposssible. However, it is still true that the MLU measure clearly represents very different developments for Italian versus English children, and the measure is provided here only as an approximate guide to overall linguistic maturity in early speech development. I

Table 1 Age, Sessions, and Mean Length of Utterance

Claudia			Francesco		
Session	Age	MLU	Session	Age	MLU
1	1;3;19	1.85	1	1;4;03	1.65
2	1;3;28	1.89	2	1;4;12	1.32
3	1;4;11	2.04	3	1;4;27	1.68
4	1;4;27	2.30	4	1;5;12	1.31
5	1;5;12	1.77	5	1;5;23	1.33
6	1;5;20	1.80	6	1;6;04	1.29
7	1;7;10	2.30	7	1;6;22	1.52
8	1;7;20	2.89	8	1;7;06	1.35
9	1;8;04	3.12	9	1;8;03	1.72
10	1;8;24	3.97	10	1;8;17	1.70
11	1;9;07	3.42	11	1;9;04	1.81
12	1;9;21	3.66	12	1;9;20	1.89
13	1;10;06	3.75	13	1;10;04	1.72
14	1;11;02	3.90	14	1;10;16	2.15
15	2;0;07	4.50	15	1;11;01	1.98
16	2;0;22	3.95[a]	16	1;11;18	2.28
17	2;1;20		17	1;11;26	2.19
18	2;2;18		18	2;0;14	2.25
19	2;3;15		19	2;0;29	2.68
20	2;4;10		20	2;1;15	2.58
21	1;5;09		21	2;2;01	3.20
22	2;6;05		22	2;2;20	4.19
23	2;7;10		23	2;3;00	3.72
24	2;9;06		24	2;3;15	3.85
			25	2;4;02	3.54
			26	2;4;14	3.52
			27	2;5;09	3.60
			28	2;5;17	4.28
			29	2;6;18	3.67[a]
			30	2;7;00	
			31	2;7;17	
			32	2;8;00	
			33	2;8;16	
			34	2;8;29	
			35	2;9;09	
			36	2;10;16	
			37	2;11;05	
			38	2;11;24	
			39	3;0;10	
			40	3;1;13	
			41	3;1;28	
			42	3;2;26	
			43	3;3;22	
			44	3;4;14	
			45	3;4;02	
			46	3;5;25	
			47	3;6;22	
			48	3;7;20	
			49	3;8;24	
			50	3;9;00	

[a] Mean length of utterance (MLU) was not calculated after this point.

must disagree with Bowerman's conclusion (1973) that MLU provides a comparable measure of linguistic maturity across different language communities.

Within the following chapters, I will specify in greater detail the criteria used for deriving data from the longitudinal records. In addition to the longitudinal analyses, Chapter VI also presents some small experiments indicative of the kind of empirical work that can be derived from longitudinal findings.

CHAPTER V

The Explicit Encoding
of Performatives

In Chapter II, we established that several months prior to speech itself, Marta and Carlotta had developed the essential procedural blueprint for carrying out speech acts. Through gestural signals employed in interaction with adults, the children indicated their communicative–performative intention. This accomplishment was apparently based on the sensorimotor developments of Stage 5, in particular concepts of agency and intermediate causes. The development of a Stage 6 symbolic capacity then permitted the use of speech with propositional content in carrying out the same imperative and declarative intentions that were previously carried out with gesture.

A basic argument of Chapter II was that performatives first exist as sensorimotor procedures, prior to the development of symbols and internal representation. Although the performative tree outlined by some linguists resembles the procedural tree necessary for gestural communication, the children do not necessarily "have" performatives in the sense of symbolic objects in a linguistic deep structure. Hence, the course of pragmatic development must rest not so much on the development of new performative procedures, but on an increased ability to control, coordinate, and reflect upon one or more of the already existing performative intentions. In short, performatives will become not only procedures for "doing," but symbolic objects that the child "has"—to manipulate, coordinate with other symbolic objects, and talk about or refer to within higher speech acts.

In this chapter we will trace this process as it occurs in the transcripts for Claudia and Francesco. This development might be termed

metapragmatics, an ability to talk about whole speech acts or coordinates of a given speech act. The clearest manifestation of a metapragmatic ability would be an explicit reference to acts of saying, utterances such as *He said "Go"* or *You can't say that.* But it also includes the mastery of elements that refer indirectly to preceding discourse, tying the present utterance to what has gone before, An example is the opening gambit *Yes, but . . .* The metapragmatic capacity will further include any explicit mention of the context coordinates of a speech act: speaker and listener, time and place of utterance, and so forth.

Obviously this set of abilities cuts across a variety of syntactic devices and will no doubt interact with a number of developmental factors not directly tied to metapragmatics. In some respects, however, the heterogeneity of the data is an advantage. If we can discern a given developmental "moment" when several heterogeneous devices appear at once, and thse devices apparently share little more than their pragmatic function, then we have more evidence that a pragmatic–conceptual development has been tapped rather than some specific formal aspect of Italian grammar.

We will take the simple, inductive approach of extracting from the longitudinal records all utterances containing an explicit reference to acts of speaking or to one or more coordinates of the speech situation, including references to the speaker and hearer, the time and place, and conjunctions or adverbials that connect a current utterance with previous discourse. A table is constructed for each of the two children, recording frequency of occurrence by session for the following types of utterances.

The first category includes references to acts of speaking. All utterances that included an explicit reference to some act of speaking, in particular those involving verbs of saying, were noted. This includes performative uses of the verb, as in the example from Claudia's records

> *Io dico **uffa.***   'I say "uffa".'

descriptive uses of the verb, e.g.,

> *Ha detto **accipicchia.***   'She said "accipicchia".'

and prescriptive uses of the verb, e.g.,

> *Non si dice **accipicchia.***   'One mustn't say "accipicchia".'
> *Parla!*   'Talk!'

Also included were uses of other verbs (e.g., *fare* 'to do') to describe verbal or vocal behavior, as in the example

> *Quello fa **glu-glu-glu.***   'That one goes "glu-glu-glu".'

The second category includes time references. All utterances that referred explicitly to time, relative to the time of the utterance itself, were noted. This included time adverbials (e.g., *now, Sunday*) and the tense of the verb (e.g., future, imperfect past). Since the vast majority of utterances were in either present or simple past tense, and both tenses were present from the earliest transcripts, only those utterances that employed a tense other than present or simple past were drawn from the records. To include all verb uses would have essentially involved duplicating the transcripts. Also, there is a peculiar problem of interpretation with simple past tense forms in Italian, a problem which is not taken up in this chapter. Volterra (1974) has noted that the earliest simple past forms, which are produced in Italian with an auxiliary and past participle, may actually be used as adjectives (e.g., *e rotto* means both 'it broke' and 'it is broken'). Hence, it is not altogether clear that the children understand the time relationship implied by the simple past form.

Also, some apparent time adverbials (e.g., *adesso* 'now') were used not as time references but as performative adverbs, as in the English sentence

Well now, my grandmother used to say . . .

Those cases were noted in which it was possible to distinguish much performative uses. These will be discussed separately.

A third category includes discourse references and connecting terms. All utterances that contained an element explicitly referring to previous discourse or tying an utterance to previous discourse or previous events were recorded. Connecting terms—e.g., conjunctions and anaphoric adverbs— are also used to carry out nonanaphoric, sentence internal operations. Both uses are discussed in this section. An example of sentence internal use of conjunctions is the term *and* in the sentence

I want bread and cheese.

However, we recorded all uses of conjunctions and potentially anaphoric adverbs to be certain of capturing all possible instances in which a device was mastered. It should be clear from the text whether these devices were used by the child to perform anaphoric functions.

Italian grammar provides a long list of such possible connecting terms, but the only terms appearing in the transcripts are shown in Table 2.

A fourth category includes references to participants in an ongoing speech act. All utterances were noted that referred to the speaker both by proper name (e.g., *Checco* 'Francesco') or by pronoun (*io* 'I'). It is ungrammatical in Italian as in English to refer to oneself by name rather than by pronoun, but it is a common child error in both languages. Also noted were utterances that refer to the listener both by name (the same child error) or by pronoun. It was not always a simple matter to distinguish between the usage of the speaker's name as a vocative (e.g., *Vieni, Paola* 'Come, Paola') and the use of the speaker's name as an argument of the second person verb (e.g., *Viene Paola* 'Paola come'). The records for

Table 2

Term	English equivalent	Example usage
Additive Terms		
più	'more'	*Non la voglio più* 'I don't want it anymore'
anche	'also'	*Anche io la voglio* 'I want it too'
pure	'also, too'	*Pure io la voglio* 'I want it too'
altra	'another'	*Un' altra birra* 'Another beer'
e	'and'	*E Paola che fa?* 'And Paola, what's she doing?
Excluding or Contrasting Terms		
solo	'only, just'	*Io voglio solo David* 'I want just David'
poi	'then'	*Poi che fai?* 'Then what are you doing?'
ma	'but'	*Ma non voglio* 'But I don't want to'
però	'however, but'	*Però non quello* 'But not that one'
Implicational Terms		
perché	'because' 'why'	*Perché stai qui?* 'Why are you here?
se	'if'	*Se siete tutti buoni . . .* 'If you're all good . . .'
se no	'if not, otherwise'	*Se no, viene il lupo* 'Otherwise, the wolf will come'

Claudia and Francesco were not transcribed phonetically, so that the types of pauses and stress used are not directly available. However, the Italian transcribers had marked the vocative with standard Italian punctuation, separating it from the rest of the sentence by a comma. These judgments were derived from intonational cues and from the context (e.g., when the name of the listener was clearly not an argument of the verb). These original interpretations are accepted in the present analysis, although the intuitive nature of the judgments must be kept in mind. In Chapter VIII, when we examine in greater detail the development of imperative and request forms, more evidence will be presented on the development of personal pronouns (both indexical and anaphoric) and person inflections on the verb. That data will be mentioned in this chapter only insofar as it is relevant to the general question of metapragmatics.

Finally, there are other linguistic devices, such as demonstrative pronouns (*this, that*) and locatives (*here, on the table*), that also perform the function of encoding coordinates of the speech situation. These developments have been examined elsewhere by Antinucci and Parisi (1973) for the data of Claudia and Francesco. They appear to be among the earliest manifestations of an ability to encode aspects of the speech situation. We will discuss the results of Antinucci and Parisi together with the data gathered for the other categories outlined above.

Antinucci and Parisi have also analyzed the development of formal propositional complexity for Claudia and Francesco, e.g., the onset of various types of adverbials and sentence embeddings. We will compare the data on metapragmatic development with these results to determine whether the developments tapped here are related to formal linguistic complexity in general.

Results

We can discern three stages in the development of metapragmatics, leading up to the eventual ability to discuss entire speech acts in metapragmatic comments such as *You can't say "good evening"*.

First, from the beginning of the transcripts through C1;5 (Claudia: 1 year, 5 months) and F1;8 (Francesco: 1 year, 8 months), we find explicit references to the speaker and hearer by name and locatives of space and direction relative to the speaker. At this stage, there are no connecting terms between speech acts. Utterances are related to previous discourse by unmarked, or zero anaphora, as in the question answering sequence *What do you want to eat? Ham.* There are no time adverbials in this period, and verbs are either in the present or the simple past tense. And, as we stated earlier, it is not even clear whether the simple past tense forms (e.g., *rotta bambola* 'doll broken') are meant as time references or as adjectives.

There is a second stage, from C1;5 to C1;9 and from F1;8 to F2;1, in which we find conjunctions and adverbials that connect a speech act to previous discourse, but only as an added comment rather than some sort of contrasting comment. For example, there are many instances of *and,* but no examples of *but.* Time adverbials appear in this period, but they encode no more information than the binary distinction *now–not now*.

In the third stage, after C1;9 and F2;1, both children begin explicitly talking about talking. Together with this new development, there are several other changes in the nature of discourse, including the onset of complex conjunctions that hold the utterance in a contrasting or implicational relationship to previous discourse (e.g., *but, if not*). Time references are now based on a continuum rather than binary *now–not now* distinctions. This includes adverbials of duration (e.g., *just a moment*) and of specific location on the time dimension (e.g., *tomorrow, noon*). Imperfect past tense appears encoding incomplete, enduring, or repeated activities. A few future tense forms also appear within this period.

Tables 3 and 4, for Claudia and Francesco respectively, present the frequency of occurrence by session for the various connecting terms, explicit time adverbials, imperfect past tense verbs, and explicit references to acts of saying. The three stages summarized above should be roughly discernible from the raw frequencies presented in the tables. But the boundaries become clearer when we examine the way a few overlapping categories (e.g., time adverbials) were actually used in the text. We will now examine these three stages in more detail, with examples from the transcripts themselves.

Metapragmatic Stage 1: Elements Present from the Earliest Speech Records

There are several devices, not recorded in Tables 3 and 4, which are present from the earliest records for Claudia and Francesco. These include demonstrative pronouns, primitive expressions for location and direction, and reference to the speaker and hearer by name. These developments are all noted by Antinucci and Parisi (1973) in an article on the first stages in semantic development for Claudia and Francesco.

The most conspicuous of these Stage 1 devices is the vocative, the use of the listener's name within an expression, in which that name is not an argument of an expressed or an implicit verb (e.g., *Paola, viene Francesco* 'Paola, Francesco is coming'). In a study of early speech in American children, Greenfield and Smith (1976) also note that the vocative is one of the first uses of a noun, occurring as a sort of general request form at first, and later used more particularly to call mother's attention in what we have called declaratives. The pervasiveness of vocatives throughout early speech is also noted by Braine (1963), who deliberately excludes vocatives from a distributional analysis of child language, presumably because they are not subject to positional restrictions. There is, of course, no reason why vocatives should obey positional restrictions on sentence constituents, since they are not constituents of the proposition itself. Antinucci and Parisi suggest that the early presence of the vocative in child language is evidence for an underlying performative structure of the type SPEAKER USES LANGUAGE TO CAUSE HEARER TO DO X. If that were the case, then the other developments that we find occurring much later would bear little relevance to the construction of the performative as a symbol structure. Antinucci and Parisi imply that the appearance of the vocative in the surface form of an utterance is sufficient evidence that the entire performative structure—speaker, hearer, communicative goal—are all represented internally, in the underlying linguistic structure, presumably on the same cognitive level as the proposition itself. However, according to the model of propositional development presented in Chapter III, we could offer an alternative interpretation. According to this model, propositions are initially constructed at two levels, so that only the encoded portion is constructed at the symbolic level while the implicit portion of the meaning remains at the level of perceptual–motor organization. At this early stage, the child need only construct the argument LISTENER at the symbolic stage in order to encode vocatives. The rest of his performative procedure remains at the sensorimotor level, where it has been a stable structure for many months.

The early transcripts also include usage of the speaker's proper name as the argument of a verb. This is also consistent with data presented by Greenfield and Smith, in which some early case relations emerge in which the listener's or the speaker's name are arguments of the verb.

It is clear that the child knows very well who his listener is from the earliest stages of speech and that this is one of the first coordinates of the speech act situation that he can encode. This result is consistent with the information drawn from eye contact and gesture in the preverbal performatives of Chapter II. The child knows who the target of his speech act is, and once he begins to use words to describe the immediate situation, he can talk about both the listener and about himself. However, we cannot conclude from this that the child is able to reflect upon his own role as a speaker. In fact, for both Claudia and Francesco, the earliest references to themselves are in the third person, using their own proper names. They have not yet mastered the *I* pronoun, nor the *tu* ('you') pronoun, which encode the roles of speaker and hearer and can shift referents from one speech act to another. Nor are there person inflections on the verb corresponding to the shifting speaker and hearer roles. The only pronominal references to speaker and hearer during thse first sessions are the adjectives *my* and *your*, which are among the first noun modifiers for both children. These occur mainly in heated discussion regarding the possession of goods, and hence are highly motivated usages. In fact, it is possible that *mine* and *yours* are limited at this stage to procedures for getting things and are never subjected to the kind of shifting deictic analysis required for the I and You forms. However, more precise observations are necessary to clarify this point.

The early records also contain a large number of demonstrative pronouns (e.g., *quello* 'that one') that refer deictically to objects (and occasionally people) in the immediate perceptual environment. These data support Antinucci's contention (see Chapter IV) that deixis is cognitively simpler than constructing all the features corresponding to a full lexical item in semantic deep structure. However, the presence of demonstrative pronouns when personal pronouns are absent also supports the interpretation that children can talk about themselves and the listener as entities, but not in their shifting roles as speaker and hearer. Clearly a capacity for pronominalization exists at this stage. Hence, the absence of personal pronouns must be due to some other factor peculiar to personal pronouns themselves rather than pronominalization in general.

There are a number of spatial locatives that are also used in the earliest transcripts, e.g., *li* 'there', *giù* 'down'. According to Antinucci and Parisi, these terms precede true adverbials. The authors define an **adverbial** as a predicate which takes a complete predicate–argument nucleus as its argument, thereby creating a particular type of propositional embedding. But locative terms that are adverbs in the standard theory can also serve as arguments of a single, nuclear predicate. When the locative is an argument of the nuclear predicate, it is not an adverbial. For example, the phrase *in the living room* is an adverbial in the sentence

Mary knit the sweater in the living room.

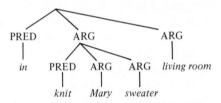

In this sentence, *Mary knits* is an event that takes place in the living room, but the predicate *knits* does not require the locative to complete its meaning. Hence, the locative is an optional, adverbial structure. By contrast, in the sentence

Mary put the sweater in the living room.

living room is an argument of the nuclear predicate, an element essential to complete the meaning of the verb *put*. The predicate relates Mary, the sweater, and the living room directly, whereas in the first example *living room* is related optionally to the entire, independent event of *Mary knits the sweater*.

Antinucci and Parisi claim that the locatives used in this period by Claudia and Francesco seem to be nuclear arguments or predicates, rather than adverbials that take an entire propositional event as their argument.

One finds examples such as

  Etta lì.   'This one here'

which can be formalized as

but there are no examples such as

  Mangia lì.   'Eat here'

formalizable as

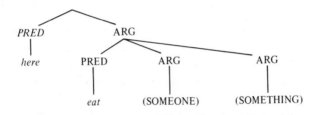

In sum, in the first stage of language development, the child can apparently reflect upon and therefore encode the individuals in a speech act, but he does not symbolize the shifting roles of speaker and hearer. He can refer deictically to objects in the situation by using demonstrative pronouns, but he does not yet use the shifting personal pronouns. The child can refer to certain spatial–directional aspects of the situation, although his spatial terms are limited until such a time as he can construct the formal relation holding between optional adverbials and their propositional arguments. Neither child produces time deictics in this early stage.

Finally, this first stage contains none of the connecting terms (e.g., conjunctions) that explicitly relate an utterance to preceding discourse or to preceding events. His utterances are anaphoric, in that they include appropriate responses to previous discourse. But there are no explicit surface markings for the relation between the present utterances and preceding events. At this point all anaphora is zero anaphora, and can thus be described with the kinds of semiautomatic presupposing procedures discussed in Chapter IV. The child does not have to learn anaphora. His utterances are already anaphoric. Instead, he will have to learn to be a bit LESS anaphoric, to make explicit the relationship between what he is saying now and what has been said before. This will involve mastering conventions that perform the link function described in the section on artificial intelligence, connecting devices and other surface indexes that help the listener locate those aspects of previous discourse to which a current utterance is directed.

Metapragmatic Stage 2: The First Connecting Terms and Time Adverbials

The devices which are present in the first metapragmatic stage are not included in Tables 3 and 4. Those devices which are covered by the two tables simply do not occur in this early period. There is a second stage from C1;5 to C1;9 and from F1;8 to around F2;2, in which several of the elements that connect discourse do begin to appear. Specifically, the terms entering the records for both Claudia and Francesco are conjunctions, adverbs, and noun modifiers that explicitly ADD the utterance as a further comment on some previous fact (linguistically or contextually established). When a child begins to say *I want another cookie,* he encodes not only his desire but the fact that this is an addition to some previous cookie. If he begins to say *And I do this* instead of *I do this,* he encodes not only his intention but its relation to some previous activity by himself or someone else. In Claudia's records for this period we find the following connecting terms and time references:

Connecting terms		Time references	
ancora		*poi*	
Più	= 'also, more,	*allora*	= 'then'
pure	another'		
altra		*dopo*	= 'after'
e	= 'and'		

In Francesco's records, we find the following terms:

Connecting terms		Time references	
più		*poi*	= 'then'
pure	= 'also, more,		
altra	another'	*mò*	= 'now'
e	= 'and'	*domani*	= literally 'tomorrow
		oggi no	not today' (See
			text for actual use)

Both children did use *più* twice prior to this stage, but in all four cases it seemed to be used much like the first word *pu* recorded for Marta (page 76). Rather than indicating "more" in the adult sense, it serves as a negation, to comment on the absence of some object or person. Hence, it is not actually *più* or 'more', but an abbreviated version of *non c'e più* 'there is no more'.

The only conjunction in this period is the additive *and.* Not one instance of *ma* 'but' was recorded. Since this single syllable appears frequently within the double syllabic word *mama,* the absence of *ma* is quite clearly the result of a semantic–pragmatic lack of some sort. *E* ('and') appears both within phrases (e.g., *I want bread and cheese*) and at the beginning of phrases to connect them anaphorically to some previous event of utterance (e.g., *E poi cavalluccio* 'And now horsie'). The adjective *solo,* which is also used in Italian to exclude possibilities (e.g., *solo io* 'only me'), is used somewhat differently in this period. Francesco used the phrase *uno solo* ('just one') together with several other quantity terms that were employed rather randomly in asking for a cookie (see Chapter VIII). Claudia's use of the term *solo* was in the alternative sense of 'alone' or 'all by itself' in the thrice repeated sentence

> *Cammina sola la macchina.*   'The car walks alone.'

used to describe a moving toy. Hence, except for the general phenomenon of negation, terms such as *but* or *just* that contrast rather than add to previous discourse do not appear in this period.

Some time deictics appear, but they are restricted to binary distinctions of *now–not now* or *now–then.* For example, Claudia (C1;7) is stringing beads and naming animals when she produced four of the five time adverbs for this period:

E poi aduccio (cavaluccio)	'And (now–then) little horse'
E poi (———)	'And then (unclear)'
Poi, lì	'Then here (stringing beads)'
allora . . .	'now . . .'

The only other time adverb in this period for Claudia is the single utterance *dopo* ('after') which appears in isolation with no clear nonverbal context. It may well have been an isolated imitation of ongoing adult speech, although we cannot be certain. Her mother expands the utterance to *Yes, Luciana's coming later.*

Francesco's time adverbs in this period are also restricted in their usage to a now/not now meaning. The adverb *poi* ('now'/'then') is used in much the same way as in Claudia's records, to bridge activities or utterances in repetitive games. The other adverbs are somewhat more idiosyncratic, and presage Francesco's later skill at mimicry of adults. For example, at F1;8 there are two uses of a time adverb *mò* ('now') that is characteristic of Roman dialect and tends to be used somewhat humorously or ironically by middle-class Romans. (Recall however that Francesco is also exposed to the speech of the lower-class Roman maid). Both uses of the term at F1;8 are in the *Well, what now?* sense in which adults often use the word, e.g.

Francesco	Adult	Francesco	Adult
pu		'more (no more)'	
	non c'e più		'there aren't any more!'
mó'!		'now!'	
pappa otte, mó'?		'food broken, now?'	

In F1;11 the same adverb appears three times in a single sentence, in a playful repetition of an adult utterance

Francesco	Adult	Francesco	Adult
	Mamma torna mò.		'Mommy's coming back now'
Mamma torna mò, *mò' torna mamma,* *mò.*		'Mommy's coming back, now she's coming back, Mommy, now.'	

Besides the two now/then terms *poi* and *mò*, there are seven occurrences of more fully specified adverbs for "tomorrow" and "today". However, as Francesco first employs the two terms, they are used simply as a negation; then later they are used to indicate now/not now. The first appearance in F1;11 is the following exchange:

Francesco	Adult	Francesco	Adult
	Fai vedere come *fai bene*		'Show how well you do'
oggi no		'not today'	
	oggi no?		'not today?'
domani		'tomorrow'	

The mother mentions to the experimenters at this point that Francesco has started using "not today, tomorrow" as a general way of refusing to do anything that does not please him. Later in the same session there is the exchange

Francesco	Adult	Francesco	Adult
	Con chi sei andato *al giardino zoologico?*		'With whom did you go to the zoo?'
omani.		'Tomorrow'	

This particular response may have been a way of refusing a question that he did not understand or could not answer. Such a functional use of an adult term is similar to Francesco's random choice of quantity terms, e.g., "one more," "lots," to make requests (see Chapter VIII). A vague understanding of time coordinates is indicated, however, in the following exchange around F1;11;18

Francesco	Adult	Francesco	Adult
	Ma gli uccellini non vengono a mangiare il pane oggi, eh?		'But the little birds don't come to eat the bread today, right?'
eeno omani		'They come tomorrow'	
	Ah, vengono domani?		'Oh, they come tomorrow?'
oggi no		'not today'	

In this latter case, *tomorrow, not today* seems to be used not as a refusal, but as a "now/not now" statement. There is, then, at least a binary distinction between present time and some other time period. An exchange in F2;1 also indicates a growing awareness of some other time, in this case in response to an adult statement of future behavior:

Francesco	Adult	Francesco	Adult
	Quando esco me la metto?		'When I go out I put it on?'
omani		'tomorrow'	

During this period, for both Claudia and Francesco, the only productive verb tenses are the present indicative and simple past tense. Each child produces one or two imitations of an adult imperfect past *C'era* ('there was'), but the sentences are not complete, and the children do not appear to understand the adult meaning. In fact, the imitation tends to indicate that the child has deliberately focused on the adult term as a curious and unfamiliar item to be played with verbally. Since the imitations are toward the end of the second period, they may presage a subsequent mastery of the adult imperfect past tense. However, it seems fair to say that the verb system in this second stage is also subject to simple binary distinctions of happens/happened.

Metapragmatic Stage 3: Talking about Talking and Accompanying Changes in Discourse

Tables 3 and 4 show a third stage beginning around 1;9;21 for Claudia (session 12, MLU 3.66) and between 2;1;15 to 2;2;20 for Francesco

Table 3 Metapragmatic Development: Claudia

Column groups: *Connecting terms* — Additive (più, altra, pure, anche, ancora, e) and Complex (ma, però, perché, se no, se); *Time terms* — poi, mo', ora, Binary (adesso, allora, dopo), Dimensional (Dimensional adverbs, Imperfect past tense); Metapragmatic comments.

Session number	più	altra	pure	anche	ancora	e	ma	però	perché	se no	se	poi	mo'	ora	adesso	allora	dopo	Dimensional adverbs	Imperfect past tense	Metapragmatic comments
1																				
2	2	2																		
3																				
4																				
5 [a]																				
6	2	2				2											1			
7	2	2				4			3							1				
8	2					2			1											
9	2	1		6		3			1											
10			2			3														
11 [b]						4													1?	
12	2				3	4	1								2	2	2	1	—	
13				11				1							—		—	1	3	
14				2		10			1			1			1		—	2	—	3
15		1	4	2		14	2		4	1		4			3		—	—	1	1
16	3	1	2	7	6	4	1	1	1			1			8		2	1	7	11
17	2	2	8		6	9	1	1	2			2			3		2	1	3	12
18	3		5		1	8	1	1	1			3			10		—	4	7	5
19	1	1	2		5	4		1	1			1			10		—	1	4	5
20	2	1		7		9	4		3		1				2		8	12	4	18
21		3			2	1	20	2	1		1	3			2		—	1	1	7
22	1	1	3		24	18	2		3		1	7	1		10		3	10	24	13
23		3	1	1	17	17	2			1	1	7			5		2	11	2	6
24	1	8	1	2	3	12	11	1	1		1	1			15		14	12	27	9

[a] Beginning of Metapragmatic Stage 2   [b] Beginning of Metapragmatic Stage 3

134

(sessions 20 to 22, MLU 3.32). Perhaps the most important event occurring in this period is the onset of explicit metapragmatic comments. The children begin to talk directly about acts of speech. This is the most clear and direct confirmation we could have that performatives are now available to the child as symbolic objects, including all the performative components of speaker, hearer, thing to be communicated, and communicative goal. In addition to this one important development, there are a number of other changes in the nature of discourse that take place at the same time. Within 2 to 3 sessions of one another, we find the following developments (i.e., within a 5 to 6 week period):

1. The appearance of explicit metapragmatic comments.
2. Two important changes indicating the development of a dimensional concept of time—the use of varied time adverbs, and the mastery of imperfect past tense.
3. The appearance of conjunctions other than *and*—e.g., *but, because, if not*—connecting terms which indicate a more complex relationship between the current utterance and preceding discourse than was evidenced in the second metapragmatic stage.
4. Across a slightly longer period (C9 to C13; F17 to F22) before and after these other developments, the basic set of personal pronouns and verb inflections are mastered (see Chapter VIII), including the shifting roles of speaker and hearer.

This rather complex set of developments involves heterogeneous syntactic devices. It would be useful to examine some of these developments in greater detail, with examples from the text, before we try to interpret the developmental causes of this third metapragmatic stage. (The acquisition of personal pronouns requires a rather lengthy examination of verb inflections and will be postponed to Chapter VIII.)

1. *Talking about Talking*

The most striking development, the one that is most undisputably metapragmatic, is the new ability to talk about talking. The first examples for Claudia (C1;10) are not carried out with adult verbs of saying, but with the verb *fare* ('to do'), used to quote a verbal/vocal performance. In this respect they are transitional from the pure action statements that children can make from the beginning of speech, e.g., *How does a doggie go?—Woo-woo* (Carlotta). This is a standard baby talk form that is found in language communities around the world (Slobin, 1967). In C1;10 we find the following examples:

aeavano cu–cu (facevano cu–cu)	'They were going "cu-cu"'
*Facciamo **aiuto**.*	'Let's do "help".'
Mettiti anche te, Paola, Eccola.	'You get over there too, Paola. There she goes.'

Table 4 Metapragmatic Development: Francesco

Session number	più	altra	pure	anche	ancora	e	ma	però	perche	se no	se	poi	mò	ora	adesso	allora	Dimensional adverbs	Imperfect past tense	Metapragmatic comments
10[a]	1	1	—	—	—	—	—	—	—	—	—	—	1	—	—	—			
11	—	—	—	—	—	—	—	—	—	—	—	—	—	—	—	—			
12	—	—	—	—	—	—	—	—	—	—	—	—	—	—	—	—			
13	—	—	—	—	—	—	—	—	—	—	—	—	—	—	—	—			
14	—	1	—	—	—	5	—	—	—	—	—	1	—	—	—	—			
15	—	—	—	—	—	—	—	—	—	—	—	—	—	—	—	—	*		
16	—	—	—	—	—	—	—	—	—	—	—	2	—	—	—	—	*	see text	
17	—	—	—	—	—	1	—	—	—	—	—	—	3	—	—	—	*	1?	
18	2	—	—	—	—	3	—	—	—	—	—	1	—	—	—	—			
19[b]	—	1	—	—	—	2	—	—	—	—	—	4	—	—	—	—		—	
20	—	1	—	—	1	4	—	—	—	—	—	3	—	—	—	—	3	—	4
21	—	1	—	—	1	1	—	—	—	—	—	2	—	—	—	1	3	—	3
22	—	3	—	—	3	10	1	—	4	1	—	1	—	1	2	—	—	3	4
23	—	3	—	—	3	7	2	—	—	—	—	1	—	1	4	—	9	1	4

	C1	C2	C3	C4	C5	C6	C7	C8	C9	C10	C11	C12	C13	C14	C15	C16	C17	C18
24	2	2	6	1	—	—	2	3	—	—	8	1	5	—	—	2	1	—
25	3	—	10	—	3	—	1	1	—	2	3	—	1	1	—	2	1	—
26	8	—	11	3	3	—	—	1	—	1	9	—	6	—	3	1	—	—
27	1	3	5	1	4	1	—	—	—	1	13	—	6	2	—	4	1	1
28	3	—	15	2	7	—	—	—	—	1	9	1	10	—	—	4	1	—
29	7	2	10	2	4	—	2	—	—	—	6	—	10	—	—	1	3	—
30	4	3	18	—	—	1	—	—	1	—	8	—	19	2	—	2	—	—
32	2	4	4	—	1	—	—	—	1	1	9	2	3	1	1	5	—	—
33	2	6	13	—	3	—	9	4	—	1	—	—	18	—	—	2	—	—
34	3	2	4	—	2	—	3	4	—	1	10	—	9	1	—	—	1	—
35	2	4	10	—	—	—	6	3	—	6	6	6	7	3	—	—	—	—
36	1	2	4	1	1	—	1	5	—	5	6	—	4	4	—	1	1	—
37	2	6	4	—	—	1	2	5	1	—	5	—	16	3	—	—	—	1
38	5	3	18	—	2	—	—	5	—	—	8	—	13	3	—	2	—	—
41	3	5	4	1	10	—	—	8	2	2	3	—	20	10	—	—	2	—
42	2	6	7	—	4	—	8	—	—	1	13	1	8	13	1	—	—	—
43	14	8	5	1	—	—	10	8	—	1	6	1	36	9	—	—	1	—
45	4	34	3	4	13	—	3	2	—	1	14	—	25	8	2	2	2	2
48	4	36	10	19	22	—	10	1	2	—	18	3	21	5	3	3	1	2
49	27	4	11	8	26	—	3	10	7	—	9	2	10	19	2	6	1	1

[a] Beginning of Metapragmatic Stage 2
[b] Beginning of Metapragmatic Stage 3

137

Facciamo **aiuto**.	'Let's do "help".'
Oppla! Facciamo	'Ooops! Let's
aiuto, facciamo **aiuto**.	do "help", let's do "help".'

In Cl;11, the examples are still carried out with *fare*, again related to animal sounds:

Mammaino fa **muh**.	'The calf's mommy goes "muh".'
Come fa Mammaino?	'How does the calf's mommy go?'
Fa **muh**.	'She goes "muh".'

In C2;0;7, Claudia has become quite concerned with being interrupted or having her turn at speaking, and she turns accusingly to an adult (who has accused her similarly on other occasions) and says

Chiacchierona!	'Big talker!' [loosely translatable as "chatterbox" or "big mouth"]

In C2;0;22, there are 11 metapragmatic references, this time involving explicit verbs of saying:

Bugia. Cosa dici, mamma, *bugia. Dici bugia.*	'Lie. What are you saying, Mommy, lie. You're saying a lie.'
Ho detto basta.	'I said that's enough.'
Che arrivate per terra. Cosa hai detto queste gambe che arrivate per terra.	'(what/that) arrived on the ground.' 'What did you say these legs are arrived on the ground.'
(Che ho detto) così.	'(what/that) I said like this.'
Ciao, accipicchia. Ciao accipicchia. Non si dice accipicchia. Non si dice accipicchia. No si dice.	'Goodbye, accipicchia. Goodbye accipicchia. One doesn't say "accipicchia". One doesn't say "accipicchia". It isn't said.'
Il cane fa **bau-bau-bau**. *Questo fa* **beh-beh**.	'The dog goes "bau-bau-bau". This one goes "beh-beh".'
Come dicevo io? Non ti voglio più vedere.	'What was I saying? I don't want to see you anymore.'

In the subsequent sessions, Claudia becomes frequently concerned with rules governing what may or may not be said, for example:

Non si dice accipicchia.	'One doesn't say "accipicchia".'
*Si dice **Ma guarda un po.***	'One says "Well, look at that!".'
*Dicono tutti **accipicchia.***	'Everybody says "accipicchia".'

This concern over the expression *accipicchia* (an Italian interjection of uncertain etymology) is apparently due to the fact that Claudia has been quite amused by the word when one of the observers first used it. Since this occurred in a period in which Claudia discovered the use of conventional interjections in general, and since Claudia was particularly fond of the observer Paola who has first used the term, she began overusing the expression until her parents become exasperated and began to chastise her. This coincided with a period of intense interest in permissible and forbidden or inappropriate expressions. A particularly interesting example of quoting a pragmatic rule is found in session C22 (about 2 years and 6 months of age):

*Non si dice **buonasera**. Quando si epre la porta ti dico **buonasera**.*	'One doesn't say "good evening." When the door is opened, I tell you good evening.'

In another example is session C19, Claudia corrects her own use of an expression:

Sono cadute, mannaggia la miseria! Ma guarda un po'. . . . non si dice 'mannaggia la miseria.'	'They fell down, darn it. Well look at that . . . one doesn't say "darn it".'

There are also several embedded metapragmatic statements such as the following (at sessions C18 and C22 respectively):

*Mamma, dici che non si dice **accipicchia**.*	'Mommy, say that one doesn't say "accipicchia".'
*Ma guarda **accipicchia**.*	'But look at "accipicchia".'
*Papà ha detto che non si dice **accipicchia** e si dice **Ma guarda un po'*** *Tu lo sai dire?* *E lui?*	'Daddy said that one doesn't say "accipicchia" and one says "Well look at that".' 'Do you know how to say it?' 'And him?'

In addition, Claudia begins to recount her fairy tales, quoting the lines for the various characters, for example (C20):

*Fulmine dice **Posso venire a cantare anche io**.*	'Fulmine says "Can I come and sing too".'
*Allora il lupo: **Vieni via!***	'So then the wolf: "Come away!"'

Similarly, in organizing games Claudia assigns speech acts to the participants, as in *You say this . . . or I'll sing **hi-hi-hi***.

For Francesco, the onset of metapragmatic references is equally dramatic. The first occurrences are in F20 (age 2;1;15). As with Claudia's first examples, the verb *fare* rather than an explicit verb of saying is used.

*Ha atto **pip** ha atto.*	'He went "pip", he went.'
*Ha atto **pip**.*	'He went "pip".'

But by the very next session (F21), explicit verbs of saying are also used, with quotes of previous or imagined speech:

*Allora io: **Totò**.* ***Via bimbo, via!***	'So then I: "Spank!" "Away, baby, away!"'
*Ho detto **Via, non si tocca pancia lì, e bimba!***	'I said "Away, one doesn't touch tummy there, there is (a) baby!"'
E' andato popó? Dimmi.	'Is car gone? Tell me.'

From F22 to F24 (F2;2;20–2;3;15), metapragmatic references still tend to describe the making of nonlinguistic sounds, for example:

*Quello che faceva **din-din?***	'That one that was going "din-din"?'
*E io ho suonato **pih**.*	'And I honked "pih".'
*Qui fa **glu-glu-glu**.*	'Here it goes "glu-glu-glu".'

However, Francesco also announces his intentions to "read" or to narrate stories, and there are two more sentences using the verb "say", e.g.,

Checca e i Suoi Piccoli.	'"Checca and Her Little Ones".'
Leggo io.	'I am reading.'
Ha detto pure Pecci.	'Pecci said it too.'

In F26 there is the first example of concern with permissible expressions, and there is another in F43. However, Francesco never becomes as obsessed as Claudia with what may or may not be said.

*Che mi dice **eh**.*	'What, you're telling me "eh".'
Dice e butte parole.	'(He) is saying ugly words.'
*Non si dice **boh**. Non si dice nemmeno **beh**.*	'One doesn't say "boh". One doesn't say "beh" either.'

Finally, Francesco begins, as did Claudia, to recount fairy tales and to quote the characters' lines. When I witnessed such a story session toward the end of the longitudinal study (F49), Francesco gave a virtuoso performance using different voices and facial expressions for each character.

2. *Time Expressions*

At the same time that explicit metapragmatic statements enter the records, the children also begin to use time adverbs that indicate points or durations along a time continuum.

In F20 to 21 (2;1;15 to 2;2;1), Francesco uses *dopo* ("after") to order possible or intended activities, e.g.,

Dopo itonna.	'Afterwards (he) comes back.'
Etto dopo.	'This one afterwards.'
'opo lo butto.	'Afterwards I throw it away.'

This is still related to the binary distinctions of now/not now, but like the word *poi* used to bridge successive activities, it specifies a before/after relation among events. In F21, Francesco says

E mettotonno (mezzogiorno).	'It's noon.'

and his mother remarks that he has begun to use the word for *noon* to refer to any specific time at which an event is supposed to take place. In F23 to 24, more time distinctions are used. *Stasera* ('this evening') seems to be used correctly in the context. Also, durations as well as time location begin as Francesco dictates *un momento* ('just a minute') to his listeners, or describes a pending activity as about to occur *un momento* ('in a minute'). By F26 (2;4;14), *tomorrow* also occurs with a further refinement, *tomorrow morning*:

Domani mattina compo una gomma.	'Tomorrow morning I'll buy a tire.'

After is joined in F25 by the reciprocal term *before* or *first*, as in

Pima io, quetto no.	'First me, not this one.'

In F29 and F30 (2;6;18–2;7), temporal conjunctions are used

Pecché te ne vai via quando hai visto il leone?	'Why did you go away when you saw the lion?'
E opo Inny-puh . . . e dopo mentre stava . . .	'And afterwards Winny Pooh . . . and afterwards while he was . . .'
Quando ritonno oppedale io cecco.	'When I return hospital I look.'

In the last ten transcripts, time adverbials multiply to include *in the summer, day after tomorrow, the next time, in the winter, every morning, always, midnight, all day long, Sunday,* and a variety of other terms. These terms are often only approximate in their range of application, and occasionally are blatantly inaccurate, as in the example

> *Domani c'era troppo traffico.*   'Tomorrow there was too much traffic.'

Since the imperfect past tense was used accurately during this period, the above error seems to reflect a problem with the exact temporal location of "tomorrow." In fact, we cannot conclude from the way in which temporal adverbs are used that Francesco has constructed an accurate time dimension corresponding to adult conventions. However, there does seem to be a general concept of dimensional time. Francesco discusses remote and near events, specific hours versus general periods, and brief versus long durations. This is a considerable advance over the simple binary distinction of now/not now that was present in the second metapragmatic stage.

Claudia's time system does not become as rich as Francesco's in the period covered by the longitudinal records, but the same major conceptual advances are made. In C12 and C13 (1;9;21 and 1;10;6), the only adverbs are *adesso* ('now'), *dopo* ('afterwards'), *domani* ('tomorrow'). However, the first temporal conjunction appears in C14 (1;11;2):

> *Che succede quando piove?*   'What happens when it rains?'

In C16 (2;0;22) there is an example specifying *quickly*:

> *Lo mettiamo? Subito ingresso.*   'Shall we put it? Quickly the entrance.'

In C18 we find the example

> *Finalmente!*   'At last!'

and several instances of the word *prima* ('first'), as in

> *Prima era questo il cacciatore.*   'First this one was the hunter.'

From C19 through to the last transcripts there are a number of "When X, Y" or "While X, Y" constructions, including the following examples:

> *Quando sono più grande di Paola*   'When I am bigger than Paola I
> *io ado in cucina.*   am going in the kitchen.'

> *Mi ha pizzicato mentre stavo*   'It stung me while I was in
> *all'orto della nonna.*   grandma's garden.'

Also, in the last transcript Claudia begins to add some of the new time locatives that multiplied in Francesco's records, such as *un giorno* ('someday') and *l'altra sera* ('the other evening'). Overall, Claudia's time adverbs tended to be those which organize present activities—*Now do this,*

First I'll go, Do it quickly—or speculations about the remote future or past. She never becomes as interested in various time locations—noon, next week, etc.—as does Francesco. However, the ability to specify orders and durations for events at all, and to embed events within a larger time span (e.g. "When X, Y" or "While X, Y") is also a major advance over a binary now/not now system in the second stage.

The other major time acquisition for both children is the mastery of imperfect past tense to express repeated or enduring past events or states (See Antinucci and Miller, 1975). Claudia's use of the imperfect past begins with three examples in C13 (1;10;6):

C'era papà Gioggio.	'There was Papa Giorgio.'
Aevano cu-cu.	'They were going "cu-cu".'
Saltavono.	'They were jumping.'

The imperfect becomes a frequent form in C16 (2;0;22), with examples such as

Che era successo, non c'entrava Giovannino là, non c'entrava.	'It was happening that, Johnnie couldn't get in there, he couldn't get in.'
La conosci una bambina che piangeva, la conosci?	'Do you know a little girl that was crying, do you know her?'

In the same session there is a gerund construction for a current, ongoing process (these meanings are usually expressed with simple present indicative in Italian):

Giampiero sta prendendo quella tua di pistola.	'Giampiero is taking that one of yours, the pistol.'

There is also a compound imperfect past constructions using the imperfect of *avere* ('to have'):

Aveva dato il pane col naso lungo.	'He had given the bread with his long nose (regarding an elephant at the zoo).'

From this point on, the imperfect past is commonly used in Claudia's efforts to tell stories or recount events. In fact, the narrative imperfect is occasionally overgeneralized in stories, to describe single perfective instances where the simple past would have been more appropriate:

Allora il lupo diceva . . .	'So then, the wolf was saying . . .'

However, it is clear that Claudia understands the durative aspect of the imperfect, since it is the only form used in "While X was happening" clauses. Also, there is an example in C22 in which Claudia uses an adverbial *at moments* to underscore the fact that she is describing an ongoing, incomplete process with the imperfect past verb:

Io andavo a cavallo	'I was going on horseback . . .'
Ma a momenti io andavo per terra.	'But at moments I was going onto the ground.'

These are both acceptable uses of the imperfect in adult Italian, covering both durative aspect (*I was riding horseback*) and repeated, incomplete activities (*at moments I was going on the ground*). The incomplete "almost" nature of the second usage is confirmed by the mother's comment

Per fortuna non ci sei andata.	'Luckily you didn't go.'

Finally, in C22 through C24, there are so many long story telling sequences that we find from 24 to 27 uses of the imperfect past verb per session.

Francesco begins to use the imperfect quite suddenly in F22 (2;2;20), with five examples, all using stative verbs:

Aevo un pallone, ea a gioia mia.	'I had a balloon, it was my pride and joy (from a nursery song).'
Eano piccoli.	'They were little ones.'
Aevo in tacca, aevo in tacca.	'I had in my pocket, I had in my pocket.'

There are only three examples of the imperfect in the next sessions, but they are no longer restricted to stative verbs:

*Quello che faceva **din-din**?*	'That one that was going "din-din"?'
Andava co zia Tata.	'(He) was going with Aunt Tata.'
Poi c'era il tetto.	'Then there was the roof.'

From F29 (2;6;18), use of the imperfect continues regularly with around two to six examples per session. The imperfect appears to express enduring states or activities, repeated activities in the past, and incomplete or intended activities in the past. By F45 (around 3;6), there is a great deal of story telling and recounting of past events, so that about 34 to 36 uses of the imperfect occur within an individual session. Finally, in the last sessions Francesco moves from these semantic uses of the imperfect past, to a pragmatic use of the imperfect as a sort of pseudoconditional. This development is not relevant to the stage being discussed here and will be examined in more detail in Chapter VII on counterfactual conditional verbs.

Instances of the future tense of the verb are rare in the transcripts for both children, although they do occur in the third metapragmatic period. The content of child speech from the second period indicates an anticipation of events yet to occur, but they are expressed with present tense verbs. The use of adverbials and temporal conjunctions in the third period indicates a dimensional concept of future events as well, including remote periods, e.g., *When I am older*. Claudia, in the third period, sings songs with future verbs, e.g., *La barca partirà* ('the boat will leave,') and in C23 there are two clear instances of remote future with a future tense verb:

E farò communione.	'And I will make communion.'
E giocherò una cosa.	'And I'll play a watchamacallit.'

There are also some uses of the future tense in Francesco's transcripts:

Allora arriverà questo bicicletti.	'Well then, it will arrive these bicycles.'
Forse pioverà.	'Perhaps it will rain.'
No, verrà.	'No, he will come (answer to *Has he come to your house?*).'

However, the children throughout both stages generally refer to future events with the inflections for present indicatives, as in Claudia's example

Io un giorno vado a scuola.	'I someday am going to school.'

or Francesco's utterance

Alle otto c dieci ie ritonno.	'At 8:10 I am returning.'
Poi quando sono ritornato dall' ospedale, tu mi prepari la pappa.	'Then when I am come back from the hospital you are fixing me dinner.'

This use of the present indicative to express intended future is acceptable in adult Italian as well, particularly in discussions of imminent events, as in the English example.

Next week I am flying to Bermuda.

Since minimal temporal adverbs and conjunctions will express the concept of future adequately, and present indicative verbs are grammatically acceptable for most future meanings, there is no communicative pressure for children to master a new set of verb inflections. On the other hand, there *is* a communicative motivation for mastering the imperfect past tense, since no other verb form will express its aspectual distinctions— duration, repeated or incomplete actions, past intentions. Claudia's example *At moments I was falling on the ground* confirms an interpretation that the child intends to communicate not only a temporal location, but an aspectual distinction.

3. Performative Adverbs

There are a number of temporal adverbs which are apparently used to modify the performative itself rather than the content of the proposition. This is a distinction that has been used by some linguists (e.g., Sadock, 1974) to demonstrate the necessity for abstract performative structures in semantic deep structure. Take the following examples:

> *For the last time, John saw his son.*
> *For the last time, eat your spinach.*

In the first sentence, the adverb *for the last time* modifies the proposition *John saw his son.* In the second sentence, the same adverb modifies the speaker's imperative act rather than the propositional content of *eat your spinach.* This becomes clearer if we cleft the two sentences to read

> *It was for the last time that John saw his son.*
> **It is for the last time that you eat your spinach.*

Another demonstration that some adverbs modify the performative clause rests in the fact that two contradictory temporal adverbs cannot modify the same clause. For example, the following two sentences are ungrammatical:

> **Today I gave a party last week.*
> **Tomorrow I gave a party yesterday.*

There are, however, certain utterances in which we do find two semantically contradictory time adverbials or tense–adverb relations, as in the example

> *Now, I gave a party last week.*

These utterances would no longer be exceptions to the generalization concerning contradictory time terms if we attributed one of the adverbials to the underlying performative clause. Hence, this last sentence would actually have a structure something like

> *Now I say to you: I gave a party last week.*

These same analyses for performative versus propositional adverbs work equally well in Italian (Parisi and Puglielli, 1972). If we apply these adverb tests to the transcripts for Claudia and Francesco, we find several examples in which temporal adverbs cooccur with semantically contradictory tenses or contradictory temporal adverbs. Following Sadock (1974) and Parisi and Puglielli (1972), we could accept these examples as evidence that these children also produce adverbs that modify their performative. The following are examples of performative adverbs drawn from Francesco's records (from 2;6;18 to 4;0):

Adesso ti do domani quelle pinze.	'Now I am giving you tomorrow those tweezers.'
Dunque, allora ti preparo il caffe.	'Then, now I prepare you the coffee.'
Adesso io fatto sola.	'Now I did it alone.'
Inni, mo'la possima volta che ti vedo . . .	'Inni, now the next time that I see you . . .'
Adesso questo motoscafo me l'ha regalato mia nonna.	'Now this motorboat my grandmother gave me.'
Allora adesso cominciamo, eh?	'So then, now let's begin, eh?'

There are similar examples in the records for Claudia:

Adesso io ho assaggiato la sigaretta di zia Anita.	'Now I tasted Aunt Anita's cigarette.'
Allora, adesso perchè . . .	'So then, now because . . .'

In addition to these examples in which propositional and performative adverbs clearly coexist within an utterance, there are also numerous uses of adverbs such as *now* and *well then* to hold a pause before speaking, as in

E allora . . .	'And then . . .'

Included among these in Claudia's records are several utterances which explicitly express the performative modified by these same adverbs, e.g.,

*E allora io dico **uffa**.*	'And now I am saying "uffa".'

This last example expresses the entire set of relationships which Sadock and Parisi and Puglielli use to describe the underlying structure for all performative adverbs. If the child can explicitly encode a performative verb with its adverb, then there is no reason to doubt that he is capable of constructing the same underlying relationship when he expresses the performative adverb only. We can therefore accept the presence of performative adverbs as further evidence that the child now has control of the entire performative structure as a symbolic object.

4. *Connecting Discourse*

During the same stage at which we find explicit metapragmatic statements, an elaborated time system, and performative adverbs, we also find some changes in the kinds of conjunctions that Claudia and Francesco use to connect an utterance to previous discourse. In the second metapragmatic stage, all conjunctions and anaphoric adverbs were restricted to additive terms—*and, another, still, more.* In the third matapragmatic stage, we find the use of contrasting or implicative conjunctions, such as *but, because,* and *if not.*

In the records for Claudia, the uses of *but* and *however,* and *because* and *if not* appear three to four sessions after the appearance of time adverbs, metapragmatic comments and imperfect tense. In Francesco's records, these same conjunctions appear only two sessions after metapragmatic statements and time adverbs, and in the same session as imperfect past tense verbs (F22, 2;2;20). Hence, these changes in the nature of discourse lag slightly behind other metapragmatic developments. When they first appear, most *but* and *because* utterances are anaphoric, commenting on some previous statement by the adult. For example, in Francesco's records (F24 and F25) we find

Perché ha fatto pípí sotto.	'Because he made peepee underneath.'
Ma questo è celesté.	'But this one is blue.'

However, not long after these new connecting terms are available, they are also used together with the temporal devices and metapragmatic comments to weave together long and sometimes logically inconsistent stories. THEREFORE, THE CHILDREN CAN NOT ONLY TIE THEIR UTTERANCES EXPLICITLY TO PREVIOUS STATEMENTS BY ADULTS, BUT THEY CAN TIE TOGETHER A SERIES OF SPEECH ACTS OF THEIR OWN INTO A NARRATIVE UNIT. Some of the clearest (and longest) include the following (from C20, 2;4):

> *Un giorno la pecorella biancolina andava sulla strada. Allora la pecorella biancolina ha detto **Il lupo cattivo arriva!** Allora il lupo cattivo diceo alla peccorella biancolina **Vieni via!** no dice **no no mi pottae via, voglio 'tare coi llini, voglio mangiare l'aranciata. No no no,** vole mangiare perchè adesso c'è il lupo. Allora il lupo: **Vieni via!** Ma io lo caccio via, gli faccio totó a le botte. Allora il topolino ha il lupo. Allora il signore canta **la la la.** E la signora che canta la canzone. Allora la pecorella biancolina scappa di corsa, andò da Fulmine, allora . . . Il Fulmine cammina cammina e gli dice . . . **Il lupo ha portato via la pecorella biancolina, allora saliamo su a pecoe sulla carrozza, e facciamo 'bilinlin, bilinlin,'** . . . Un giorno la pecorella biancolina . . . Ho raccontata la pecorella . . . Ma un giorno la pecorella biancolina . . . Hai capito?*

One day the little white sheep was going down the road. So then the little white sheep said "The bad wolf is coming." So then the bad wolf was saying to the little white sheep "Come away!" "No" he says "No don't carry me away, I want to stay with the little pigs, I want to eat orange juice, no no no." He wants to eat because now there's the wolf. So then the wolf: "Come away!" But I toss him away, I make him "toto," a spanking. So then the little mouse has the wolf. So then the

man sings "la la la." It is the lady that sings the song. So then the little white sheep runs away fast, he went to Fulmine . . . So then . . .
Fulmine walks, walks, says to him . . . "The wolf has carried away the
little white sheep . . . so then let's climb up on the sheep . . . on the
carriage, and we'll go 'bilinlin, bilinlin'." One day the little white
sheep . . . I have recounted the little sheep . . . But one day the little
white sheep . . . Did you understand?

This particularly lengthy example actually continues, with some inter-
ruptions, for much of session C20. Claudia is apparently trying to put
together one of her familiar fairy tales. There are other examples in which
Claudia narrates some story of her own concoction, partially based on
actual events. One such example involves an incident in which a little boy
with the same name as her younger brother is hit by a car but narrowly
escapes.

Francesco returns throughout the transcripts to the story of Little Red
Riding Hood (*Capuccetto Rosso*). The last such episode occurred in the
final session (F50), just before his fourth birthday. Even in this final version, Francesco also gets lost in the details of the story, although to a lesser
degree than Claudia. An interesting example from a Piagetian point of
view is a portion of the Riding Hood story in which Francesco is led into an
incorrect outcome, apparently because of the kind of failure to conserve
quantity that Piaget has noted in other preoperational children. Francesco
begins by correctly stating that Little Red Riding Hood took the long road
to grandmother's house, which should have led him to the familiar conclusion that the wolf arrived there first. But he is so struck by the length of
Riding Hood's road that he generalizes greater length to greater velocity,
and has her arrive first:

> *Ma Capuccetto Rosso arriva piú prima perche la strada era
> lungo, sta cosí* (gestures). *Allora, è arrivata Capuccetto Rosso . . . Il
> lupo gia stava dentro, era giá mangiato la nonna. Mó scappa il lupo.
> Capuccetto Rosso, il lupo scappa dietro. Poi a un certo momento
> passava il cacciatore, Capuccetto Rosso, il lupo . . . PAM!*

> But Little Red Riding Hood arrived first because the road was
> long, it was like this (gestures). So then, Little Red Riding Hood
> arrived . . . The wolf was already inside, the grandmother was already
> eaten. Now the wolf escapes. Little Red Riding Hood, the wolf escapes
> behind. Then at a certain moment the hunter was passing . . . Little
> Red Riding Hood, the wolf . . . BANG!

From these examples the limits of the new discourse system should be
clear. The children can now sew together a long passage that is logically
faulty from our point of view. There are great gaps in the overt logic of a
structured story. The child's attention is drawn to various characters and
events, often out of sequence. However, he is able to use the new discourse

tools as a sort of verbal needle and thread, tying together only partially organized events as if they formed a consistent unit.

Despite the inconsistencies in the actual narrative products, it is noteworthy that all the heterogeneous devices treated in this chapter are in fact used together, to serve a shared discourse function. The fact that these devices are acquired within the same developmental period, and that the child is capable of orchestrating them into long narrative passages, indicates that they are the product of some more general pragmatic–conceptual development. We have suggested that this development may be related to a preoperational ability to manipulate speech acts as symbolic objects. Actually, the development that brings about all the new events in this third metapragmatic stage may be even more general than that. Before we consider the possible cognitive changes that have brought about a metapragmatic capacity, we will first examine some other linguistic acquisitions that occur in the same time period.

Discussion

The pragmatic devices discussed in this chapter are syntactically quite heterogeneous, involving verbs, adverbs, embedded sentences, conjunctions and pronouns. Yet as Tables 3 and 4 indicate, they do fall into three developmental "moments." Given the syntactic heterogeneity of these metapragmatic changes, it is quite unlikely that they are the artifact of formal syntactic development. However, it is possible that they bear some relation to a more abstract set of formal, logical developments. Antinucci and Parisi (1972; 1973) have analyzed the data for Claudia and Francesco from the point of view of formal, propositional complexity. An examination of their results indicates that there are indeed strong parallels between the metapragmatic stages outlined here and stages in formal semantic structure. However, the relationship between the metapragmatic and semantic developments do not suggest a cause and effect relation. On the contrary, there is reason to believe that both trends are the result of some still more general, cognitive development.

Figures 1 and 2 compare the metapragmatic stages discussed here with Antinucci and Parisi's outline of developments in formal propositional complexity (for Claudia and Francesco, respectively). At the period corresponding to metapragmatic Stage 1, there are only simple, nuclear propositions with no optional structures (e.g., adverbials, sentence embeddings). Metapragmatic Stage 2—additive elements connecting discourse, and binary distinctions of time — coincides   with the onset of adverbials and noun phrase modifiers. This extends only to adverbials as the authors define them (see page 128), as optional elements that take an entire

Age (years)	Formal semantic development	Metapragmatic development
1		
1;1		
1;2		
1;3	——Beginning of data collection.	——*Stage 1:* (from onset of records):
1;4		Vocatives; demonstrative pronouns,
1;5	——First noun modifiers; first	no personal pronouns; spatial loca-
1;6	adverbials.	tives, no time terms; no connecting
1;7		terms.
1;8	——First implicit embedded sentence	——*Stage 2:* Binary time terms, no
1;9	(e.g., *voglio andare* 'want to go').	imperfect past; additive connecting
		terms only.
1;10		——*Stage 3:* First dimensional time
		adverb; first *because*
1;11	——First relative clause.	——First *but:* first imperfect past verb;
2	——First adverbials with sentential	first metapragmatic comments;
	arguments.	performative use of adverbs.
2;1		——First *if not;* person pronouns
2;2	——First explicit embedded sentences.	established
2;3		
2;4		
2;5		
2;6		——First *if*

Figure 1. Claudia: Comparison between formal semantic development as established by Antinucci and Parisi (1972) and metapragmatic development.

nuclear proposition as an argument. As we stated earlier, locative terms and other elements which are adverbs in the standard theory do appear as arguments WITHIN a nuclear proposition during this first stage. Finally, metapragmatic Stage 3—including explicit metapragmatic comments, dimensional time concepts, and complex, nonadditive connecting terms—coincides roughly to the onset of explicit sentence embeddings (e.g., relative clauses, *that* clauses). Implicit propositional embeddings expressed with double verbs (e.g., *fare vedere*—'cause to see'; *vado a fare*—'I go to do') appear slightly prior to metapragmatic Stage 3.

Do these parallels mean that the metapragmatic developments examined in this chapter are simply epiphenomena of logical, propositional development? I think not. The relationships do overlap in some cases. For example, the use of time adverbs will require a more general capacity to construct adverb–proposition relationships. Many of the explicit metapragmatic comments involve explicit sentence embedding. Simple conjunctions such as *and,* according to Antinucci and Parisi, are actually adverbials that take two propositional nuclea as their arguments. Hence, the use of conjunctions should require a general adverbial capacity.

Age (years)	Formal semantic development	Metapragmatic development
1		
1;1		
1;2		
1;3	——Beginning of data collection.	——*Stage 1:* (from onset of data collec-
1;4		tion) Vocatives; demonstrative
1;5		pronouns, no personal pronouns;
1;6		spatial locatives, no time terms; no
1;7		connecting terms.
1;8	——First noun modifiers; first	——*Stage 2:* Binary time terms, no
1;9	adverbials.	imperfect past; additive connecting
1;10		terms only.
1;11	——First implicit embedded sentences	
2	(e.g., *voglio andare* 'want to go').	
2;1	——First adverbials with sentential	——*Stage 3:* First dimensional time
2;2	arguments.	adverbs and metapragmatic com-
		ments.
2;3	——First explicit embedded sentences.	——First *but*; first *because*; first *if not*;
2;4		imperfect past tense.
2;5		
2;6		
2;7		
2;8		——First *if.*

Figure 2.   Francesco: Comparison between formal semantic development as established by Antinucci and Parisi (1972) and metapragmatic development.

However, many of the metapragmatic developments bear a much less direct relationship to formal semantic development. For example, why should the development of the imperfect past tense be related to sentence embedding? What is the possible relation between sentence embedding and a shift from binary time adverbials (now/not now) to dimensional time adverbials (e.g., *Sunday, last week*)? Also, many of the metapragmatic comments do not in any direct way require an embedded sentence, e.g., *Ha fatto **glu-glu-glu*** ('It went   glu-glu-glu') or *Non si dice **accipicchia*** ('One doesn't say "accipicchia"'). And yet both types of metapragmatic comments appear simultaneously. I think that a case can be made that these developments do share some broad structural characteristics. But the relationship is not direct enough to permit the conclusion that metapragmatics "is caused by" semantic development. Instead, all these developments may reflect a very general increment in the capacity to coordinate symbol structures. I will suggest (1) that the second metapragmatic stage is brought about by a cognitive capacity to coordinate two mental units or "chunks"—propositions, speech acts, or other mental events; (2) the third metapragmatic stage reflects a new cognitive capacity to coordinate three or more mental "chunks," in such a way that the third unit is coordinated with a relationship established between the other two.

First, with regard to the second metapragmatic stage, Antinucci and Parisi define the adverbial capacity as the ability to coordinate a propositional nucleus with any optional structure "outside" the nucleus. This broad definition—PROPOSITION + X—describes adverbs such as *in the living room* in the sentence *Mary knit the sweater in the living room*. It also includes simple conjunctions such as *and* which perform the additive function PROPOSITION + PROPOSITION. This definition would also include one linguistic proposal for the underlying structure of noun modifiers. Antinucci and Parisi (among others) suggest that a sentence such as *The red dog ran* is produced from two propositions: *The dog ran* and *The dog is red*. And, in fact, noun modifiers do appear at the same time as adverbials and simple conjunctions in the records for Claudia and Franceso. Also, it becomes clearer why time references—even the simple now/not now distinction—cannot appear prior to the development of an adverbial capacity. Whereas spatial locatives can serve as arguments of a nuclear proposition, e.g., *Etto li*—'This one here,' temporal adverbs always modify a state or event. Even the minimal structures NOW–EVENT X or NOT NOW–OBJECT Y IN STATE Z are formed with an optional adverb plus a predication. And in fact, spatial locatives do appear in the first stage, while the most minimal temporal adverbs are delayed until the second metapragmatic stage. Therefore, all the developments noted for the second stage can be explained as manifestations of a general adverbial capacity. However, this capacity has been defined so broadly by Antinucci and Parisi, that it should also extend to nonlinguistic manipulations of symbol structures, coordinations of two noncommunicative predications or mental events and relations. Since we have only linguistic data for Claudia and Francesco, this question must be left to future research.

Next, with regard to the third metapragmatic stage, Antinucci and Parisi have restricted their discussion to various types of sentence embeddings, implicit and explicit. Embeddings are actually an extension of the adverbial capacity, except that nuclear propositions are now taken as arguments of complex sentential structures rather than single adverbial predicates. At this point, the metapragmatic developments of the third stage bear a much less direct relation to formal propositional development. For example, why should the conjunction *and* occur when adverbials appear, while *but* is delayed until the child is capable of sentence embedding? At least on the surface, the utterances *And Paola is coming* and *But Paola is coming* are equivalent in propositional complexity. And what possible relationship is there between an imperfect past utterance such as *They were little ones* and a capacity to nest propositions?

One possible explanation is, of course, that these are all fortuitous correlations, coincidences set in motion by the general principle that anything a child does gets better as he gets older. This is a plausible hypothesis, and could be tested by comparing speech records for other children in other language communities, to see if the coincidence occurs again. But there remains the intriguing possibility that these seemingly disparate developments are set in motion by a more general factor. We have sufficient data here to speculate, at least, about the kinds of conceptual developments that may underlie the third stage in metapragmatics.

The best starting point is a reexamination of developments from Stage 2 to Stage 3 within a single grammatical category—in particular, the shift from time binarily quantified to time more finely quantified, and the shift from additive *and* to contrasting conjunctions such as *but*.

Let us first examine the shift from binary to dimensional time. By definition, a binary distinction involves two coordinates, X and Y, such that $X \neq Y$. More information could be added to a binary distinction, such as information about the way in which the two elements are related, or the distinctions that keep them from being identical. X and Y might be held together by an ordering relation, or by some further logical operation. X might be subordinate to or part of Y. But the minimal information required to construct a binary distinction is the knowledge that two elements are related, but not the same. The first formulations of a time relationship by Claudia and Francesco express little more than this minimal binary distinction, now vs. not now. Within the same developmental period, the children proceed to a minimally ordered now/not now relationship, a now/then relationship in which Event X follows Event Y. For example, while Claudia is stringing beads and counting toy animals she says *Poi cavalluccio* ('Then little horsie'). But there is no sense of a divisible time continuum along which different events can be located.

A continuum requires the presence of at least three points—X, Y, and some point Z. The three elements must share some common characteristic, such that Z stands between X and Y with respect to that characteristic. Hence a dimensional construct is more complex than a binary construct in two important ways: (1) It requires at least three mental "chunks" rather than two, and (2) it requires a transition function relating one of the three chunks to the other two with respect to some shared property.

This difference in complexity explains why binary constructs should precede dimensional constructs in development. It should also be clear why locational time adverbs—*Sunday, last week, tomorrow*—require a dimensional concept of time, and hence, appear later in development than now/then adverbs. The same notion of dimensionality is also responsible for the acquisition of imperfect past tense verbs. Enduring, incomplete, or repeated activities require a continuum that can be segmented. Hence, it is not surprising that temporal locatives and imperfect tenses appear in the same developmental period. They are both apparently based on the construction of a dimension or continuum along which events can be ranked.

While it is not so immediately obvious, the same cognitive shift may be responsible for an ability to handle complex rather than additive conjunctions. The conjunction *and* requires a simple linkage of two propositions, objects, or events. It is nothing more than a binary distinction, two things which are separate but related. The proposition *but* requires more processing. If I say "X, but Y," I not only link the two propositions according to some variable, but I posit some further contrast regarding that variable. As R. Lakoff points out (1971), one cannot say *but* about two propositions that bear no apparent relation to one another. Note the example

It is raining today, but I like cream cheese.

On the other hand, one cannot posit *but* of two propositions that are perfectly compatible. Take the example

It is raining today, but the sidewalks are wet.

According to this analysis, the use of the conjunction *but* has the same requirements in complexity that are required to construct a continuum: there are three "chunks" of information—two propositions and a third piece, a contrasting presupposition—such that the presupposition is related to the two propositions according to some shared characteristic.

Hence, in broad formal terms both dimensional time concepts and the use of complex conjunctions require a shift from 2-chunk linking operations, to 3-chunk operations in which the third piece is placed within, between, or along the relation between the first two.

This overall shift from link relations to within–link relations brings us to the distinction between embedded propositions (Stage 3) and propositions modified by external, optional, adverbial elements (Stage 2). In the case of adverbials or simple conjoined sentences, the mental operation involved is again a type of binary linkage between a proposition and either an external predicate or an external proposition. In sentence embedding, however, there is a relationship of "within" that must be established. Two linked propositions take up two mental "slots" or "chunks." To perform the operation of embedding, however, the unity of one of the propositions must be temporarily broken and held in mind—hence requiring two pieces—while the second proposition is built inside it. (We are referring here to the hierarchical relationship, and not to the surface icon of half a phrase, interruption, second half of phrase.) To carry out this operation, one must have at least three processing slots available, since the unity of the superordinate proposition is temporarily suspended.

The same kind of shift will be required to turn performatives into propositional content for metapragmatic utterances. The child must be able to focus on the proposition–slot and a performative procedure simultaneously, while creating a new propositional structure out of the two. Metapragmatics requires an ability to focus on two different procedural levels in one mental act. Until his processing space for symbol units increases, the child can focus only on his proposition, leaving the performative at the procedural level.

Finally, the same increment in processing capacity would explain why children now operate on an entire discourse as a unit, narrating long stories tied together with the new conjunctions, time adverbials, performative adverbs, etc. The same ability that permits the construction of a time continuum also permits the construction of a discourse continuum, in which speech events are ordered and coordinated with one another. IN A SENSE, THE CHILD IS NOW OPERATING IN ANAPHORIC OR DISCOURSE SPACE, A NEW SYMBOL WORLD LAID OUT ON THE TIME–SPACE COORDINATES DERIVED FROM SENSORIMOTOR ORGANIZATION. It is important to note, however, that metapragmatics is not the same thing as metalinguistics. These 2-year-olds are talking about speech acts, real and visible (or at least audible) events. They are not reasoning about the nature of language itself as an abstract system. These children probably could not tell us what makes a word a word, or why a cow is called a cow. They can simply tell us that a speech event has taken place, and they can operate on that speech event to coordinate it with larger discourse structure.

We have posited a a very general kind of shift in processing capacity. While the shift from sensorimotor to preoperational organization required a qualitative change in levels, the developments posited here may require a quantitative increase at the SAME preoperational level. Although the similarities are of a very abstract sort, it appears that complex conjunctions, dimensional time, sentence and discourse embedding all require a similar increment in the number of internal units that can be simultaneously maintained and coordinated with one another, particularly when the coordination involves a relationship placing a third element inside, between or within the other elements.

We suggest that something new is now happening in the mapping space, the area in central processing where symbolic arrays are constructed for communication (or problem solving, or some other operative scheme). There is a new capacity for coordinating packages of mental events. First, this shift in the capacity for coordination is clearly of a conceptual nature, since these children have been moving around efficiently in a world of more than two perceptual chunks for some time now. Second the particular conceptual shift noted here at metapragmatic Stage 3 is not the first change in the chunking capacity to take place in the mapping space. We suggested in Chapters III and IV that the shift from one to two to three-word speech may involve the child's expanding capacity to construct lexical packages. What we see here at a later stage may be a vertical decalage of that first expansion, involving a resegmentation and coordination of a larger kind of package, containing complete mental events or propositions. Hence, this new development may not necessarily reflect an increment in the number of mental slots, but in the kind of construction possible within each mental slot. The space limits were first applied to lexicalization, and then as the child gains a more stable and flexible control over procedures for lexicalization, the chunking capacity is applied upward at the level of predication. This could of course, as psycholinguists have suggested for some time, be a purely language specific development. But in all sorts of perceptual–motor activities we see similar developments. In learning to type, we begin with a letter-by-letter approach, moving up to little subprograms that execute whole words, then phrases. And that is only one example of the progressive reintegrations that occur in acquiring perceptual–motor skills.

It is not clear how or why human cognition operates according to such "chunking" limits, although the phenomenon has been documented in the psychological literature for years. An example is Miller's classic article on the magic number 7 plus or minus 2 (Miller, 1970). Typical illustrations of mental "chunking" can be found in the function of mnemonic devices for recalling unrelated material. For example, music students can recall the lines of the G-staff by reciting the sentence "Every Good Boy Does Fine," hence retrieving the notes E, G, B, D, and F in their correct order.

It should not surprise us, then, if the same principles govern the child's reconstruction of his sensorimotor world at the level of internal representation. When quantitative increments take place, they may be followed by qualitative reorganizations of mental structures, including linguistic structures. This position is put forth explicitly by Pascual–Leone (1970), with particular regard to Piagetian stages in cognitive development. Pascual–Leone defines a central computing space "M," which determines the number of schemes that can be handled simultaneously in one mental operation. Quantitative increases in this central computing space will result in resegmentations of mental processing, reflected in stage shifts similar to those observed by Piaget. Pascual–Leone does not suggest, however, that these quantitative shifts are in some way genetic, arbitrary, or hormonally induced. In fact, qualitative improvements may in themselves bring about quantitative changes in processing capacity. As the child gains experience in using schemes at one qualitative level, his level of performance becomes smoother, and hence less taxing to focal attention and central processing. This gradual equilibration may in itself contribute to an expansion of the number of schemes that can be handled at a given moment in planning. Much of Pascual–Leone's work has been devoted to the boundary between preoperations and concrete operations. However, it should apply equally well within the preoperational period, and may be one of the most fruitful lines of future research in this developmental stage.

Finally, if this rather abstract cognitive model is an accurate interpretation of the pragmatic–semantic changes recorded here, then it also adds further support to our contention in Chapter III that the figurative component of thought is involved in the construction of propositions for linguistic communication. The kinds of chunking and repackaging problems noted here would be characteristic of the static, holding aspect of thought, creating objects for higher operative procedures.

To summarize, across the preoperational period the child becomes capable of handling not only his proposition, but a performative and one or more presuppositional structures as symbolic objects for a single communicative act. In this chapter we have examined the transition from performative procedures, to the manipulation of performatives as symbol structures. In the next chapter, we will examine the same transition with regard to presuppositions and the topic–comment organization of discourse. In particular, we will examine the transition from a presupposing procedure for selecting new information from old, to the mastery of conventions that mark the new–old relationship in the surface form of utterances. In both these developments, the child, who first learned to operate WITHIN discourse space, becomes capable of operating ON large segments of discourse.

CHAPTER VI

Word Order and the Mastery of Presuppositions[1]

In Chapter IV on presupposing as a sensorimotor procedure, we suggested that early, one-word speech obeys presuppositions concerning new versus old information. The child selects the most informative element from a structured situation, and encodes that element in his one-word utterance. Hence his utterance presupposes that situation, treating the uncoded elements as the topic for the one-word comment. The presupposed portion of the message is not marked or encoded in any way. It is merely implied through use, a case of zero anaphora.

It was also suggested in Chapter IV that this presupposing procedure derives from low level orienting and figure–ground mechanisms. Hence, it is almost an automatic process; the presupposed material need not be constructed at the level of symbolic representation. In fact, according to the model outlined in Chapters III and IV, there is very little that CAN be constructed at the symbolic level during the one-word period. The child is limited to one word at a time not because of some language specific deficit, but because both figurative and operative aspects of "central computing space" are still limited in the number of "chunks" that can be constructed and operated upon. Given such severe limits, it is then not very surprising that the child constructs and maps precisely those aspects of the situation

---

[1] My profound thanks go to my friend and co-worker Brian MacWhinney for his help in rewriting this chapter. Many of the best ideas in it are either his to begin with, or originated in discussions with him. Any generally bad ideas, mistakes in interpretation, or inclarities are mine alone, despite Brian's best efforts to get rid of them.

that attract his attention most. It would be far more surprising if he did the opposite, encoding those aspects of the situation that he himself takes for granted. Under the constraints of one-word speech, when the child must encode either the topic or the comment, a decision to encode old, given information would require suppressing or ignoring the priorities established by the figure–ground and orienting mechanisms. In other words, a system for encoding new information, or comments, could be based entirely on sensorimotor procedures. But a system for encoding topics instead of comments would require conscious, reflective control over these same procedures for presupposing.

We also proposed, in Chapter III, that the shift from one- to two- to n-word speech may reflect a general increase in the number of units that can be constructed at the symbolic level. If this model is correct, what should we predict about the proposition–presupposition relationship in multiword utterances? One possibility is that the child will simply extend the old figure–ground strategy by blurting out the new or most interesting information first, and adding other information on as a sort of after-thought, until he runs out of processing space. Hence, the order of elements in an n-word utterance would parallel the order of attentional priority held by these items, from most to least important. However, given all the uses that adult languages make of word order (some of which we will examine shortly), it is unlikely that a child could maintain such a mapping system for very long. If he is to master the language of his community, he will have to gain control over his own presupposing procedures, suppressing the priorities assigned by the attentional system and rearranging constituents according to some other principle.

In this chapter, we will look at the way Italian children master the relationship between word order, and the highlighting of new and/or important information. Up until now a simple distinction between new and old has been sufficient to describe proposing versus presupposing in early speech. But in adult grammar the problem is much more complex. Before we can begin our developmental analysis, we will have to examine the topic–focus system in adult grammar, and in Italian grammar in particular.

The chapter will be divided into the following sections:

1. On defining topic and comment.
2. Previous approaches to word order and to topicalization in child language.
3. How word order works in Italian.
4. Longitudinal data for Claudia and Francesco.
5. Some pilot experiments on word order and topicalization in child language.

On Defining Topic and Comment

In all languages, there is interaction and competition between the pragmatic system for highlighting important information, and the semantic system for expressing reference, case relations, and other propositional structures (see Slobin, 1975). Both systems are competing for access to a limited linear channel and a rapidly fading short term memory. Both systems are limited in the devices they can use to signal their respective kinds of information. For the most part, they are restricted to some combination of four kinds of signals:

1. Lexical items.
2. Word order.
3. Morphological markers on individual words.
4. Intonation contours.

Different languages have resolved this competition in different ways (see Fillmore, 1968). One solution is to "divide the spoils," using some of the above signals for semantic purposes, and reserving others for pragmatic purposes. For example, in English the pragmatic system makes extensive use of intonation contours, particularly contrastive stress, while word order is used primarily to express semantic relations. In highly inflected languages such as Hungarian, semantic information is carried by morphological markers, and word order is used far more for the highlighting and backgrounding of information (see MacWhinney, 1975a). In some African languages that make semantic use of tones, contrastive stress for pragmatic purposes is not possible, and pragmatic information tends to be expressed through word order and special morphemes or both (Antinucci, personal communication).

This "competition" model of syntax has very strong implications for the ORIGIN of syntax, in language history and in ontogenesis. WE PROPOSE THAT THE ASPECT OF LANGUAGE CALLED SYNTAX CAN BE VIEWED AS A SECONDARY SYSTEM, DERIVED THROUGH THE INTERACTION BETWEEN SEMANTICS AND PRAGMATICS, COMPETING FOR ACCESS TO THE LINEAR, ACOUSTIC–ARTICULATORY CHANNEL. This position contrasts sharply with several traditional approaches to syntax, notably Chomskian transformational grammar. Chomsky (1972) and Jackendoff (1972), among others, view syntax as the primary component of the grammar, providing the essential structural relations among sentence constituents. The semantic component merely interprets this basic syntactic structure, inserting meaning at various stages in sentence derivation (or mapping). Hence, the semantic component does NOT contribute the structural relations among sentence parts. The semantic relation of agent–action, for example, does not generate the relationship subject–verb. Propositional meanings, including categories of agency, animacy, etc., tend to be assigned early in derivation, at the deepest level of syntactic deep structure. Pragmatic meanings, including the assignment of focus, tend to be inserted late in sentence derivation, through the assignment of phonological features such as intonation, and through certain stylistic re-arrangements of surface order that are currently considered to be "postcyclic." The pragmatic component, like the semantic component, plays no role in the assignment of primary structural relations among sentence parts.

The Chomskian position provides strong predictions about the primacy of syntax in child language development, suggesting that "pure" syntactic structures are either innate or acquired very early. Our position, on the other hand, makes an opposite prediction. We suggest that pragmatic and semantic structures (insofar as they are derived from basic, prelinguistic cognitive functions) will appear first in language development. Through his efforts to map these structures onto a limited, linear channel, the child will gradually acquire syntactic structures and/or transformations as solutions to the mapping problem.

As we shall see, a number of psycholinguists have already suggested that syntax derives from the problem of mapping semantic structures (e.g., Schlesinger, 1973; Brown, 1973). In this chapter, we want to emphasize the importance of pragmatic functions, particularly the topic–comment or given–new relationship, in this same developmental process. This will require an examination of the competition between pragmatics and semantics in the acquisition of syntax. But it will also require examining competition WITHIN the pragmatic system, between devices for topicalizing old information and devices for focusing new information.

We have, then, two tasks in this section. First, we will examine in more detail the inner workings of the adult topic–focus system, including several points at which topicalization and focusing actually compete for the pragmatic share of channel access. Second, we will look at the interaction between this pragmatic system and the semantic system, and their respective contributions to syntax. After these two rather lengthy excursions, we should be ready to examine the interaction of pragmatics, semantics, and syntax in the child data.

Let us turn first to the problem of defining topic, and comment or focus. In Chapter IV we treated these two concepts as polar opposites, along a single dimension of "informativeness." The child selects the most informative or important element in a structured situation and encodes that element in his one-word utterance. Hence, the less informative portion of that structured situation becomes the implicit topic for that one-word comment. At this stage, then, "topicalization is a passive process. It is assigned by default, as the by-product of focusing and commenting on new and/or important information.

In adult speech, the topic–comment system becomes far more elaborate, and topicalization and focusing both become active processes. Within a single lengthy utterance we can find topics and subtopics, comments and metacomments. Furthermore, the adult often takes great pains to foreground the topic—the exact opposite of the child's tendency to topicalize by default. Indeed, it begins to look as though the highlighting of information is not a simple unidimensional process at all in adult speech. We can distinguish at least three different models to explain the complexity of the adult system.

1. Perhaps there are actually two, or four, or twelve, or fifty different, discrete distinctions that are coded in the name of this single function. These discrete bits of information probably bear some functional resemblance to one another, which has allowed them to be handled as though they were manifestations of the same topic–comment function. But a more detailed analysis of the different individual devices and the different reasons for assigning topic and focus might reveal a multitude of separate semantic–pragmatic structures. [For example, Castelfranchi (personal communication) has proposed that contrastive stress and clefting are used to express two different kinds of presuppositional information.]

2. Alternatively, there may indeed be one PROCESS of foregrounding information. But it may be an analogue process rather than a digital one, involving tuning various parts of a proposition to their proper degree of emphasis or informativeness. Hence, a digital propositional structure would be tuned to different shades of emphasis in the same way that light and shadow are added to a charcoal sketch.

3. Yet another possibility is that there is only one, discrete topic–comment process. But it may be a recursive process that can be applied repeatedly within a single utterance, creating topic–comment divisions that serve in turn as the topics for yet another, "higher" comment.

All three of these possibilities are supported by the fact that individual languages such as English and Italian provide a large set of heterogeneous devices that seem to serve no purpose other than topicalizing and focusing information.

Let us look at a few examples of multiple topic–focus divisions as they are applied to a pragmatically neutral proposition DRANK (man, beer):

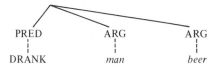

Let us assume for the moment that all the information in this proposition, including the identity of the referents for *man* and *beer* and their relationship in the act of drinking, is new to both speaker and listener. We will start with the most neutral expression possible for expressing these pragmatic conditions. Then we will begin adding devices that increase the amount of topicalization and/or focusing within the same proposition.

In English, there is no way to express the pragmatically neutral information without implying, if only by default, a minimal topic–comment division. The most neutral sentence we can generate to express these components is

(1)   *A man drank a beer.*

Whether we like it or not, this sentence could be interpreted by the listener to imply that *a man* is the topic, and *drank a beer* is a comment about that man. In English surface structure, default topicalization is assigned obligatorily through the assignment of the role of surface syntactic subject.

However, the listener might also consider the active, declarative sentence in the way that we intended it, as the unmarked form with respect to topicalization. In markedness theory (e.g., Trubetskoy 1939), when a surface distinction cannot be avoided even though no corresponding semantic distinction is intended, one surface form is generally made to serve as the neutral, or unmarked form. For example, when an English speaker has to use a third person singular pronoun, but does not wish to specify sex, the male pronoun *he* is generally chosen to serve as the unmarked, sex-neutral form (i.e., a shorthand version of the speaker's real meaning, which is actually "he or she"). Similarly, when an English speaker is introducing entirely new information, and has no real topic–comment division in mind, the active, declarative can serve as the unmarked form for topicalization. This means that the active declarative form is pragmatically ambiguous, between a marked and an unmarked interpretation of topic and focus, in the same way that the pronoun *he* is often ambiguous between a male referent and a referent whose sex is either unknown or irrelevant.

Suppose that the speaker does not want to risk the possibility that the listener will interpret his sentence as an effort to mark *a man* as the assumed, or topicalized portion of the message. There are two possible motives for such concern. One is that he does NOT want to topicalize *a man,* and thus wants to take that argument out of the default topic slot. The other motive might be that he DOES want to topicalize the object, *a beer,* which would require taking that argument out of the default comment slot. One of the speaker's options, given this situation, is to select a marked surface order such as the passive, e.g.,

(2)   *A beer was drunk by a man.*

This sentence places *a beer* in the topic slot, treating it as the assumed or given portion of the message, while *was drunk by a man* becomes the comment. The passive transformation is always a marked form with respect to topicalization, while the active declarative is ambiguous between the unmarked form and a potential marked form. Hence we could say that *a beer* in sentence (2) is topicalized more strongly, or to a greater degree, than *a man* in sentence (1). This interpretation would fit the analogue model for topicalization and focus outlined above.

Suppose we now replace the indefinite articles in expression (1) with definite articles, e.g.,

(3)   *The man drank a beer.*

(4)   *A man drank the beer.*

(5)   *The man drank the beer.*

In sentences (3) and (5), we have specified a particular man, presumably known to both speaker and listener. In (4) and (5) we have specified a particular, recognized beer. The same arguments with definite articles are more strongly topicalized than their equivalents with indefinite articles. It is obvious, for example, in sentence (5) that neither the man nor the beer are in themselves new information. The only thing that is new is the relationship between them. Another way of saying this is that sentences (3) to (5) are, in their entirety, comments on the presupposed existence of specific, known referents. According to the above analogue model, we might say that there is a greater DEGREE of topicalization or backgrounding applied to the two arguments of the predicate DRANK. Alternatively, using one of the digital models proposed above, we could also view sentence (5) as a nested topic–comment structure, in which *there is a man* and *there is a beer* are the lowest level topics, commented upon by the entire proposition *the man drank the beer.* That entire proposition is in turn divided into another topic–comment structure with *the man* assigned the role of topic and *drank the beer* assigned the role of comment. The complete nested structure would have been produced by the recursive application of a single topic–comment mechanism, which "hands out" different surface expressions for that relationship each time it is applied.

There are a number of other surface devices that increase the amount of topicalization or "giveness" of one or more elements, while increasing the focus or emphasis on other elements. In English, an operation for increasing focus is the cleft transformation, e.g.,

(6)   *It was the beer that the man drank.*

(7)   *It was the man that drank the beer.*

(8)   *What the man did to the beer was to drink it.*

Hatcher (1956) and Jackendoff (1972), among others, have suggested that the question test provides linguistic evidence for the topic–focus function served by such forms. For example, (6) is an appropriate answer to

(9)   *What did the man drink?*

(7) answers the question

(10)   *Who drank the beer?*

and(8) is an appropriate response to

(11)   *What did the man do to the beer?*

Each question establishes the focal point for its answer, and in answers (6) through (8) that focus is expressed via the mechanism of clefting. The same foci could also be expressed, in response to the same questions, through the use of contrastive stress. For example, questions (9) to (11) could be answered by the respective sentences

(12)   *The man drank the* **beer**.

(13)   *The* **man** *drank the beer.*

(14)   *The man* **drank** *the beer.*

It is also possible to assign compound foci, illustrated by the question

(15)   *Did the woman drink the lemonade?*

and its answer:

(16)   *No, the* **man** *drank the* **beer**.

(see Sgall, Hajicova, and Benesova, 1973). In all these cases, the pragmatically neutral proposition DRANK (*man, beer*) can be divided into presupposed information, and asserted information that comments on the presupposition through the use of a stressed or cleft element. The question test is a linguistic technique for making such presupposed topics explicit for each type of cleft or stressed comment.

Let us consider these devices from the point of view of the three possible topic–focus models outlined above. As we noted, Castelfranchi (personal communication) has suggested that clefting and contrastive stress each map a different kind of presupposition–proposition relationship. The choice of surface mechanisms is automatically dictated by the type of presupposed information and "identifying assertion" contained in deep structure. This interpretation would be in keeping with the first, digital model in which the multitude of surface topic–focus expressions are independently motivated by a multitude of underlying distinctions. Alternatively, we could consider clefting and stress with an analogue model, in which portions of the neutral proposition are tuned "up" as focal elements or "down" for a greater degree of topicalization or giveness, depending on the analogue contours of importance, informativeness, etc. intended by the speaker.

Finally, with the second digital model we could describe sentences (6) to (8), (12) to (14), and (16) as nested topic–comment structures produced by the recursive application of a single topic–comment operation at increasingly higher levels.

Pronouns also serve a topicalization function, since the use of a pronoun as in the use of a definite article specifies that the referent should be known to both speaker and listener. The same thing can be said for elliptical expressions, e.g., *Drank the beer* alone as an answer to *What did the man do?*. In analogue terms, an argument expressed by a pronoun—or an argument left out of the surface expression entirely—carried a greater degree of giveness than the same argument expressed explicitly with a noun. In digital terms, pronominalization and ellipsis would be assigned during the recursive application of the topic–comment device within the proposition.

There are also a variety of adverbials, conjunctions, and other lexical items that serve as links between a propositional comment and the presupposed topic for that comment. For example, the sentences

(17)   *Now the man is drinking a beer.*

(18)   *The man is drinking a beer again.*

(19)   *This time the man is drinking a beer.*

(20)   *But the man is drinking a beer.*

(21)   *The man is even drinking a beer.*

each contain an element cuing the listener to connect this utterance as a comment on previous, topicalized material.

All that we have done so far is to illustrate the complexity of the adult topic–focus system. We have provided no evidence to support any of the three proposed models for representing the topic–focus system. And there is certainly a great deal more that could be said about any one of the surface mechanisms for expressing topic and focus (see the last six volumes of the "Proceedings of the Regional Meeting of the Chicago Linguistic Society" for detailed discussions of all the above devices). There are sundry syntactic peculiarities attached to each of the expressions treated here, all of which are beyond the scope of this chapter. The point for present purposes is that the topic–focus system that seemed so simple at the one-word stage is extremely complex in adult speech, permitting multiple, nested topic–focus arrangements within a single utterance, e.g.,

(22)   *It was **this** beer, not the other one, which was drunk by the man who had only **recently** returned from Cincinnati* (as opposed to the guy who came back from there a month ago).

However, despite these complexities, when the topic–focus system is discussed in the literature, it is almost always discussed with a pair of reciprocal terms, implying one or at most two dimensions. There has been a proliferation of terms for describing this system, referring to the same general divisions, but with enough subtle differences to cause considerable confusion. It might be useful at this point to list a few of the terms that occur most often in the literature, examining the major differences in usage.

Table 5 certainly does not exhaust all the terms that have been used, in all their possible combinations. But it does at least represent a few of the most widely cited versions. The first set of definitions (1 through 7) treat the left- and right-hand terms as though they were opposite poles of a single dimension. What is not new is by definition old or given. The assignment of one role implies the assignment of the other by default. Beyond this shared characteristic, however, pairs one to seven vary in their range of application. Sets such as NEW–GIVEN and NEW–OLD are restricted to a particular attribute of messages, involving degree of novelty. Sets such as COMMENT–TOPIC, FIGURE–GROUND, and BOUND–FREE are more broadly defined. In these latter sets, novelty may be only one of several considerations involved in selecting a piece of information as COMMENT, FIGURE, etc. Emotional import, uncertainty, and a number of other factors may be involved as well. But in all the bipolar analyses,

Table 5   Topic Focus Terminology

Bipolar Terms		
1. NEW INFORMATION	OLD INFORMATION	Chafe, 1970; Baroni, Fava and Tirondola, 1973; Chapter IV, this volume.
2. NEW INFORMATION	GIVEN INFORMATION	Haviland and Clark, 1974
3. COMMENT	TOPIC	Sechehaye, 1926; Vygotsky, 1962; DeLaguna, 1927; Feldman and Hass (in press); Hornby, 1972; Chapter IV, this volume.
4. FIGURE	GROUND	MacWhinney, 1974; Chapter IV, this volume.
5. BOUND INFORMATION	FREE INFORMATION	Rommetveit, 1974
6. CONVERSATIONAL DYNAMIC ELEMENT	CONVERSATIONAL STATIC ELEMENT	Firbas, 1964
7. RHEME	THEME	Halliday, 1970
Bifunctional Terms		
8. INFORMATION FOCUS	THEME	Halliday, 1970
9. EXPRESSIVE FOCUS	LOGICAL FOCUS	MacWhinney, 1975(b)
10. SECONDARY TOPICALIZATION	PRIMARY TOPICALIZATION	Fillmore, 1968
11. FOCUS	TOPIC	Chomsky, 1972; Jackendoff, 1972
12. EMPHASIS	THEME	Dezso, 1970

the polar terms refer to mutually exclusive roles, a sort of linguistic YIN and YANG.

The second set of definitions (8 through 11) are taken from authors who treat the left- and right-hand terms as separate though interacting functions, motivated by different kinds of considerations. For example, Halliday defines **theme** as the selection of a point of reference in discourse, while **information focus** deals with the emotional impact, or informational weight of a given item. These two roles, as defined by Halliday, are not mutually exclusive. In fact, Halliday has a third term, **rheme,** which is the polar opposite of theme. While a single element cannot be both theme and rheme, it can at least in principle be both theme and information focus. For example, in the sentence

(23)   *John got the job.*

Halliday would presumably give the element *John* both the role of theme and the role of information focus. Nevertheless, it does generally happen that the theme corresponds with giveness in Haviland and Clark's sense, while information focus is usually assigned to a conversationally new element. Hence, there is statistical overlap between the bipolar and bifunctional definitions. However, according to the bifunctional analysis the overlap is coincidental and not intrinsic to defining the terms. Theme overlaps with giveness because the same theme tends to be held constant through a long series of turns in a single conversation—e.g., we begin talking about John and we continue talking about John, reminded of new anecdotes about him, etc. Similarly, information focus tends to be assigned to new or contrasting information because new things are inherently interesting. However, Halliday notes that at the beginning of a conversation, when nothing is necessarily given, we still assign the role of theme to some element during our opening remarks. And we can also place contrastive stress (and therefore information focus) on some element that has been the theme of several preceding utterances. Hence, despite the fact that there is a statistical overlap between information focus and newness, and between theme and giveness, Halliday would insist that the two are assigned for different and autonomous reasons, and therefore are not mutually exclusive roles.

MacWhinney (1975b) puts forth a similar analysis, suggesting that "expressive focusing" (similar to Halliday's information focus) and "logical focusing" (similar to Halliday's theme) are separate functions. In the 1975 paper, MacWhinney provides a detailed list of the different motivations for choosing expressing focusing, logical focusing, or both. For example, an element may require expressive focus because it is new, because it is emotionally important (regardless of its novelty), or because it contrasts with or denies previous expectations. "Logical focus" is more difficult to define, but involves a great deal more than simple "absence of newness." In general, logical focusing involves the selection of a central point of view or reference point in an utterance, which takes the rest of the utterance as its "logical scope" (similar to Halliday's rheme). There is a great deal of overlap between MacWhinney's concept of logical focus–logical scope and our earlier analysis of topic–comment. For example, he states that in neutral active declarative sentences, the syntactic subject is assigned the role of "default logical focus" and the rest of the predicate is the "default logical scope." This is identical to our earlier analysis of default topic and comment assignment in the unmarked active declarative sentence. However, the motives for selecting a logical focus involve more than giveness in discourse. For example, MacWhinney has speculated that the choice of logical focus may be related to the psychological function of perspective taking or identification. According to this analysis, agents tend to be selected more often as the logical foci of sentences because we can more easily project ourselves into the point of view of agents. Also, Mac-Whinney notes that emotional factors, similar to those underlying expressive focus, can also contribute to the selection of logical focus. To illustrate, he gives the following examples:

(24)   *Chimps communicate like the deaf.*

(25)   *The deaf communicate like chimps.*

(in which both sentences describe research on Washoe and other chimpanzees who have learned a portion of American Sign Language, a language spoken in American deaf communities). The two sentences should be semantically equivalent. Yet it is far more offensive to attribute "chimpness" to the deaf than vice-versa. If we chose the logical focus strictly on the basis of identification with a given element, we would presumably choose the deaf over chimps and construct sentence (25). But the emotional impact of attributing chimpness to human beings makes (24) a preferable construction. Hence, we see two different motivations contributing to the selection of logical focus. And neither of these are in any way related to the selection of expressive focus.

To summarize, the bipolar approach maintains that topic and focus are mutually exclusive roles, opposite poles of a single, albeit very general dimension of informational highlighting and backgrounding. In the bifunctional approach, topic and focus are separate roles, assigned on the basis of different kinds of considerations. In the bifunctional approach, the two roles are not mutually exclusive, and can at least in principle be held by the same component of a message. In actual use it is true that the two roles are generally assigned to separate portions of a message, corresponding to a "new," "comment," "focal" portion versus a "given," "topicalized" or "backgrounded" portion. According to the bipolar positions, this statistical distribution is inherent in the nature of the two terms.

According to the bifunctional positions, the statistical distribution is coincidental.

Returning to the three models for representing a complex topic–focus system, the bifunctional approach would require a model similar to digital model (1), in which discrete and very different structures underlie each of the many surface devices for topicalizing and focusing information. The analogue model, in which a proposition is tuned up and down along a single dimension of informativeness or conversational highlighting, obviously applies only to a bipolar definition of topic and focus. The same can be said for the second digital model, in which a single, recursive topic–comment mechanism is applied repeatedly within an utterance creating different sets of topic–comment relationships requiring different surface expressions.

However, the recursive topic–comment model could in some ways handle the arguments put forth by Halliday and MacWhinney, regarding the very different motivations for creating logical foci and expressive foci. For example, take the sentence

(23)   ***John** got the job.*

in which *John* is in the subject–topic slot, but also receives contrastive stress. Presumably the same argument has been assigned both the role of theme or logical focus, and the role of information or expressive focus. However, an alternative interpretation, preserving the bipolar YIN/ YANG approach to topic and focus, would suggest that *John* is the topic at one level, and the comment or information focus at another. In this case, *John* would be the theme or topic of the sentence

(26)   *John got the job.*

But this entire sentence would in turn be a comment on further, presupposed information that could be paraphrased as

(27)   *Someone got the job.*

If topicalization is applied recursively (creating both bipolar roles each time it is applied), then the same component can play both topic and focus roles, but ONLY if it holds each role at a different level in an embedded message structure. In other words, topic and focus would be mutually exclusive roles with respect to message levels, but not with respect to the utterance taken as a whole.

Taking this multilevel approach, we can translate MacWhinney's and Halliday's bifunctional systems back into a bipolar model. The division into logical focus–logical scope, and theme–rheme, could be considered to be one of the products of a topic–comment mechanism. Hence, within the utterance *John got the job, John* is the topic and logical focus and *got the job* is the comment or logical scope. However, when the topic–comment mechanism is applied a second time, the entire structure *John got the job* is made to serve as a comment on a presupposed, topicalized structure *Someone got the job*. That relationship is expressed on the surface by assigning contrastive stress to John. In MacWhinney's terms, at the next level up *John got the job* is the logical scope, and *Someone got the job* is the logical focus.

We can, then, propose a compromise position, in which topic and focus maintain their mutually exclusive YIN/YANG, through recursive applications within a single utterance. This would account formally for the statistical fact that topic and focus are almost always assigned to different surface elements. However, Halliday and MacWhinney have quite correctly pointed out that the motivations for selecting an element as topic or as focus are often distinct and varied. We may wish to topicalize an element for one reason (e.g., our sense of identification with its referent) while we wish to emphasize or focus it for a different reason. It may be that languages have evolved heterogeneous and varied topic–focus devices precisely because there are many reasons for assigning the two roles within a given utterance. With a recursive topic–comment model, we could respond to the different reasons for assigning the two roles by assigning them several times within a nested message structure.

Regardless of whether topic and focus are bifunctional or bipolar, however, they are always separate roles. They can, then, potentially compete for a given surface slot—for example, the opening position in a multiword utterance. At the one-word stage, there does not seem to be any competition for the limited mapping space between these two separate portions of a message. From the child's point of view, the topic is obvious. It is by definition given, serving as the background for more interesting figures that are inherently more worthy of discussion. However, the child's comment will function as a comment ONLY if his listener shares the sensorimotor topic. Since very young children talk almost exclusively about the here and now (e.g., Greenfield and Smith, 1976), the adult listener usually has no trouble retrieving the presupposed, topicalized material. However, as the range of events that the child tries to talk about expands, the possibility of communicative misfire also increases (see examples from Francesco on page 100). In fact, after repeated frustration in trying to make a one-word comment work, the child may be forced to encode material that he previously took for granted (e.g., BALL! BALL! BALL! . . . GIVE!). In such cases, the topic becomes worthy of attention a posteriori, because a comment has failed. Here we see the beginning of competition for channel access between focus and topic. The focused material competes for the one-word slot on the basis of its inherent interest and informativeness. The topic competes for the same slot in response to a need to provide the listener with assumed information.

In adult speech, we generally calculate IN ADVANCE the amount of topicalization that can be assumed, and the amount that must be provided to insure that a comment will work. It is because of our capacity to foresee the listener's needs that topicalization becomes a much more active process, competing for channel access with the comment portion of a message. This process involves selecting links, conventional devices that can be added to an utterance to help the listener locate the presuppositions for a given proposition. These links include several of the topicalization and focusing devices discussed in sentences (1) through (27) above. In the terms presented in Chapter I, topicalization in early child speech is carried out almost entirely by P_3 presupposing. Topicalization in adult speech involves turning P_3 presuppositions into P_1 and P_2 presuppositions, signalled for the listener's benefit with surface markers.

Rommetveit (1974) gives an example of a single P_3 presupposition that can require varying degrees of explicit topicalization depending on the amount of shared information that the speaker can assume in his listener. Two football fans are watching a televised game, in which player Bob Wilson makes a brilliant touchdown. Speaker A cries out immediately

(28)   *Magnificent!*

Both speaker and listener are completely wrapped up in the game. They share exactly the same here and now context, including the semantic content of the game (e.g, Bob Wilson just made a touchdown) and the pragmatic weighting of that content (e.g., the touchdown was important, brilliant, and stands out as a figure against all the background moves of the game). In that context the one–word comment carries perfectly. There is no risk that the uncoded topic (Bob Wilson's touchdown) will be lost. Rommetveit suggests that very young children, unable to see the world from a divergent listener viewpoint, always assume such a shared here and now context for their brief utterances—even when the assumption is invalid. Adults, however, have enough experience with different listeners and different viewpoints to judge whether a one-word comment will carry or not.

In the case of our two adult football fans, suppose that the speaker says nothing during the touchdown itself. Later, over beer and popcorn, he says

(28)   *Magnificent!*

If the listener is equally preoccupied with Bob Wilson's play, the comment may carry as easily as it did before. However, given the passage of time and events, it is also possible that the listener may interpret the utterance as a comment on the game as a whole, or perhaps even as a comment on the beer and popcorn. At this point, it is more likely that the speaker will specify the topic, with something such as

(29)   *That play was magnificent!*

Given the shared experience of the game, this topic–comment structure will probably work, since the listener will know immediately which play is under discussion. However, 24 hours later, discussing the same game with a colleague at the office, the speaker might decide to add still greater topic specificity to his utterance, saying

(30)   *That touchdown by Bob Wilson in the*
          last quarter was magnificent!

To make the same point to his wife, who did not watch the game and knows very little about football, the same speaker may have to prepare his comment with topicalization involving a detailed history of football, a definition of touchdowns and other plays, and so forth. Indeed, so much topicalization may be required that he will decide not to bother with the comment at all.

Rommetveit notes that many aspects of this topic–comment function are conventionalized within the grammar. For example, the phrase *the touchdown by Bob Wilson,* with a definite article, assumes a shared frame of reference with the listener, while *a touchdown by Bob Wilson* makes fewer assumptions. However, given the infinite variety of possible topic–comment divisions of information, each varied for the amount of shared background information that can be assumed, the language system cannot account in advance for all the relationships it will have to encode. Much will have to depend on ad hoc, private signals as well as standard conventions. The success of these ad hoc signals will, in turn, depend on the intimacy and skill of the two interlocutors. Rommetveit concludes that

> The bridge by which the novel information is linked to what was known beforehand and by which it thereby becomes part of an expanded or modified social world will in each case be exactly as fragile as the pre–established commonality between speaker and listener upon which it is founded . . . [p. 32].

To summarize, topicalization competes for channel access in order to insure that the listener has sufficient information for comments to work. Foci or comments compete for channel access by virtue of their inherent importance, novelty or informativeness. Let us now return to the child who has just entered the two-word stage. This child has just developed the capacity to encode both topic and comment within a single utterance. How will he order these two units? Assuming for the moment that the child knows nothing about semantic–syntactic constraints such as "agents are mapped before actions," we have proposed that the child will extend his one-word strategy, blurting out the interesting or novel information first, and adding other units on in decreasing order of interest. However, aside from the multitude of semantic–syntactic ordering rules that he will soon encounter, there is also another, opposite pragmatic constraint. If the listener is ill informed, it may be more prudent to express the topic first, and follow with a comment. Otherwise the listener will spend the first half of the utterance wondering where in discourse space to stick the incoming information. Of course, with two-word utterances he will not have to wait very long, and can probably keep the first unit in mind until he has enough information to make sense of it. But as the average length of the child's utterances expand, there is an increasing risk that the listener may lose track of the point of the utterance (the comment) before he finds out where it belongs. Hence, within the pragmatic system alone, there are two possible mapping strategies reflecting competing pragmatic pressures:

1. Encode the comment first, in isomorphic relation to its attention value.

2. Suppress the attention priorities and encode the topic first, to prepare the listener for the comment.

According to the cognitive model presented here, the first strategy would require little conscious control of proposition-presupposition relationships. It would essentially be a sensorimotor procedure, reflecting the automatic workings of well-developed orienting and figure–ground mechanisms. The second strategy, on the other hand, would require suppression of the earlier sensorimotor procedure, plus an awareness of the listener's informational needs. We therefore predict that—in the absence of clear adult semantic–syntactic ordering models—strategy 1 will develop earlier than strategy 2.

Note that this prediction is made "in the absence of semantic syntactic models." It would be difficult to find a child growing up in a situation in which competing pragmatic pressures function in the absence of other, nonpragmatic uses of word order. As we shall see later, there is a brief period in the acquisition of Italian in which such a situation may exist. For the most part, however, pragmatic strategies interact and compete with strategies for mapping semantic relations, e.g., the relationship between agent, action and object. Also, children are generally exposed to high frequency, conventional syntactic patterns from the adult language, as well as highly specific but also frequent word associations such as *Hi Daddy!* [see Braine (1973) and MacWhinney (1975b) for a discussion of word based patterns]. This brings us to our second task, examining the relative contributions of the semantic and pragmatic components to surface syntax.

Earlier we gave several examples of the way that various languages divide channel use between the semantic and pragmatic components. For example, English tends to reserve word order to signal semantic case relations, while intonation—particularly contrastive stress—is used primarily to focus information. Hungarian expresses case relations through inflections on individual words, and therefore can make greater use of word order for pragmatic purposes. There is another kind of solution to this competition for channel access. In those instances in which pragmatic and semantic roles tend to overlap, they may both be assigned the same high priority syntactic device. In most cases, they can coexist peacefully on this bit of territory. When conflicts do arise, special conventions can be provided to signal the divergence of roles. In English and Italian, the best example of this is the assignment of surface syntactic subject. As we noted earlier, under neutral conditions the role of pragmatic topic is obligatorily assigned to the subject of an active declarative sentence. It is also true that, under neutral conditions, the semantic agent is also assigned the position of subject of an active declarative sentence. This interaction results in three types of sentence subject:

1. Semantic agent.
2. Pragmatic topic.
3. Syntactic subject (out of one or more arguments of the predicate, the argument that must agree with the predicate in person and number).

When we do not wish to assign all three types of subjects simultaneously, we can select an alternative surface form like the passive or cleft, as illustrated in examples (2) and (6) to (16). Several psycholinguistic studies have indicated that the passive is more difficult to process and/or remember than the active. And it also seems to be the case that clefts and passives are late acquisitions in child language (e.g., Brown, 1973). But since the three types of subjects do generally overlap, and since there are also a number of other devices for manipulating topic-focus relations (e.g., contrastive stress), we are not often required to invoke these unusual surface forms.

Most linguists agree that the three types of subjects exist, that they overlap under neutral conditions, and that special transformations such as passives and clefting have probably evolved to remove the agent-subject from its neutral position of "default logical focus" or "default topicalization." However, there is much more controversy regarding the process by which these three structures are derived.

In the Chomskian position outlined earlier, pragmatic roles are assigned late in sentence derivation. Chomsky's argument rests in part on his contention that syntactic subject is a primary, purely formal role that is assigned directly by the base component.[2] He has even argued that the concept of syntactic subject is an innate idea, a "substantive linguistic universal" that is found in all human languages. As such, subject is distinct from both semantic agent and pragmatic topic, and cannot be derived from them.

Fillmore (1968), on the other hand, suggests that syntactic subject is a

---

[2] We are speaking here of the deep structure syntactic subject, which does not always occupy the role of surface syntactic subject, agreeing with the verb in person and number. On the other hand, it is not a semantic or a pragmatic role either. In a sense, perhaps we should consider Chomsky's deep structure subject role to be a fourth type of subject.

secondary, derived structure, a surface option that some languages (e.g., ergative languages) do not even use. In languages that do assign an obligatory role of surface subject (i.e., the argument that agrees with the verb), subjectivalization is a rule, a transformation that operates on a preestablished semantic structure. This rule operates according to a case hierarchy, such that under neutral conditions subjectivalization is applied to the agent if there is an agent. If there is no agent, subjectivalization is applied to the experiencer case. If there is no experiencer, the instrument is subjectivalized. And so forth. Givon (1974) and MacWhinney (1975b) have noted that this subjectivalization hierarchy proceeds from most to least human, or most to least like the speaker. This is an illustration of MacWhinney's contention that logical focus is motivated by the speaker's ability to identify with a given argument in a proposition, hence "taking its points of view."

According to this second position, then, the role of syntactic subject could be viewed as a convention regulating the interaction between the assignment of pragmatic topic, and the expression of semantic case roles. In Fillmore's grammar, topic assignment could be viewed as the starting point in the mapping process, insofar as subjectivalization under neutral conditions involves moving down a semantic hierarchy to select an argument for topicalization. In fact, the semantic hierarchy itself may not be a formal, arbitrary structure at all. It may be possible to generate the hierarchy from such psychological principles as the speaker's identification with the various arguments of the verb. In this sort of model, in contrast with Chomsky's, the pragmatic component makes primary structural contributions to syntax.

One approach to this controversy is to determine the starting point that children use in acquiring pragmatic topic, semantic agent, and syntactic subject. We will now take a brief look at the history of word order and topicalization in child language, to see how these questions have been handled up until now.

Previous Approaches to Word Order and Topicalization in Child Language

In examining the literature on acquisition of word order, we note that the concepts of syntactic subject, semantic agent, and pragmatic topic have been emphasized in precisely that historical order.

Psycholinguistics in the 1960s was heavily influenced by Chomsky, particularly by his radical proposal that the child comes into the world equipped with innate ideas about the nature of syntax. One of these innate ideas—a supposed starting point for language acquisition—was the concept of deep structure subject. McNeill (1966) suggested that the speech of very young children would directly reflect their first (and therefore, innate) hypotheses about syntax, and would thus respect deep structure ordering constraints among the major sentence constituents. McNeill (1970) noted that the early speech of Adam (see Brown, 1973) employed only 9 of 27 possible orders for Subject, Verb, and Object, and that those 9 orders correspond to the combinations of constituents permitted in the formation of English deep structure (including utterances in which only two elements are expressed). McNeill claims that if the child did not know a priori about sentence constituency and order constraints, the 27 possible SVO orders would be randomly distributed in his early speech.

Slobin (1966) contributed to speculation about innate order strategies in reviewing Gvozdev's observation that Russian children pass through a stage in which they rigidly preserve one kind of word order. This is particularly interesting since Russian, unlike English, is an inflectional language with relatively free word order. Also, the order that is the most statistically frequent in adult Russian is not the one that children prefer during this first stage. Since the preferred ordering strategy could not have been derived from simple imitation, Slobin suggests that these children are trying out one of a stock of innate strategies, one that will eventually be discarded in favor of the inflectional system for marking subject–verb–object relations.

The case for innate syntax was weakened in 1969, when Bowerman described the early speech of two Finnish children (also learning an inflectional language with flexible order) and one English child. Bowerman noted that the speech of the Finnish children is relatively order free, and that the number of occurrences within each type of constituent order corresponds directly to the frequency of each order in parental speech. Indeed, even the English child in Bowerman's sample showed more variation in order than might have been expected from earlier studies. Bowerman also reexamined the Brown data originally described by McNeill, and concluded that Adam's early utterances show more "noise" in ordering and segmentation than indicated by McNeill's interpretations. While McNeill was quite correct in his overall statistical reports, the exceptions to the norm are such as to preclude an interpretation in terms of absolute order strategies. Bowerman concludes that it would be more correct to speak in terms of statistically preferred orders than absolute mapping rules such as those that occur in adult speech. No mention is made in Bowerman's book of possible pragmatic factors influencing the various order strategies. It is possible that the Finnish children are not really modelling adult frequencies in a statistical sense, but that the distribution of various pragmatic reorderings is similar for child Finnish, and for adult speech to children in Finnish. This would occur if child and adult were discussing the same here-and-now context, with more or less the same pragmatic weightings given to various objects and events.

Both Bowerman (1973) and Brown (1973) caution against immediately attributing an SVO preference—even when one does appear—to an underlying syntactic rule. The same early sentences in English that obey SVO could also be described with an Agent-Action-Object rule. In adult English subjects are often NOT semantic agents; but apparently in the child samples studied by Bowerman and Brown early subjects are almost always either agents or vehicles (which from the child's point of view could be considered agents as well). The fact that an adult observer can classify the child's utterances into abstract syntactic categories such as subject and object does not mean that these categories are functional for the child. Bowerman suggests that when either a semantic or a syntactic hypothesis can be used to explain the same child data, the semantic hypothesis is less abstract and hence a more parsimonious interpretation.

Finally, Bowerman has stressed one tenet of Chomskian transformational grammar that had been deemphasized in earlier studies—namely, that the order of elements in syntactic deep structure varies from one language community to another. Hence, deep structure order must be LEARNED regardless of whether or not is is available through imitation of adult surface structures. If the child, according to a Chomskian grammar, must learn one kind of unobservable structure, then there is no reason why he cannot also learn the rest of the underlying transformational system. Bowerman suggests that in applying the term INNATE to the child's idea of word order, one must clearly be referring to some very general kind of ordering concept rather than to a specific innate strategy for relating particular kinds of constituents.

Roeper (1973a,b) responds to Bowerman's criticism with one of the more Baroque innatist hypotheses available in the child language literature. He agrees with Bowerman that, in orthodox transformational theory, the order of elements in deep structure varies from one language to another. Hence, children need not and indeed should not come into the world with one, single, fixed order in mind. However, Roeper notes that in German, English, and other languages for which transformational grammars have been written, the order of constituents in deep structure is invariably reflected within surface relative clauses. Roeper suggests, then, that children may come into the world with an innate strategy for scanning the order of constituents in relative clauses, in order to derive the order of constituents in the deep structure of their particular language.

An ongoing study by Slobin and colleagues (see Slobin, 1975) compares comprehension of subject, verb, and object relations through word order versus inflections. Data have been gathered from four language communities: Italian, American English, Serbo-Croatian, and Turkish. Preliminary results indicate that if any strategy is innately prior or more natural for children, it is the highly regular, agglutinating inflectional system of Turkish. Children acquiring Turkish perform better in comprehension of syntactic relations than subjects acquiring the more irregular Serbo-Croatian inflections. And they are also superior to children learning the regular English word order relations and the more flexible Italian word order rules. These results are undergoing further analysis, and more complex interactions may emerge. But it does seem fair to conclude that our original fascination with innate word order mechanisms may have been premature.

Sinclair and Bronckardt (1972) have examined comprehension of word order by French children. Order is somewhat less flexible in French than in Italian, but there is more pragmatic variation than in English. It is perhaps for this reason that Sinclair's results are so surprisingly complex. French children use a variety of strategies in deriving agent and object from various Noun–Verb–Noun orders presented in the experiment. Some of these strategies are clearly related to developmental level. For example, there is a tendency for very young children given a command such as *Make the cow and horse push* to use himself as the agent in pushing both the cow and the horse. Other strategies bear a less clearcut relationship to developmental level. Sinclair and Bronckardt have not considered the possible effect of pragmatic ordering rules on the children's interpretations. It may well be that some children are influenced by so-called stylistic uses of the various orders to focus on elements in the sentence. In any case, the results of the Sinclair and Bronckardt experiment, like those of the Slobin project, indicate that the mechanisms brought to bear on acquisition of order are much more complex than the earlier studies of English had led us to believe.

In more recent proposals for acquisition of word order, there is a tendency to seek a cognitive or semantic basis rather than a purely syntactic set of strategies. Sinclair (1974) has suggested that the child's concept of ordered constituents may be based on earlier sensorimotor action patterns—the literal ordering of objects in time and space, lining them up together in play, etc. Brown (1973) and Bowerman (1973) both point to the fact that early English speech obeys semantic ordering principles such as Agent–Action. They suggest that these semantic rules may in turn reflect perceptually natural arrangements based on the way the child actually perceives agents, actions, and results in time. Finally, McNeill (1974) seems to have radically altered his earlier position concerning word order development, suggesting now that the child's notion of ordering may be derived from preverbal action schemes that are interiorized and extended to ordering in speech.

To summarize thus far, in the 1960s it was suggested that the syntactic subject is the starting point for language acquisition. In the late 1960s and early 1970s, it was proposed instead that children may use semantic notions such as agent to form their first hypotheses about grammar. In this chapter, we will suggest that pragmatic factors of topicalization and focus also influence the acquisition of syntax, from the very first two-word combinations.

Although most of the major articles on semantic bases of language acquisition ignore pragmatic factors, this is NOT the first time that pragmatic factors have been mentioned in word order research. Gruber (1967) and Menyuk (1969) both noted that the speech of English-speaking children from 2 years of age onward can be described with a TOPIC–COMMENT ordering rule. Gruber went so far as to suggest that children may begin with the pragmatic concept of topic, as a heuristic that eventually leads them to a grammar based on the more abstract syntactic notion of subject.

Note, however, that the ordering rule described by Gruber is TOPIC–COMMENT, or GIVEN–NEW. On the basis of the model presented in Chapter IV, we have suggested instead that a more natural order for the child's first two-word utterances would be COMMENT–TOPIC or NEW–GIVEN. Is our prediction already disconfirmed by Gruber's findings? Probably not. First of all, Gruber was describing the speech of a 28-month-old child, well beyond the initial stages that will be discussed here. Second, Gruber and Menyuk were both describing the speech of children learning English, a language in which pragmatic TOPIC–COMMENT, semantic AGENT–ACTION, and syntactic SUBJECT–VERB all follow the same high frequency order in adult language. Much of 1960s psycholinguistic research was devoted to demonstrating that frequency—the sine qua non of behaviorist theories of language learning—is not sufficient to account for all aspects of language development. But no one has EVER demonstrated that frequency has no effect on acquisition. It is more likely that all three types of structural principles—pragmatic, semantic, and syntactic—interact with environmental frequency to determine the course of language development.

Finally, there have been a few experimental studies examining the role of topicalization in child language. We will discuss these studies together with our own experiments at the end of this chapter.

How Word Order Works in Italian

Yngve (1960) has claimed that there are no naturally occurring "left-branching non-agglutinative codes" in human language. If hierarchical syntactic–semantic relations are to be retrievable from a linearly ordered sentence, then a language must use one or both of two options

1. Identify the hierarchical roles of constituents by inflections (e.g., accusative case markings for objects).
2. Identify the hierarchical role of a constituent by its order with

respect to other constituents (e.g., the object follows the verb in English declarative sentences).

Chomsky (1957) has noted that there are no completely "order free" languages. All languages show statistical preferences for certain orders, and take order into consideration in transformations. However, inflectional languages tend to take greater stylistic liberties with variations in order than can be permitted in a noninflectional language. Italian has lost the case markings of its parent language, Latin, retaining only the rule of verb agreement for the subject. Hence, it is officially classified as a noninflectional code based on standard SVO order. However, casual Italian speech permits much greater flexibility in word order than one might expect from Yngve's rules. Under certain circumstances, all possible noun–verb–noun orders can be used grammatically to express a given semantic–syntactic relationship. But when variations do occur, information about syntactic relations is always available in some combination of the following:

1. Indications from the nonverbal context and from previous discourse.

2. The presence of a clitic (a particular type of pronoun which stands for the object) to the left of the verb, as in *Il libro lo compro io*-'The book (it) am buying I'.

3. Contrastive stress and/or pauses marking the pragmatic role of a constituent.

4. Clearcut semantic distinctions (i.e., a naturalness hierarchy) between the subject and object NP's, so that only one interpretation of subject and object roles is possible, e.g.

Giovanni mangia la mela.	'John eats the apple.'
La mela mangia Giovanni.	'The apple eats John.'

5. Number inflections on the verb that automatically assign the role of subject to whichever NP agrees with the verb.

6. First or second person inflections on the verb, which automatically assign the subject role to either the speaker or the hearer, respectively.

All of these factors are apparently involved in a decision to use an alternative word order. Since so many of these factors depend on a realistic discourse context, it is difficult to elicit native speaker judgments for the grammaticality of different word order types. Antinucci, Parisi, and Castelfranchi are currently carrying out an exhaustive study of the pragmatics and semantics of Italian word order. The authors currently believe that the rules may be formulable only within the framework of a larger, discourse grammar specifying topic and comment relations, and other presuppositions from one sentence to another.

Table 6 presents permissible and unpermissible orders, with and without contrastive stress, for sentences presented out of context (from

Table 6 Grammaticality of Various NVN Orders in Italian

SVO	*VSO	*SOV
NVN	VNN	NNV
*OVS	*VOS	*OSV
_S_VO	*V_S_O	*_S_VO
_N_VN	V_N_N	_N_NV
OV_S_	VO_S_	O_S_V
SV_O_	VS_O_	S_O_V
NV_N_	VN_N_	N_N_V
*_O_VS	V_O_S	*_O_SV

Antinucci et al.). In all the cases presented, the subject and object NP's are not semantically interchangeable (e.g., *Lenin quotes Marx* for those in possession of the correct historical sequence).

These 18 possibilities can also be varied for the presence or absence of the object clitic always in a fixed position to the left of the verb. Such clitic pronouns can be anaphoric, in that they stand for an object NP that is not expressed in the surface form of the sentence, e.g., *Lo compro* 'It I buy'. Or they can be cross–referential, serving as a redundant marking for an object NP that is expressed in the same sentence, e.g., *Il libro lo compro* 'The book it I buy'. By varying the combinations in Table 6 for presence and absence of a cross–referential clitic, the number of possibilities is raised to 36. It appears from Antinucci et al. that once the pronominal cross-referent is added (and in some cases with appropriate pauses between constituents), most native speakers will accept practically all of the 18 possible order–stress combinations. It is noteworthy, however, that natives will often add some comment of the type "That one is okay in a context in which. . . ." Finally, Antinucci et al. plan to vary the sentences for the interchangeability of NP's within semantic roles (e.g., *John kisses Mary* versus *John eats the apple*), raising the number of combinations to 72. However, there seem to be degrees of interchangeability between NP's. For example, *The lion ate the sheep* is mildly resistant to role switching, while *The lion ate the cottage cheese* is far more resistant. Such scalar relations would raise the table to an indefinite number of possible combinations.

Some sentence types, for example the Italian equivalent of WH-questions, are more resistant to reordering. The presence of an indirect object also seems to affect the amount of movement that can be tolerated in a sentence. And if there are embedded clauses, standard word order is more likely to be preserved. Predictably, intransitive verbs with subject only can reverse subject order more freely than sentences with transitive verbs.

Finally, in addition to the possibility of alternative orders, Italian also has all the devices that English uses to signal particular topic and focus relations. A neutrally ordered sentence can signal special emphasis through the simple addition of contrastive stress on the item to be emphasized. There are passive transformations, e.g.,

(31)   *Marx é citato da Lenin.*   'Marx is cited by Lenin.'

And there are clefting transformations, e.g.

(32)   *É Lenin che cita Marx.*   'It is Lenin that cites Marx.'

Also, in casual Italian speech the subject of the sentence is often deleted altogether, producing sentences such as

(33)   *Cita Marx.*   *'Cites Marx.'*

Hence, the decision to encode or delete the subject provides another option for expressing logical focus. This option is not available to English speakers, who must obligatorily provide some sort of explicit surface subject in all but simple second person imperative sentences.

At this point it should be clear that Italian word order is not "freer" than English word order. Instead, it is a system with surface flexibility, regulated by a much more complex set of factors than English. Nevertheless, Italians manage this complex interaction of factors with speed and ease; misunderstandings based on the use of nonstandard orders are rare. When they do occur, it is usually the case that the listener fails to make the same presuppositions as the speaker. For example, at a dinner party attended by several anthropologists, a friend and I overheard the phrase

(34)   *Siamo andati in un posto dove*   'We went to a place where
       mangiano i selvaggi.   (they eat) the natives.'

We turned around startled, prepared to hear a story of cannibalistic horrors. Instead, the anecdote dealt with a simple discussion of vegetable cookery, in which the natives were the subject rather than the object of the subordinate clause. Our first, incorrect interpretation had been prepared by (1) a failure to follow the thread of the conversation, and (2) the greater probability of an "eat human" interpretation in a conversation among anthropologists. Under other conditions, the syntactically ambiguous sentence should have been clear on semantic and pragmatic grounds.

Italian children also manage to disentangle the web of interdependent relations, computing syntactic, semantic, and pragmatic factors to understand and produce various sentence orders. It will no doubt take psycholinguists years to determine how they go about it. In the present study, we will restrict ourselves to the acquisition of optional subject final orders versus standard SVO, with particular regard to the presuppositional relations underlying emphasis and topicalization.

In the longitudinal data, we will begin by examining the transcripts of Claudia and Francesco to determine the frequency of various types of constituent ordering. Then we will look at a series of factors that may be influencing word order patterns. Keeping in mind the hypotheses put forth in Chapter IV, we are particularly interested in trends that indicate an increase in conscious, reflective control over the process of presupposing.

Finally, in the last section we will present some pilot research on topicalization in 3- to 6-year-old children. These data will be discussed together with results from related projects by other authors.

Longitudinal Evidence

The longitudinal records of Claudia and Francesco were examined for the frequency of various major constituent word orders across development, to determine the sequence in which the standard SVO order and the emphatic subject-final orders are acquired. Since the transcripts were not phonetically transcribed, there is no information concerning contrastive stress either in the children's utterances or in parental speech. Data collection therefore involved a simple count of the incidence of all the following order patterns:

| SV | SVO | SOV | VSO | VO only | SO |
| VS | OVS | OSV | VOS | OV only | OS |

The subject and object roles were assigned on the basis of the way that sentences were used in context; in later sessions, when verb and noun morphology were acquired, the decision to assign the role of subject was also influenced by marking for verb agreement (see Chapter VIII). Contextual information was almost always sufficient to assign the function of subject or object to a given NP. Naturally, these decisions represent an interpretation from the adult point of view. Bloom (1970), Bowerman (1973), and others have used the same method of "rich interpretation" to assign underlying sentence roles. It is possible to obtain high interjudge reliability for such ratings. However, such decisions are clearly based on a mixture of different kinds of information, regarding the use of a given constituent as semantic agent, pragmatic topic, and syntactic subject. It is not entirely clear which of these roles (if any) has any reality from the child's point of view. We will return to this point later.

Since the goal of this analysis was to determine the onset of standard versus alternative SVO orderings, several kinds of utterances are excluded from the count. Copulative sentences (e.g., *This is pretty, That's a doggie*) were considered separately. Also, the Italian equivalent of WH-questions (e.g. *Che fai?* 'What are you doing?') were excluded from the word order count, since the orders for these sentences are fixed in adult language, with

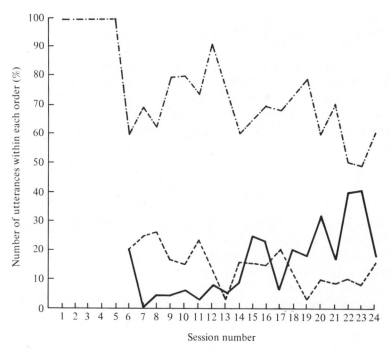

Figure 3. Claudia: Word order preferences in percentages of total utterances across all sessions. V only: – • – • ; SV:——; VS: – – –.

little possibility for pragmatic variation except for special open slot questions such as the English exchange *I am going to Boston—To do what?* For the same reason, sentences with overtly embedded sentence complements were excluded from the count. Such sentences are rarely reordered in the adult language, and they appear late in child speech. We might note at this point that when WH-questions and embedded sentences did appear in the child protocols, they mirrored the high frequency adult order patterns from the beginning. Had we included these fixed patterns in the analysis, they would have artificially inflated the frequencies for one type of ordering. However, it will be possible to determine whether optional ordering patterns are affected by the onset of one or more of these fixed patterns.

Objects clitics are not considered to be object NP's for present purposes. First, their order is fixed to the left of the verb in all major constituent combinations (e.g., *Lo faccio io* 'It I do'), and children respect this obligatory order from their first uses of clitics. Second, since clitics can be either anaphoric (e.g., *Lo faccio io* 'It I do') or coreferential (e.g., *lo faccio io quello* 'It I do it'), the presence of one of these pronouns does not preclude the presence of the object NP for which it stands within the same utterance. Hence, an analysis separating sentences with and without clitics would reveal little about the development of major constituent ordering. The results presented below therefore conflate sentences with clitics and sentences without. The interaction of word order with the use of clitics will be discussed separately.

Finally, the results below do not include a small class of utterances without either implicit or explicit verbs. These include utterances such as *Hi, Daddy* and deictic utterances with the unique Italian deictic term *ecco,* as in *Ecco palla* '(Behold) ball'. In almost all such utterances, children used the same high frequency order observed in adult speech.

To summarize, the data presented below are restricted to utterances using some combination of subject, verb, and object, under conditions that would permit either standard or optional ordering. Tables 7 and 8 present the frequency of each order type by sessions for Claudia and Francesco respectively. Figures 3 and 4 illustrate the percentage of subject-first, subject-final, and subject-free utterances across development, for each child (collapsing transitive and intransitive utterances). The term **subject-first** refers to sentences in which the subject is in standard position. **Subject-final** is a shorthand term to refer to sentences in which the subject follows the object and/or the verb. For example, a VSO order will be called subject-final.

The data are rather complex, and we shall have to wind our way through them a little at a time. To begin with, the developmental sequences illustrated in Figures 3 and 4 are strikingly different from the patterns of development reported for English-speaking children. As Brown (1973), Braine (1973), and others have observed, the earliest speech of

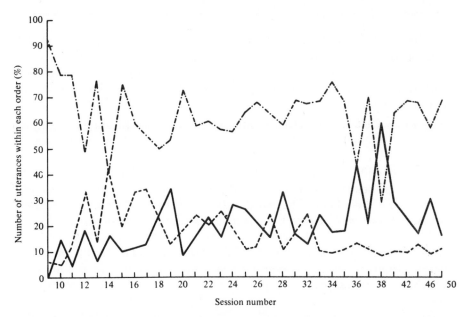

Figure 4. Francesco: Word order preferences in percentages of total utterances across all sessions. V only: – • – •; SV:——; VS: – – –.

Table 7   Frequency of Utterances of Each SVO Order
Claudia

Session	SV	VS	OV	VO	SO	OS	V only	SVO	SOV	OVS	OSV	VSO	VOS
1		1		3	1		3						
2		2	1	4	1		10						
3				6			11						
4				2		3	7						
5							3						
6	2	3		1	2	1	7	1					
7		6	3	9	1	1	10					2	
8	10	19	2	10		1	13	2		1			
9	3	7	1	29			22			3			
10	5	14	3	22			75	2		1		1	1
11	2	16	2	7			52					2	
12	2	8	2	18	1	1	36	4		1			
13	2	1		14			24						
14	9	18	3	20			81	3		1		3	1
15	16	13	5	36			32	14		4		2	1
16	24	20	5	32	1		71	13				1	
17	9	23		23			82	3				7	3
18	19	15	3	19			68	9			1	1	
19	9	1	1	25			45	7					1
20	19	12	4	31	1		43	25				1	
21	16	9		24	1		65	4					
22	19	12	6	33			46	16	1	1		2	
23	13	33	5	69			70	21		1	1	3	2
24	34	12	3	25			52	32		2		1	1

children acquiring English shows a high percentage of SVO or SV constructions, with variants dropping out monotonically until the children preserve word order as rigidly as adults. With Italian children, there is a very different pattern. We can discern four rough stages, summarized as follows:

1. From C1 to C12 for Claudia (ages 1;3 to 1;9) and from F1 to F19 for Francesco (ages 1;4 to 2;0), there is actually a statistical preference for subject-final constructions.

2. Around MLU 3.0 for both children, a long period of alternating "strategies" begins, with subject-final predominating in some sessions, and subject-first in others. The word "strategies" is placed in quotes here because it may well be that the alternation is entirely random.

3. Then, fairly late in development (around MLU 4.0), both children spend several sessions in which SVO is more rigidly preserved. During this period, there is also a tendency to express the subject in sentences in which adults would delete them. For example, in Francesco's records we find

> *Io mangio alle otto e dieci,*   'I eat at eight-ten, I return.'
> *io ritonno.*

Table 8   Frequency of Utterances of Each SVO Order
Francesco

Session	SV	VS	VO	OV	SO	OS	V only	SVO	SOV	OVS	OSV	VSO	VOS
1							3						
2							3						
3			2				18						
4							5						
5			1				26						
6							9						
7							6						
8						1	14						1
9			4		1		10						
10	3	1	1		1		15						
11		3	3				13	1					
12	2	3	2	1	1	2	5	1		1			2
13	2	5	5			1	20						
14	3	11	1		1	2	13			3	1		
15	1	3	3				19	1		1			
16	5	14	8		2	3	22	1		1		2	
17	1	14	15		1	4	12			1			3
18	1	7	7				16	2		1		1	3
19	17	2	12		1	1	19	2		2		1	2
20	4	8	9			1	44	2		3		1	2
21	14	16	26	1	1		38	1		1		2	10
22	11	13	22				36	9		1		1	2
23	12	23	29		1	1	28	5		1		2	2
24	13	9	27	2			19	12		1		3	1
25	12	5	20	1			30	10		1		2	
26	8	9	34		1		41	16		2			1
27	5	14	13				28	5				1	
28	22	7	20	3			23	10				1	1
29	9	12	15	7			27	3				1	1
32	3	12	6	1			28	3					1
33	10	9	21	1			30	7			1		
34	10	6	29				41	7		3			
35	8	6	17	2			30	7		1		1	
36	21	9	13		1	2	27	18	1	1		1	1
37	15	9	22				60	9			1		
38	39	10	15				21	27				1	
41	11	5	12	1			24	4	1				
42	12	5	19	1			37	7				1	
43	5	8	15	2			20	4					
45	27	11	18				46	2	1				
50	17	12	44	3			53	6				3	1

Such repetition of the subject pronoun would be quite unusual in adult speech.

4. After the above "conservative" period, both children take on adult patterns of optional ordering and subject deletion.

The first question that comes to mind is, where does this early preference for subject-final orders come from? As we noted earlier, the subject of the sentence is usually the pragmatic topic of that sentence. Hence, a first hypothesis, based on our discussion of topic and comment at the one-word stage, is that what appears to be a subject-final strategy may in fact reflect a more basic tendency to put new information or "comment" first, adding the topic on at the end with leftover processing space. But before we accept this interpretation, we must consider a number of competing hypotheses concerning environmental frequency, and semantic–syntactic ordering constraints.

As Bowerman (1969) and MacWhinney (1975b) have recommended, we will first consider the possibility that adult frequency for various orders has influenced the child's speech. We have already noted that where the adults do provide highly consistent order models, Claudia and Francesco seem to adopt that order. This is true for word–based patterns such as *Hi, Daddy* and *ecco palla*. It is true for the Italian equivalent of WH-questions and for embedded sentences. It is then quite possible that the first order patterns adopted by Claudia and Francesco for subject, verb, and object reflect high frequency patterns in the speech addressed to the children. To check this hypothesis, three transcripts were randomly selected from Francesco's and Claudia's records. The frequencies of the various orders in adult speech are presented in Table 9.

These adult counts were made with exactly the same criteria as the child counts, excluding WH-questions and embedded sentences, copulative sentences, and ritualized verb free patterns such as *hi* and *ecco*. Sentences with and without clitic pronouns were considered together. The adult transcripts show a clear preference for VO as opposed to OV orders, and this preference is reflected in the tendency for both children to preserve VO ordering. However, there does not seem to be a model for the subject-final preference by children. In two of the three transcripts, there is some preference in adult speech for subject-final over subject-first when there is no object, or when the object is expressed with a clitic only. But when the object is expressed with an NP, then SVO ordering predominates. Collapsing across the various NP conditions, we find that adults are equally likely to use subject-final and subject-first. Hence, the children could not have derived their S-final preference through simple modelling of adult frequencies. Furthermore, this finding must be weighed

Table 9 Adult Order Patterns in Three Transcripts

Session	SV	VS	OV	VO	SVO	SOV	OVS	OSV	VSO	VOS
24 (C)	20	34	14	72	14	1	1	0	2	0
22 (F)	15	14	3	35	17	0	0	0	2	0
21 (F)	11	21	3	43	5	0	1	0	1	0

against the fact that by far the most common sentence type in adult Italian is a sentence with no expressed subject whatsoever. Models for subject position can be found in only 30 to 40% of adult utterances. This makes it even less likely that children acquire their early preference for S-final by imitating high frequency adult forms.

Although simple frequency alone will not account for this early S-final strategy, it is still possible that adult S-final sentences are in some way more salient, and therefore more likely to be imitated. Since SVO is the neutral order, and the various S-final orders generally involve special focusing and topicalization, it is possible that S-final sentences contain contrastive stress and hence are more likely to be noted by the child. Is the subject more likely to receive contrastive stress in adult speech in sentences with alternative orders? Since the transcripts for Claudia and Francesco are not phonetically transcribed, this cannot be determined for adult speech to children. However, referring back to Table 6 (the Anti-nucci et al. analysis of order and stress patterns for isolated sentences without clitics), we find that subjects are generally NOT stressed when they appear in alternative orders. Of the four possible combinations in which an S-final subject is stressed, only one (VOS) is grammatical. However, this analysis pertains only to sentences with expressed object NP's. The subject CAN receive contrastive stress in postverb position in sentences in which there is no object or in sentences with clitic objects only. Hence, it is at least possible that adult S-final sentences are particularly salient to the child because they are more likely to receive contrastive stress.

There is another reason why S-final sentences might be more perceptually salient. Since alternative orders are always adapted either to topicalize the object strongly, or to focus strongly on the subject, these orders are almost always used in pragmatically interesting or highlighted circumstances. For example, a subject-final order is likely to occur when there is an argument over who will carry out a given act, e.g.,

(35)   *Lo fai **tu**? No, lo*   'Are YOU doing it?' 'No,
       *faccio **io**!*   I'M doing it!'

Hence it is possible that children hear alternative orders in circumstances that are particularly likely to hold their attention.

We are, then, still left with the hypothesis that children pattern their early S-final sentences on pragmatically salient adult speech. Antinucci (personal communication) has carried out an informal analysis of order patterns for one 15 minute tape of adult–adult speech. He finds that only 8% of utterances are subject-final. Compare this with the adult–child records in which 50% of sentences with expressed subjects have pragmatically salient alternative orders. This presents an interesting candidate for the growing literature on "motherese" (e.g., Drach, 1969; Snow, 1972; Shatz & Gelman, 1973). In examining the speech of English mothers and their children, investigators have noted that adults (and sometimes older children) present simplified versions of their language to young children, exaggerating the prosodic contours and reducing the syntactic complexity of their utterances from the adult–adult standard. In most cases, such simplification will work to provide the child with a clear and accurate model of basic grammatical structure. But it should be kept in mind that most adults are NOT following a child development textbook in designing their utterances. Rather, they use the same tools that they would use with other adults to make a sentence more emphatic, explicit, or clear (Wertsch, 1974). Fortunately for children, such efforts usually result in a textbook model of English (or Italian) syntax. But when an Italian adult follows his pragmatic instincts in trying to speak clearly for an unreliable listener, he will fall back on topicalization and focusing rules which, in this particular case, contrast with the neutral declarative order patterns of Italian (i.e. SVO). In trying very hard to be understood, e.g.,

(36)   *Lo faccio io? Lo fai tu?*   'Shall I do it?' 'Shall YOU do it?'

the Italian adult ends up by presenting his children with the wrong model for mastering standard Italian SVO order. By contrast, an English speaking adult who follows the same kind of pragmatic instincts for emphasizing sentence constituents will present HIS child with an acoustically clear SVO model in almost every instance.

Hence we are left with the interesting and plausible hypothesis that adult pragmatic ordering rules interfere with the child's acquisition of pragmatically neutral SVO order. However, there is reason to believe that the situation is still more complex, and that this hypothesis alone will not suffice.

First of all, if the children are simply imitating acoustically clear sub-ject-final models, we might expect them to imitate stressed intonation contours as well. Again, the transcripts for Claudia and Francesco do not have intonational information. To obtain some idea of the stress patterns accompanying subject-final and subject-first orders by children, I returned to several of the original tapes for Francesco. Around F24, when the subject-final strategy has been replaced and Francesco alternates between S-first and S-final orders, the stress patterns sound very much like those of Italian adults, with intonational highlighting on an NP containing new information, or information that is being questioned or argued about. However, in the earlier sessions, when S-final predominates, there is a peculiar intonation pattern that is quite unlike adult stress. It is quite clear in these tapes that S is NOT the stressed element in subject-final sentences. In fact, it appears that the opposite is true, giving the sentences a bizarre and unadult quality. Where there is something like contrastive stress, it seems to fall on the first major constituent of the sentence. One of the most illustrative examples is in an utterance without a verb (and hence excluded from the original count):

Checco pure.   'CHECCO too.'

To imagine the unnaturalness of this utterance for an adult, the reader is invited to try saying **Me** too several times to himself, providing stressed intonation on the pronoun rather than the adverbial too. The effect is strange in English, and it is equally strange for an Italian adult. Of course, this pattern will have to be examined in a detailed phonological analysis of the same transcripts before any conclusions can be drawn. My own observations are clearly insufficient. However, there are indications that (1) some kind of pragmatic stress pattern does exist in the earliest records, and (2) the emphasis pattern appears to have little directly to do with the adult S-final construction.

Further support for the hypothesis that early S-final is not an emphasis pattern for the child comes from an examination of the context of use for S-final versus S-first utterances in Francesco's records. Four transcripts were selected at various points in the acquisition curve in Figure 4: F17, when S-final still predominates; F21, when strategies begin to alternate; F38, when SVO is rigid and frequent; F50, when patterns are clearly adult-like. All subject-free, subject-final, and subject-first sentences were examined in the light of their nonverbal context (e.g., Francesco and the adult are reading a book) and/or the parental utterance immediately preceding and following the child's utterance. The child's utterances were considered to be contrastive in the context if the nonverbal situation involved a contrast of subject (e.g., an argument over who would read the book), and/or if the child's utterance provided the sentence subject as new or contrasting information in response to adult speech. This classification of utterances yields the results presented in Table 10.

These figures indicate that the S-final construction IS used for contrast in F38 and F50. In the early records, however, there is no clear indication that S-final constructions are pragmatically different from S-first utterances. When this small analysis is considered together with the

Table 10 Pragmatic Contrast as a Function of Child Order Patterns

	F17		F21		F38		F50	
	No. of utterances	Percent which contrast	No. of utterances	Percent	No. of utterances	Percent	No. of utterances	Percent
V only	27	0	65	6	36	14	100	0
S-first	2	0	15	37	66	15	23	18
S-final	18	16	29	42	11	63	10	62

indications from contrastive stress, it seems clear that the early S-final strategy by Italian children is NOT, in any clearcut way, an attempt to express emphasis on the final major constituent. Also the peculiar stress pattern that is given to S-final sentences suggests that they are not direct imitations of adult stressed S-final utterances. Hence, whereas it is possible that adult pragmatic efforts to simplify speech account for the ABSENCE of an SVO model for children, it does not seem likely that children adopt their initial S-final strategy by imitating adult pragmatic efforts.

To summarize thus far, it is unlikely that the early tendency for Claudia and Francesco to use subject final orders is a simple reflection of adult frequency. It IS possible that adult subject-final sentences are more noticeable because of their pragmatic salience. However, an examination of both contrastive stress and pragmatic use in the children's early utterances indicates that the early subject-final pattern is not at all similar to the adult subject-final pattern. The children are in no way focusing or stressing the subject in early VS sentences, whereas their later VS sentences do tend to focus the subject and/or topicalize the object. In fact, there is some indication that contrastive stress generally falls on the first element in early subject-final utterances. This lends still stronger support to our first hypothesis, that early in the two-word stage children extend the strategy of the one-word stage, by blurting out the most new, interesting, and informative element first.

However, we still have not considered the possibility that the various stages in ordering are affected by competing semantic–syntactic factors. Why does the initial subject-final tendency drop out around F20 and C13? What kinds of semantic and syntactic developments accompany this shift?

In both children, the S-final preference drops off around MLU 3.0. However, this does not seem to be attributable to a simple increase in number of words. The first sentences by both children encoding subject, verb, and object together are definitely S-final constructions (see Tables 6 and 7). In Francesco's records, the first 3-term sentence is subject-final, and S-final continues to predominate in 3-term sentences until F22. In Claudia's records, 3-term sentences are evenly divided between subject-first and subject-final until around C15 to 17. HENCE, THE CHILDREN ARE NOT FORCED INTO THE ADULT ORDER PATTERN SIMPLY BY INCREASED SENTENCE SIZE.

ANOTHER FACTOR WHICH DOES NOT SEEM TO AFFECT THE S-FINAL PREFERENCE IS MASTERY OF CLITIC OBJECT PRENOMINALS. It is difficult to determine precisely when this morpheme is acquired. Roger Brown (1973) has described the acquisition of inflections as a sort of "ivy growing up between the semantic building blocks of Stage 1." He reports that the acquisition of inflections in English involves a monotonic increase in the usage of a morpheme in obligatory contexts, rather than sudden "moments" in which inflections are used properly. This is true in the case of Italian clitics as well, and is further complicated by two other factors. First, the earliest object clitics in the records are poorly articulated "schwas" that cannot be clearly distinguished in terms of number or gender, nor are they always distinguishable from reflexive *si* clitics, or other Italian open vowel sounds. Second, the notion of obligatory context is not entirely applicable to Italian object clitics, since they not only substitute for object NP's (anaphoric clitics) but also may cooccur with them within a given utterance (coreferential clitics). However, by C7 and F12, schwas used correctly in object clitic position can be found, and their use increases gradually from then on. There is no direct relationship to the eventual switch in word order strategies. For example, the schwas do not become phonetically clearer at the time when order strategies reverse.

Sentences were also divided into transitive and intransitive to determine whether this distinction affected the decrease in S-final utterances. However, both S-first and S-final utterances appear to be evenly distributed between transitive and intransitive. This is true in the earliest records, and there is no apparent switch at any point in the transcripts.

To summarize thus far, there are at least three syntactic–semantic developments which clearly are NOT related to the switch from S-final ordering. There is no clear relationship to increase in MLU. Mastery of clitic pronouns is a long and gradual process that begins early in the S-final period and continues without affecting ordering in any obvious way. There does not seem to be any shift in the frequency or use of transitive versus intransitive verbs, so the initial preference for S-final (more permissible in the adult language with intransitive verbs) cannot be attributed to an initial predominance of intransitives. We have already mentioned that embedded sentences appear relatively late, well after the shift from VS to SV. When they do appear, SVO is respected from the outset.

Recall that copulative sentences were excluded from the count. In adult speech (including the speech addressed to Claudia and Francesco) there is considerable variation in order for copulative sentences (e.g., *Maria é bella* 'Mary is pretty' versus *É bella Maria* 'Is pretty Mary'). In Francesco's earliest records, orders were fairly evenly divided between Noun–Predicate Adjective versus Predicate Adjective–Noun, and Noun–Predicate Nominative versus Predicate Nominative–Noun. Around the same time that S-final drops out as a preferred order, there is an increase in both N–PA and N–PN orders. This is consistent with a switch toward higher probability for a Subject–Predicate order after MLU 3.0. However, it is unlikely that there is a cause and effect relationship between these two events. It is more likely that they are parallel manifestations of some underlying shift.

In short, there is no evidence that grammatical devices related to major constituent ordering affect the switch from S-final to S-first in any direct way. However, there is one interesting coincidence that may be related to the shift in subject orders. For both Claudia and Francesco, during the period in which the dominant order is S-final, it is also the case that the speaker and hearer are always referred to by proper names instead of personal pronouns. For example, instead of saying *I eat,* the child says *Claudia eats.* Furthermore, during the period in which both children begin to alternate between subject-final and subject-first from one session to another, they also begin to alternate between using the speaker and hearer's names, and using the subject pronouns *io* 'I' and *tu* 'you'. Finally, the use of proper names to map speaker and hearer drops out entirely (at a time corresponding to metapragmatic Stage 3, as discussed in the previous chapter). During the period of alternation between names and subject pronouns, both children generally assign correct subject–verb agreement. Prior to that time, subject–verb agreement is the accidental product of the fact that the children use one unmarked form of the verb to serve almost all functions. Since the unmarked form of the verb is generally the third person singular, and since first, second, and third person subjects are all encoded as proper names, there is subject–verb agreement in the vast majority of relevant sentences. However, the notion of subject–verb agreement is only meaningful when the child clearly has productive control over person and number for both verbs and nouns. Hence, it would be correct to conclude that subject pronouns, subject–verb agreement, and alternation between SV and VS all begin around the same time. During the period in which the children alternate between SV and VS, and between subject pronouns and proper names, both types of sentence subjects can appear either before or after the verb. However, it is interesting that the first utterance in which Francesco uses both types of subject, *Checco* (Francesco) is found in the S-final position, and *io* is in S-initial:

> *Io talo, batte Checco qua.*   'I cut, hits Checco here.'

Finally, during the brief period in which Francesco and Claudia use an abnormally high percentage of rigid SVO sentences, they also use an abnormally high percentage of subject pronouns (particularly *io* and *tu*), encoding the subject in a context in which an adult would delete it. Hence, there is a sort of parallel conservatism in the tendency to preserve SVO and the tendency to encode subject pronouns explicitly where they are contextually obvious.

All of these concurrent developments may of course be sheer coincidence. While two children are better than one, it would certainly be useful to replicate this finding with a larger sample. However, there is a speculative but intriguing interpretation for these results. PERHAPS THESE CHILDREN DISCOVER SVO, SUBJECT PRONOUNS, AND SUBJECT–VERB AGREEMENT AROUND THE SAME TIME BECAUSE THEY HAVE JUST DISCOVERED THE CONCEPT OF SYNTACTIC

SUBJECT. Prior to that time, semantic agents were mapped like other arguments of the predicate, in accordance with their relative usefulness as a comment or topic.

This interpretation would be quite consistent with recent formulations by Fillmore (1968) and Chafe (1970) that "subjectivalization" is a transformation on underlying semantic structure, one which works differently in accusative languges such as English and Italian versus ergative languages such as Chinook and Dyurbal. Fillmore's term "secondary topicalization" (similar to emphasis or expressive focus) would therefore be an earlier acquisition than "primary topicalization," which refers to the creation of a sentence subject.

Let us assume for the moment that this interpretation is correct, that in the early stages Francesco and Claudia have no concept of syntactic subject. Therefore the so-called subject–final strategy cannot have anything directly to do with the mapping of subjects. What looks from the adult point of view like a syntactic strategy would necessarily be an epiphenomenon of some other type of mapping principle. We still could not conclude whether the child's principle is a pragmatic rule or a semantic rule. On the one hand, an apparent S-final tendency could be produced by a rule for mapping the pragmatic focus first and the pragmatic topic second. On the other hand, the same surface pattern could result from either an agent-final rule or from some kind of a predicate-fronting rule.

There is support for the semantic PREDICATE–ARGUMENT ordering rule from several sources. Park (1974) has reported that the earliest sentences of his German subjects tend to reflect some principle of verb fronting (although this stage rapidly gives way to verb-final utterances). Radulovij (1975) has noted that in the very first samples for her subjects there is also a tendency for verb fronting, although this is followed soon thereafter by an extremely conservative period of SVO ordering. It is even true that one of Braine's English subjects (Braine, 1973) produced an early pivot–open pattern that could also be explained as verb–initial. This English case is particularly surprising, since so many authors have reported a high preference for SUBJECT–VERB or AGENT–ACTION from the outset for English-speaking children. MacWhinney (1974) observes that the first stage for his Hungarian subjects could be described by either a VERB–ARGUMENT rule or by a FIGURE–GROUND rule. He notes that it is very difficult to choose between the semantic and pragmatic descriptions, since the two consistently overlap. In addition to the fact that agent-subjects often tend to be pragmatic topics, it is also true that verbs tend to contain novel, interesting, or important information.

Is there any way that we can pull the semantic and pragmatic alternatives apart? We have no conclusive evidence, but there are some reasons for preferring the pragmatic COMMENT–TOPIC strategy to the semantic VERB–ARGUMENT strategy. First of all, while it is certainly true that

V–NP or PREDICATE–ARGUMENT orders predominate in the early transcripts for Claudia and Francesco, NP–V or ARGUMENT–PREDI-CATE orders do occasionally occur. While this finding weakens the case for a true semantic rule, it would not detract from a pragmatic COM-MENT–TOPIC rule, since it could well be, in certain contexts, that verbs furnish old information while the new information is found among the arguments of the verb.

A better solution still would be to redo the entire longitudinal analysis in terms of new information, old information, comment and topic, instead of the intuitive, mixed SVO analysis reported here. Unfortunately, the transcripts of Claudia and Francesco were made only with semantic considerations in mind. There is often incidental pragmatic information, suggesting that one piece of information is particularly new and important (e.g., Francesco and his mother are arguing over who will carry out a given act, hence the agent is focused information). However, there is frequently too little information in the transcripts for reliable pragmatic analyses. Around the time that I had completed the preceding analyses and was puzzling over the question of pragmatic evidence, I came across a study by Baroni, Fava, and Tirondola (1973) at the University of Padova. These authors reported on a longitudinal study of word order acquisition by six Italian children. The period described in the study corresponds to the level of linguistic maturity of Claudia and Francesco when S-final was a dominant strategy. The authors report that child speech in this period is in apparent violation of adult ordering norms. Although their data are not analyzed in terms of adult categories such as subject–object, their exam-ples look very much like the early S-final speech of Claudia and Fran-cesco. Baroni et al. designed, transcribed, and analyzed their study entirely in terms of the pragmatic distinction between new versus old information, as determined from both the verbal and nonverbal context. While there are still problems with determining new versus old informa-tion a posteriori (problems which we will return to in the next section), the fact that they had this distinction in mind prior to data transcription means that there is more pragmatic context available in their transcripts for assigning topic and focus roles. First, the authors excluded from their analysis certain word–based, ritualized patterns that do not permit alternative ordering (e.g., *ecco palla* 'behold ball'). When these word-based utterances are removed, the remaining data can best be described with a single ordering rule:

NEW INFORMATION FIRST—OLD INFORMATION SECOND

[See MacWhinney (1975b) for a more detailed description of the interac-tion between word based patterns and pragmatic ordering.] The Baroni et al. analysis included not only the agent–action–object meanings that pre-dominate in our data, but also locative patterns, predicate nominatives, predicate adjectives, genitives—the range of case structures that were analyzed together as "copulative sentences" in our data. These findings are compatible with the small contrastive stress and context analyses carried out in Francesco's transcripts, although the Baroni et al. data are probably more trustworthy than ours for such pragmatic analyses.

The Baroni et al. study, together with data on early verb fronting in several languages, lend support to our hypothesis that the child's first ordering strategy will be NEW-OLD or COMMENT-TOPIC. After this initial stage, children learning various languages seem to go in different directions, probably influenced by the different semantic–syntactic mapping constraints of their particular language. These findings can also be taken as support for the Fillmore-Chafe[3] position, in which primary topicalization or subjectivalization develops out of the effort to coordinate pragmatic and semantic demands on a limited, linear mapping system.

Gruber (1967) was perhaps the first writer in recent psycholinguistic history to suggest that children acquire the pragmatic topic/comment division first, and use those two concepts as heuristics leading them to an eventual mastery of the syntactic subject–predicate distinction. And yet, as noted earlier, Gruber's own observations suggest a universal TOPIC-COMMENT ordering, the opposite of the pragmatic rule observed here. Again we should stress that Gruber was analyzing the speech of a 28-month old child, well beyond the very early stage described here as verb fronting or comment fronting. Perhaps his data reflect the same kind of semantic AGENT-ACTION ordering that Bowerman and Brown have discussed for their English data. It is also possible that the supposed TOPIC-COMMENT rule may result from the second pragmatic strategy we proposed earlier, in which topic is ordered first in response to the listener's needs.

To sort out the difference between semantic and pragmatic ordering strategies, it might be worthwhile to reexamine earlier studies reporting "peculiar" or varying order patterns. For example, Bowerman reported that her Finnish children varied word order freely, with the probability of each order directly reflecting the probability of that order in adult speech. She did not, however, examine possible pragmatic differences in the use of various word orders. It may be that these seemingly free uses of order actually reflect underlying topic–focus constraints on ordering, distributed unevenly across major semantic constituents. Another example of a peculiar child order pattern comes from Slobin's report on Gvozdev's Russian data, in which the Russian child strongly preferred a word order

---

[3] Lakoff (1975) has recently suggested that the entire syntax may be perfectly predictable from the assignment of semantic and pragmatic roles, and the constraints imposed by the linear acoustic–articulatory channel for mapping those roles. His recent position would be an even stronger statement of the position that notions such as syntactic subject are derived from efforts to coordinate pragmatic and semantic roles.

that was NOT the statistically most frequent order in adult speech. It would be interesting to determine the pragmatic function of the particular word order chosen by this child.

Recall, however, that children in several of these studies were quite able to discern and use high frequency ordering patterns in adult speech, including specific word-based patterns (such as *Ecco palla* in Italian), and semantic patterns such as AGENT-ACTION. We are not about to suggest a universal and/or innate pragmatic strategy that should hold for all children in all places learning all languages. Rather, the acquisition of word order probably reflects an interaction of internal pragmatic and semantic constraints, and high frequency environmental models, all competing for limited channel use during communication. The one point we have tried to stress in this chapter is that pragmatic factors can make crucial contributions to the acquisition of syntax. Indeed, questions of topicalization and focus are probably so important in language acquisition that we cannot hope to make sense of word order data without them.

Which brings us to a final point. Pragmatic factors are extremely difficult to study, particularly in post hoc analyses of free speech data. While we can occasionally assign topic and focus roles on the basis of objective contextual factors (e.g., arguments over who will do what, what we shall do next, etc.), we often risk circular analyses in which we assign pragmatic roles on the basis of linguistic factors, and then analyze the same linguistic factors on the basis of their pragmatic use. There is a way out of the circle, but it requires a lot of hard experimental work. The only way to be at all sure of pragmatic roles such as topic and focus is to assign them ourselves, and then watch the child's reaction. We will now examine a few pilot experiments designed along such lines. The results of these experiments are still inconclusive, although interesting. Above all, they are interesting as illustrations of methods and problems in studying pragmatic factors in development.

Some Pilot Experiments on Word Order and Topicalization in Child Language

In the longitudinal data presented so far, our approach has been to observe major constituent ordering in child speech, and infer the pragmatic use of various orderings from the verbal and nonverbal context. This approach has yielded some interesting possibilities, and does conclusively support our contention that pragmatic factors affect the acquisition of syntax. But the assignment of pragmatic roles on the basis of semantic and contextual information is often difficult when the real "here and now" speaker–listener context has been distilled on paper. We can be more certain of the pragmatic role for a given piece of information IF WE PROVIDE THAT ROLE OURSELVES, in a controlled, experimental context.

The first experiment to be examined here is a sentence imitation task, administered in a situation highly biased in favor of one interpretation of semantic agent, syntactic subject, and pragmatic topic and focus. The child was asked to imitate a series of sentences describing this biased situation. Some of these sentences were compatible with the context, and others were not. The goal of the study was to determine whether the child would change incompatible sentences models to correspond to the established semantic–pragmatic conditions.

Subjects were 60 Italian children attending middle-class preschools in the Rome area. The children ranged in age from 3 to 6 years, with a mean age of 4;6. Each child was tested individually at the school by two experimenters, in a room near the child's classroom. The child was seated at a table with an array of small plastic animals and a toy telephone. The telephone was battery operated, and communicated with another receiver several feet away, handled by the Italian assistant. The child was immediately introduced to a large handpuppet of a lion, who was busy chasing the small plastic animals around the table in an attempt to "eat them all up." The child was then instructed that the phone would ring, and that he would hear a sentence that he must repeat exactly. When the child had repeated the sentence (regardless of his version of the model), the lion would then proceed in an effort to catch and eat the animal described in the model sentence.

It might be useful to note at this point why we chose such an elaborate and questionable telephone procedure. The answer is simple, although we do not know the reasons for the problem. Italian children simply refuse to imitate. Unlike their American counterparts, who willingly obey the instruction "I'm going to say something and you say it after me," Italian children stare at an adult who issues such an instruction as though he were mad. I had been told prior to piloting that I would not succeed in eliciting straight imitations. My colleagues, as I soon discovered, were correct. The telephone technique, on the other hand, provided the Italian children with a reasonable context for repeating sentences to an experimenter. Unfortunately, although this technique enabled us to elicit sentence imitations, it also provided us with a number of interesting but unwanted examples of reported discourse, e.g., *The lady said that* (*x*). In fact, I recommend this technique as a means for eliciting reported discourse.

The children heard a series of active, declarative sentences describing the lion's consummatory activities with sheep, cows, giraffes, etc. Recall that the lion was approximately 20 times the size of his small prey. It is hence quite unlikely that the child would mistake the eater for the eaten. The first stimulus sentences were not directly related to word order, but served as ancillary data for a separate study of conditional and subjunctive verbs (see Chapter VII). Included in these first sentences were examples such as

| *Il leone vorrebbe mangiare la pecora.* | 'The lion would like to eat the sheep.' |

After these training sentences, each child was given nine sentences in which the major constituent order was varied, with contrastive stress on one or another of two NP's. Sentences were without coreferential clitic pronouns. The 18 possible order/stress combinations in Table 6 were randomly divided into two sets, so that half the subjects received one set and half received the other (no child would sit still for a full 18 items). The sentences included the following:

*Il leone mangia la **pecora**.*	'The lion eats the SHEEP.'
*La **mucca** il leone mangia.*	'The COW the lion eats.'
*Il **leone** mangia la giraffa.*	'The LION eats the giraffe.'

The various animal objects (giraffes, cows, etc.) were randomly varied within each order type to prevent a differential effect in terms of the "eatability" of the object NP itself.

There are some definite experimental flaws in this task. First, there is the problem that the telephone situation tends to elicit reported discourse (e.g., *The lady said the lion eats the sheep*). Since so little is known about the operation of pragmatic factors in direct versus reported discourse, it is hard to know how to handle these responses. Second, one of the most unnatural aspects of the task lies in the fact that the child is asked to repeat declarative sentences, which are then acted out by the lion. Hence, the children are tempted to talk directly to the lion, reformulating the sentences into imperatives, e.g., *Eat the sheep, lion*. However, it was certainly clear that the children enjoyed the task immensely. Hence, if some of these problems can be worked out this technique will be a useful tool for future research.

To summarize, the situation was strongly biased for three interpretations:

1. That the lion was the semantic agent (i.e., the animal doing the eating).

2. That the lion was the syntactic subject of the verb "eat".

3. That the lion was the old information, or topic, held constant from one sentence to another, while the object NP was the focus, varying across all model sentences.

It was hypothesized that children would have more difficulty imitating those sentences whose surface form clashed with the above interpretations. It was further hypothesized that changes in imitation of the model would be in the direction of bringing the sentence into line with the above interpretations.

The first hypothesis was partially supported, in that sentences incompatible with both the agent and focus in the situation were correctly imitated significantly less often (χ^2–5.726, $p < .05$). However, the greatest difficulty in this particular task lay not with the pragmatic focus, but with matching the semantic agent–object relations in the sentence with those in the situation. Focus alone did not interfere with correct imitation, since there was no significant difference in imitation of compatible stressed O sentences versus incompatible stressed S sentences ($\chi^2 = .737$). In short, the interactions of semantic interpretation and syntactic order preoccupied children in this age range far more than contrastive stress.

The second hypothesis was not supported. Children generally did not or could not reconstruct incompatible sentences to correspond to the interpretations provided in the situation. They had difficulty imitating incompatible sentences (as predicted by hypothesis 1), but they did not or could not "fix" those incompatible sentences in the expected direction. The pattern of errors in imitation (i.e., changes in the model) indicates that there simply wasn't time to make all the changes necessary to bring an incompatible sentence into line. The most common change in the model involved the reestablishment of NVN order. Out of a total of 48 imitations involving reordering, only one imitation changed an NVN to something else. 47 imitations changed the order of an NNV or VNN sentence, and in all but two of these the child reestablished an NVN order. It is interesting that the child did not always recreate the correct SEMANTIC situation in their changes to NVN. 17 of the imitations placed the lion in standard object position, while 30 placed the lion in standard subject position. Hence, we could conclude that many children were primarily interested in reestablishing standard syntactic order, regardless of semantic interpretation.

Changes in contrastive stress usually involved dropping the contrastive stress altogether. This was done in 31 cases (not including instances in which the child did not repeat the sentence or the contrasted element at all). We had hoped that the children would try to switch the contrastive stress on S to a contrastive O, but children switched stress in only four cases. In 10 instances, stress was provided for both NP's, e.g., *The **sheep** eats the **lion***.

It is interesting that most (i.e., 31) of the changes in stress took place in NVN models. The other models, with varied orders, were more likely to be imitated intact, parrot fashion, if they were imitated at all. This difference is significant at $p < .01$, in a χ^2 table comparing NVN with other orders, for number of stress errors versus number of order changes ($\chi^2 = 25.282$):

NVN	Other	
31	14	Stress errors
1	47	Order errors

One interpretation of this rather complex order and stress data is that the children are in a situation of information overload. In trying to disentangle the layers of information concerning order, stress, and situational presuppositions, they seem to tackle the problems one at a time. Overall, incompatible sentences are harder to imitate than compatible ones. However, when both order AND stress contrast with expectations, children will try to reestablish order. If order is already NVN, then the children may try to rearrange stress. On either end of these error patterns, there is the option of perfect imitation. If a sentence is completely compatible with the situation and with standard patterns, it is imitated correctly. If sentence and situation are a hopeless mismatch, the child either refuses to answer or parrots without analysis.

If it is true that the children were simply overloaded by all the conflicting factors, it may be useful to repeat the study several times, varying only one or two factors at a time. For example, the same sentence imitation task could be administered varying order only, with no contrastive stress. In another experiment, compatible and incompatible contrastive stress could be provided while holding order constant. Then we could begin again with order–stress interactions, but for a few possibilities at a time, so that each interaction could be tried with several items rather than just one, increasingly the likelihood of teasing out statistically significant patterns. Plans are currently underway to begin this series of experiments, in both English and Italian.

The above study was designed in part to complement an ongoing study of order and stress relations, in a comprehension task with Italian children. The study is being carried out by Antinucci and associates as part of Slobin's (1975) cross-cultural project in four language communities. In the Slobin et al. task, children are presented with two toy animals, either of which could reasonably serve as the semantic agent. Then the child is told to act out a series of instructions such as *The cow pushes the sheep, the cow the sheep pushes,* and so forth. In Serbo-Croatian and Turkish, these items are administered both with correct semantic inflections (e.g., nominative and accusative) and without inflections. In Italian and English, which do not have case inflections, the same items are administered with contrastive stress, and without contrastive stress, e.g., *the cow the **sheep** pushes* versus *the cow the sheep pushes.* Although the data for Italian have not been analyzed in detail at this writing, preliminary analyses indicate that stress plays an important role in the interpretation of various order patterns by the youngest Italian children, i.e., 2-year-olds. (Antinucci, personal communication).

In the Slobin et al. (1975) study, the child is presented with pragmatic-semantic conventions in a neutral situation, and his interpretation of those conventions is assessed. In the study reported here, on the other hand, the child is provided with the interpretation, and permitted to adjust the surface conventions. Hence the two types of data should be complementary.

Another study is currently underway with Brian MacWhinney (see MacWhinney and Bates, 1975) examining topic–focus relations in language acquisition for English, Italian, and Hungarian children. These three languages provide particularly interesting contrasts, since English is a noninflectional language with relatively rigid word order, Italian is a noninflectional language with relatively free word order, and Hungarian is an inflectional language with much more order variation than either English or Italian. The first experiment in this comparative study follows the same model outlined above, in that the situation is biased in favor of one topic–focus interpretation, and the child's linguistic reaction to that situation is assessed.

In this task, the child is presented with a picture book containing 11 sets of 3 pictures, and simply asked to describe what he sees. In each set, one major semantic constituent is varied across all three pictures while the others are held constant. For example, there is a set varying the agent of an intransitive verb (a mouse crying, a rabbit crying, a teddy bear crying) versus another set varying the intransitive verb while holding the agent constant (e.g., a little boy swimming, the same boy running, the same boy again skating). In the first study, the following sets have been provided:

1 agent—3 intransitive verbs
3 agents—1 intransitive verb
1 agent—3 transitive verbs—1 object
1 agent—1 transitive verb—3 objects
3 agents—1 transitive verb—1 object
1 agent—1 transitive verb—1 object—3 datives
1 agent—1 transitive verb—3 objects—1 dative
1 noun—3 locative prepositions—1 location
1 noun—1 locative preposition—3 locations
1 noun—3 attributes (two sets)

Obviously this list is not exhaustive of all possible semantic–syntactic combinations. We plan to vary others in future research. The above contrasts were chosen for the first project as the most likely to elicit different pragmatic–syntactic–semantic interactions in the three target language communities. The three independent variables in the study are, then, age, language, and semantic–syntactic structures (e.g., variant agent, varied dative, etc.). We have compiled a rather lengthy list of dependent variables, i.e., possible topic–focus devices in the child's description of the pictures, as they differ in descriptions of the first "neutral" picture versus the successive biased pictures in each set. These devices include those in Table 11. We are collecting an adult sample in each language as well, to determine language differences in use of these various devices when developmental factors are eliminated. We are interested in determining whether some topic–focus devices (e.g., ellipsis) are inherently easier, earlier developments than others. However, we expect that developmental preferences will interact with the way that various devices are used in the parent language.

A similar, though more limited, study has been reported by Hornby and Hass (1970). They presented children with sets of two pictures, also varying one of several possible case relations while holding other elements constant. The authors did not look at the full range of possible topic–focus devices that we have rather ambitiously proposed to try. Restricting their analysis to contrastive stress, Hornby and Hass report first, that contrastive stress is more likely to be applied in the second picture than in the first. This amounts to saying that the technique works. Second, the

Table 11

Topic–Focus Device	Example
1. Ellipsis (deleting one or more of the topicalized elements in successive pictures).	A. *The boy is swimming.* B. *Skating.*
2. Pronominalization.	A. *The boy is skating.* B. *He's swimming.*
3. Contrastive stress.	A. *The mouse is crying.* B. *The **bunny** is crying.*
4. Definite versus indefinite articles.	A. *A boy is skating.* B. *The boy is swimming.*
5. Adverbials, conjunctions, and other lexical items linking and contrasting successive descriptions.	A. *The boy is skating.* B. *Now the boy is swimming.*
6. Restrictive relative clauses.	A. *The boy is skating.* B. *The boy who was swimming is skating.*
7. Neutral SVO versus alternative orders.	A. *The mouse is crying.* B. *Is crying the bunny.*
8. Topic comment sentences with coreferential pronouns.	A. *The boy is skating.* B. *The boy, he's swimming.*
9. Transformations shifting topic focus relations (including passives and clefts).	A. *The mouse is crying.* B. *It's the bunny that's crying.*
10. Topicalizing sentences followed by separate comment sentence.	A. *The mouse is crying.* B. *There's a bunny. He's crying.*

tendency to use contrastive stress varies systematically with the particular case relation that is being contrasted. The likelihood that an element will be stressed mirrors the topicalization hierarchy noted by Fillmore (1968) and Givon (1974), in that agents are most likely to receive contrastive stress when varied, followed by experiencers, and so forth down the case hierarchy. This study is complemented by a study of the acquisition of stress by Weiman (1974), who reports that the developmental order in which contrastive stress for various elements is acquired also reflects the semantic case hierarchy.

Data are still being collected for the MacWhinney and Bates project, so at this writing there is very little to report other than our methods and predictions. We have a number of possible variations of the experiment in mind. For example, the data should be compared with administration of the same stimulae in entirely random order, to determine in more detail the effect of our imposed topic–focus set. Also, we are interested in the amount and type of intervening material that can be administered between the child's first mention of a component (e.g., the bear) and the time when he decides that he must retopicalize or reintroduce that element into the discussion once again. For example, if the child has talked about the bear, and then about a series of other agents (e.g., the fox, the rabbit), does he realize that he cannot pronominalize the bear without risking confusion among the other possible antecedents? This question is related to the broader problem of the interaction between topicalization and egocentrism in children, a matter that we will take up in more detail later (see Chapter X).

There are enormous methodological problems in such research, as we have quickly discovered. In virtually all other types of psycholinguistic work with children, we seek to randomize interitem effects. In this research we are trying to establish and use interitem effects. The problem is that children tend to find and use all kinds of interitem relations beyond the ones intended by the experimenter. In pilot research, we are continually refining our stimulae to remove these irrelevant response sets. But children seems to have an inexhaustible supply of ways for interrelating factors that we had hoped to introduce as entirely "new information." Similarly, when we work to establish a given element as "old information," children can find some way to recognize the familiar old bear, or boy, or bunny as an entirely new character.

This is a rich area for future research, and we are optimistic. But pragmatic factors are remarkably slippery objects for experimental as well as longitudinal research. On the one hand, in naturalistic free speech data it is often difficult to determine a posteriori the pragmatic roles served by various portions of a message. On the other hand, in experimental research there is the risk that our manipulations of the context will destroy the naturalness and spontaneity that characterizes pragmatic processing. The best solution is a combination of both longitudinal and experimental research, in a complementary approach that we have tried to illustrate here. Since we have reviewed more methods than data in this experimental section, we should leave the reader with one strong methodological conclusion: Pragmatic research will contain more surprises and take more time than almost any area of child language study. But since we can ignore these factors only at the risk of studying half a phenomenon, we had best plunge in.

Summary

The results of the longitudinal and experimental studies can be summarized as follows:

First, the longitudinal records for Claudia and Francesco yield an unusual developmental pattern for standard versus optional SVO ordering In the first transcripts, there is a tendency to preserve subject-final orders, although subject-first orders do occasionally occur. This is followed by a long period of session by session alternation between subject-final and subject-first preference. Around MLU 4.0, both children pass through a brief "conservative" period in which they strongly prefer SVO ordering, and express the subject under conditions in which an adult would delete it. Finally, both children display patterns indistinguishable from those of the adults.

We suggested that this initial subject-final strategy could reflect the first pragmatic strategy proposed earlier in the chapter—namely, the child extends his earlier, one-word strategy of encoding comments only, by encoding the comment first and adding other information on with remaining processing space. Such a strategy would produce what looks to the adult like a subject-final tendency, since subjects so often tend to overlap with topics, or old information.

Before accepting this interpretation, we examined a number of competing hypotheses, beginning with the possibility that the S-final tendency reflects statistical frequencies in adult speech to children. However, in the transcripts for Claudia and Francesco, adult speech is divided evenly between S-final and S-first. This is particularly interesting, since adult speech to adults contains far lower frequencies for the S-final form. We suggested that, in efforts to be particularly clear and emphatic with children, adults tend to overuse the S-final surface form, thereby presented their children with the wrong model for standard surface ordering.

We also considered the possibility that the adult S-final utterances, although no more frequent than S-first, were somehow more salient. Since the S-final form is used pragmatically to mark emphasis, it is likely to be used in situations that engage the child's attention. Also, it is more likely that an S-final sentence will contain contrastive stress, another factor contributing to the attentional pull of such utterances. However, in examining the way that Francesco uses contrastive stress in early sessions, it became clear that he was not imitating adult stress patterns. In fact, there was a tendency to stress the first element in both S-final and S-first sentences, yielding unusual patterns very unlike those used by adults. Second, in examining the way that Francesco used S-final versus S-first sentences in context, it became clear that S-final is not a strong contrastive form until much later in development. Both these findings weaken the argument that the child is imitating pragmatically salient adult ordering. But both these small analyses strengthen the hypothesis that in the early stages, Francesco is using a COMMENT–TOPIC rule.

We examined the period in which both children switched from S-final to alternating orders, to determine whether the switch had been caused by some kind of semantic–syntactic development. Increase in MLU, use of clitic pronouns, use of transitives and intransitives, and acquisition of embedded sentences were all unrelated to the shift in ordering strategies. Copulative sentences, i.e., predicate nominatives and predicate adjectives, tended toward a higher frequency of N–PA and N–PN forms around the time that the child began to use more S-initial orders. This suggests that both SVO ordering and N–PN/PA ordering have been affected by some third factor.

The only syntactic development that clearly coincided with the switch from S-final to S-initial was a switch from the use of proper names to express speaker and listener, to the use of subject pronouns. Furthermore, the use of subject pronouns coincided with productive marking of subject–verb agreement. We proposed that these three developments—standard ordering, subject pronouns, and subject–verb agreement—can all be explained by the possibility that the child has just discovered the concept of syntactic subject. Hence, prior ordering tendencies are unrelated to constituents such as S, V, and O. The apparent S-final tendency would have to be the byproduct of some other semantic or pragmatic ordering principle.

We considered two possible rules that might generate the subject ordering patterns observed in Claudia and Francesco. First, COMMENT–TOPIC ordering rules would increase the likelihood of subject-final patterns, since subjects tend to be pragmatic topics, or old information. However, since predicates tend just as often to contain new or important information, the COMMENT–TOPIC rule could also be described as a VERB–ARGUMENT rule.

Support for a verb fronting rule comes from data for German, Serbo-Croatian, Hungarian, and even English children, at least during the earliest stages of language development. Yet, as MacWhinney notes in his analysis of Hungarian, the same verb-fronting patterns could also be generated by a pragmatic rule such as FIGURE-GROUND. Returning to the Italian data, we noted that there are a good many exceptions to a verb-fronting rule, in those sentences in which subject does precede the verb. But these sentences need not necessarily be exceptions to a COMMENT-TOPIC rule, since agents can also be comments in certain contexts. The problem is to find sufficient contextual evidence to assign comment and topic roles to a larger percentage of utterances in these early samples.

Baroni, Fava, and Tirondola (1973) have performed just such an analysis on the early data for six Italian children. They report patterns similar to those observed for Claudia and Francesco. However, their analysis was carried out entirely in terms of new information versus old information. They conclude that, when high frequency word-based patterns such as *ecco palla* are omitted, the corpus can best be described with a NEW INFORMATION FIRST—OLD INFORMATION SECOND mapping rule.

There is, then, support for the hypothesis that—in the absence of clearcut semantic-syntactic constraints—the first ordering principle adopted by children will be COMMENT-TOPIC. It is perhaps a mistake to call this strategy a rule, since it is probably an automatic extension of an earlier strategy at the one-word stage, in which the child simply talked about the element that seized his attention. As such, this tendency is probably NOT a true linguistic rule, based on controlled reflection on symbol structures. Later, as the child encounters semantic-syntactic constraints for his particular language, and pragmatic constraints for insuring that the listener has sufficient topicalized information, the child will gain a reflective, preoperational control over these early sensorimotor tendencies, producing sentences in which the more interesting comments are made to follow their topics in order of mention.

Recall that around MLU 4.0, Claudia and Francesco each passed through a conservative period, in which SVO was more rigidly preserved, and subject deletion was held to a minimum. This period may reflect a preoccupation with the newly established concept of syntactic subject. In an experiment with 3- to 6-year-olds, we strongly biased a situation in favor of one interpretation of semantic, pragmatic, and syntactic subject. We then gave the child a series of sentences to imitate, some of which were incompatible with the situation in terms of order and/or contrastive stress. The prediction was that incompatible sentences would be more difficult to imitate, and that children would change the incompatible model sentences to correspond to the correct interpretation. The first hypothesis was supported, in that incompatible sentences were significantly more difficult to imitate. However, when the children did change the model sentence they tried above all to reestablish NVN order, even at the risk of producing another semantically and pragmatically incongruous sentence. It appears that 3- to 6-year-olds are quite preoccupied with standard syntactic orders. Hence they are more similar to Francesco and Claudia during the later, conservative stage in major constituent ordering.

In a complementary study, Slobin, Antinucci, and associates are providing children with various contrastive stress and order models, and assessing their interpretation of those models. Antinucci reports that, in preliminary data analyses, Italian 2-year-olds are strongly affected by contrastive stress in their interpretation of semantic roles. Hence, it is likely that the 2-year-olds, unlike the older children in our study, are still at a stage in which pragmatic factors play a predominant role in semantic interpretation and ordering of semantic–syntactic constituents.

We offered a number of examples from research by other authors, and from our own ongoing research, of methods for assessing the role of topic and focus in language development. In Chapter X, we will present a few more ideas for future research. It is far too early to come up with universal conclusions about the influence of pragmatics on language acquisition. However, it should at least be clear at this point that pragmatic factors are NOT a sort of overlaid system, applied late in sentence derivation and late in language acquisition. The topic–comment, presupposition–proposition relationship can be a powerful factor in explaining the mapping system for any given language, and in explaining the way that children acquire the mapping system.

Finally, this chapter—like the preceding chapter on metapragmatics—was included to illustrate the passage from sensorimotor to preoperational control of performative and presuppositional structure. By the end of the preoperational period, the child should be able to operate on all three aspects of the pragmatic system—performative, proposition, and presupposition—as symbolic objects. However, until around 5 years of age, according to Piaget, the child's internal operations are missing several of the properties of closed, logical systems. In the next section we will examine the changes that take place in the pragmatic system when the child enters into the so-called "concrete operational" phase in cognitive development.

PART THREE

Pragmatics in the Concrete Operational Period

In the last two sections, we examined the transition in communication from implicit pragmatic procedures to explicit pragmatic signals. In the following section, we will examine a return to implicit pragmatics—but of a very different sort.

In the sensorimotor period, the child could not control or manipulate his own pragmatic procedures. Like the action patterns in his early sensorimotor play and exploration, performatives and presuppositions were something the child DID, not mental objects that the child HAD. Hence, the child himself did not recognize the pragmatic relations implicit in his communicative routines. During the preoperational period, the child attains a reflective control over his own procedures, manipulating them like other symbol structures, and referring to them with explicit speech signals. In Chapters VII, VIII, and IX we will examine a new, still higher level of pragmatics, in which the child controls not only his own pragmatic structures, but the listener's interpretation of those structures. With all this information available to him, and with an enlarged and more efficient processing capacity, he can recombine performative–proposition–presupposition relations to create a camouflaged utterance, indirect speech acts which successfully convey a different meaning and/or goal than is signalled in the surface form of the utterance alone.

Why should these pragmatic achievements be concrete operational? Piaget defines concrete operations as the capacity to perform reversible transformations on a set of internal mental objects or relationships. These transformations include transitive operations (e.g., the seriation of sticks according to length), and classification into hierarchical relations (e.g., the ability to answer class inclusion questions such as *Are there more dogs or animals here?*). Much of research on concrete operations has concentrated on conservation, the ability to conserve a constant quantity, weight, etc. across time as it undergoes perceptual transformations. For example, when a round ball of clay is rolled into a long, thin strand, preoperational children will often claim that there is now more clay because it is longer, or perhaps less clay because it is thinner. A concrete operational child understands that the operation on the clay is reversible; one could theoretically undo the action and return to the original ball of clay. The amount has remained the same under transformation. The system of reversible operations was implicit in the logic of action at the sensorimotor level. By the end of the sensorimotor period, children can move out in a trajectory and then return to the point of origin by reversing their paths, or taking an equivalent path. In fact, Piaget suggests that this implicit logic is the source of the interiorized action patterns that later make up logical thought. The child reconstructs the same relationships at the level of symbolic representation, applying them to his new mental world.

If we apply the concept of reversibility to pragmatic procedures, there are two reasons why camouflaged speech is concrete operational.

1. The child must consider simultaneously both his own perspective, as encoder, and that of the listener, as decoder. He must be able to follow a progression that can be paraphrased as "I know I mean X. The listener will hear Y but has sufficient additional information to know that I mean X." To take the positions of encoder and decoder simultaneously, the child must be able to perform reversible communicative operations.

2. Even without consideration of the listener's perspective, from the child's own perspective the combination of these various types of information—from performative function, surface form, propositional content, presuppositions, and conversational postulates—requires an elaborate symbolic array and the ability to transform that array without losing track of the initial configuration. While he reconstructs his meaning into an indirect or camouflaged surface form, he must be able to retrieve the initial pragmatic-semantic divisions in that information. The operation "X becomes Y but is still X" is essentially a type of conservation.

In the following three chapters, we will examine two kinds of implicit or camouflaged meanings in Italian: first, the use of counterfactual conditional verbs, to permit simultaneous assertion and suspension of truth; second, the use of various indirect surface forms to serve as requests or commands. Both of these will require a social concept of polite versus offensive speech, as a motivation to resort to indirect speech acts. The concept of politeness will, in turn, require knowledge of the listener's perspective.

In the following chapters, a combination of longitudinal and experimental evidence will be presented. First, we will examine the longitudinal history of conditionals and polite forms in the records for Claudia and Francesco. Then, for both conditional verbs and polite requests, experiments with a larger sample of preschool children are presented. These experiments should serve to confirm or disconfirm the sequence of developments derived in the longitudinal study, and to test whether children actually understand the pragmatic implications of the forms examined in the production data.

The details of the experiments are given within individual chapters. Chapter VII contains both longitudinal and experimental evidence on conditional verbs. For polite forms, the longitudinal and experimental results are presented separately, in Chapters VIII and IX respectively. This division was necessary because of the extraordinary length and detail required to establish acquisition of politeness versus other request forms.

CHAPTER VII

Counterfactual Conditionals[1]

Of the various research projects described in these chapters, the study of the acquisition of conditionals was among the most interesting to Italian adults. It seems to be widely recognized that conditionals are problematic, a late development in child speech. Parents and preschool teachers assumed that we were interested in resolving that recognized problem. And yet it is not immediately clear why the linguistic forms for counterfactuals and hypotheticals should be such late acquisitions. As early as 12 months of age (Chapter III), children will "pretend" that one object or activity is another. Piaget (1962) has noted that his own children often showed clear awareness of the pretense by laughing during the game. For example:

> Jacqueline ... at 1;3 ... saw a cloth whose fringed edges vaguely recalled those of her pillow; she seized it, held a fold of it in her right hand, sucked the thumb of the same hand and lay down on her side, laughing hard. She kept her eyes open, but blinked from time to time as if she were alluding to closed eyes. Finally, laughing more and more, she cried *Nene* (No, no). (p. 96)

In the sequence, Jacqueline not only laughs, thereby permitting us to infer that she knows this is a "counterfactual" game, but at the end of the sequence she even provides a linguistic expression of the untruth of the game—"No, no." The action patterns could be paraphrased as *This is a blanket. I am sleeping.* Above these two sensorimotor propositions, the child places the linguistic markers "not true."

A more striking example, in a somewhat older child, can be found in the Padova data discussed in Chapter VI. A child whose speech was at a fairly

---

[1] Portions of this chapter have appeared in Elizabeth Bates, "The Acquisition of Conditionals by Italian Children." In *Proceedings of the 10th Regional Meeting of the Chicago Linguistic Society.* Chicago: Chicago Linguistic Society, 1974. Pp. 27–37.

elementary two-word level filled his mouth with food, looked up at the teacher with full cheeks and said

    Sputo? . . . Finta.   'I spit? . . . Fake.'

Apparently the difficulty in acquiring counterfactuals is not simply the fact that they express imaginary situations, nor even the fact that they encode the awareness of suspended truth in the surface form of an utterance. Children at the very beginning of speech and symbolic activity can encode or act out all these same relationships, as a series of separate units. As the results of this study will show, we did replicate the long-standing parental finding that conditionals are late and difficult developments for Italian children. But the reasons for this delay in development are not obvious.

How Conditionals Work

The conditional verb inflection in Italian is reserved only for counter-factuals. In English, the same counterfactuals are expressed with modal verbs, which are also used to express other functions. Hence, in English a study of the acquisition of conditionals would be difficult to separate from a more complete study of modality. Because of the delimited use of conditional inflections, Italian is an excellent target language for a study of the acquisition of counterfactuals and hypothetical conditionals.

In Italian, as in English, "If/then" sentences can appear with either the indicative or with conditional and subjunctive verbs, as in the examples

(1)   *Se piove, resto a casa.*   'If it is raining, I am staying
                                       home.'

(2)   *Se piovesse, resterei*   'If it were raining, I would stay
        a casa.   home.'

The difference between the two is a subtle one, but a difference with important implications for logical and pragmatic development.

In linguistic analyses of these two types of conditionals, there is general agreement that both structures serve to connect a possible world relation between two propositions to a set of verifying conditions in the real world. However, the particular nature of this possible–real relationship is a matter of some controversy.

Some recent analyses of the counterfactual describe the possible–real relation with a 2-valued logic, permitting only "true" or "false" statements. Lakoff (1970) has suggested that the counterfactual is used when the speaker presupposes that both the antecedent (X) and the consequent (Y) are false in the real world. He offers the sentence

(3)   *If Harry had known that Sheila survived, he would
    have gone home.*

and claims that the listener can deduce from this the two propositions

(3a)   *Harry did not know that Sheila survived.*

(3b)   *Harry did not go home.*

Dowty (1972) uses a similar approach in a discussion of causal predicates in general. He claims that the negative presuppositions of the counterfactual in

(4)   *If John hadn't put the lampshade on his head, Mary wouldn't have left the party.*

includes both of the following:

(4a)   *John did put a lampshade on his head.*

(4b)   *Mary did leave the party.*

Furthermore, given the causal connective inherent in the "if/then" structure, the listener can also deduce the entailed sentence

(4c)   *John's putting the lampshade on his head caused Mary to leave the party.*

Dowty's interpretation receives support from a psychological study mentioned by Fillenbaum (1973) regarding recognition memory for counterfactual conditionals. Fillenbaum found that subjects who had originally seen the sentence:

(5)   *If the man had not been late, he would have caught the train.*

will falsely recognize the sentence

(5a)   *The man missed the train because he was late.*

as having been among the original stimulus items.

Karttunen (1971) takes issue with Lakoff on the claim that both the antecedent and consequent are presuppposed to be false in a counterfactual conditional. He suggests instead that the counterfactual presupposes only that the antecedent condition X is false. The consequent can be true on other grounds. He points out qualified versions of the same sentences Lakoff used:

(3c)   *If Harry had known that Sheila survived, he would have gone home, which he did anyway.*

(3d)   *If Harry had known that Sheila survived, he would still have gone home.*

Lakoff also admits that 3c and 3d are possible. He has suggested that these qualifying phrases cancel the presupposition that the consequent is false. Karttunen disputes this, demonstrating that one cannot similarly cancel the presupposition of the antecedent with qualifying phrases, e.g.,

(3e)   *If Harry had known, as he did, that Sheila survived, he*
           would have gone home.

Karttunen concludes

> As I see it, although a counterfactual conditional presupposes the negation of the
> antecedent, it only suggests, in the absence of a disclaimer, that the consequent is false
> too.

As an alternative explanation, he cites the work of Geis and Zwicky (1971) on invited inferences. For example, given the sentence

(6)   *If you mow the lawn I'll pay you $5.*

the speaker never ASSERTS the sentences

(6a)   *If you don't mow the lawn, I'll pay you $5.*

(6b)   *If you don't mow the lawn, I won't pay you $5.*

Yet listeners will invariably infer that (6b), the logical inverse, is also true. This conclusion by the listener is not a deduction that follows the rules of predicate calculus, but an inference that was INVITED by uttering (6) in normal circumstances. It is this same sort of process, Karttunen suggests, that underlies the inference that the consequent is false in a counterfactual conditional.

A different solution to the issue of presuppositions in counterfactuals would be to accept a three-valued rather than a two-valued logic for truth conditions. Given an "If X, then Y" statement, the speaker must take a stand regarding the following THREE possibilities for the truth of X:

1. X is not true in the real world.
2. X is true in the real world.
3. X is either true or false in the real world.

The third possibility is best paraphrased as *I don't know.* Insofar as possibility (3) describes objective truth conditions, it can be reduced back to a two-valued logic—either true (possibility 2) or false (possibility 1). But in pragmatic terms, all three of these possibilities are descriptions of the speaker's beliefs rather than objective truth. Hence, possibility (3) is a description of speaker ignorance, and cannot be reduced to (1) or (2). Instead, it is a separate and distinct belief condition.

Puglielli and Giliberti (1972) have analyzed the Italian conditional according to such a pragmatic, three-valued system. They claim that the semantic core for all counterfactual conditionals is a conjoined proposition

ENTAIL (Proposition X, Proposition Y)

This same structure is also shared by present indicative "if/then" sentences, and by "Because X, Y" sentences. The difference in meaning among these three structures lies not in the semantic core, but in a set of presuppositions concerning the relation between this conjoined proposition and the speaker's beliefs. For example, given the proposition

$$\text{ENTAIL} \begin{pmatrix} \text{`it is raining'} \\ piove \end{pmatrix} \begin{pmatrix} \text{`I am staying home'} \\ resto\ a\ casa \end{pmatrix}$$

a speaker may construct the following three sentences:

(7)   *Perché piove, resto a casa.*   'Because it is raining, I am staying home.'

(1)   *Se piove, resto a casa.*   'If it is raining, I am staying home.'

(2)   *Se piovesse, resterei a casa.*   'If it were raining, I would stay home.'

Sentence (7) can be used only if the speaker believes that the antecedent *It is raining* is true. Puglielli and Giliberti, in a rather unusual use of the term "presupposition," describe this condition as an imperative, an instruction to the listener:

ASSUME THAT I ASSUME (*It is raining*).

This instruction to assume that the speaker believes (X) is the standard conversational rule regulating most declarative utterances, and hence is not an unusual or special constraint on the conjoined ENTAIL proposition. By contrast, the speaker may use the ENTAIL proposition to construct sentence (1) ONLY if he does not know whether or not it is raining. Hence the instruction to the listener in (1) is

ASSUME THAT I DO NOT ASSUME (*It is raining*).

This instruction can also be paraphrased as a statement by the speaker, *I don't know.* This is the third possibility in the three-valued logic described above.

The counterfactual sentence (2), by contrast, requires both the second and third possibilities in the three-valued logic. According to Puglielli and Giliberti, counterfactuals in Italian are always pragmatically ambiguous. Sentence (2) can be used either in a situation in which the speaker does not know it is raining, or in a situation in which he knows that it is not raining. The instruction to the listener covering both cases is

DO NOT ASSUME THAT I ASSUME (*It is raining*).

This instruction is a sort of warning to the listener not to infer that the antecedent is true. But it does NOT require, as Karttunen would have it, that the antecedent is false. To use Geis and Zwicky's terminology, the counterfactual serves to block the invited inferences of indicative "if/then" statements: The listener may not infer that either the antecedent or consequent are true, but he may also not infer that the speaker is NECESSARILY ignorant. This inherent ambiguity makes the conditional particularly useful for certain pragmatic uses such as polite forms and hedges. For example, Puglielli and Giliberti suggest that the sentence

(8)   *Vorrei restare a casa.*   'I would like to stay home.'

causes the listener to construct an empty antecedent condition (X), something such as *If you wouldn't mind* or *If it were possible.* The speaker does not specify the nature of this antecedent condition. Nor is it necessary that the listener go to the cognitive work of reconstructing some complete and specific condition holding on the sentence. It is sufficient that the listener reconstruct the fact that information Y is contingent on some factor X whose truth cannot be assumed. In a sense, such conditionals are a sort of deictic reference to a set of conditions shared by the listener and the speaker.

Another, similar usage often found in Italian newscasts is a sentence such as

(9)   *Tanaka incontrerebbe Mao*   'Tanaka would meet Mao next
          il mese prossimo.   month.'

This sentence also calls up an empty antecedent, one that might be paraphrased as *If my information is correct, and you may not assume that it is . . .* For such a pragmatic use of the conditional to work, it is essential that the antecedent is not necessarily false, but simply suspended or hedged. If the antecedent were unambiguously false, as Karttunen suggests, then we would have the newscaster in the position of saying *If my information is correct, and my information is not correct . . .* Such a usage would not be permissible in that particular context.

To summarize, Puglielli and Giliberti claim that there is a single semantic core—the conjoined proposition ENTAIL (X,Y)—which can be used to construct three different sentence types, differing only with respect to the listener's instructions on how to relate the proposition to the real world:

1. ENTAIL (X,Y) INSTRUCTION: ASSUME THAT I ASSUME (X)
                 RESULT: "Because X, Y"
2. ENTAIL (X,Y) INSTRUCTION: ASSUME THAT I DO NOT
                               ASSUME (X)
                 RESULT: "If X, then Y" (indicative).
3. ENTAIL (X,Y) INSTRUCTION: DO NOT ASSUME THAT I
                               ASSUME (X)
                 RESULT: "If X, then Y"
                               (X in subjunctive, Y in conditional).

As has been pointed out, the complete counterfactual structure underlies sentences in which only the conditional clause is expressed, so that the listener must recover the implicit "if" clause required by the conditional verb inflection.

In the study of acquisition of conditionals by children, we will assume that the Puglielli and Giliberti analysis of Italian is correct. However, some further qualifications must be added if we are to describe adequately the various uses of the conditional to which children are exposed. The conditional–subjunctive system seems to be a fairly unstable part of Italian grammar, subject to considerable variation in substandard dialects. Just as the English subjunctive

(10)   *If I were you, I wouldn't do that.*

is deteriorating in some dialects to

(10a)   *If I was you, I wouldn't do that.*

the Italian subjunctive/conditional verbs are also the source of common grammatical "errors" by adults. The correct Italian form for the above sentence would be

(10)   *Se io fossi te, non lo farei.*   'If I were you, I wouldn't
                                                do that.'

One common "error" is to place the entire sentence in the subjunctive, e.g.,

(10b) *Se io fossi te, non*   'If I were you, I were not
          lo facessi.   doing that.'

More common is the tendency to substitute the imperfect past for one or both of the two verbs, yielding possibilities such as

(10c) *Se io ero te, non lo*   'If I was you, I wouldn't
          farei.   do it.'
(10d) *Se io ero te, non lo*   'If I was you, I wasn't doing it.'
          facevo.
(10e) *Se io fossi te, non*   'If I were you, I wasn't doing it.'
          lo facevo.

A still more common substitution is occasionally found in the casual speech of middle-class Roman adults. In sentences requiring compound perfect past forms, e.g.,

(10f) *Se io fossi stato te,*   'If I had been you, I wouldn't
          non lo avrei fatto.   have done it.'

both verbs can appear in the imperfect past, as in sentence (10d). It is interesting that this is the only substitution for the conditional and subjunctive which is occasionally accepted by middle-class speakers. The compound past form is the most clearly counterfactual of all the above cases, in that its placement in the past renders the possible truth of the antecedent even more unlikely. One reading of the imperfect past tense is "action or state that was intended but did not come into being." Hence, the imperfect past does approximate the truth conditions of *If I had been you . . .* insofar as it asserts a relationship between two propositions that did not necessarily occur. Most of my middle-class informants recognized (10d) as "bad grammar," but I did observe its use in casual speech, particularly when the speaker was affecting a light or humorous style. A few Roman informants (e.g., Antinucci, personal communication) actually insisted that the form is now acceptable.

In the present study, all subjects are middle-class children of educated parents. We can assume at the very least that most parents recognize the above patterns as substandard. If they use the above patterns, they would be likely to use them only for the compound past version (10f) and only in casual speech.

The use of conditionals of any type was relatively rare in the adult speech recorded in transcripts for Claudia and Francesco. Indeed, some of the pragmatic forms examined in this volume (e.g., formal second person pronouns) never appear in the adult transcripts at all and yet children do acquire them. Presumably—unless these surface forms are innate in Italian children (a most unlikely prospect)—they are hearing them somewhere, probably in more formal and/or more complex conversations between adults. In four sessions chosen randomly from Francesco's records, there were only two conditional verbs addressed to him. Both of these were standard conditionals rather than a substandard use with the imperfect past. But given the general incidence of imperfect past as a conditional form in Roman middle-class speech, it is likely that middle-class children have been exposed to both forms.

This leaves us with the same dilemma that Roger Brown (1973) has discussed with regard to the double negative in English. There is a tendency for grammatical forms typical of substandard English to appear as "errors" in the speech of middle-class children. Have these children simply learned a substandard variant when they persist in such "errors" as the double negative? If the error is learned, then why do children invariably begin with the form which we recognize as substandard, and then change over to the standard form? Is it possible that children have reinvented the error for themselves, perhaps for the same reasons of structural economy that introduced the change into the substandard dialect?

The English conditional, which is carried out with the modal verb "would," seems to be more stable in middle-class speech than the Italian conditional. However, in English both the imperfect past and the conditional can be expressed grammatically with the same modal verb

(11)   *If I could, I would go to the store for my mother.*

(12)   *When I was a little girl, I would go to the store
          for my mother.*

In several other languages, e.g., French, the imperfect past form of the
verb is used in either the antecedent or consequent clause in counterfactual sentences. Perhaps the imperfect past and the conditional share
some common semantic structure, which accounts for the adult variants,
and for the tendency for children to rediscover the substitutability of the
imperfect in conditional frames.

These options must be kept in mind as we examine the acquisition of
conditionals by middle-class Roman children. While "error" patterns may
be learned from adult models, it is also possible that they are generated
creatively from a shared semantic base underlying both the conditional
and alternative verb forms.

Longitudinal Results

In the longitudinal records for Claudia and Francesco, there is in fact no
evidence that the counterfactual conditional inflection has ever been
acquired at all. No verbs appear in the subjunctive (except for certain
imperative structures—see Chapter VIII). There is one instance of a conditional verb by each child, in both instances the very same expression
(F32; C15):

    Che sarebbe?   'What would that be?'

This question is semi-idiomatic in adult usage, and it appears in the child
transcripts at a time when the children have been using adult interjections
and other idiomatic expressions. It is likely that both these isolated
instances are either imitations or contextually appropriate, learned
expressions. In the same session that Claudia says *Che sarebbe?* she also
hears a knock at the door and says

    Chi sarà?   'Who will that be?'

a similarly idiomatic phrase, used by adults in the same sort of context.

While the counterfactual conditional verb itself does not appear, there is
evidence for the build up of part of the counterfactual structure. The basic
unit is a predicate ENTAIL with two propositions as arguments. As outlined earlier, this structure plus a presupposition with instructions to the
listener, underlies

1. Because X, Y.

2. If X, then Y (indicative).
3. If X, then Y (conditional/subjunctive).

It appears from the longitudinal transcripts that these three types of ENTAIL (X,Y) structures are acquired in precisely the above order. (For exact frequencies per session for "because" and "if" connectives, see Tables 2 and 3 in Chapter V.)

The first to appear is the "Because" structure, coming in for both children in the third metapragmatic stage discussed in Chapter V. In Italian the same word *perché* is used for both 'because' and 'why'. Claudia says this the first time in an isolated question, during the following exchange (C9, age 1;8;4):

Claudia	Adult	Claudia	Adult
	Andiamo!		'Let's go!'
Perché?		'Why?'	

She does not follow up on the question in any way, and there are no further examples until C12 (age 1;9;21). The isolated question *perché?* is used more often in Italian than in English, with a more flexible pragmatic range. It is a way of refusing to do something one is told, or of challenging an act or statement by another person. While the same uses are possible in English, it is my impression that they are far more common in Italian (as is also the case for the conjunction *ma* 'but'), particularly in interacting with children. While this one example is certainly insufficient to build a case one way or another, it is possible that Claudia has first learned the pragmatic use of *perché* (e.g., as a refusal), without learning its full semantic range. (Francesco does the same thing with quantifiers and time adverbs—see Chapter IV.)

Claudia then uses *perché* in C12, in an incomplete statement. She is narrating Little Red Riding Hood, and says

   . . . *perché* . . . *cane cattivo*   '. . . because . . . bad dog'

Finally, in C14, there is a full-fledged conjoined proposition with *perché* as a connective, although the causal relation between the two propositions is so obscure that it is not certain whether Claudia understands the entailment relation:

   Paola, è andata dentro la   'Paola, it went inside the ball,
      palla, perché Gippi non ha   because Gippi didn't want to
      voluto mangiare la pizza.   eat the pizza.'

Later in the same session we find another statement, which seems to be appropriate in its context:

Perché è brutto il cane.	'Because the dog is ugly.'

Also in the same session, the connective *se no* makes its first appearance. While *se no* literally means 'if not', it is used in Italian in the same way as the English terms "or else" and "otherwise." In this session, it is found four times in the following example:

Se no, metti a posto questo,	'If not, put this on in place, this
questo. Giovannino se no ci	one. Giovannino if not he is
ha freddo. Se no ci ha freddo,	cold. If not he is cold, if not
se no ci ha freddo. Lo mettiamo?	he is cold. We put it?'

The connective *se no* appears commonly in adult admonishments, warning dire results if certain conditions are not met. It is similarly used by Claudia in the next example (C21):

Se no mi dai le botte?	'If not you'll spank me?'

The connective "if" itself does not appear until C22:

Se me la dai la gomma, mi fa	'If you give me the gum it hurts
male al pancino, se no io vado	my tummy, if not I go to the
all'ospedale perché si.	hospital, because yes.'

The use of 'if' and 'if not' respectively is not logically consistent in this example, but there does seem to be a clear notion of contingency. In the next session there is a clearer example:

Claudia	Adult	Claudia	Adult
	E che ti ha detto il signore?		'And what did the gentleman say to you?'
'Se mi lasci il tuo fratellino io ti do un paio di scarpe.' E io ho detto 'No no, non ti lascio il fratellino.'		' "If you leave me your little brother, I'll give you a pair of shoes." And I said "No, no I am not leaving you my little brother." '	

Other indications of a concept of contingency are the two examples in C17 and C22 respectively:

Ma è possibile.	'But it is possible.'
Forse sta qui. No, lì.	'Perhaps it is here. No, there.'

The context in C17 is not clear, and it may once again be more or less idiomatic, imitative of a common Italian expression of bewilderment. The example in C22 is quite clear, however, since Claudia not only poses a possibility, but then disproves it (i.e., *perhaps it is here. No, there*).

The build up of a concept of contingency is quite similar in Francesco's records. he also produces "because" and "or else" first, with the actual connective "if" coming in much later. The first examples if F22 (age 2;2;20) are in incomplete utterances:

. . . pecché lo potto qui, qui le scale. Cammina, perché cammina.	'. . . because I carry it here, here the stairs. It walks, because it walks.'
. . . io, pecché il pupo mio . . .	'. . . I, because my baby . . .'
Perché a metto bene.	'Because I put it well.'
Se no si ompe.	'If not it breaks.'

In F24 there are several more examples, although some of them are still fairly unclear:

Pecché, pecché adono qui	'Because, because they fall here.'
Io ado via, pecché . . . ado ai malati.	'I go away, because . . . I go to the sick people.'
. . . pecché hai peso il cacciavite?	'Why did you take the screwdriver?'
Edi quella donna . . . pecché . . .	'You see that lady . . . because . . .'
Papa . . . pecché a (oato) io quetto (a) la neve.	'Daddy . . . because I (found) this (in) the snow.'
Pecché ha fatto pipí sotto.	'Because he made pipi underneath.'
Quetto é otto, pecché, pecché . . .	'This is broken, because, because . . .'

In F25 there is a particularly interesting example of contingency. Francesco has been reacting badly to the impending arrival of his parents' second child (see Volterra, 1975). This has been manifested in hostile acts toward smaller children and the invention of his own fictitious baby. In F25 he goes over to close the door. When an adult asks him why, he responds

Se no entra il ragazzino brutto.	'If not the ugly little boy comes in.'

Then, by F26, Francesco has begun to ask "why" repeatedly, sometimes to the exasperation of the listening adult. A few examples include the following:

*Pecché fa **bum** il cannone?*	'Why does the cannon go "boom"?'
Perché si ape così?	'Why is it opened like this?'
Perché batta (basta)?	'Why enough?'

The first actual "if" construction comes in at F32 (around 2;9):

Se piangi a scuola, niente.	'If you cry at school, nothing.'

In this instance he is recreating adult warnings about the results contingent upon given behaviors. A fairly regular usage of the complete "if" structure begins several sessions later (see Table 3, Chapter V).

Finally, in the last half of his fourth year, we find several examples that could be interpreted as the use of an imperfect past tense verb to express a counterfactual conditional:

Io l'ho messo di là, se no i cuginetti strillavono forte (F36).	'I put it over there, otherwise the little cousins were yelling loud (F36).'

Francesco	Adult	Francesco	Adult
	La macchina a scuola l'hai portata mai?		'Did you ever bring the car to school?'
No, perché i bambini piccoli lo rompevano(F38).		'No, because the little children were breaking it (F38).'	

Volevo vederla ancora (F42) (uttered in a context in which he still wants to see it).	'I still wanted to see it (F42).'
Perché è messo qui in questo barattolo, perché il lupo se no (se) lo mangiava . . . (P45).	'Because it is put here in this container, because the wolf if not was eating it up (F45).'
Be, ma un ombrello me s'è rotto, mio papà s'è comprato solo quello e allora se l'ombrello era aggiuttato te lo davo (F48).	'Well, but an umbrella broke on me, my father bought himself just these and so if the umbrella was fixed I was giving it to you (F48).'

The last example in particular (*If the umbrella was fixed . . .*) is a full fledged example of the substandard Roman use of the imperfect past in compound conditional–subjunctive structures (i.e., *If the umbrella had been fixed . . .*).

In F49, there is a further usage of the imperfect past to establish the "pretend" conditions for a game. While there is no adult model, including substandard Italian, in which such sentences are grammatical, they are commonly observed when older children are assigning roles or contexts in dramatic play:

> *Adesso era la festa, adesso* 'Now it was, now it is your
> *è la festa tua, le candeline* party, the little candles where
> *dove sono? Era la festa di* are they? It was the party of
> *... era la festa di Gioia.* ... it was the party of Gioia.'

> *Io sono il marito, e tu* 'I am the husband, and you
> *eri la mia moglie.* were my wife.'

The source of this schoolyard idiom is not certain, but informants suggest that it is derived from the use of the imperfect past tense in fairy tales and other stories, e.g., the famous opening line of Pinocchio:

> *C'era una volta ... un* 'There once was ... a piece
> *pezzo di legno!* of wood!'

In these last transcripts for Francesco, there are also uses of adverbials like *forse* ('perhaps') or modal verbs to indicate contingency (F38):

Francesco	Adult	Francesco	Adult
	... adesso non piovè.		'... Now it isn't raining.'
Forse pioerà.			'Perhaps it will rain.'
	Chi è?		'Who is it?'
Dev'essere Alessandra.			'It must be Alessandra.'

If Francesco has a stable concept of contingency, and even uses the imperfect past in conditional–like structures, why are there no examples of a true counterfactual conditional with appropriate markings? We did some follow up observations of Francesco in the six months after the last session (F50). The imperfect past still appeared to be a preferred structure, although his mother noted that conditional verbs had appeared, particularly in restricted pragmatic uses as polite requests. The conditional elicitation task was administered to Francesco at age 4;6, and his responses were again in the imperfect past. The only observation of a counterfactual conditional by Francesco during this research period occurred before his fifth birthday, in a telephone conversation between Francesco and experimenter and family friend Virginia. When asked if he would like to have a brown puppy with a black nose, Francesco responded in a plaintive tone:

> *Vorrei!* 'I would like!'

Some additional longitudinal evidence for counterfactual conditionals comes from a diary account of Iuri, the son of one CNR colleague. According to his parents, conditional verbs appeared in Iuri's speech as early as 2;6, but in a highly restricted usage. First of all, the verb was almost always in the second person (e.g., *vorresti* 'would you like'). Second, it was used, sometimes in play monologues, to describe situations in which something was needed or missing. For example, in playing with crayons Iuri looked about for a missing color and said

> *Vorresti l'arancio.*   'You would want the orange.'

At age 3;4, Iuri was administered the conditional elicitation task, and like Francesco his answers were also in the imperfect past. However, this must be qualified with an observation by his father when the child was approximately three years of age. Iuri placed three fingers vertically against a table, moved them, and said to his father:

> *Se un uomo avesse tre gambe,*   'If a man had three legs, what
>   *che farebbe?*   would he do?'

These reports may be taken as evidence for the earliest observed age at which a true counterfactual conditional can emerge.

To summarize the longitudinal findings, the acquisition of conditionals follows an order that reflects the difficulty of the three presuppositions for ENTAIL (X,Y) structures.

First, *perché* appears (C9–12; F22), simultaneous with or followed shortly by *se no.* These two can be formalized as

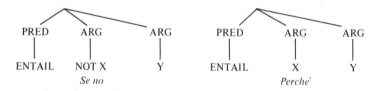

together with the presupposition (in instruction form)

ASSUME THAT I ASSUME (X)

Second, "If" structures appear in the present indicative (C22; F32). These can be formalized as

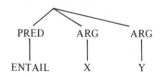

together with the presupposition

ASSUME THAT I DO NOT ASSUME (X)

Third, counterfactual conditionals are the last structures to appear, after four years of age. These can be formalized as

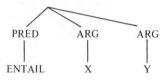

together with the presupposition

DO NOT ASSUME THAT I ASSUME (X)

It is not clear whether the imperfect past and the counterfactual conditional inflection have the same underlying structure, or whether the imperfect past is in some sense a partial version of the counterfactual. There is, in fact, too little longitudinal evidence to conclude when the late developing counterfactual is actually acquired. The following experiment was designed to elicit conditional verbs from a larger sample of children, ranging in age from 2;0 to 6;2, in the hope that more data will provide more precise information about the sequence of developments leading to conditional inflections.

Experimental Evidence

Procedure

The subjects were 74 Italian children, ranging in age from 2;0 to 6;2. Both sexes were evenly represented at all age levels. All subjects attended predominantly middle-class preschools in the Rome area, and were judged by their teachers to be normal in intelligence and linguistic development (i.e., children with apparent learning disabilities were excluded from the sample). Subjects were tested in the preschool setting, after the experimenters had spent two to three days in the classroom so that the children were accustomed to their presence.

The procedure was patterned on the familiar task of looking at picture books with an adult. Pilot testing was carried out with various types of pictures, but the eventual format was based on a Hallmark children's book entitled *If I Were . . .* The book contains a small mirror on the back page. Each page has an animal or human figure, with a hole cut in the face area. Hence the mirror is visible to the child in place of the figure's own face.

The presence of the small mirror not only made the task more interesting for the child, but seemed to help focus his attention on subsequent *If you were an X . . .* questions. Since the original illustrations in the Hallmark book were highly stylized and difficult for children to identify, simplified drawings were substituted over the mirror frames. There were six figures chosen as the most easily recognized by the subjects in pilot testing: a monkey with a banana, an elephant, a cowboy, a fish, a cat with a ball, and an airplane. On the final page, the child was shown the mirror only, and asked to identify himself.

At the beginning of the task the child was seated next to the Experimenter so that he and the adult could "look at this book together." Close proximity to the child, from his perspective, also aided the Experimenter in determining whether the subject had seen his face in the small mirror. For each of the 6 figures, the format was roughly as follows:

Adult	Child	Adult	Child
Questo che cos'è?		'What is this?'	
	una scimmia.		'a monkey.'
E che sta facendo la scimmia?		'And what is the monkey doing?'	
	Mangia la banana.		'He eats a banana.'
E qui chi vedi?		'And here who do you	
Chi c'è qua?		see? Who is in here?'	
	Lauretta.		'Lauretta.'
	(own name)		(own name)
Allora, se tu fossi		'Well then, if you were	
una scimmia, che faresti?		a monkey what would you do?'	
	Mangio la banana.		'I eat a banana.'
E se io fossi una		'And if I were a monkey,	
scimmia, che farei?		what would I do?'	
	Mangi la banana.		'You eat a banana.'
E se Valeria (other Experimenter)		'And if Valeria (other Experimenter)	
fosse una scimmia, che farebbe?		were a monkey, what would she do?'	
	Mangia la banana.		'She eats a banana.'

It should be noted that while an English-speaking child could respond grammatically to the above questions with the infinitive alone, minus the modal verb (e.g., *Eat a banana*), an Italian must choose some type of inflection for the verb, with both person and tense, if he is to respond at all. If the above question were asked of a middle-class adult, the verb would be inflected as a conditional.

Finally, on the seventh item the child was shown the mirror alone, framed as a handmirror with a human hand holding it. Here the format was as follows:

Adult	Child	Adult	Child
E questo, che cosa è?		'And what is this?'	
	Uno specchio.		'A mirror.'
E chi ci vedi dentro? Chi c'è?		'And who do you see inside? Who's there?'	
	Lauretta (own name)		'Lauretta.' (own name)
Ah sì? E se tu fossi Lauretta, che faresti?		'Ah yes? And if you were Lauretta, what would you do?'	
	Mi specchio.		'I look at myself.'
E se io fossi Lauretta, che farei?		'And if I were Lauretta, what would I do?'	
	Ti specchi.		'You look at yourself.'
E se Valeria fosse Lauretta, che farebbe?		'And if Valeria were Lauretta, what would she do?'	
	Si specchia.		'She looks at herself.'

This last question is obviously a sort of trick, to examine the child's comprehension of the presupposition that the listener does not necessary believe in the child's identity. It was hoped that the children would handle these questions differently from the preceding hypotheticals with other kinds of figures.

While the format was always roughly the above, it was decided early in pilot testing that to induce maximal performance in children as young as 2;0, it would be necessary to keep the format flexible. If the child insisted on skipping pages, he was permitted to do so, and then later an attempt was made to return to earlier items. If he had trouble identifying the figure, he was helped with phrases such as

> *Don't you see his long long trunk and his ears?*
> *What has a long nose like that?*

With regard to the *What is* (X) *doing?* question, generally any verb that the child himself spontaneously provided was acceptable. This was to insure that subsequent performance with inflections was not affected simply by familiarity with a verb chosen by the Experimenter. However, a few children continually went back to the same verb—e.g., *to eat*—for all the pictures. If this occurred, the Experimenter would encourage production of another verb with questions such as

> *What else does a kitten do? Do you see the ball*
> *he has? What is he doing with it? Is he playing?*

The child's attention was always explicitly drawn to the mirror inside the figure's face on the first one or two items, as outlined above. However, it was noted in pilot testing that the session was lengthened and the children grew bored with the task if the mirror was mentioned every time the page was turned. On the other hand, if after the first few items the child's attention began to wander, a return to the question *And who do you see in here?* would often rekindle interest. Hence, the Experimenters used their own discretion in adding that question to all but the last item with the mirror alone.

Questions were repeated whenever the child was confused or distracted. The two Italian Experimenters were encouraged to use their own judgment in adding "entertainment" to the task to keep the child's interest—e.g., labelling parts of the cowboy's clothes, adding sound effects to go with the child's choice of action verbs. However, in all cases the format did involve the questions (*1*) *What is it?*, (*2*) *What does it do?*, and (*3*) *If (you/I/she) were an (X), what would (you/I/she) do?* This yielded 21 possible responses requiring conditional verbs, seven in each of the three persons. Whatever problems a flexible format may have presented for subsequent interpretation were, we decided, outweighed by the fact that it was possible to elicit so many responses to this difficult task from children as young as two to three years of age.

Responses were recorded with a Grundig portable cassette recorder, and transcribed later in the same day. In addition, an Experimenter jotted down the child's verb responses as she heard them to check against later transcriptions.

Results

Table 12 presents the types of verb inflections used in response to conditional questions, by children in 5 different age groups with 15 subjects per age level (2;0 to 3;2, 3;2 to 3;11, 3;11 to 4;9, 4;9 to 5;6, and 5;6 to 6;2. There are only 14 subjects in the 5;6 to 6;2 age range, since the schools closed down before we could test the last 6 year old). Figure 5 illustrates the total incidence of verb response types as a function of the five age groups, for (1) simple present indicative verbs, (2) conditional verbs, (3) combined frequency of all verbs not in the present indicative, and (4) all verbs in neither present indicative nor conditional (herein referred to as alternative verbs). Tables 13 and 14 present the results of statistical tests on some of the age differences and interactions illustrated in Figure 5.

As should be clear from the figures and tables, children at various age levels exercise a variety of options in responding to the "if" questions. Roughly three stages can be characterized.

First, from 2;0 to 3;11 (30 subjects) children either cannot respond at all, or they respond almost exclusively with the simple present indicative, e.g., *I am eating a banana.*

Table 12 Types of Responses to Conditional Questions: Totals Within Age Levels

	Age levels				
Type of response	2;0 to 3;2 Level 1 (15 Subjects)	3;2 to 3;11 Level 2 (15 Subjects)	3;11 to 4;9 Level 3 (15 Subjects)	4;9 to 5;6 Level 4 (15 Subjects)	5;6 to 6;2 Level 5 (14 Subjects)
Noun or pointing (no verb)	55	0	0	0	0
Present indicative	114	228	168	182	90
Infinitive	14	10	20	25	4
Modal and infinitive	0	7	1	0	2
Future	2	0	7	8	30
Imperfect past	12[a]	9	50	44	19
Subjunctive	0	0	0	5	1
Conditional	3	9	56	52	131

[a] All 12 responses by one subject.

Second, from 3;11–5;6 (30 subjects) conditional verbs appear, but they are outweighed by responses either in the present indicative, or in a variety of verb forms, including the following:

(a) imperfect past   *mangiavo*   'I was eating . . .'
(b) future   *mangerò*   'I will eat . . .'
(c) infinitive   *mangiare*   'to eat . . .'
(d) infinitive + modal   *devo mangiare*   'I must eat . . .'
(e) subjunctive   *mangiassi*   'I were eating . . .'

Table 13 Some Statistical Results of Age Differences on the Conditional Elicitation Task: Overall Age Effects

	By 5 age levels (15 Subjects)		By 2 Age Levels (Older versus younger halves)	
Verb categories	F–ratio	Probability[a]	F–ratio	Probability[a]
Present indicative	3.942	.05	.986	n.s.
Conditional verbs	8.656	.01	16.665	.01
Total of alternative verbs (imperfect past, future, etc.)	1.53	n.s.	3.121	n.s.
Conditional + alternatives (all verbs other than present indicative)	7.286	.01	18.915	.01
Imperfect past only	1.042	n.s.	.689	n.s.

[a] All values are upper limits; n.s. means not significant.

Table 14 Statistical Differences Between Specific Age
Levels on Conditional Elicitation Test

Verb categories	F–ratio
Conditionals:	
First 30 versus second 30 subjects	9.433**
Second 30 versus last 14 subjects	8.915**
Fourth versus fifth age levels only	6.341*
Present Indicatives:	
Fourth versus fifth age levels only	4.941*
Alternative verbs:	
First 30 versus second 30 subjects	7.073**
All verbs not in present indicative:	
Second versus third age levels only	7.507*
Fourth versus fifth age levels only	2.241^a
	Proportional t-statistic
Present indicative versus all	
other verbs, fourth versus fifth levels	6.25**
Conditionals versus alternative verbs,	
fourth versus fifth age levels	5.57**
Present indicative versus	
conditionals, fourth versus fifth levels	7.24**

^{a} not significant
  * $p < .05$.
 ** $p < .01$.

These five forms have been termed alternative verbs, and are so labelled in Figure 5.

Third, from 5;6 to 6;2 (14 subjects) the conditional becomes the most frequent response type. The use of alternative verbs decreases, and the use of simple present indicative drops radically.

Let us first examine the overall age trends within the response types illustrated in Figure 5. Then we will look at the results from the point of view of the three developmental stages just outlined.

1. *Overall Age Trends*

A. PRESENT INDICATIVE VERBS

The age effect for present indicative verbs (e.g., *mangio* 'I eat') is significant at $p < .05$ ($F = 3.942$) across the five age groups. However, the effect is not linear. An analysis of variance comparing the youngest versus the oldest halves is not significant ($F = .986$). As can be seen from Figure 5, this is due to the fact that indicatives first increase drastically, and then decrease as conditionals and other verb responses begin to appear. The initial increase is due to the fact that many of the youngest children can-

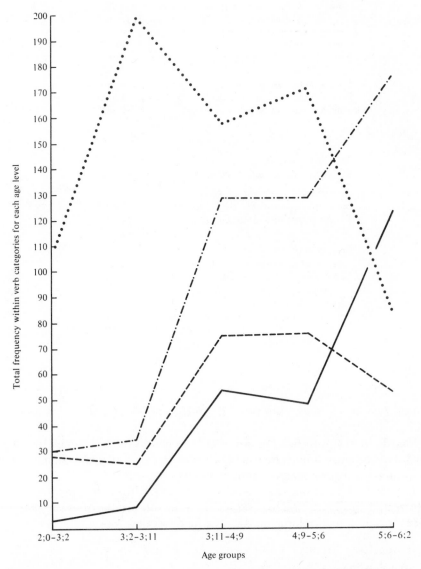

Figure 5. Age trends in types of responses to conditional questions. Conditional verbs: ——; present indicative verbs: •••; alternative verbs: — —; all nonpresent indicatives: –•–•–.

not respond at all to the conditional questions, so that the increase in present indicative responses represents an increase in the ability to understand the question in the first place. Hence, it seems fair to conclude that the first kind of response to appear is the present indicative.

B. CONDITIONAL VERBS

The use of conditional verbs increases significantly across all age levels ($F = 8.656$ for five age groups, $p < .01$; $F = 16.665$ for older versus younger halves, $p < .01$). The most significant increases occur between the second and third age levels (around 3;11) and again between the fourth and the last age groups (around 5;6).

C. ALTERNATIVE VERBS

The tendency to respond with alternatives to the conditional (e.g., future tense, imperfect past, etc.) increases significantly between the first and the second age levels ($F = 7.037$, $p < .01$). However, the overall age effect for alternative verbs is not significant ($F = 1.53$ by five age levels; $F = 3.121$ by older versus younger halves). As can be seen from Figure 5, this is due to the fact that alternative verbs first increase, and then decrease gradually from ages 3;11 to 6;2 in the period in which the conditional inflection itself is mastered.

Taken together, these trends yield three developmental periods, which will be referred to as the Indicative Stage (2;0 to 3;11), the Alternative Stage (3;11 to 5;6), and the Conditional Stage (5;6 to 6;2).

2. Developmental Stages

A. INDICATIVE STAGE

Regarding the Indicative period, there were a number of 2-year-olds who could not even answer with simple present indicative verbs. While all the children in the sample were able to follow the task of naming the figure in the book and providing an action verb (e.g., *This is a monkey* . . . *Monkeys eat bananas*), several of the youngest children completely blocked when asked the conditional question *If you were a monkey*. . . . In some cases the Experimenters would repeat the questions several times, attempting to draw the child into some minimal deduction, for example:

> *What did you say the monkey does? He eats a banana? Well then,*
> *if you were a monkey what would you do?*

This still did not draw a verb response from some children. It is interesting that two of the youngest subjects attempted to resolve the dilemma by responding not to our question, but to the general demand characteristics of the book task. When unable to come up with any other response, they labeled parts of the picture. A sample exchange is the following:

Adult	Child
What is this?	
	A monkey.
And what does the monkey do?	
	Eat a banana.
Well then, if you were a monkey, what would you do?	
	This is his ear.
If I were a monkey, what would I do?	
	This is his foot.

The reasoning behind this exchange might be paraphrased as "I don't know what this lady wants, so I'll give her what they usually want when we look at books."

Another type of response with very young children involved a sort of verb deixis. When asked *If you were a monkey what would you do?*, some subjects would point to the picture and say *Questo* 'This'. No amount of probing could induce the production of an inflected verb.

When children in this age range did use verbs in responding to the conditional question, they tended overwhelmingly to use present indicative verbs. Furthermore, the use of present indicatives increased significantly from the first age group (2;0 to 3;2) to the second (3;2 to 3;11). As suggested above, this shift is due to the fact that an increasing number of children begin to understand something in the conditional questions; the earlier, deictic responses may instead have been attempts to cover an inability to decode the question itself.

How much of the counterfactual question do children in this first age level understand? Within a certain margin of error the subjects respond with the appropriate person inflection, e.g., *If you were . . . —I eat . . . —If I were . . . —You eat . . .* It is therefore not likely that the children were merely repeating their previous description of what monkeys do (e.g., *He eats . . .*) It is possible, however, that the children who answer in the present indicative have understood only the juxtaposition of YOU/MONKEY/VERB. Or perhaps they may have understood the IF morpheme sufficiently to draw up minimal relations of implication of the type ENTAILS (You are monkey) (You do X), without processing the counterfactual presupposition. Finally, it is also possible that children from 2;0 to 3;11 do comprehend the counterfactual conditional including its presuppositions, but cannot reproduce it themselves in their responses.

However, if the latter interpretation were correct, it would be difficult to explain the fact that it will be almost two years before these children master the conditional inflection for themselves.

B. ALTERNATIVE VERB STAGE

In the next developmental stage (3;11 to 5;6), the children use a variety of verbs in addition to the old present indicative pattern, including the newly appearing conditional inflections. This distribution of verb response types is not a reflection of individual strategies by different children. Rather, the responses tend to vary within the protocols for each child. Of all those subjects who produced some verb other than the present indicative, all but one used at least two different types of inflections among his responses. One 5-year-old boy used five different response types, including conditional, present indicative, future, infinitive, and subjunctive. The only exception was a very articulate 6-year-old girl who used the conditional 21 times. Hence, children in this age range appear to have a highly unstable system for responding to conditional questions.

Although the frequency of the simple present indicative remains high, it begins to drop off slightly as alternative verbs start to appear. All nonindicative verbs, including both conditional and the alternative "errors," increase significantly between the Indicative period and the Alternative period ($F = 7.507, p < .05$). For conditionals alone, the increase is significant at $p < .01$ ($F = 9.433$), and for alternative verbs, the increase is significant at $p < .01$ ($F = 7.073$).

Within the category of various alternative verbs (e.g., imperfect past, infinitives, etc.) no one type of inflection is frequent enough to reach significance by age levels. The imperfect past tense is a more frequent alternative than others, and has a nonsignificant age effect by five age levels ($F = 1.042$). However, all of these errors show a similar pattern, in that they increase and then decrease at the same developmental periods.[2]

Since the alternative verbs and the conditionals appear at the same time, increase at the same level, and are used interchangeably within the protocols for individual children, we can conclude that during this second stage all these verbs are functional variants of one another, related to some common semantic–pragmatic base.

C. CONDITIONAL VERB STAGE

A third developmental period begins between 5;6-6;2 (the oldest children in the sample). This stage is characterized by mastery of the conditional inflection itself, and a decline in all type of nonconditional

---

[2] It is possible, however, that more data would reveal some developmental differences in preference for one alternative verb vs. another in responding to conditional questions. For example, infinitive + model might precede the use of future tense. See Table 10.

responses, both alternatives and present indicative, as illustrated in Figure 5.

Between the fourth and the last age levels (15 and 14 subjects, respectively), the use of present indicative verbs drops significantly ($F = 4.941$, $p < .05$). At the same time, there is a nonsignificant increase ($F = 2.24$) in the combined incidence of all nonindicative responses (both conditional and alternative verbs). Note the crossover between the two response types in Figure 5. This relationship was tested for significance with a t-test applied to the proportion of present indicatives to total verb responses, in the fourth versus the fifth age group. The finding was significant at $p < .01$, with a t-statistic of 6.25.

Considered alone, this finding might indicate that whatever semantic structure had brought on the use of all these verbs at the second stage, had simply become more stable and/or been mastered by more children in the third stage. However, there is another interaction, between conditional inflections and alternative verbs, which indicates that something qualitatively different has occurred to characterize the third stage. Conditionals increase significantly between the fourth and fifth age levels ($F = 6.431$, $p < .05$). There is, at the same time, a nonsignificant decrease in the frequency of alternatives to the conditional. Since conditionals and alternatives increased together in the second stage, we might consider them functional equivalents for the children. But this final cross-over between conditionals and alternatives indicates that something new has been acquired, causing children to prefer the conditional over other, previously equivalent verb forms. The cross-over in response styles illustrated in Figure 5 was tested for significance by a t-test on mean proportions of conditionals versus conditional + alternative responses in the fourth versus fifth age group. The finding was significant at the $p < .01$ level, with a t of 5.57.

There is one further cross-over in response styles between these two age groups. As illustrated in Figure 5, conditionals finally increase to the point where they exceed present indicative responses for the first time across all five age groups. This relationship was also tested by a t-test applied to mean proportions of conditionals to conditionals + present indicatives, again significant at the .01 level, $t = 7.24$.

Several tentative conclusions can be drawn from these latter findings.

First, although present indicative and alternative errors do persist through the last age groups, it seems fair to place mastery of the conditional inflection at about age 6.

Second, until the last age level the conditional and the various alternative verb responses could be considered functional equivalents of one another, sharing the same underlying meaning which simply increases linearly over time. However, in the last age group the conditional continues to increase while the alternative verbs drop off, suggesting that some new semantic–pragmatic distinction has been acquired that causes the conditional to be a preferable response. If this had not occurred, we might have concluded that the alternative verbs are a simple reflection of adult substandard dialects. If some children were learning the substandard dialect (e.g., substituting imperfect past tense for conditional) and others were mastering the standard form, then we would expect both forms to increase together across development, in parallel, as the counterfactual concept becomes more stable. In the second developmental stage, this is in fact what happens—although the two forms do coexist in the protocols of individual children. But between 5;6 to 6;2, there is a sudden preference for the standard forms. We have suggested that this occurs because a new distinction has been learned. An alternative hypothesis would be that children have suddenly become aware that the substandard is less preferable from a social point of view, even though it means the same thing. However, even if the development were merely one of social reinforcement, we would still have no explanation for why the substandard—if that is what these alternative verbs are—is actually preferred by the younger children. Furthermore, the imperfect—which is an adult substandard variant—cooccurs with other forms that have neither standard nor substandard models in the conditional usage, e.g., the infinitive. These facts lead us to prefer the interpretation that middle-class 6-year-olds have acquired some kind of semantic–pragmatic distinction between alternative verbs and conditionals, a distinction which middle-class 4-year-olds do not have.

This interpretation is supported by the longitudinal findings for Francesco. He began using the imperfect past in conditional frames, through to the last recorded sessions around 4;0. But observations made within the next year indicate that he has begun to use the standard conditional inflection. The social environment had not changed during this period in any apparent way, and his parents were unaware of any effort to reinforce one type of verb over another. We will return to this question shortly.

It had been hoped that the last item on the conditional task, with the mirror alone, would result in a different sort of performance than on the preceding six items. The questions to the child were

1. *If you were* (child's name), *what would you do?*
2. *If I were* (child's name), *what would I do?*
3. *If Valeria were* (child's name) *what would she do?*

In essence, a child who understands the presuppositions of the conditional is being asked to accept that the Experimenter doubts the child's identity. We had predicted that this item would provoke more active denials than previous items. Also, it was hoped that there would be a difference between performance on *If I were you . . .* and the anomalous *If you were you . . .* If the child employs the indicative "if" presupposition in answering these questions (i.e., ASSUME THAT I DO NOT ASSUME (You are you); ASSUME THAT I DO NOT ASSUME (I am you)), then all the questions should be equally difficult to answer. The speaker's purported ignorance on both counts should provoke protest. On the other hand, if the child employs the counterfactual presupposition in answering these questions (i.e., DO NOT ASSUME THAT I ASSUME (You are you); DO NOT ASSUME THAT I ASSUME (I am you)), then the first question should be more difficult to entertain than the second.

The results were, however, disappointingly ambiguous. It was certainly true that the last item (including all three questions) produced more non-verbal distress than the animals and other figures. Children hesitated at length, or gave embarrassed smiles. But this may also have been due to the difficulty of finding an appropriate verb for one's own activities. In fact, virtually all the children employed a verb drawn directly from the concrete situation, e.g.,

Guardavo nello specchio.	'I was looking in the mirror.'
Ti vedi nello specchio.	'You see yourself in the mirror.'
Si specchierebbe.	'She would look in the mirror.'

The overall pattern of verb inflections on this item was the same across development as that for other items, proceeding from indicatives, to alternatives, to conditionals.

Although a few children did actively deny the role switches required by the task, they did so long before the final item, e.g., *I am not a monkey, I'm a little girl.* The only explicit denial on the last item came from a 3-year-old who accepted the question *If you were you...* but rejected *If Valeria were you...* , responding

Io sono Nicola.	'I am Nicola.'

These few active denials are what one would expect if the children had applied an indicative "if" interpretation (e.g., *If you are a monkey...*) to the conditional question. The indicative interpretation would leave the possibility mandatorily open, while *If you were a monkey* informs the listener that the speaker may in fact believe that this is not the case. By the same token, *If you are Nicola...* leaves the child's identity as either true or false from the speaker's point of view, while *If Valeria is Nicola ...* shows that the speaker insists on the possibility that someone else has the child's identity.

Hence, there is some scant evidence that an indicative presupposition has been applied by some children; there is no clearcut evidence that counterfactual interpretations begin at any given age. As the task was set up, the children apparently applied the same strategies that had worked on the previous six items, despite the challenge to their own identity. This is the unfortunate result of the fact that the *If you were Nicola* item was always the last item administered. While these results are inconclusive, they do point up the value of a more detailed and controlled investigation of the two types of conditional presuppositions in research subsequent to the present study. In the final chapter, we will discuss some possible follow-up studies to the conditional elicitation task.

3. On Alternative Verbs—Some Supporting Data

Whenever a new experimental method produces an interesting and unexpected finding, there is some reason to suspect than an experimental artifact may be involved. A few observations on the use of conditionals outside the above experimental situation lend comforting support to the reality of the phenomenon of alternatives to conditional verbs.

First, there is evidence from the sentence imitation task described in Chapter V. The task itself was based on word order and emphasis, but it was necessary to establish a bias in favor of one emphasis presupposition before administering the order items. Prior to the actual order and emphasis items, we gave the children several "warm up" sentences to familiarize them with the procedure and to help establish the interpretation that the lion puppet was the agent, chasing and eating various small animals (see page 201). We decided to include some sentences with conditionals and subjunctives among these items to provide additional data for our other experiments. Sample sentences include

Se il leone avesse fame, *mangerebbe la pecora.*	'If the lion were hungry, he would eat the sheep.'
Io vorrei che tu prendessi *la pecora* (addressed to the lion).	'I would like for you to take the sheep (addressed to the lion).'

While most imitations involved either dropping or correctly imitating the verb, we did find a large number of responses substituting some of the same alternative verbs discussed above for the conditional or the subjunctive in the model sentence. Out of a total of 679 imitations of a conditional or subjunctive verb, for 60 subjects ranging in age from 3;0 to 6;2, the following substitutions were found:

Verb form	Number of substitutions
Present Indicatives	56
Imperfect Past Tense	18
Subjunctive Mood	15
Modal + Infinitive	31
Infinitive only	14

The future was the only one of the alternative verbs recorded in the conditional elicitation task which was not also spontaneously substituted in imitations of conditional–subjunctive sentences.

Further supporting evidence comes from a spontaneous incident that occurred while we administered the conditional elicitation task itself. One of the preschools cooperating in the data collection was an experimental school in the outskirts of Rome. The school was run according to a free format, and since testing took place during the spring, children were almost always outdoors. This meant that some children were tested on benches in the corner of the school grounds, and in accordance with the teacher's preferences, children were allowed to gather nearby to watch if they so chose (these were not children who would themselves be used as subjects). They observed quietly when requested to do so, but as soon as the testing of two young subjects was completed, some of the older children (ages 3;6 to 5) began to play the same game among themselves, e.g., *If you were a monkey, what would you do?* During their game, we overheard several of the same nonconditional verb alternatives being used spontaneously by the children, outside of the specific constraints of the experimental situation itself.

One final supporting observation arose during pilot testing of some experimental procedures with an American sample. The conditional elicitation task itself would be, as was stated earlier, fairly useless with English-speaking children, since a truncated sentences such as *Eat a banana* would be a grammatical response to any conditional questions. However, in trying out various sentence imitation tasks, several conditional–subjunctive sentence frames were administered to 12 American children ranging in age from 2;9 to 5;0. The sentences included

> *If the boy were happy, he would laugh.*
>
> *If I had a cookie, I would eat it.*

A predictable result was the tendency to substitute *was* for *were* in the subjunctive clause *If the boy were happy.* This is consistent with trends in adult American English, particularly substandard forms, and raises the same questions about the relation between substandard adult language and middle-class child language. Another, more surprising occurrence made less sense until pilot testing with the Italian sample began. Three imitations recorded for the conditional clause in English were the following:

> *If the boy was happy, he was gonna laugh.*
>
> *If the boy was happy, he's gonna laugh.*
>
> *If I had a cookie, I was gonna eat it.*

There is to my knowledge no common adult model in English in which a past progressive can be substituted for a modal conditional, although as was pointed out in the introduction, the imperfect past and the modal conditional can be executed with the same modal verb "would" in English. It is possible that these three substitutions, far from being random, were generated from a shared semantic base, a structure that underlies conditional verbs and other imperfect tense forms in English as well as Italian. This possibility would warrant further investigation in a study of modal verbs as they are acquired by English-speaking children.

Summary and Discussion

The longitudinal evidence presented in this chapter suggests that a concept of contingency between conjoined propositions is first expressed between 2 to 2;6 years of age, with the conjunctions *because* and *if not* (in the sense of *or else*). The indicative "if/then" structure is expressed months later, and the counterfactual conditional makes a minimal appearance in Francesco's records at 3;6 to 4 years of age. When the counterfactual does occur, it is expressed with imperfect past tense verbs rather than with subjunctive and conditional inflections.

The experimental evidence suggests that response to counterfactual conditional questions occurs first in the present indicative, from 2;0 to around 3½ years. Then, from 3½ to 5½ years, a variety of verbs are used in counterfactual responses, including present indicative, conditional, imperfect past, future, infinitive, and infinitive + modal. Finally, between 5½ to 6 years the conditional inflection itself predominates, and the various alternative verb forms drop off in frequency.

If the linguistic model proposed by Puglielli and Giliberti is an accurate account of adult competence, then the essential development between the first *because* at age 2 and the complete counterfactual *if* at age 5½ is a pragmatic one. Given a core logical structure of the type

ENTAIL (Proposition X) (Proposition Y)

the child must learn to manipulate the relations between his own assumptions about the truth of X, and the listener's view of those assumptions. These assumptions in turn are based upon a separation between the possible world context of (X,Y) and the real world status of X.

Because sentences provide information about the real world only. Both speaker and listener share an assumption of fact or truth. Indicative conditionals provide information about a possible world only. The speaker indicates to the listener that he does not know whether the antecedent is true or false. But counterfactuals signal a potential CONTRAST between the real world and conditions in the possible world. And perhaps more important, the counterfactual permits a contrast between the speaker's assumptions and the listener's. Since counterfactuals are pragmatically ambiguous between (1) the speaker's belief that the antecedent is false, and (2) the speaker's ignorance about the truth or falsity of the antecedent, then the speaker can use counterfactuals as "hedges," to avoid taking a stand. Presumably the speaker knows the state of his own beliefs; but by using a pragmatically ambiguous form, he can prevent the listener from knowing those beliefs.

Precisely what is it in this web of pragmatic relations that makes the counterfactual a late development in children? It cannot be reduced to a separation between real and possible worlds. In the play sequences described at the beginning of the chapter, very young children indicate a clear awareness that their play is pretend. Jacqueline, for example, can distinguish her own blanket and real sleeping from the blanket symbol and pretend sleeping.

Not only do children realize very early the distinction between real and pretend, but they are also capable, in very primitive utterances, of signalling the property "unreal" in their speech. Jacqueline concludes her sleep game with *no-no*. The child at the Padova institute threatens to spit food at the observer, and then furnishes the reassuring comment *fake*.

What is the difference between these primitive counterfactual sequences and the linguistic counterfactual conditional? The answer may in part be attributable to the number of relations and real–possible contrasts that are encoded SIMULTANEOUSLY by a counterfactual statement. We can see from the longitudinal evidence, and from the sequence of stages in the experimental data, that the components of the counterfactual are acquired separately, prior to their use together.

First, the distinction between real and possible is built up gradually as the child explores the nature of his symbolic world. Although the opening play sequences are quite convincing, it should be stressed that symbolic play is almost always encoded in the present indicative in Claudia and Francesco's transcripts, as if the events were current and real. Francesco commandeers various adult roles frequently in the transcripts:

Io Pecci.	'I'm Pecci.'
Io sono il dottore.	'I am the doctor.'

Just as adults can be entirely absorbed in a television drama without the necessity of continually remembering its unreality, children can throw themselves into pretend play without continually considering the contrast between this game and the real world. Yet they are perfectly aware, if asked, that it is a game. The difficulty seems to lie in simultaneously marking the hypothetical situation and its relation to the real world.

Another portion of the counterfactual structure is the entailment relation between two propositions. This structure is first expressed by Claudia and Francesco around 2 to 2½, with *because* sentences which restrict both propositions to the real world. Then, months later, the same relation is expressed with indicative "if" sentences that relate both propositions to the possible world. Finally, the counterfactual makes a minimal appearance around 3½ to 4 years, signalling the same entailment relation in the possible world, plus a warning that the two propositions may have a different status in the real world.

Third, the counterfactual will require an ability to know when and why it is necessary to signal the "unreality" of a situation. The child must be able to predict what kinds of inferences a listener might draw unless otherwise warned. If we accept the use of alternative verbs (e.g., imperfect past, future) as an effort to signal the counterfactual, then we can infer that children can "role-take" to some degree by 3½ to 4 years of age.

In summary, by four years of age children can construct

1. An entailment relationship between two conjoined propositions.
2. A potential contrast between real and possible truths.
3. The listener's perspective with respect to those truths.

This is a complex set of developments, several operations within a single utterance. And yet it occurs one or two years prior to the boundary for concrete operations established by the Geneva group (i.e., 5 to 7 years). Recent research at the Piagetian institute (e.g., *La Prise de Conscience*, 1974) has begun to establish substages in the construction of concrete operations, such that the late preoperational period includes partial, "first draft" versions of the set of operations completed between 5 to 7 years. Presumably, the operations required to construct pseudoconditionals with alternative verbs would belong to this late preoperational period.

Note, however, that the complete counterfactual conditional, with the proper verb inflections, is acquired precisely at the 5 to 7 year age boundary. Of course it is possible that this development is simply a refinement of the mapping rules for the existing counterfactual structure. But given the coincidental occurrence at around six years of age, and the significance of the rise in conditional inflections and drop in alternative verbs at that point (see Figure 5), it seems more likely that there is some further cognitive development in conditional verbs, which was missing in the construction of alternative verbs.

Let us assume for the moment that the period of alternative verbs is a period of partial structures, successive approximations of an eventual concrete operational ability. What is the difference between the alternative verbs and the conditional itself?

First of all, there is a common factor linking all the various alternative verbs on the conditional elicitation task. All of them share the condition "not now" (in contrast with the present indicative used at an earlier stage), and all are open ended in terms of aspect or duration. This is particularly true of the two most common "errors," the imperfect past and the future. Notice that all past tense verbs appearing in the conditional task are imperfect past. No child ever says *Ho mangiato una banana* 'I ate (perfective) a banana'. The future tense also displaces the reality of the event out of the present, without specifying a single moment at which the event could be verified. The modal structures accomplish more or less the same thing, insofar as

Posso mangiare una banana.	'I can eat a banana.'
Devo mangiare una banana.	'I have to eat a banana.'

are conditions that hold in the present, but are not events taking place in the present. They are open ended in terms of completion of the event. By the same token, the infinitive in Italian can be a truncated response to a modal question, for example

Che vuoi fare?	'What do you want to do?'
Mangiare una pizza.	'To eat a pizza.'

Therefore the responses to the conditional questions that occur with the infinitive only may be truncated versions of an intended Modal and Infinitive. A correct adult response to *If you were a monkey . . .* would necessarily place the modal in the conditional

Potrei mangiare una banana.	'I could eat a banana.'
Dovrei mangiare una banana.	'I would have to eat a banana.'

Hence, an answer such as *I can eat . . .* is still a creative error on the part of the children. It is, as with the imperfect and future, an approximation of a true counterfactual conditional. Finally, there are responses in this period occurring in both the conditional and the subjunctive, which are correct adult forms for encoding counterfactual propositions, except that the children place the subjunctive on the wrong proposition in this case.

Perhaps these alternative forms are attempts to encode the counterfactual presupposition DO NOT ASSUME THAT I ASSUME (X), but they are transitional moments in which the child's concept of the hypothetical is still tied to a concrete, "real time" concept of reality. What these children may be doing is approximating the truth value conditions of the counterfactual with a creative use of the time dimension. McCawley (1971), among others, has analyzed the semantic structure of tense and aspect with symbols of the type

True at time $\bar{T}$.

True before Time $\bar{T}$, not true at time $\bar{T}$.

These units can be combined into simple or compound tense structures.

Since they are based upon contrasting truth conditions, the tense structures are likely candidates for approximating the conditional.

But there is an important difference between the pure truth conditions of the counterfactual, and the time-based truth conditions of the alternative verb forms. The important difference is that the time continuum, from the child's point of view, is basically egocentric. The concept of time was built out of the child's subjective experience of ongoing, intended, or completed acts. Hence time is as seductively real for the child as the space/action coordinates used to construct it (H. Clark, 1973).

We noted in Chapter IV that Claudia and Francesco had acquired a notion of dimensional time, evidenced by time adverbs, imperfect and future tense. But at that point, the child's internal map of both time and space was still subjective, or ego centered. Piaget gives an illustration of the same phenomenon at the sensorimotor level, an example in which a child attempting to maneuver out of a difficult spot tries unsuccessfully to lift his own foot out of the way with his hands, apparently confused at the distinction between self as object and self as subject in a series of displacements. Eventually, children will take account of their own position as an objective factor in resolving sensorimotor problems of space and action. The same difficulties, Piaget emphasizes, will be encountered again at the level of internal representation. If we keep in mind the essentially subjective nature of the preoperational child's concept of time, the transitional period noted here in acquisition of conditionals begins to make more sense. The succession of verb forms used in the construction of the counterfactual reflects a progressive "decentration" from time, and time/truth relations.

The process may be illustrated as follows. Consider the time dimension topologically as a line with EGO at the center. When a contingency relationship is expressed in the present indicative, it is located with the speaker, at time of utterance. The *if* morpheme expresses the *I don't know* qualifier regarding the speaker's knowledge of the truth, but since it is in the present indicative, the proposition (X) is potentially verifiable in the here and now.

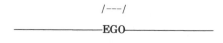

Present Indicative
Mangio la banana

When the child begins to grasp the meaning of counterfactuals, i.e., the instruction DO NOT ASSUME THAT I ASSUME (X), he approximates the suspension of truth by locating the contemplated events ANYWHERE but at the time of utterance. This is the case whether the response is in an undefined imperfect past, an undefined future, or somehow realistically pending but incomplete, as in *I can eat a banana.* The combination of displaced time and incomplete aspect avoids giving the events expressed in the two propositions a single verifiable "moment" on the time continuum. Yet the speaker implies that the antecedent is not true "now," without insisting that the antecedent is false.

These displacements from an egocentered time can be illustrated topologically as follows:

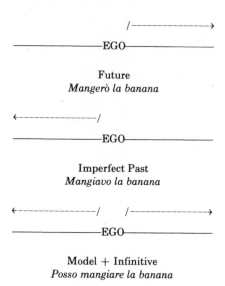

Future
Mangerò la banana

Imperfect Past
Mangiavo la banana

Model + Infinitive
Posso mangiare la banana

In short, the child has used a more familiar and perhaps psychologically easier system to do the work of a counterfactual. But the counterfactual does not actually mean "True at time unknown/Not true now." The conditional requires a complete suspension of truth conditions, to which the particular time of utterance should be irrelevant. The above tense relations are, instead, displacements of truth in time. To consider the counterfactual objectively, the child must be cognitively decentered from the time line, so that causally linked events (X,Y) are contrasted with all possible points along that line. This relationship can be illustrated as

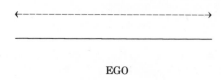

EGO

Conditional
Mangerei la banana

This sort of truth operation along an objective time continuum is a reversible operation. The same operation holds equally in both temporal directions. By contrast, the pseudoconditionals are irreversible operations in time. They read differently from left to right than from right to left. This difference between the two types of conditionals is reminiscent of stages in the acquisition of seriation. At the late preoperational stage, before concrete operational seriation, children asked to line up a series of sticks from smallest to largest will create partial groupings, with two or three sticks properly ordered. But a complete serial ordering, which holds the same relationship in both directions across the whole set, is not possible until the concrete operational period. Perhaps the use of alternative verbs is also a kind of partial grouping, an irreversible one-way operation along the time continuum.

Recall again the example of the sensorimotor child pulling on his own foot to get it out of the way. If cognitive constructs such as decentering and coordination of arrays have any dynamic reality, then the child in this transitional period can be seen as slowly trying to attain the new system, falling regularly back into a less accurate but easier way of doing things. The difficulty that Italian children apparently experience with counterfactual verbs may well reflect the difficulty of just such a building process—falling back, perhaps within a single utterance, on a cognitively easier way of manipulating truth conditions—or leaving them in the present indicative and ignoring the counterfactual work altogether.

Which brings us to a second point. If counterfactuals are so difficult to build, what is the point of doing them at all? Indeed, the tendency of substandard dialects is to dispense with them altogether, settling for an approximation executed with tense and aspect. First, the counterfactual has a relatively low information value compared with the internal content of the proposition itself. It encodes, as was stated earlier, a warning to the listener regarding beliefs about the proposition. This pragmatic effect can be created just as reliably with the substandard forms. In most contexts, the real-time interpretation permitted by an imperfect past (e.g., *If I was you, I wasn't going*) is impossible. Hence, the listener will be forced to recover the counterfactual meaning as the only other possible interpretation. Whenever the antecedent condition or the consequent is marked with a contrasting or illogical tense form, the listener is warned that the speaker's beliefs about this declaration may not be the usual ones. If these more common time forms accomplish the same pragmatic function, then the true conditional may be a cognitive luxury, an extra option that can be dispensed with without radically altering the pragmatics of the conditional situation. This would be another example, like those mentioned by Brown, of child language and substandard dialects converging (no doubt for very different reasons) to eliminate weak or uneconomical structures in the language.

On the other hand, there are languages in which there is no available special marking for counterfactuals, even in the standard form, beyond some tense–aspect combination with real-time implications. This does not mean that native speakers do not mentally create the distinction between a true counterfactual and a displaced truth condition in time. It simply means that the distinction between the two must be implicit in the surface form of the utterance, without a special signal. It is likely that children learning such languages go through the same cognitive steps illustrated here between four to six years of age. However, such a language would not be useful to us as a tool for examining this kind of shift in the child's underlying pragmatic system. Precisely because Italian makes this distinction, it permits us to operationalize the shift from egocentric pseudoconditionals to true counterfactual meanings.

In conclusion, the counterfactual is essentially a pragmatic–conceptual development, which does not become stable until the beginning of concrete operations, when the child can consider divergent viewpoints, perform complex coordinations on truth conditions, and carry out reversible operations up and down an objective time continuum. In the next two chapters, we will look at some other late developing pragmatic operations that may also depend on complex internal operations on divergent perspectives. In particular, we will look at the shift from explicit commands to implicit or polite requests, including requests that involve conditional verbs.[3]

[3] Many of the ideas in this chapter were generated during discussions with two people. In particular, I want to thank Ben Lee for discussions about the relationships between this data and preoperational vs. concrete operational thought, and Francesco Antinucci for talks about the structure of the Italian system of tense and aspect.

CHAPTER VIII

Acquisition of Polite Forms: Longitudinal Evidence

*L'erba **voglio** non cresce*
Nemmeno nel giardino del Re.[1]
ITALIAN PROVERB

It seems fair to say that desire is an early development in small children. In Chapter II, we examined the development of the understanding that other human beings can be used as instruments in fulfilling those desires. We also noted the variation in signals that our two older subjects adopted to convey their wishes. Recall the example of Marta, as she persuaded her father to open a small purse:

> Marta is unable to open a small purse, and places it in front of her father's hand (which is resting on the floor). Father does nothing, so Marta puts the purse in his hand and utters a series of small sounds, looking at Father. Still he does not react, and Marta insists, pointing to the purse and whining. Father asks *What do I have to do?* Marta again points to the purse, looks at Father, and makes a series of small sounds. Finally, he touches the purse clasp and simultaneously says *Should I open it?* Marta nods and says *Sì.*

What is striking about this sequence is the variety of means at Marta's command, despite the absence of language. Different signals are substituted within the function frame. Gestures and vocalizations are alternated, augmented, or recombined up and down a gradient of efficiency. Given such an ability to sustain a communicative goal while varying the means,

---

[1] "The herb 'I want' doesn't grow even in the king's garden." Italian proverb used in admonishing small children to say "please" or "I would like . . ."

255

the child must certainly enter into language development actively searching the new signal system for still more efficient tools in getting things done. In this chapter, we will examine the development of commands and requests by Italian children, from the first one-word commands through to the mastery of subtle linguistic devices for fine-tuning and efficient but polite request. The order in which these devices are acquired should tell us something about the structural complexity of early versus late imperative forms, and about the growing social sensitivity of the child.

In this chapter, we will present longitudinal evidence regarding the child's acquisition of polite and/or indirect means of expression. In the next chapter, the same question is treated with an experimental study involving a much larger number of children. In both chapters, a major theoretical issue is the distinction between the FORM and the FUNCTION of a given speech act. As we shall see shortly, the imperative function can be expressed with surface imperative forms, but it can also be expressed as a surface declarative or interrogative. Furthermore, children will acquire additional devices to soften the impact of all three surface forms.

The longitudinal evidence to be examined here is rather complex, involving several overlapping issues. The best way to proceed through the maze of evidence is to begin with the acquisition of devices for expressing explicit surface imperatives. Then we will look at the acquisition of politeness conventions, and at the expression of imperative and declarative FUNCTIONS with a variety of surface speech acts. The chapter is divided as follows:

I. EXPLICIT IMPERATIVES

A. First we will outline in some detail how the imperative verb inflections and second person pronouns work in Italian, including the formal versus informal levels of address.

B. Then results will be presented on the acquisition of imperative inflections by Italian children, and on the acquisition of formal versus informal pronouns of address (with corresponding verb inflections). This will necessarily require careful examination of the development of pronouns and verb inflections in general.

II. IMPLICIT AND/OR POLITE SPEECH ACTS

A. First we will outline the kinds of indirect and polite request and command forms available in Italian, as well as implicit forms for declarative statements.

B. Then results will be presented on the acquisition of polite and indirect request forms, and implicit declaratives, in the longitudinal transcripts.

III. Discussion

> The results for explicit versus implicit imperative forms are discussed together, and a possible structural model underlying the two is suggested.

Explicit Imperatives

How Explicit Imperatives Work in Italian

The Italian system for marking explicit imperative verbs is more complex than the English. In English, an imperative verb is inflected as a second person present indicative, with no difference between plural or singular. An exception is the verb "to be," which takes the form *You are . . .* in the indicative, and *You be . . .* in imperatives.

Italian has a separate morphology for imperative verbs, and the imperative, like the indicative, is also marked separately for singular and plural, and for formal versus informal levels of address. Compare the following English and Italian versions of a command to eat:

Pronoun	Italian verb	English verb
you-singular informal	*(tu) Mangia!*	'(you) Eat!'
you-plural informal	*(voi) Mangiate!*	'(you) Eat!'
you-singular formal	*(Lei) Mangi!*	'(you) Eat!'
you-plural formal	*(Loro) Mangino!*	'(you) Eat!'

The plural formal *Loro*, which literally means 'they', is disappearing from recent usage, replaced in many idiolects by the pronoun *voi* as the plural of both *tu* and *Lei*. But the difference is regional, or in many cases a matter of personal preference. Hence, many children are exposed to all four forms. Also, it should be noted that while *Lei* and *Loro* formal imperatives as listed above are grammatically correct, many Italian informants find them pragmatically jarring. The occasions that call for formal address almost always require one of the more indirect, polite request forms discussed further on.

The informal singular *tu* takes a different verb form in negative commands. It is formed with the negative morpheme *Non* followed by the infinitive, e.g., *Non mangiare* 'Don't eat!' The other you-pronouns appear in negative commands with *Non* plus the same imperative verbs as above.

The use of formal versus informal pronouns of address is also complicated by the fact that Italian (unlike French or Spanish) has no unique lexical item for you-singular formal. Instead, the pronoun *Lei* is used for both the you-singular formal and for the pronoun corresponding to the English *she*. This usage is attributed historically (see Brown and Gilman,

1960) to the use of indirect, third person address forms with social superiors, involving terms such as *La Vostra Signoria* 'Your Lordship'. These feminine gender terms were shortened to the feminine pronoun *lei*, so that addresses such as

> *La Vostra Signoria desidera*   'You Lordship desires to eat?'
> *mangiare?*

became

> *Lei desidera mangiare?*   '(You/she) desires to eat?'

Hence, all the verb markings for formal second person pronouns are identical to the corresponding third person inflections. Since there is of course no third person imperative, the *Lei*-pronoun appears with a verb in the subjunctive mood when it is used in explicit imperatives. Historically, such a *Lei*-imperative would be similar in structure to something such as

> *If your Lordship would desire to eat . . .*

The borrowing of the subjunctive means that the *Lei*-imperative for irregular verbs is unambiguously marked, since irregular verbs undergo clearcut changes in the subjunctive. For regular verbs, however, there is a great deal of potential ambiguity among the endings for *tu*-imperatives and *tu*-indicatives, versus *Lei*-imperatives and *Lei*-indicatives. In Italian, the "you" pronoun is deleted from imperatives unless some special emphasis is desired. This is of course true in English as well, so that for us a verb appearing without a pronoun subject (or any other subject) is inevitably an imperative (this excludes colloquial, anaphoric forms such as *Really makes you wonder, huh?*). In Italian, however, indicative or other descriptive verbs can also appear without pronouns, so that several interpretations are possible for a verb appearing without a subject. For example, for commands formed with verbs that have an *-are* ending in the infinitive (e.g., *Mangiare* 'to eat'), the following interpretations are possible:

Verb	Interpretation	English gloss
Mangia	*Lei mangia.*	'You-formal are eating.'
	Lui/lei mangia.	'He/she is eating.'
	Tu mangia!	'You-informal eat!'
Mangi	*Tu mangi.*	'You-informal are eating.'
	Lei mangi!	'You-formal eat!'

For *-ire* or *-ere* verbs appearing without subjects, the following interpretations are possible:

Verb	Interpretation	English gloss
Senti	*Tu senti.*	'You-informal are listening.'
	Tu senti!	'You-informal listen!'
Senta	*Lei senta!*	'You-informal listen!'

Hence, only the *a* ending for *-ire/-ere* verbs is unambiguous when it appears alone, without a subject pronoun.

As it happens, Italians proceed with these surface ambiguities with very little difficulty. For English imperatives, we generally depend upon the context to tell us which *you* is indicated for the verb without subject (although note the invention in some dialects of the term *you-all*). Italians also depend upon the context, not only to identify the referent of *you*, but also to decide whether a command or a statement has been made, or whether the *you* or *she* interpretation of *Lei* was intended. One type of communicative misfire that does occasionally occur can be found in conversations in which a female is being discussed or is present in the room. If the interlocutors are using formal address with one another, then a sentence such as

    Lei vuole andare?   '(You/she) wants to go?'

may necessitate a response such as

    Lei chi? Io?[2]   '*Lei* who? Me?'

If the speaker was referring to the woman, he must either repeat the name of the woman or point; if he was referring to the listener, he can only disambiguate his utterance by pointing. However, given the amount of potential ambiguity in the system, it is more interesting that such misfires are quite rare. They usually serve as anecdotes for amused or befuddled foreigners.

Just as Italian adults disambiguate verbs by reference to the context, children also seem able to master the system by dependence on situational meaning. However, the ambiguities do make it difficult for us as observers, in assessing the child's productive competence at a given point in development. For example, all children tend to begin their syntactic careers with one unmarked verb form for any given verb. In Italian children, the form chosen is usually the third person singular, present indicative (e.g., *Mangia* 'eats'). For some other verbs, the child may choose a different inflection as the unmarked form, but he will usually restrict himself only to that inflection for all possible functions of the verb. This tendency to use one inflection only is occasionally reverted to even after

---

[2] The same phrase is often used as a joking remark, to let the listener know that *tu* is permissible, i.e., *Lei who? Surely you don't mean me!*

other inflections begin to be acquired. This means, from our point of view, that the number of possible interpretations of the child's underlying intention is even greater than with an adult sentence. There are at least seven possible interpretations for the following two sentences:

Sentence	Interpretations	English gloss
Mangia le patate	1. *Lei mangia . . .*	'You-formal are eating.'
	2. *Lui/lei mangia . . .*	'He/she are eating.'
	3. *Tu mangia!*	'You-informal eat!'
	4. **Tu mangia . . .*	'You-informal are eating.'
Mangi le patate	5. *Tu mangi . . .*	'You-informal are eating.'
	6. *Lei mangi!*	'You-formal eat!'
	7. **Tu mangi!*	'You-informal eat!'

The starred examples (4) and (7) are ungrammatical from an adult point of view. They are permissible as second person interpretations only for young children who still use unmarked verbs. In fact, for such children sentences (4) and (7) could also mean 'We eat', 'They eat', 'I eat', and so forth. We can usually specify which PERSON of the verb the child had in mind by referring to the context. But the context alone is not sufficient to determine whether a child has mastered a given second person CONVENTION. To assess the mastery of second person inflections, we need the following types of evidence.

First, there is evidence that an early unmarked verb strategy has dropped out if no mismatches between an expressed noun or pronoun subject and its verb have appeared for several sessions. If that is the case, we can infer that the tendency to map *tu*-imperatives with a third person or otner unmarked verb has probably dropped out as well. This would eliminate interpretation (4) in the above list.

Second, there is evidence that an explicit *tu*-imperative marking for positive commands is intended when the unambiguous Non + Infinitive form for negative *tu*-commands has also been mastered. We can conclude that at this point the child does have the concept of special imperative markings, and that the error in interpretation (7) is less likely.

Third, there is evidence that marking for *Lei*-formal is intended by the child if an irregular subjunctive verb appears in an imperative (e.g., *Tenga!* 'Take', instead of *Tieni* 'You are taking'), or if an *-ire/-ere* regular verbs appears in an imperative with the unambiguous *a* ending (e.g., *Senta* 'Listen!'). Also, the accompanying use of titles rather than names (e.g., *Signora, mangi!*) is evidence that a formal marking was intended. Unless such evidence is present, it would be imprudent to attribute the you-formal interpretations, (1) and (6), to the above sentences.

Explicit Imperatives—Longitudinal Results

The longitudinal records for both Claudia and Francesco indicate that the imperative INTENTION is well established by the first one-word utterances. This is of course what would be expected, since we have witnessed the gradual development of imperative intentions well before speech in Marta and Carlotta (Chapter II). It is also true that both Claudia and Francesco, from the earliest sessions, employ a variety of means for communicating imperative intent, and that they alternate these means from one situation to another, or within a given situation. This is also predictable from the preverbal commands of Carlotta and Marta, as they vary, augment, or recombine signals until a goal is satisfied.

Two things do change across time in the longitudinal records. There is an increase in the formal elaboration of linguistic means, including a refinement of imperative verb inflections. And there is a gradual shift in function from signals varied along a dimension of efficiency to signals varied along a dimension of politeness.

Since appropriate imperative inflections were acquired gradually, we could not restrict our analysis of imperatives to those that were inflected properly. Instead, we took from the transcripts ALL utterances in which a noninterrogative verb was used in a context implying imperative intent. (The interrogative utterances were examined separately, with polite and implicit request forms). As we have just explained, ambiguity of verb inflections in Italian made it difficult to determine the moment when a given imperative CONVENTION was intended by the child. The majority of verbs in the early records are -ire/-ere verbs, which take the same i ending for both the present indicative and the imperative tu. Hence, for those verbs it was impossible to decide if the child was aware of a set of rules for marking imperatives. Furthermore, in the tape recordings it was not always a simple task to distinguish the e sound of the third person indicative from the i of the second person. Hence, it was difficult to establish even the transition from unmarked verbs to ANY kind of distinction at all between second and third person markings. Verbs of the -are type provide less ambiguous evidence of imperative intent, but they are fairly infrequent in the earliest speech records. Therefore, to determine how explicit imperatives are acquired, we must first examine the acquisition of subject–verb agreement and pronoun use in general. We can then evaluate the more ambiguous imperative inflections to determine whether the two children understand the difference implied by surface markings.

First, in the earliest sessions for both children, specific verbs tend to occur with only one type of person inflection. Claudia's first person entries for the first five sessions are all accounted for by the word oio (which gradually becomes voglio 'I want'). Since no other o endings occur, it is quite likely that this word is a memorized routine for stating wishes rather than a productive inflection. The third person entries for the first sessions are all *da* 'give', which is first used as a comment while passing objects back and forth (as was the case with Marta in Chapter III). Then, after session C3 (age 1;4;11), *da* appears as a command, that is, in a context in which Claudia is trying to get something. Finally, two second person verbs, *api* ('open') and *vedi* ('see') are also used with that inflection only, until session C6.

The earliest sessions for Francesco are almost identical to those of Claudia, in that the same verbs appear, restricted to the same inflections. *Oio* ('I want') accounts for all first person entries until F6 (1;6;4). *Da,* ambiguously marked as either third person singular or *tu*-imperative, occurs first as a comment on exchanging objects, and then in the context of a command. *Api* ('open') and *edi* ('see') occur in second person only, and are the only second person verbs to appear for several sessions. During this period, for both children, it seems fair to conclude that inflections are regarded as an integral part of a given lexical item, rather than a productive morpheme.

Around the sixth session (C6, age 1;5;26; F6, age 1;6;4), we find these same verbs appearing with several verb inflections. However, the person inflection used does not always match the person apparently intended in the context. For example, Francesco uses third person *ape* as a command, second person *api* as a comment upon his own activities, and first person *apo* as a command. Claudia, who has begun using some *-are* verbs in C7, extends the *a* ending to *ire* verbs as well, saying *apa* when commanding the experimenter to open a box. She also uses third person *ape* as a command. Similar errors occur for other verbs, although *aprire* is statistically more frequent.[3] It appears that, during this second period, the children are aware that verbs can receive different markings, but they have not yet understood the relation between verb inflection and person. In fact, the inflections seem to be assigned randomly, although more information might indicate some idiosyncratic strategies in the assignment of different endings.

Between sessions 9 to 13 (ages 1;8;4 to 1;10;6), Claudia begins to use person inflections correctly and productively. First person plural and singular, second person singular (*tu*), and third person singular and plural all appear in appropriate contexts. At the same time, the subject pronouns *io* ('I') and *tu* ('you-informal') begin to be used correctly with some of these inflected verbs (see Chapter VI). However, this is still the period in which Claudia generally refers to herself as *Claudia* in some sentences, and *io* in others. With a few exceptions, she inflects the corresponding verbs to

---

[3] **Aprire** is used with high frequency by both children in early sessions, not only to indicate 'open' versus 'close', but to request or describe a variety of state changes in objects.

match the surface subjects, with third person verbs for sentences with Claudia as subject (e.g., *Caddia domme* 'Claudia sleeps') and first person verbs for sentences with *io* (e.g., *Io apo* 'I open'). Since the referent for both these noun phrases is the same, WE CAN CONCLUDE THAT CLAUDIA UNDERSTANDS THE CONCEPT OF SURFACE SUBJECT–VERB AGREEMENT.

Francesco takes more time than Claudia in working out subject pronouns and verb agreement. While he too begins using different kinds of inflections in the sixth session, errors in person-assignment persist through F15 (1;11;1). After F15, verbs are almost all appropriately marked for first person singular, second person singular, and third person singular. But there are no plurals, and the only subject pronoun that occurs at all is *io*. Like Claudia, Francesco refers to himself as either *Checco* or *io* during this entire period, through to F21 (age 2;2;1). He also tends to mark the verb to agree with the surface subject, although he makes more errors than Claudia. An example of the two marking rules is found in F14, in the single sentence

> *Io talo, batte Checco qua.*   'I cut, Checco hits here.'

or in two consecutive sentences such as

> *Metto.*   'I put.'
> *Mette Checco qua.*   'Checco puts here.'

By F21, the use of Checco as a sentence subject has dropped out entirely. In the same session, first and second person plurals are also established. Francesco begins to use the pronouns *tu* ('you-informal') and *noi* ('we') during this period, and ceases using the listener's name (e.g., *Mommy sleeps*) as the subject of an imperative sentence. WE THEREFORE PLACE MASTERY OF THE PERSON INFLECTION SYSTEM FOR FRANCESCO AT F21 (2;2;1).

A few more developments remain before the pronoun–verb system is completed. By C13 and F21, the children have all the pronouns that English-speaking children ever have. However, they must still acquire the informal second person plural *voi*, and the formal second person singular *Lei*. Claudia begins using *voi* productively by the penultimate session (C23), and never does indicate an understanding of formal address during the period in which she was studied. Francesco begins to use *voi* productively at F34, near his third birthday. At the end of his fourth year, there are also a few occurrences of formal second person address. These will be examined in detail shortly. These latter types of second person inflections—plural and formal—are probably later than the other person inflections partly because they are not at all essential to most conversational interaction. After all, native speakers of English do without them altogether.

Somewhere during this gradual acquisition of the person–verb system, the children must distinguish between imperative versus indicative second person inflections. However, it is not at all clear when this occurs. Many of these verbs, regardless of their inflections, have been made to function as imperatives from the first sessions. The -ire/-ere verbs have the same ending (i) in both the indicative and the imperative for you-informal, and hence provide no clue to the child's syntactic intentions. -are verbs receive i in the indicative and a in the imperative, and thus would provide less ambiguous evidence of imperative conventions. But they are fairly infrequent in the early longitudinal records. The unique form of the negative tu-imperative (Non and Infinitive) is unmistakable evidence that the child does intend to differentiate imperative verbs from others, but it may also have been acquired well after a more general understanding of imperative inflections has developed.

Claudia begins to use a number of -are verbs around C9 to C12, at the same time that person inflections are acquired. Since she marks almost all -are imperatives correctly with an a ending, it is possible that she has mastered both kinds of surface marking rules at once, surface imperative inflections and subject-verb agreement. If there were a set of utterances using the same -are verb with both a imperative and i indicative, we would have conclusive evidence that imperative inflections are mastered. Unfortunately, there are only a few -are second person indicatives for these five sessions. The only -are verb appearing with contrasting indicative and imperative is dare ('to give'), as in

> Dammi.   'Give me.'
>
> Mi dai?   'You give me?'

However, dai! is one of a small class of irregular -are verbs (along with fare 'to do') in which the i ending is also acceptable as a straight imperative, e.g.,

> Fai questo!   'Do this!'

It is therefore not good evidence that regular imperative inflections have been acquired. Otherwise, Claudia either DESCRIBES first and third person activities (hence indicative) or COMMANDS second person activities. We find no second person descriptions or questions (e.g., Mangi? 'Are you eating?') with these same -are verbs. Also, since a few person inflection errors do still occur in this period, we cannot conclude that Claudia understands imperative inflections as such.

Later, from C14 through C24, examples are found of the same -are verbs used contrastingly in indicative versus imperative utterances. For example, Tira! ('Throw!') and Canta! ('Sing!') appear as commands, where Tiri? ('Are you throwing?') and Canti? ('Are you singing?') occur in interrogative requests. Also, regarding evidence from negative commands,

Claudia uses the negative imperative for the first time in C18:

Non la toccare!   'Don't touch it!'

This imperative form is distinct from a descriptive statement with the same verb:

Non si tocca.   'One doesn't touch it.'

Such declarative statements serve as negative imperatives in the adult language, and that is precisely how Claudia uses them in this same period. Putting this evidence together with the other contrasting indicative/imperative uses of -*are* verbs, WE CAN CONCLUDE THAT SURFACE IMPERATIVE INFLECTIONS ARE ACQUIRED BY CLAUDIA SOME TIME BETWEEN C9 (1;8;4) AND c18 (2;2). This is a very imprecise analysis, but the only one possible given the ambiguities in the data.

It is equally difficult to establish the onset of surface imperative conventions for Francesco. Except for the verb *da,* which is among the first verbs and does not seem to be inflected productively, -*are* imperatives are incorrectly marked with an *i* ending, which is the standard second person inflection for all -*ire* verbs, and the second person indicative of -*are* verbs. In fact, this tendency to overgeneralize the single *i* ending may be interpreted as evidence that Francesco does not understand the concept of separate imperative markings during this period.

From F20, there are a number of correct -*are* imperatives, e.g.,

Levalo!   'Take it off!'

although the tendency to overgeneralize -*ire* endings does not drop out entirely until F29. Also, regarding evidence from negative commands, Francesco's first properly inflected *tu*-negative occurs at F25:

Non buttare!   'Don't throw!'

HENCE, AS WITH CLAUDIA, WE CAN ONLY INDICATE A RANGE WITHIN WHICH IMPERATIVE INFLECTIONS ARE MASTERED, SOMEWHERE BETWEEN F20 TO F25 (ages 2;1;15 to 2;4;2).

The gradual and uncertain acquisition of Italian imperative verbs leads to the conclusion that children do remarkably well without them. The reason why they are so late and so infrequent in the data is that both Claudia and Francesco have a large repertoire of other signals and linguistic devices that convey their wishes. Hence, they need not resort to the difficult verb system to assure understanding. We will examine some of these other devices in the next section, on implicit imperatives.

Before continuing on to a discussion of implicit imperatives, there is one last development in imperative conventions that occurs in the last 13 sessions from Francesco (up to age 4;0). While imitating adult roles in play, he uses formal address, irony, and exaggerated politeness together, indicating the presence of a sophisticated pragmatic system. With regard to formal address, there are two examples, in F37 and F38 respectively (ages 2;11;5 to 2;11;25) that might be interpreted as *Lei*:

Meccanico! Lorenzo! Aggiusti la mia macchina, perché la macchina mia é quasi rotta. (F37)	'Mechanic! Lorenzo! Adjust my car, because this car of mine is almost broken.' (F37)
Senta, io passo prima io, lei passa dopo. Voi state con Alessandra, eh? (F38)	'Listen, first I'll pass then (she/you-formal) pass. You-all stay with Alessandra, okay?' (F38)

The F37 examples occurs while Francesco pretends to visit his father's mechanic, and the verb *aggiustare* ('to adjust, to fix') appears with the correct inflection for second person formal *Lei*. Francesco had used this same inflection on several -*are* imperatives much earlier in the records, before F29. But this was apparently an overextension of that high-frequency *i* ending and had disappeared between F29 to F37. Until this example, all -*are* verbs had been correctly inflected with the informal imperative *a*. Either the use of *aggiusti* is a sudden regression to an old error pattern or a deliberate formal marking. In the F38 example, the verb *sentire* is inflected with the formal *a* ending. This inflection for -*ire* is unambiguous and can be used correctly only for formal address. Since Francesco has been using the informal *Senti* for months, it seems likely that he is deliberately using the formal inflection. Also, Francesco uses the pronoun *lei* in the second clause *Lei passa dopo*. The pronoun takes the third person indicative verb, but this would be acceptable for formal address as well if it were intended as a suggestion rather than an explicit imperative. As is so often the case in Italian, the use of *lei* is ambiguous between 'she' and 'you-formal', particularly since there were several females in the room to whom Francesco might have referred.

In the last two sessions, however, there are two examples of formal address that could not be interpreted as anything else:

Ma Signora, Signora, Signora . . .	'But Mrs., Mrs., Mrs. . . .'
Signora Alessandra, che fa? Non si sbriga? (F49)	'Mrs. Alessandra, what are you-formal doing? Aren't you-formal hurrying?' (F49)
Tenga, Signorina. (F50)	'Take this, Miss.' (F50)

In F49, Francesco is playing grown up with his 5-year-old cousin Alessandra, whom he generally calls *Lalla*. He chooses to use her full name in this utterance, together with the emphasized title *Signora*, and two verbs marked correctly as second person formal. The verb *sbrigarsi* ('to hurry oneself') is an obligatory reflexive, and the reflexive particle *si* must appear in different positions for the informal command *Sbrigati!* and the formal suggestion *Si sbriga*. Francesco chooses the latter. This one utterance, then, has four separate elements that mark it as formal address. Finally, the utterance in F50 has an irregular verb in the subjunctive, which is clearly and unambiguously intended as a *Lei*-formal—particularly since the *tu*-imperative of the same verb (*Tieni!*) has been used since before 2 years of age. This formal verb is then paired with the formal title *Miss* as a vocative.

Since these uses of formal address occur in play, with listeners that are usually given the *tu*, they cannot be the result of social training that conditions responses to particular individuals. To use formal address in this manner, Francesco must understand the principle of formal situations. There is an anecdote provided by his mother during this period, in which Francesco tries to persuade his parents to grant an important favor by using their first names plus the pronoun *Lei*:

> *Carmela, Lei e Renato . . .*   'Carmela, you-formal and
>   Renato . . .'

In this use of formal address, Francesco places himself on a par with the other adults, as their equals. Hence, he adds weight and authority to a particularly important request.

In the examples offered up until now, we have seen the growth of explicit, surface imperative CONVENTIONS as they are used to express imperative INTENTIONS. However, in child speech as in adult speech there is not always a one to one correspondence between convention and intention. We will now examine the acquisition of indirect and/or polite forms for expressing performative functions.

Implicit or Polite Imperatives and Other Mixed Forms

How Implicit Performatives Work in Italian

While the Italian explicit imperative system is an elaborate one, Italian provides some simpler devices for polite forms than does English. In both languages, very indirect requests can be conveyed by expressing discomfort, desire or a state of need, e.g.,

(1)   *Gee, it's cold in here.*

as a request to close the window. However, midway between the explicit imperatives and such implied desires is a set of conventions for toning down the assertiveness of commands and requests while clearly maintaining their force as an imperative act. Whereas *Gee, it's cold in here* might possibly be misinterpreted as a simple descriptive statement, a sentence such as

(2)   *Would you close the window?*

is a request in virtually any context. One can imagine contexts in which the latter is a simple question, e.g.,

(3)   *Doctor, I've been wondering about the effect of night air*
           on Richard's viral pneumonia. Tell me, if you were in
           my position, would you close the window?

But while (1) requires a special context in order to be a command, (2) requires a special context in order NOT to be one. The tendency of conventions such as (2) to shift within certain contexts does not detract from the fact that they are part of the grammar. In fact, Italian and English differ in some interesting ways in the conventions for creating this special class of requests.

English polite forms tend to occur with modal verbs, e.g., *Would/could/ should you close the window?* In similar request frames, Italians may use conditional verbs, as well as some modal verbs such as *potere* ('can') and *volere* ('want'). In both languages, the interrogative is usually judged as more polite than the simple imperative. However, in Italian, a simple indicative question can also be used as a request, without conditionals, modal verbs, or any other special marking. Compare the following:

(4)   *Dammi quel libro!*   'Give me that book!'

(5)   *Mi dai quel libro?*   'You are giving me that book?'

English polite interrogative requests must be carried out with modal verbs. Hence, a translation capturing the pragmatic sense of (5) would necessarily be something such as *Can/would/could/will you give me that book?* There is no polite way to say *Are you giving me that book?* as an English request. One can, in a very impolite and menacing tone, say

(6)   *Young man, are you eating your spinach?*

In the special context of a mother trying to get vitamins into her child, (6) will indeed imply a command. But it is hardly a polite request, and it is not a convention. In fact, with a different context the same sentence could imply a request NOT to eat something. This becomes clearer if we substitute a different foodstuff while preserving the same tone of voice:

(7)   *Young man, are you eating those cookies?*

Unlike (6), sentence (7) is likely to make a small boy stop eating immediately. The Italian version of (6)

(8)   *Mangi i biscotti?*

if it is used as a request rather than a true question, can only be interpreted as a conventional, polite request to eat the cookies (please). (We will overlook here the point that a sarcastic snarl can, in both Italian and English, reverse the politeness of any request convention.)

The imperative is not the only performative function that can be expressed with a variety of speech act forms. Both Italian and English also have means for implying an assertion or declarative with the use of imperative and/or interrogative conventions. English has sentences such as

(9)   *Ya know what, I just saw an elephant.*

(10)   *Look, an elephant!*

(11)   *That's an elephant, isn't it?*

These sentences are marked on the surface as questions or commands. But insofar as their goal is to direct the attention of the listener to some fact or event, they do function as declaratives. In Italian there are similar devices, e.g.

(12)   *Hai visto quell'elefante?*   'Did you see that elephant?'

(13)   *È un elefante, no?*   'That's an elephant, no?'

(14)   *Guarda l'elefante!*   'Look at that elephant!'

The fact that such conventions exist, and that they shift in meaning and degree of ambiguity from one context to another, has been a disturbing issue in recent linguistic semantics. We will examine here whether these conventions are as disturbing for children as they are for linguists, and when and how they are finally acquired and used by Italian children. If an examination of the longitudinal records yields a developmental sequence distinguishing explicit and implicit forms, we will have some measure of the underlying complexity for these various kinds of speech acts.

Implicit Speech Acts and Polite Forms: Longitudinal Evidence

In both English and Italian, the three performative functions of imperative, declarative, and interrogative each have a matching explicit surface convention. However, each of these three functions can also be expressed by "borrowing" one of the other two conventions, yielding nine possible form–function mixtures. For example, the imperative can be expressed as an imperative (*Give me that*), an interrogative (*Would you give me that?*), or as a declarative (*I'd like to have that.*). The interrogative can be expressed as a simple question, or as a command for information (e.g., *Tell me* (X)), or as a declarative statement that information is needed. And one can carry out the declarative function of conveying information through an explicit statement, or through a question (e.g., *Did you know that* (X)?) or through an attention–imperative such as *Look at the way it's started raining out there!* Sadock, in his 1974 book and in several articles, has discussed these form–function mixtures with a series of fanciful titles such as the "queclarative," the "whimperative," and so forth.

In addition to these form–function mixtures, we also have a number of other devices for softening the impact of a given illocutionary force, including polite words such as *please,* the use of conditional verbs (see Chapter VII), shifts in level of address, and so forth. Finally, there are still more creative uses of language to hint remotely at desires, at the need for information, at the suggestion that something might be true, etc. without ever introducing the CONTENT of the intended request, question or statement in ANY form, however softened or indirect. For example, Ervin–Tripp (1975) points out the use of the question *Would you like another drink?* as a hint that the guests should go home.

We cannot hope to look at all speech act conventions and intentions in this one chapter. We will concentrate on four combinations: expression of imperative intent with interrogative and declarative form, and the use of imperative and request form to express declarative intent. In examining this set of form–function mixtures we will also look at the use of *please* and other polite devices for reducing the impact of a command or request. The data are presented in three sections:

1. WISH STATEMENTS   This section covers the expression of imperative function with surface declaratives, or with abbreviated phrases naming only the desired object or state. Examples range from one-word utterances encoding the desired object (e.g., *tata* 'dollie') or relationship (e.g., *mio!* 'mine!'), to simple statements of desire (e.g., *voglio carta* 'I want paper'), through to more complex statements that some need exists (e.g., *Qua ci vogliono le chiavi* 'Here we need the keys'). If they occur in the transcripts, this category will also include declaratives embedding a command for action (e.g., *I wish you would close the window*) and declaratives vaguely hinting at a desire without actually naming it, e.g., *Gee, it's cold.*

2. REQUESTS   We have reserved the term "request" to cover all instances in which a wish or a desired course of action are marked with interrogative intonation. This includes one-word commands to the listener (e.g., *Api?* 'Open?'), requests for permission for one's own activities (e.g., *Guido io?* 'Am I driving?'), and indirect questions indicating a desire that some activity be done or not be done, e.g., *'Perche voi non mangiate il*

caffe? 'Why aren't you-all drinking your coffee?' In short, this section examines imperative functions conveyed with interrogative surface form.

Since polite terms such as *please* generally appeared in this type of request, we will also use this section to examine polite words occurring in isolation, e.g., the phrase *per favore* used in itself as a request.

3. INDIRECT DECLARATIVES   In this section, we have collapsed two form–function mixtures, the expression of declarative intent with imperative form, and the expression of declarative intent with interrogative form. Recall that in Chapter II we defined the declarative function as a particular kind of imperative calling the listener's attention to some object, event, proposition, etc. In keeping with this definition, we have included in this section all nondeclarative sentences used when giving, taking, or showing objects (e.g. *da* or *grazie* when showing off or taking a doll), as well as sentences such as *Guarda!* 'Look!', or *Hai visto la bambola?* 'Did you see the doll?'.

The only imperative conventions or intentions excluded by these three sections are the explicit imperatives, with verbs, examined in the previous section. Hence, in this chapter, we will have covered all forms of what Austin calls "behabitives," speech acts designed to produce or change some behavior in the listener.

We will now examine the above three categories individually.

1. *Wish Statements*

The earliest expressions of imperative intent look very much like declaratives, in that they simply indicate the object of a desire or the fact that a desire exists. Recall that in the preverbal data for Carlotta and Marta, the same signals—pointing, reaching, calling—occurred in both imperative and declarative performatives. Similarly, in the early one-word speech of Claudia and Francesco, intended imperatives are equally ambiguous, in that they simply verbalize the referential act of pointing by naming the object or event (e.g., *acqua* 'water', or *giu* 'down'). These "implicit imperatives" cooccur in the first sessions with only two explicit verbal imperatives: *da* ('give') and *api* ('open'). As they are used in this period (always with one and only one verb inflection), these two verbs have a wide range of meaning. *Da* refers to any exchange or refusal of objects, or the initiation of some activity, and *api* refers to a wide variety of state changes in objects rather than just opening and closing. In fact, these explicit imperative verbs are so abstract in their range of application that they might be translated as little more than DO SOMETHING. Hence, in the earliest transcripts, there is more variety and frequency in wish statements than in explicit imperatives as defined here. It may be that at this point the child understands more about end states than about the means for reaching them, and so he encodes the goal and leaves the choice of means up to the adult.

After the one-word utterances naming desired objects (e.g., *water*) or states (e.g., *down*), both Claudia and Francesco quickly discover *Oio* (*Voglio* 'I want'). It is used as a sort of pivot that can be paired with an infinite set of names for objects, events, or states. An example is the following exchange in Francesco's records:

Francesco	Adult	Francesco	Adult
Lì		'There.'	
	Lo so che stanno lì.		'I know they're there.'
	Che cosa vuoi?		'What do you want?'
Oio lì.		'I want there.'	

As the children master adverbials, genitives, and locatives, they can describe more aspects of a desired end state, so that we then find wish statements such as *Ancora* ('more'), *Là* ('there'), *mio* ('mine'), *a Checco* ('to Francesco'). Just as Marta reissued her consecutive commands in the purse sequence, Claudia and Francesco will consecutively verbalize various aspects of a desired event until the goal is reached:

> *Birra! . . . Ancora!*   'Beer! . . . More! . . .
> *. . . A me! . . .*   to me! . . .'

In short, as soon as a new syntactic device is acquired in this early phase, it is immediately used in the service of wish statements. By F13 (1;10;4), Francesco has learned a set of quantity terms that he uses only in the context of requests, and that he does not seem to understand beyond their pragmatic use. In trying to acquire cookies, he alternates

> *Uno solo pane!*   'Just one bread!'
>
> *Due!*   'Two!'
>
> *Tanti!*   'Lots!'
>
> *Uno solo!*   'Just one!'

In F17 this occurs again in a request for candy:

> *Lula a me!*   'Sugar to me!'
>
> *Uno uno solo!*   'One one only.'
>
> *Uno solo mamma lì.*   'Just one Mommy there.'
>
> *Mio! A me!*   'Mine! To me!'

There is no particular reason why commands should contain verbs, particularly when the adult's choice of means in fulfilling the desire is either obvious, or irrelevant. It is true, however, that in societies such as this, adults tend to consider such explicit goal statements to be impolite. They are, in fact, based on an assumption that 'My wish is your command." As the child begins to understand what politeness means, he will have to alter his concept of efficiency in imperatives. The most economical but informative command may no longer be the most efficient.

In later sessions, we can infer from changes in the form of wish statements that the children have begun to understand this notion of politeness. The simple *I want* never disappears, but there is a growing tendency to modify it. In the earliest sessions, successive expressions of the same wish served only to increase the amount of information about the goal—to me, more, beer, mine, etc. Later on, however, a series of modification of a given wish add information about the request–act itself rather than the goal. For example, there are utterances adding a clause stating the reason for the request, e.g.

Io voglio il vino, che ci ho sete. (C16)	'I want wine, 'cause I'm thirsty.' (C16)
No, non la voglio, ho mangiato giá stamattina posciutto. (F43)	'No, I don't want it, I already ate ham this morning.' (F43)

Also, there are phrases that soften the wish by pointing out that others have had the same, or by including others in what is to come, e.g.,

Pure io voglio acqua. (C15)	'I want water too.' (C15)
Non la vogliamo più la tigre. (C16)	'We don't want the tiger anymore.' (C16)

Quantifiers, conjunctions and adverbials can also be added to modify the wish:

Adesso a me. (C17)	'Now to me.' (C17)
Un altro po'.	'Another little bit.' (C17)
Ma, ma questo é mio.	'But, but this one is mine.' (F30)
Ci voglio provare un pochino io. (F36)	'I want to try a little bit myself.' (F36)

Or the wish can be stated generically as a need (as opposed to a desire):

Qua ci vogliono le chiavi. (C23)	'Here the keys are needed.' (C23)
Ma io devo fare Babbo Natale, se no . . . (F36)	'But I have to do Santa Claus, otherwise . . .' (F36)

All of the above phenomena have also been noted by Garvey (1975) in the requests of American preschool children.

In adult pragmatics, a simple statement of desire can be polite if (1) it is understood from the context that maximal efficiency is required, and no rudeness is intended—e.g., *Scalpel!*; (2) the wish also encodes a presupposition that power rests in the listener, and that his compliance is in no way assumed. In English a standard device for the second condition is a modal verb, as in *I would like a cookie.* In Italian, this function is generally indicated by a conditional verb (see Chapter VII), as in

> *Vorrei un biscotto.*   'I would like a cookie.'

Neither of the children ever utters a conditional request in the longitudinal records. However, there are a number of wish statements in the late records for Francesco that are expressed in the imperfect past. Examples are

Io volevo attaccare il carro attrezzi. (F33)	'I wanted to attach the tow truck.' (F33)
Io lo volevo vedere. (F42)	'I wanted to see it.' (F42)
Volevo vederla ancora. (F42)	'I wanted to see it still.' (F42)
Io volevo vede se il vinaio è aperto perche se no, io voglio andare a piglià la gomma che ci ho fame, eh! (F42)	'I wanted to see if the bar is open, because if not, I want to go get me some gum because I'm hungry, yeah!' (F42)
Io volevo quella . . . (F45)	'I wanted that one . . .' (F45)

The choice of the imperfect past, as discussed in Chapter VII, functions very much like the conditional, in that it suggests that the wish is not necessarily active at the present time. A similar form is found in American English, as in the sentence

> *Mr Jones, I wanted to talk to you about the Douglas report . . .*

We cannot be certain that Francesco intended such a reduced force request in the above examples. The first example (F33) is particularly unclear since he is describing what he had been doing with his toys. The other four examples, however, are in contexts that indicate a still active desire. The first two examples in F42 follow consecutively in a situation where Francesco is still trying to look at something in the adult's control. It therefore seems plausible that Francesco did intend to soften the force of these wish statements by choosing the imperfect verb convention. Note also that the imperfect itself was acquired many months earlier, yet does not appear in these request forms until the fourth year.

Finally, the knowledge that it is impolite to state explicitly one's desires can also be used for intentional rudeness or emphasis instead of intentional politeness. In the later records, Francesco gives several examples that deliberately encode stubbornness, or anger with the observers, for example

No. Io voglio fare questo,
    non mi importa niente. (F36)
	'No. I want to do this one,
	    I don't care.' (F36)

Adesso voglio vedere tutti
    seduti! (F49)
	'Now I want to see everybody
	    seated! (said with a menacing
	    tone while playing teacher).'

Io voglio tutte le fragole,
    me le mangio tutte io. (F43)
	'I want all the strawberries,
	    I'm gonna eat them all up
	    myself.' (F43)

Io voglio solo David tutto
    il giorno! (F35)
	'I want just David all day
	    long!' (F35)

These emphatic wish statements coincide in development with the use of the imperfect *volevo* in softened wishes. This lends support to the interpretation that Francesco has learned to modify or "fine tune" requests up and down a scale of politeness. As we shall see further on, there are a number of other indications of sophisticated pragmatic speech in the same developmental period (F33 to F50, from 3 to 4 years of age).

2. Requests

The interrogative request has been described as a false interrogative, the use of a questioning intonation and word order as a means of masking imperative force. If it is true that the interrogative convention is borrowed to soften commands, then we should expect such requests to be acquired later, after both the standard interrogative and the standard imperative have been established. Based on data concerning the late development of interrogative requests in English-speaking children (Bates, 1975), we had predicted that their acquisition would be delayed in Italian children as well. The longitudinal data for Claudia and Francesco quickly established that this was not the case at all. These so-called polite requests developed well before 2 years of age. The question that remained was whether the children understood the social function of this particular category of commands, and whether they used it as a camouflage for a stronger imperative form.

Francesco's first explicit verb commands appear at F3 (1;4;27). The first verb request with a question intonation appears in F4 (1;5;12):

Ape?	'Open?'

There are very few such requests during the next 11 sessions; explicit verb commands and wish statements are both much more frequent. However, the first interrogative requests that do exist at this stage actually precede the first real questions recorded for Francesco. Interrogatives requesting information, as opposed to those requesting behavior, are not apparent until F11 (1;9;4).

From the time that explicit subjects and verb inflections are provided, the interrogative is used not only as a command, but to request permission for the speaker's own activities, e.g.,

Suona Checco?	'Francesco plays?'
Pende Checco?	'Francesco takes?'

As soon as he has mastered first person plural, in F21, plural requests appear, e.g.,

Annamo popó?	'We go car?'

When second person plural (*voi*) is mastered months later, it also appears immediately in requests. The same is true of reflexives, appearing in requests for permission, e.g.,

Si pottono mettere i bambini lì?	'Can babies be put here?'

Finally, in the last sessions of Francesco, he implies a command indirectly with questions such as

Perché voi non mangiate il caffe? (F42)	'Why aren't you drinking your coffee?' (F42)
E perché tu non te ne vai a casa? Perché stai qui? Non devi stare qui? (F42)	'And why don't you just go home? Why are you here? You shouldn't be here.' (F42)

This last type of question differs from conventional requests, in that they fail several of the tests for request idioms (Sadock, 1974). For example, one cannot say *per favore* ('please') with a sentence such as the examples at F42. Rather, this is the use of a question to imply a desire, with irony or sarcasm, as in the English example offered earlier, *Are you eating your spinach?* We will return to this point later.

Claudia's acquisition of requests, as with person inflections and a variety of other developments, proceeds more rapidly than Francesco's. However, the sequence of developments is the same. The first explicit verb command is at C2 (1;3;28), while the first interrogative command is at C6 (1;5;16). After this session, interrogative requests are used regularly. As soon as first person plurals are available, they are also used in requests (C9). The same is true of second person plurals. Like Francesco, Claudia uses the request form to ask permission for her own activities as well as to command the activities of others, e.g.,

Pende Caudia?	'Claudia takes?'
Mangia Caudia?	'Claudia eats?'

As soon as reflexives are acquired, they are used in requests, e.g.

> *Si puó sentire Bella Belinda?*   'Can Bella Belinda be heard?'

Longitudinal records for Claudia end earlier than for Francesco, and we have no examples of the nonconventional question–commands such as Francesco's *Why don't you go home?* However, in the last session (C24, 2;9), Claudia becomes very irritated that the adults are not listening to her, and with an angry and sarcastic tone of voice she says

> *Mi fate parlà'?*   'Will you-all let me talk?'

To summarize, from the longitudinal records we can conclude that interrogative requests are very early developments. In fact, they begin as soon as, or even before, true questions are acquired. Also, various request types—first person plural, second person plural, reflexives, etc.—are adopted within the request frame as soon as they are acquired. Requests are, however, slightly later than simple verb commands, and the explicit commands and wish statements are far more frequent than requests throughout the research period. Two questions remain. Do the interrogative requests serve a different function than the straight commands for these children? And do the children realize that requests are a more polite form than commands?

With regard to the first question, there is evidence that requests are recognized as functionally different from commands. Not only are they used less frequently, but they tend to be reserved as a last resort when simple commands fail. In C9, we have two clear examples that requests serve to increase the value of a command. In one, Claudia is trying to convince the Experimenter to play a telephone game with her and says

> *'Ciamo potto nonna!*   'Let's do "Hi grandma"!'

The Experimenter does not comply, and Claudia says

> *Paola, 'ciamo potto nonna?*   'Paola, we do "Hi grandma"?'

Later, we have the following exchange between Claudia and her mother (C9):

Claudia	Mother	Claudia	Mother
Dammi a mano.		'Give me your hand.'	
	Come si dice?		'How do you say?'
Poppoe, a dai a manina?		'Please, you give me your little hand?'	

In F24 (2;3;15), we have two similar sequences for Francesco:

> *Famo questo gioco!*   'We play this game!'
>
> *Famo questo gioco?*   'We play this game?'

Mette ciuccio mio!	'Put my pacifier!'
Mette tu a ciuccio mio!	'*You* put my pacifier!'
Mette tu ciuccio mio?	'You put my pacifier?'

At the very least, then, the interrogative form is used by these children to increase the efficiency of a command. In Claudia's case, 19 out of her first 20 requests occurred with the listener's name as a vocative, e.g.,

Api, Paola?	'Open, Paola?'

In the same period, 30 out of 72 commands—fewer than half—were accompanied by vocatives. It appears that requests, like the vocative, are used when a more economical signal fails, and additional communication is needed to draw attention to the speech act.

We can, then, conclude that interrogative requests serve a somewhat different function than explicit imperatives. It is less certain, however, whether the children see the interrogative as more polite. There is a close relationship between the efficiency and politeness of a command once one understands the principles involved. In fact, by withholding the child's goal a parent can use the efficiency dimension to train in politeness. Claudia receives a considerable amount of sociolinguistic training, and as discussed in Chapter V, she was conscious very early of her own speech acts and those of others. By C9 (1;8;4), Claudia has learned to say *please* whenever Mother says *How do you say? Please* was not used spontaneously until very late in the records, but even when she is responding to mother's prompting, Claudia does tend to use *please* within an interrogative frame (as in the *Give me your little hand please* example above). Francesco received much less explicit training, at least during the experimental sessions, and his first uses of *please* are later than Claudia's. But in F28 (2;5;17), his first *please* is also the result of parental prompting:

Francesco	Adult	Francesco	Adult
Dove stanno *le chiavi tue?*		'Where are your keys?'	
	Come dici? *Per piacere?*		'How do you say?' 'Please?'
Pacere.		'Please.'	

While these first overt acts of politeness may be the result of explicit training, and hence more a matter of efficiency than courtesy, there are some indications that the children are acquiring the politeness dimension. As in the case of wish statements, requests in the later sessions tend to be qualified with quantifiers and reasons. In the example given above for Claudia, *la mano* is changed to *la manina,* the diminutive term. Most such examples appear later in the transcripts. The following requests are used after a series of less elaborate requests have failed to convince the Experimenter to give her bracelets to Claudia (C22):

Mi dai i bracciale un momento per favore, Virginia, me li dai?	'You give me the bracelets a minute please, Virginia, you give 'em to me?'

The quantifiers in these requests tend to diminish size, period of time requests, or amount. These efforts are not more economical, nor are they more efficient UNLESS one understands the power relations involved in politeness. The diminishing quantities imply diminishing force of an imperative. To make a command more EFFICIENT, one generally increases either its information content or its attentional pull. But to make a command more POLITE, one must consider the possibility that the listener might be offended, or prefer a more modest approach by the speaker. Hence, this new tendency to ask for less instead of more is evidence that, toward the end of data collection, Claudia and Francesco have changed over to a new dimension of politeness. However, this still does not tell us whether the very first uses of interrogative requests were intended by the child as more polite. We will present evidence in Chapter IX to suggest that they do not.

We stated above that Francesco begins, in the last 10 sessions, to demonstrate mastery of the concept of formal address. There is further evidence of pragmatic skill in that time period (F37 to F50; 3 to 4 years). Francesco had developed a crush on his preschool teacher, and during the last four sessions he spends a great deal of time pretending to be his teacher, using all the adults and small cousins present as his class. While playing this role, he issues a variety of complex speech acts—warnings, threats, promises, and indirect commands. I was present at one of these sessions (F49), and was also impressed by the skillful mimicry in gesture and intonation that accompanied examples such as the following:

Silenzio! Perche la Signorina Simonetta, i suoi bambini sanno che bisogna fare in silenzio . . . i bambini miei sanno che bisogna fare in silenzio.	'Silence! Because Miss Simonetta, her children know that it is necessary to behave in silence . . . My children know that it is necessary to behave in silence.'
Be', se siete buoni . . . Sei diventata buona?	'Well, if you-all are good . . . Have you become good?'
Vuoi stare in silenzio? Adesso voglio vedere tutti seduti.	'Do you want to be quiet? Now I want to see everybody seated.'

Ma se siete cattivi no, eh?	'But if you're bad no, okay?'
Ancora non avete detto **Buonasera.**	'You still haven't said "Good Evening".'
Se non state buoni . . .	'If you're not good . . .'
Nessuno puo andarsene via. Dovete stare tutti zitti.	'No one can go away. You have to all shut up.'
Perché sì, perché a scuola si parla con bassa voce.	'Because yes, because at school one speaks with a quiet voice.'
Adesso silenzio! Se i bambini chiàcchierano . . .	'Now quiet! If the children are chattering . . .'
Tutti! Virginia, con le braccia conserte. Pure lei con le braccia conserte.	'Everybody! Virginia, with your arms folded. Her too, with her arms folded.'
Però adesso se state buoni, non l'adopriamo il lupo.	'However, now if you are good, we won't use the wolf.'

The warnings include implying a result by stating the condition (*If you're not good . . .*), attributing the command to another authority (his supposed co-teacher Signorina Simonetta), or implying a command by referring to some well-known rule (*You still haven't said Good Evening*). As they are discussed by Sadock (1974) and others, these utterances indicate a highly flexible set of pragmatic rules for the use of sentence types, including some creative and nonconventional forms.

But as Ervin–Tripp (1975) has pointed out, there are limits to just how creative a child of this age can be with his requests. Francesco, in the above examples, always expresses either the behavior expected of the listener (e.g., *You'll have to be quiet . . . You still haven't said Good evening*) or the desired end state (e.g., *I wanted to see that one . . .*). The means chosen to express either of these two alternatives are indeed elaborate, using all possible surface combinations, tenses, clause structures, etc. But I have found no examples of expression of imperative intent (in any surface form) in which neither the goal nor the means are mentioned. According to Ervin–Tripp, adults use these obscure hints often, e.g., *Do you want another drink* to ask guests to leave, or (somewhat less subtly) *Are you alone* to elicit an invitation. If Francesco or Claudia ARE using such obscure hints, they are so obscure as to be totally unrecognizable in the transcripts. It seems fair to conclude that Francesco can rearrange the means for expressing an illocutionary force, but he cannot mask both the FORCE and the CONTENT and still achieve an imperative goal.

Some semantic proposals (e.g., Gordon and Lakoff, 1971) would predict no greater pragmatic complexity for Francesco's last developments (at 3½ to 4 years of age) than for the use of interrogative in commands (at 1½ years of age). We will now examine one final class of implicit speech acts that also occur very early, and then suggest a structural model that explains the wide developmental lag between the first mixed speech acts, and Francesco's later pragmatic developments.

3. Indirect Declaratives

According to the analysis of preverbal declaratives in Chapter II, the declarative is, at all stages, an imperative that commands a particular act of attending or knowing on the part of the listener. This category contains all sentences used while offering or exchanging objects, through to sentences that explicitly command or request attention to an object or event. In the records for Claudia and Francesco, we find a smooth transition from sentences that verbalize the object exchange, to sentences that otherwise command a knowing act.

A first stage reaches from F1 to F11, and from C1 to C6. Examples in this period are identical to the sensorimotor declaratives discussed for Marta and Carlotta, in that the children are handing objects back and forth, or pointing objects out to the adult. The sentence types that are used with such behaviors are the following.

A. *Da* ('Give'), which occurs when then child is giving an object, as well as when he is receiving it.

B. *Tazie* (*Grazie* 'Thanks'), which is used like *da* to accompany an exchange of objects in either direction. Unlike the adult word *grazie*, this term is used as a pivot that takes nouns in combinations such as *azie palla* 'thanks ball'.

C. Vocatives, or the use of the listener's name to draw attention to an act of giving or pointing.

D. Nouns and demonstratives which name the object itself or refer to it with a deictic word while pointing, giving or showing.

These utterances function like the sensorimotor declaratives, in that their goal seems to be some tangible evidence of attention by the adult, such as accepting the object or turning and commenting.

A second stage begins at F11 (except for two earlier examples at F7) and at C7 (1;9;4 and 1;7;10 respectively), and extends to the beginning of the third metapragmatic stage discussed in Chapter IV (C12 and F21). In this phase, the act of attention itself is explicitly commanded from the listener, with a verb of seeing or listening. In the meantime, the concrete exchange of objects that predominated in the first phase are now coded separately, with specific verbs such as *Prendi* ('Take') and *Tieni* ('take' or 'have'). These words are used only unidirectionally, for giving an object, and bidirectional exchange words such as *tazie* disappear. *Da* is now used only as a command for objects or actions from the adults.

Among the verbs of attention that the child use are the following:

A. *Vedi!*	'See!'
B. *Gadda! (Guarda!)*	'Look!'
C. *Ha itto? (Hai visto)*	'Did you see?'
D. *Senti.*	'Listen.'

The fourth term, *Listen,* appears slightly later than the three visual commands, within two or three sessions. All of these verbs commands are paired with both names of objects, and with sentences describing events, as in

Hai itto pipí la bambola?   'Did you see peepee the dollie?'

Also, all four terms often appear alone, either to accompany nonverbal deictic acts, or to be followed later by some further comment. These declarative commands are statistically very frequent, averaging 15 or 16 per session after they first appear.

The above are examples of declarative functions expressed with an imperative surface form, or attention commands. Around the same time that interrogative requests appear to express declaratives, in what might be called attention requests, e.g.

Hai visto come si fa la *capriola?*	'Did you see how a somersault is done?'
Lo vedi Roberto?	'See Roberto?'
Vedi?	'You see?'

Like the interrogative commands, these interrogative declaratives function to increase the efficiency of the speech act, insisting on attention in those cases in which a noninterrogative command for attention has failed. For example, in the early records for Francesco there is the following sequence:

Uce!	'Light!'
(no response from adult)	(no response from adult)
Hai itto uce?	'Did you see light?'

Finally, we can discern a third change in the nature of indirect declaratives when the children begin to command attention not only to events and objects in the immediate context, but to facts verifiable outside the speech situation. After the onset of the period discussed in Chapter V as the third metapragmatic stage, both Claudia and Francesco begin to call attention to facts, past events or ideas by using the phrase *Sai che . . .* —'You know that . . .' This ability to call attention to intangible events, with a verb describing a nonperceptual act of knowing, may be linked to the increase in the symbolic processing capacity discussed in Chapter V. Also, recall that in Chapter II we stated that it is difficult to pinpoint the shift in declarative goals from SPEAKER ATTEND to SPEAKER ASSUME. The shift from *See* (X) to *Know* (X) may be symptomatic of just such a change in the goal of the declarative performative.

Summary and Discussion

To summarize the rather complex longitudinal findings, we can conclude the following:

1. Explicit verb inflections are mastered fairly late by Italian children. Nevertheless, both children from the earliest records already have a variety of means in their repertoire for expressing imperative intent.

2. The ability to express a given sentence function with a mixture of surface sentence types is apparently established before two years of age. Interrogative commands tend to appear together with—or even slightly before—true questions. At the same time, interrogatives are also used in requests for attention, and hence in the service of declarative goals.

3. Around 2½ years of age, there is a tendency to soften imperative force by using *please,* and by reducing the dimensions of a request. This development suggests a shift from an efficiency dimension to some kind of politeness dimension.

4. At a much later stage, between three to four years of age, pragmatic skill extends to indirect commands, implied threats and promises, the use of imperfect tense to soften commands, and formal second person pronouns and verb inflections. However, in the age range examined here, neither Francesco nor Claudia are able to construct very indirect hints that do not specify the imperative goal in some way.

The data are not perfectly compatible with some current proposals for the pragmatics of commands and requests. Notably, Gordon and Lakoff (1971) suggest that the marking of commands with other, nonimperative sentence types is based on the use of Gricean conversational postulates. For example, there is a postulate that speakers will not sincerely ask a question if they already know the answer, or if they are not really seeking information. A sentence such as

Do you know what time it is?

cannot be answered with

Yes, I do.

The listener knows that such information by itself is useless, and that speakers do not normally request useless information. Therefore, the speaker must have a different reason for using the sentence. If the question interpretation is blocked, the listener constructs the presupposition

Speaker wants to know the time.

and responds to the presupposition rather than the apparent question.

This sort of an analysis has profound psychological consequences. According to the Gordon and Lakoff approach, at the age of 18 months Francesco and Claudia must go through a series of steps in which they

(1) Build an imperative intention.

(2) Consider the listener's reaction.

(3) Consider the conversational postulates.

(4) Choose a form that violates the conversational postulate so that the listener will be forced to reconstruct the actual imperative intention and/ or choose a form that mentions one of the felicity conditions for the imperative intention.

From what we know about cognitive development, it seems unlikely that an 18-month-old is capable of this series of operations. And yet both Claudia and Francesco use a set of linguistic forms which, according to Gordon and Lakoff, must be generated from such a process.

Furthermore, there are a number of pragmatic developments that do not take place until two years later: implied commands such as *Why aren't you drinking your coffee,* indirect threats such as *If you're not good . . . ,* quasi conditionals such as *I wanted to see that one . . . ,* and formal second person address. Claudia never acquires these devices in the period covered in the longitudinal study. Francesco does not acquire them until about 3½ years, and Francesco is by many standards an exceptionally precocious child. According to both the Grice and the Gordon and Lakoff analysis, many of these later sentence types are also explained in terms of conversational postulates and presuppositions about the listener. It does seem plausible, on the basis of the elaborate pretend play that Francesco is also capable of at 3½, that the pragmatic operations described above do underly these later skills. But the two to three year gap between these late developments and one-word interrogative requests suggests that the two have very different pragmatic structures.

An alternative speech act analysis is presented by Sadock (1974), in *Toward a Linguistic Theory of Speech Acts.* He suggests that some implicit speech acts are carried out by reference to the conversational postulates, as Gordon and Lakoff describe. Others, however, have become a conventional part of the language and are generated directly by the performative deep structure. Sadock compares these two kinds of speech acts to the difference between idioms, e.g.,

Helen spilled the beans.

and metaphors, e.g.,

Helen put the red meat on the rug.

a literary metaphor with roughly the same meaning as "spill the beans." It is possible, according to Sadock, to distinguish idioms from metaphors by subjecting them to certain syntactic tests. For example, the metaphor can be passivized while the idiom cannot:

*The beans were spilled by Helen.
The red meat was put on the rug by Helen.

The passivized idiom can be used only for humorous purposes, in which case it is a deliberate violation of grammatical rules. This analysis is similar to Chafe's (1970) discussion of idioms as postsemantic processes that cannot take all the transformations that other propositions undergo.

Sadock provides a number of similar tests to separate idiomatic request conventions from indirect or implied requests. For example, idiomatic requests can take a sentence internal *please,* while other implicit requests cannot:

Would you open the window?
Would you please open the window?

Do you have a cigarette?
*Do you please have a cigarette?

The Italian interrogative command is such a request idiom, in that it reacts differently to syntactic tests that do other, indirect or nonidiomatic commands. Sadock's proposal would generate

Apri (per favore) la finestra?　　'You are opening (please) the
　　　　　　　　　　　　　　　　　window?'

from the performative hypersentence in deep structure. The nonidiomatic request

Perché non apri (*per favore)　　'Why aren't you (*please)
　　la finestra?　　　　　　　　　opening the window?'

would instead be derived from a Gricean process contrasting surface illocutionary force with a conversational postulate, forcing the alternative interpretation that the sentence is a command rather than a question.

An analysis that separates idiomatic from nonidiomatic speech acts would be supported by the developmental data for Italian, insofar as the conventional request is acquired early, while the implied request appears two years later. But why is the idiomatic performative structure of *Apri la finestra?* so easy to acquire?

One defect in Sadock's analysis is that it seems less economical than the Gordon and Lakoff approach. The Gricean analysis has a more conservative deep structure (despite its psychological complexity). It requires only a small stock of standard performative verbs—ask, declare, command— plus a limited set of conversational postulates. All possible implicit performatives are then created by various contrasts between the performative verb and the conversational rules. Sadock's proposal, by contrast, seems to require assigning a different performative structure to every speech act idiom—one for explicit commands, one for interrogative requests, another for true questions, etc. There is the risk of multiplying the performative verbs indefinitely, and consequently increasing the stock of transformations for each type of performative verb.

Sadock partially resolves this problem by suggesting that performatives contain complex verbs, with decomposable internal structure. This proposal is similar to the analysis of the performative outlined by Parisi and Antinucci (see page 16) and to a recent proposal by McCawley (1973). Different surface forms, e.g., requests versus commands, would have a similar force or meaning in Sadock's system insofar as they have several components in common. For example, both interrogative requests and explicit commands share the components CAUSE(DO(Listener, X)). The different surface forms would be the result of other components which are NOT the same for both structures. Since transformations—e.g., interrogative, imperative—are sensitive to specific components rather than to the whole performative structure, requests and true questions take the same transformation because they both have the component which triggers interrogative surface forms. Hence, the grammar requires only a limited set of performative components that can be placed in different combinations, plus a limited set of transformations that operate only on particular components.

Following Sadock's suggestion, we can describe a limited set of performative components that would generate all the sentence types of Italian 2-year-old grammar, without invoking conversational postulates or other elaborate presuppositions.

1. *Wish Statements versus Explicit Commands*

The deep structure for imperative intentions described in Chapter II was as follows:

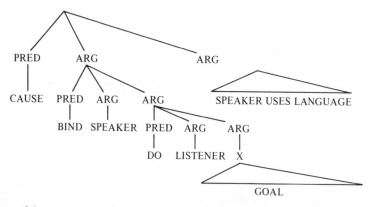

To map this structure, there are two major options:

A. Encode the course of action or the means to the goal, the branch DO LISTENER X.

B. Encode the goal or wish itself, for example the branch HAVE SPEAKER X.

One could also, of course, encode both, but time and economy select against overly long sentences. The choice of encoding the means versus encoding the goal may depend upon the situation. If the means or course of action is either obvious, or unknown, or irrelevant, the child will probably state his desire instead. If the goal itself is obvious, or if stating the goal has thus far failed, the child may encode the desired activity or means. The first imperatives for both Claudia and Francesco select between these two options according to the context and are often alternated within a single context. This process is similar to the nonverbal imperatives of Marta, which alternate signals until the goal is reached.

2. Declaratives versus Imperative Statements

The structure of the declarative as outlined in Chapter II is similar to the imperative, except that the predicate of *listener* is either ATTEND or ASSUME:

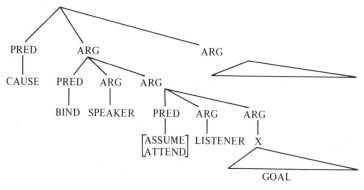

To map this structure, the speaker again has two major options:

A. Encode the course of action, in this case an epistemic act of knowing, seeing, listening, etc.

B. Encode the goal of the commanded act, in this case the object or fact to be known.

These are the same two options that regulated wish statements versus command. If the DO LISTENER X component is selected for mapping, the sentence will be a surface imperative. If the X component itself, the goal, is selected for mapping, the sentence is a declarative. In the earliest transcripts for Claudia and Francesco there are no transformations distinguishing imperatives from declaratives. There are only DO utterances versus X-goal utterances. When the imperative transformation (e.g., verb inflections, postverb object clitics) does develop, it is applied immediately to both DO-ATTEND predicates as well as to DO–CAUSE predicates; hence both "true" imperatives and imperative statements (e.g., *Guarda l'elefante*) appear at the same time. By the same token, the declarative transformation applies both to the objects of ATTEND predicates and to the objects of CAUSE predicates, so that both "true" declaratives and wish statements appear at the same time.

With this analysis, there is no need for extra structures distinguishing "false imperatives" or "false declaratives," particularly since we have no evidence that these early expressions are "false" from the child's point of view. Instead, we have two transformations that map two separate aspects of a performative: the act requested of the listener (including attention acts) or the goal of that act (including the object to be attended). Since the child commands attention as sincerely as he commands any other behavior by the adult, there is no reason to conclude that the first form-function mixtures require double level camouflage structures of the Gricean sort. At this point, we can also analyze to the use of interrogative forms to express any of the three functions.

3. *Questions versus Other Interrogative Forms*

The performative structure outlined by Parisi and Antinucci for interrogatives is also an imperative, like the ones discussed above, except that the DO–proposition for the listener requests another speech act. The speaker essentially commands the listener to perform a declarative speech act regarding some topic. If the interrogative transformation (or mapping rule, in Parisi and Antinucci's terms) is sensitive to this entire performative structure, then the interrogative performative would not generate requests or interrogative declaratives that do not command speech acts from the listener. However, it is possible that, following Sadock's proposal, only a subset of the components of this interrogative performative triggers the question intonation. Perhaps the interrogative has a more abstract function than a specific command for speech acts.

The interrogative is usually employed, in declaratives or imperatives as well as in questions, when some signal is required from the listener to assure that the message is received. Recall in the chapter on sensorimotor performatives that once imperative gestures were firmly established, the children often failed to establish eye contact while communicating. If the command then failed, eye contact was reestablished, presumably to seek information explaining the communicative failures—e.g., Mommy wasn't listening. The interrogative seems to function in Italian speech much like eye contact in the sensorimotor period, as a search for feedback concerning the effect of the message. It is a request for confirmation, verbal or nonverbal, that the message was received. This would explain the way interrogative requests and statements function in the early transcripts for Claudia and Francesco. Recall (see page 277) that the question intonation was used in a command as a "last resort," when straightforward commands had failed. The interrogative form of the subsequent command requires a confirmation by the listener. In fact, this function might be described with a compound predicate CONFIRM, which might have an internal structure something such as

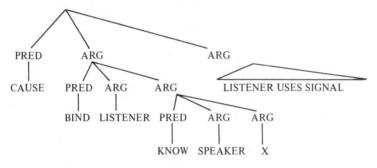

This CONFIRM predicate may dominate either the interrogative goal— i.e., the listener's speech act—or the declarative goal LISTENER ATTEND-ASSUME, or the imperative goal of LISTENER DO-CAUSE. The transformation (which at this stage is restricted simply to a questioning intonation) would then be sensitive only to the CONFIRM predicate, as it appears in any of the three types of performatives.

Since all three types of interrogatives appear around the same time, with requests for listener speech acts coming slightly later than requests for other behaviors, it does not seem useful to call requests "false interrogatives". Neither does it seem useful to explain them with a process of "borrowing"—a transformation to camouflage some other kind of intent. The CONFIRM predicate makes any kind of speech act more efficient for the child because it insures the listener's attention. Later, the child may also learn that this form is ranked higher along a politeness dimension, and that it reduces the force of a command or assertion by granting the listener power to confirm or deny. But as it functions in the early speech records, the interrogative request is in fact a particularly strong means for expressing imperative intent, and is used when explicit imperative forms fail. (See Chapter IX for further evidence supporting this interpretation.)

The above system will generate virtually all of Claudia's performatives and all of Francesco's until about 3½–4 years of age. Up until that point, there is no need to invoke Gricean postulates as part of the performative system, at least with regard to indirect requests. But around 3½–4 the above system begins to break down. We have suggested that once the child decides whether to map the goal or the action expected of the listener, the mapping system applies automatically. If he selects the goal, he will express his sentence as a declarative. If he selects the action, his sentence will be mapped as an imperative. Finally, if there is a CONFIRM predicate dominating either a DO–ATTEND or a DO–CAUSE complex, the surface sentence will be an interrogative. In Francesco's later transcripts, such an automatic mapping system obviously no longer applies. He is still restricted to saying something about either the action or the object–goal of that action. But he can express either one of these with virtually any surface form—*if* clauses, reflexives suggesting that the act has not been done yet, citations of someone else's desires, conditionals, and so forth. At this point, it does seem that Francesco can freely manipulate the means for expressing his imperative intent, masking the illocutionary force in any number of ways as long as the content is specified. This is also the period discussed in Chapter VII, in which children begin to issue counterfactuals albeit with alternatives to the conditional verb. We suggested in that chapter that even such partial mastery of the conditional, suspending truth at a given time, requires some kind of role-taking concerning the likelihood that the listener will draw undesirable inferences. If that is true, then it would not be surprising if the child could apply the same limited role-taking ability to the use of Gricean conversational postulates for softening and camouflaging pragmatic intentions.

A recent paper by Aksu (1973) on the acquisition of requests by Turkish children, suggests that the same sequence of developments occurs in Turkish. The more indirect, creative request forms are the last ones acquired, while idiomatic requests come in much earlier. Why, then, do interrogative requests develop fairly late in English-speaking children? There is one fairly simple explanation which should have been obvious without cross-cultural comparison. The English interrogative request can only be carried out with modal verbs. It is not grammatical in English to request opening the window with *Are you opening the window?* Brown (1973) reports that modal verbs are among the last acquisitions of basic grammar by his American subjects. And this finding is certainly compatible with our results in Chapter VII on conditional verbs. It is quite likely that the delay in interrogative requests in English is an artifact of the delay in acquiring modal verbs. Ervin–Tripp (1974) suggests that the request *Can I have . . .* is acquired as an idiomatic or memorized form by English children before they can handle other modal verbs. And Holzmann (1972) reports that Brown's subject Adam does in fact make five one-word interrogative requests in the earliest speech records. One of them, coincidentally, is the same as Francesco's first interrogative request:

Open?

Apparently, Adam discarded this kind of request until much later, when modals were acquired. Perhaps he discovered that such requests are simply not grammatical in English. But these few early attempts indicate that, like the Italian children, Adam was capable of using the CONFIRM predicate in his request intentions as early as one-word speech.

Insofar as it is possible to summarize across the few languages in which indirect requests have been studied, I suggest a tentative three-stage model.

1. First, there is a period from the beginning of language development up to about 3½–4 years of age, in which from the CHILD's point of view there are no indirect speech acts. The child decides which aspect of his desire he wishes to encode in a given utterance, and the mapping mechanism automatically transforms the selected components into their appropriate surface form. If the child selects the components containing the activity desired of the listener, the utterance is encoded as a surface imperative. If he chooses instead to encode the object or goal of the listener's act, the utterance is encoded as a surface declarative (i.e., as a wish statement). These two rules hold equally regardless of whether the child is mapping a command to attend (i.e., a declarative intent) or a command to some other action (i.e., an imperative intent). If the performative intention contains the additional structure CONFIRM, the utterance will appear in interrogative surface form and/or with a vocative, depending on the child's degree of frustration in achieving listener attention.

This analysis is, as we have stated, a version of Sadock's model. It generates only idiomatic surface structures, with no recourse to complex presuppositions or conversational postulates. However, the same general model could also generate other idiomatic surface forms, beyond the three specified here. Both Sadock, and Chafe (1970), have presented models for representing idioms as "post-semantic processes" (Chafe's term). This means that idioms serve, like single lexicalizations, to map a set of components directly. As such, they cannot be broken or moved by the syntax as easily as other, nonidiomatic phrases. Recall Sadock's example

Helen spilled the beans
*The beans were spilled by Helen.

It is possible that children in this first stage may learn several direct, idiomatic mapping rules for various portions of a performative, without analyzing or understanding the internal syntactic structure of such idioms. For example, as Ervin-Tripp (1975) suggests, English-speaking children may learn the phrase *Can I have . . .* as a request idiom when they are otherwise incapable of producing modal verbs. Similarly, Francesco's pragmatic use of quantifiers (e.g., *Some! Lots! Just one!*) would be an example of an unanalyzed idiom in the service of performative intentions. A child could in this fashion acquire a fairly good repertoire of such idiomatic direct mappings without having the flexible, conscious control over form–function relations that Francesco shows at 3½–4 years. In fact, it may be that gradual experience with idioms leads the child into an understanding that form can be detached from function.

2. In the second stage, as illustrated by Francesco's later transcripts, the child is free of the idiomatic, direct mapping constraints of the earlier period. He understands the distinction between form and function in the same sense that he learned to separate means from ends during the sensorimotor period. As a result, he can manipulate the means for expressing performative content with great facility, using virtually every surface syntactic device at his disposal. This capacity may also be related to the newly acquired ability to role-take, i.e., to take the perspective of the listener. The child now understands that he and the listener share certain rules about the goals of speakers and the nature of conversations, and hence, that the listener can recover the child's intent despite variations in form.

However, since the child's role-taking ability is limited at this stage (see Chapter X), he is also limited in his ability to manipulate the listener's expectations. At both the first and the second stage, the child must either express the act commanded of the listener, or the object of that act, or both. The Stage 2 child can manipulate the surface form for such utterances, but he cannot construct utterances that mask both form and content while successfully achieving their goal. Francesco, in the period covered by this research, remains at the second stage.

3. At this third stage, the child will be able to manipulate both form and content in achieving communicative goals. As his role-taking capacity increases, his ability to deceive, wheedle, seduce, and persuade will expand accordingly. The more he knows about his listener, the more he can play upon that knowledge without committing himself to an out and

out (and hence, refutable) request. As noted, Francesco never gets quite this far. Although he is a pragmatically precocious child, when the matter at hand involves cookies, he invariably mentions cookie, mother going to get them, and so forth.

Both Garvey (1975) and Ervin–Tripp (1975) have discussed this third stage. They both report that completely indirect hints are extremely rare in preschool children. Neither is quite sure when a full fledged capacity for such utterances is established. An educated guess is that this stage begins when concrete operations are well-established (e.g., 7–8 years of age), and the child is confident and versatile in role-taking skills.

The second stage can be generated fairly easily from a pragmatic–semantic model based on a standard set of conversational postulates, permitting allusions to felicity conditions, violations of standard expectations, etc. The third stage, on the other hand, virtually defies formalization. A grammar generating all possible hints, seductions, and persuasions would require a "human nature" component, an encyclopedia of motives, habits, quirks, irritations, and preferences of all potential listeners. This is clearly a point where the boundary between linguistic knowledge and world knowledge breaks down.

One last question remains. Piaget has noted that children are often capable of deception when they are barely capable of one-word speech. For example, his daughter used the word for *potty* as a trick to be allowed out of her play pen. Our own data (Bates et al., 1975) confirms this observation. Furthermore, children who cannot carry out the elaborate persuasions noted above often ARE capable of outright lying. Why are some devious behaviors so much easier than others?

Recall our discussion in Chapter VI of the difference between the ability to pretend at one year of age, and the ability to suspend reality in a counterfactual conditional statement at 5 years of age. We suggested then that the difference may lie in the number and nature of simultaneous operations required for suspending, reversing and yet asserting truth in a given communicative act. Perhaps the same generalization applied here as well. It is one thing to deceive or tease. It is another to do so while simultaneously constructing and coordinating performative, presuppositional and propositional structures in a single communicative act. This is admittedly an ad hoc formulation. Again we must invoke a tiresome but eternally necessary statement: there is need for a great deal of future research.

In the experiment presented in the next chapter, explicit judgments of politeness are elicited from children. In the longitudinal data, we can only infer from production and context whether the child understands that some forms are more polite. For example, it is not at all certain—in fact it is unlikely—that the interrogative commands are recognized as polite forms at age 1½. In the next chapter, it will be possible to confirm or disconfirm whether the sequence of acquisitions observed here will hold across a larger sample, and whether children control the politeness dimension with respect to these various forms.[4]

[4] I want to offer special thanks to Virginia Volterra and to Susan Ervin-Tripp for their suggestions and criticisms of an earlier version of this chapter. I have included several of their ideas in this final version. Misrepresentations are of course my own.

CHAPTER IX

Acquisition of Polite Forms: Experimental Evidence

In the preceding chapter, we described a sequence of developments for both explicit and implicit imperative forms, between 1½ and 4 years of age. Furthermore, we suggested that during this period, at around 2½ years of age, there is a shift in usage from speech acts ordered along a dimension of efficiency (i.e., economy and informativeness), to speech acts ordered along a dimension of politeness. We inferred the acquisition of a politeness concept from the fact that Claudia and Francesco began to reduce rather than augment the force of failed imperatives. For example, Claudia used diminutives (e.g., *biscottino* instead of *biscotto*) to modify an unsuccessful request. And both children used quantifier terms (e.g., *Un altro pochino di birra* 'another little bit of beer') and time adverbials (e.g., *Mi dai un momento le chiavi?* 'You give me the keys for just a moment?') to reduce the dimensions of various requests and commands. Apparently, Claudia and Francesco have discovered that by asking for less, one increases the probability of compliance by the listener. This discovery, while clearly linked to the goal of request efficiency, also requires some minimal capacity to predict the forms that an adult will find acceptable. Further confirmation that something like a politeness concept has been acquired rests in the fact that this tendency to reduce requests begins at the same point at which Claudia and Francesco begin to use the ritual term *please*, albeit usually with adult prompting.

If our inferences from the longitudinal data are correct, a general concept of politeness or acceptability for speech acts has been acquired by age 3. This suggestion is also supported by the metapragmatic data presented in Chapter V, in which Claudia and Francesco reflected upon and talked about their own speech acts and those of others, again around 2½–3 years of age. However, we cannot be certain whether Claudia and Francesco apply the judgment of politeness to all the various request forms that are polite or rude from an adult point of view. For example, we suggested that at 1½ years of age, they may not be at all aware that their interrogative requests are considered to be "softened" imperatives. Some of the models available for describing indirect speech acts (e.g., Grice and Gordon and Lakoff) involve a good deal of reasoning about the acceptability of utterances and the listener's expectations. If we are to make any use of these models in describing child speech, it will be important for us to determine if and when children are capable of reasoning about the pragmatic value of various request forms.

The experiment described below was designed to test the ability of 3–6-year-old children to produce and judge different types of request forms. The experiment should give information about the following questions:

1. Will the sequence of developments observed in the longitudinal records be confirmed in production data for a larger sample of children? What are the request forms that 3–6-year-olds use when explicitly instructed to "ask nicely"?

2. Can children make passive judgments of relative politeness for various request forms? If so, are such judgments acquired in a block, or are they extended gradually across time to different request forms?

3. Can children who do make accurate passive judgments of relative politeness also explain or reason actively about why one item is "nicer" than another?

Method

The subjects were 60 Italian children between the ages of 2;10 and 6;2, attending middle-class preschools in the Rome area. On the basis of teacher assessment, children with apparent learning disabilities or speech deficits were not included in the sample. Subjects were evenly divided according to sex, and there were roughly 10 children within each six-month age span (e.g., 10 subjects from 2;10 to 3;5, 10 subjects from 3;5 to 4;0, etc.) Testing took place in the preschools, after the Experimenters had spent at least two schooldays in the classroom so that the children were accustomed to their presence.

Children were brought for individual testing into a familiar room near their classroom, and were seated at a table with an array of puppets and a visible supply of wrapped caramels. First, the child was introduced to "Signora Rossi," a handpuppet of an elderly, grey haired woman. The old woman puppet was chosen to make the politeness task more reasonable to the children, since Italian culture requires greater deference to older men and women. Also, it was hoped that some children might spontaneously address "Signora Rossi" with formal levels of address.

Subjects were told that the candies belonged to Mrs. Rossi, and that if the child asked her, she would give him a caramel. When the child had made his first request, the Experimenter pretended to whisper something with Mrs. Rossi, and then said (in Italian):

> *Signora Rossi ha detto che ti dará senz'altro una caramella. Pero, sai, è un po' vecchia, e le piace quando i bambini sono **molto** gentile. Chiédila **ancora piú gentilmente** per il dolce.*

> 'Mrs. Rossi said that she will surely give you a candy. But, you know, she's a bit old, and she likes it when children are VERY, very nice. Ask her again EVEN MORE NICELY for the candy.'

Regardless of the child's next response, he was always given the candy by the puppet immediately after the second attempt. If the child was not frustrated or bored with the game, the Experimenter then offered him a second piece of candy "If you will ask even MORE nicely still." Again, the child's request was rewarded with a caramel regardless of its forms.

The purpose of this part of the experiment was to determine the child's own productive control over degrees of politeness in requests. In addition, this task served as a training exercise to prepare the child for the next part of the experiment, in which he himself must "be like Mrs. Rossi" and reward politeness in speech.

After the child's own requests were elicited, he was introduced to two more handpuppets, a pair of identical green frogs. Several kinds of human and animal puppets had been tried in pilot testing. But the nature of the task absolutely requires that the child watch the puppet, to be certain which had issued what request form. Hence, we chose the puppets that were most likely to retain the child's visual interest, and the frogs were clearly superior for this purpose. The subject was told that now he and the Experimenter are in charge of Mrs. Rossi's candy, and that the frogs are each going to ask for some. The child must listen very carefully and decide who asked the nicest. He must give a piece of candy only to the frog who spoke in the nicest way. The frog puppets were useful instruments in this phase of the experiment as well, since they have large gaping mouths into which the child could place the caramel "reward."

Each child heard eight pairs of requests from the puppets. An Italian assistant manipulated the frogs and made the requests. An effort was made to control tone of voice as much as possible between item pairs, except for the interrogative versus declarative intonation contours on one item. Obviously the use of controlled, recorded stimulae would have insured less interference from tone of voice phenomena. However, pilot efforts by this Experimenter and by Slobin's research team (Slobin, personal communication) indicate that children will not respond to recorded stimulae. Also, Feldman (1971) has discovered that processing of pragmatic material is markedly different for taperecorded speech versus sentences spoken aloud by someone in the room. In the light of these problems, we were necessarily restricted to live presentation.

To control for left- or right-hand preferences (since the children pointed to the "nicest" frog), the more polite request was randomly assigned to either the left- or right-hand frog. To control for a tendency to choose the first or last request heard, items were also randomly assigned in terms of which of the stimulae came first.

The eight pairs of requests were the following:

(1) *Dammi un dolce.*   'You (informal) give me a candy.'

     Dammi un dolce per favore.   'You (informal) give me a candy please.'

(2) *Voglio un dolce.*   'I want a candy.'
     Vorrei un dolce.   'I would like a candy.'

(3) *Dammi un dolce.*   'You (informal) give me a candy.'

     Mi dai un dolce?   '(Me) you (informal) give a candy?'

(4) *Posso avere un dolce?*   'Can I have a candy?'
     Potrei avere un dolce?   'Could I have a candy?'

(5) *Mi dai un dolce?*   '(Me) you (informal) give a candy?'

     Mi daresti un dolce?   '(Me) you (informal) would-give a candy?'

(6) *Senti, mi dai un dolce?*   'You (informal) listen, (me) you (informal) give a candy?'

     Senta, mi da un dolce?   'You (formal) listen, (me) you (formal) give a candy?'

(7) (Child's name), *mi potresti dare un dolce tu?*   '(Child's name), (me) you (informal) could give a candy you (informal)?'

     Signor/Signorina (child's name), *mi potrebbe dare un dolce Lei?*   'Mr./Miss (child's name), (me) you (formal) could give a candy you (formal)?'

(8) *DAMMI UN DOLCE!* (harsh intonation)   'YOU (INFORMAL) GIVE ME A CANDY!' (harsh intonation)

     Dammi un dolce! (soft intonation)   'You (informal) give me a candy!' (soft intonation)

The items were presented in two different random orders, with half the subjects receiving one order and half the other, except that the *please* item was always first, and the intonation item was always last. Since the task was unprecedented in the literature, and involved complex instructions, extensive pilot testing had been carried out with both Italian and American samples. In the pilot studies, if the intonation item was not the last item, children would insist on attending to tone of voice differences in all subsequent items, despite the effort to control out intonational differences on all but that item. To avoid setting off this strategy, the intonation item was placed last. Also, pilot results indicated that if the *please* item was the first administered, children who could not otherwise understand the task would immediately grasp the concept and go on to make other pragmatic judgments. This was not surprising, since *please* was also among the first polite forms in the records for Claudia and Francesco. To insure maximal performance by all children, the *please* item was always the first one heard.

After each item, the child was asked

Perché era piú gentile lui?   'Why was this one nicer?'

Che ha detto di meglio?   'What did he say that was better?'

This not only elicited the child's reasons for judging, but it also helped to focus his attention on the instructions to judge speech rather than some irrelevant factor.

The experiment therefore yielded three types of information about the acquisition of politeness in speech:

1. Passive judgments of politeness for eight pairs of items, contrasted for presence or absence of *please,* harsh versus gentle intonation, conditional versus present indicate verbs, interrogative versus imperative surface forms, and formal versus informal address.

2. Reasons for choosing one request as more polite than another.

3. One or more spontaneous requests by the child himself, constrained to elicit his "nicest" request forms.

We will examine the data in that order.

Results

Passive Judgments of Politeness

Overall, the test was effective in eliciting judgments of politeness for children in this age range. For example, the distribution of right versus wrong answers (collapsing across all subjects) was significantly greater than could be expected by chance, at the $p < .001$ level ($\chi^2 = 23.836$). We can at the very least conclude that the technique worked, and that children are capable of judging the politeness of speech forms in this task.

More interesting, however, were the developmental differences across and between items. Table 15 summarizes the total number of correct choices made by children for each type of item, within six different age levels. Figure 6 illustrates developmental changes across all eight items, again for these six age levels. The developmental trend is significant. A one-way analysis of variance on total scores for each subject, by three age levels, is significant at $p < .05$ ($F = 5.223$); comparing only two age groups, younger and lower halves, a one-way analysis of variance is significant at $p < .01$ ($F = 10.615$).

We should note here that there were absolutely no SEX differences in performance on this task ($F = .037$). Hence, if there are different cultural expectations for girls versus boys with respect to polite speech, they do not affect the child's passive control of the meaning of politeness. It may, however, be the case that boys and girls differ in the degree to which they USE this knowledge in their everyday activities. We have no data to answer that question here, but it is an idea that merits future study.

Let us now examine the developmental results for different types of polite forms. As Figure 6 indicated, overall performance on the task seems to increase gradually from 2;10 to 6;2, with children performing at a better than chance level somewhere in the middle of the curve, around 4½–5 years. This does NOT mean, however, that the concept of politeness itself is

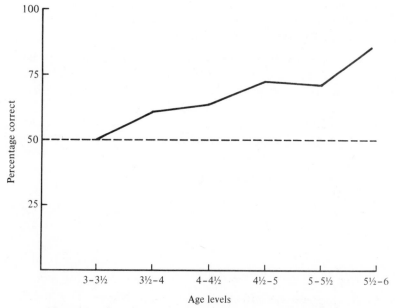

Figure 6. Performance on all politeness items by six age levels.

Table 15 Number of Correct Politeness Judgments: Type of Item by Age

Age groups (10 Subjects per cell)	Please (1 item)	Intonation (1 item)	Interrogative versus imperative (1 item)	Conditional versus indicative (3 items)		Formal versus informal address (2 items)		Total
				Total	Average	Total	Average	
3–3½ years	7	6	8	11	3.67	9	4.5	41
3½–4 years	8	7	6	18	6.0	8	4.0	47
4–4½ years	10	7	3	18	6.0	11	5.5	49
4½–5 years	10	9	7	19	6.33	11	5.5	56
5–5½ years	10	9	7	16	5.33	12	6.0	54
5½–6 years	9	10	7	24	8.0	15	7.5	65
Total	54	48	38	106	35.33	66	33.0	312

Table 16 Order of Difficulty for Types of Politeness Items
and Age at which Item Is Discriminated Correctly

Item	Percentage correct for all subjects	All subjects: χ^2 of right vs. wrong answers	Age at which discrimination reaches significance	χ^2 right vs. wrong by age level
"Please"	90	$p < .01$	2;10–4;0 years	$p < 0.05$
Intonation	81.4	$p < .01$	4;0–5;0 years	$p < .01$
Imperative vs. interrogative	63.3	n.s.		
Conditional	59.2	n.s.	5;6–6;2 years	$p < .01$
Formal address	52.9	n.s.	5;6–6;2 years	$p < .05$

delayed until 4½. Rather, some kinds of pragmatic judgments are acquired later than others, so that the low scores of the younger children reflect their inability to handle only the more difficult items.

Table 16 presents the order of difficulty of item types, for all subjects, as well as the age level at which each type of item is discriminated at a better than chance level. These results confirm in part the longitudinal findings presented in the previous chapter. The subjects in the youngest age group—2;10 to 3;11—apparently have already acquired a concept of politeness or niceness in speech, manifested in the ability to choose *please* as a more polite term. Claudia and Francesco also used *please* correctly at this age level. The choice of harsh versus soft intonation does not reach significance until after 4;0, but there is good reason to believe that this distinction was actually understood earlier. During testing several of the younger children giggled at the harsh intonation and chose that puppet while offering reasons such as *Cause I like him.* It is likely that their choice in those cases was based less on a sociolinguistic judgment than on amusement at the harsh tone of the "rude" frog. Also, it must be kept in mind that this was necessarily the last of the eight items; it is possible that the younger subjects had tired of the task by the time they reached this item. With regard to the longitudinal transcripts, there is no information in the records about tone of voice for Claudia and Francesco. However, one of the earliest politeness distinctions in the longitudinal results was a tendency to reduce the dimensions of a request in a variety of ways— quantity, amount of time, size of item, etc. As should become clearer when we examine the spontaneous requests of children in the experiment, it is likely that a reduced tone of voice was also a "polite" device at this 2½–3-year-old stage.

Neither the conditional nor the formal address items were successfully discriminated until the last age group, from 5½ to 6 years of age. In the longitudinal transcripts, Francesco had begun to use formal address earlier than this, between 3½ to 4 years of age, the same period in which he also used conditional-like requests with imperfect verbs. Hence, the age boundary yielded by the experimental study for acquisition of conditional and formal address judgments is two years beyond the use of those two functions in requests by Francesco. However, the SEQUENCE in which Francesco acquired these forms is the same as the sequence yielded by the experimental study, insofar as conditionals and formal address are the last of the distinctions to be acquired. How do we account for the developmental lag? Francesco was precocious by most norms, which could account for some of the age difference. And experimental studies generally yield developmental ages beyond those observed in natural settings, possibly because of variance added by complex instructions, the child's uneasiness with experimenters, and so forth. It seems safest to conclude that the age range established here for the more difficult pragmatic devices reflects the upper limit for acquisition of those structures. Many Italian children, like Francesco, may acquire politeness judgments for these structures much earlier. However, the sequence of developments yielded by both the longitudinal and the experimental study is probably a stable one, and can be generalized to other settings.

There is one striking exception to the sequential data in the two types of data. In the experiment, the single item contrasting interrogative with imperative form never reaches significance in any of the age groups. In addition, although successful discrimination of other items tends to increase gradually across time, similar to the curve in Figure 6, the age curve for this one item shows a peculiar U-shaped pattern (see Figure 7).

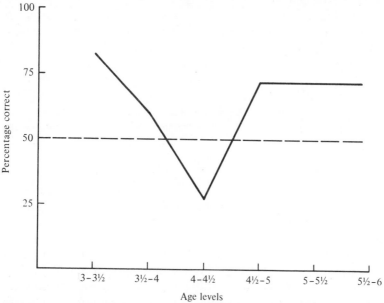

Figure 7. Correct discrimination by six age levels for interrogative versus imperative request.

Among the younger children, from 3 to 4½, the tendency to choose the interrogative *Mi dai?* as more polite than the imperative actually DECREASES with age. Then later, between 4½ to 5, performance on this item increases once again. Although this trend falls short of significance on this item, it does lend possible support to the interpretation made earlier concerning the use of interrogative intonation as a polite form. In Chapter VIII we noted that the interrogative request appears in the transcripts long before any of the other adult polite forms. We questioned at this point whether the interrogative request actually functioned as a "polite" device for 1½-year-old children. Instead, it was suggested that this was a more efficient kind of request, a stronger form which requires the adult to confirm the message verbally.

Note that the tendency to depress the *Mi dai?* request coincides with the acquisition of the first polite forms in the experiment (*please* and intonation). It is possible that the new concept of politeness at first tends to select against the interrogative request, since that form has been for some time the most efficient and hence strongest speech act type in the child's repertoire. While the drop in discrimination across time does not reach significance, IT IS AT LEAST CLEAR THAT THIS TYPE OF REQUEST—THE FIRST POLITE REQUEST BY ADULT STANDARDS TO APPEAR IN THE LONGITUDINAL RECORDS—IS NOT CONSIDERED BY THE YOUNGER CHILDREN TO BE A "NICER" WAY TO ASK FOR THINGS.

To summarize the results for the different item types, we can conclude that a concept of politeness is already established within the 3-year-old age group, as demonstrated by their performance on the *please* item. However, this concept of politeness is extended to different surface forms at different points in development. Discrimination of harsh versus soft intonation comes in somewhat later than *please*—although this finding may be distorted by the fact that children found the harsh intonation amusing and attractive. Judgments of conditional verbs and formal address as more polite did not go beyond the chance level until the oldest age group, between 5½ to 6 years. This sequence of developments is similar to the sequence found in the longitudinal records. The one exception is the item comparing interrogative and imperative surface forms. Italian children do not judge the interrogative to be more polite, even though longitudinal evidence suggests that they have been using the interrogative request since 1½ years of age. In fact, there is a tendency for the interrogative item to be rejected more often than the straight imperative among some of the younger children. Since the first polite "rule" in the longitudinal records seemed to involve a general tendency to reduce requests, it is possible that the interrogative is rejected by children precisely because it has functioned for months as a particularly strong and efficient imperative form. At any rate, it is at least clear that the interrogative is not a more polite or camouflaged form for young Italian children.

Reasons for Choosing Items

After each passive judgment of a pragmatic item, we had also asked the children *Why was he nicer? What did he say that was better?* The responses by children to these questions can be classified into six categories:

1. No response, including both the failure to respond at all, and answers such as *I don't know* or *I forget.*

2. Absolute judgments, including answers such as *Because he is better* or *Because I like him,* or even *Just because.*

3. Absolute linguistic judgments, responses such as *Because he talked better* or *Because he said a nicer word,* without naming or describing a particular word or pragmatic device.

4. "Minus polite" responses, responses in which the child answers by describing a request, but substituting a less polite form for the one he had passively judged to be better—e.g., a child who correctly chose *I would like a candy* and explained his choice as *Because he said 'Gimme a candy'.*

5. "Plus polite" responses, responses in which the child answers by describing a request, but substituting a more polite form or an equally polite form for the one which he had actually heard—e.g., a child who correctly chose *Could I have a candy?* and explained his choice as *Because he said 'please'.*

6. Correct judgments, responses correctly describing or identifying the pragmatic element that made the request more polite, e.g., *Because he said 'I would like'.*

Table 17 presents the incidence of these six response types across age groups, from the youngest 10 subjects to the oldest 10 subjects.

Table 17   Reasons for Choosing One Item as More Polite:
Six Response Types by Age

Age group (10 subjects per cell)	Correct identifications		Plus polite	Minus polite	Absolute linguistic judgment	Absolute judgment	No response
	No. of responses	Percentage correct					
3–3½ years	1	2	4	8	2	17	48
3½–4 years	4	8	4	8	7	18	38
4–4½ years	7	14	1	26	3	17	24
4½–5 years	18	32	16	14	11	9	18
5–5½ years	24	44	4	13	11	9	19
5½–6 years	38	58	4	7	21	3	8
Total	92	29	33	76	55	73	155

As can be seen from Table 17, the judgments were acquired in the same order (1) through (6) in which they were just presented. Nonresponses and absolute judgments both tend to decrease in direct relation to age, indicating that children are better able to give some kind of concrete reason for their choice as they grow older. However, the category for absolute linguistic judgments (e.g., *Cause he said a nicer word*) contains no specific content other than the fact that something nice was said. Yet responses in this category tend to INCREASE in direct relation to age. These are not, then, a kind of nonresponse. Instead, these responses probably mean that the child knows that he chose a LINGUISTIC device when he made his judgment, but that he cannot remember or reproduce it.

At the other end of the developmental continuum, the ability to identify correctly the element chosen as more polite also increases in direct proportion to age, with a much higher incidence of correct explanations in the oldest half of the subjects. (See Figure 8 comparing correct explanations with nonresponse.) A one-way analysis of variance comparing total correct explanations in younger versus older subjects is significant at $p < .001$ (F-ratio $= 17.068$).

It should be stressed that this last finding is not simply a function of the fact that older children can make more correct PASSIVE judgments of

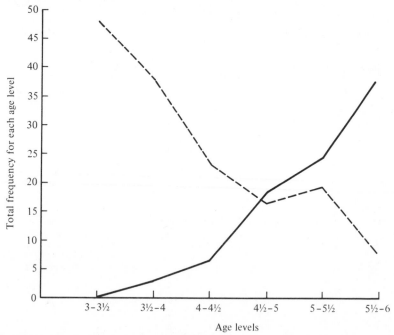

Figure 8. Total number of correct explanations of politeness judgments within each age level versus total number of nonresponses. Correct explanations: ———; nonresponse: - - -.

politeness than the younger subjects. Among the younger children, in only 8% of the cases in which the child did correctly discriminate an item could he also provide the correct reason why that sentence was better. In 45% of the cases in which older children had chosen correctly, they were also able to supply accurately the reason for their choice. This means that the ability to reason actively about a passive judgment is increasing with age, but not as a direct function of passive competence.

The two remaining categories, "Plus Polite" and "Minus Polite," are particularly interesting in terms of uncovering the process by which children acquire the pragmatic system. While the other categories increase or decrease in a linear relation to age, these two categories bear a U-shaped relation to age. Both types of responses tend to increase between four to five years, and then drop off among the oldest children. Also, between four to five years there is a trade off between the "Minus Polite" category and the "Plus Polite" category.

Explanations that subtract polite elements from the stimulus sentence ("Minus Polite") increase steadily until age 4 to 4½, and then begin to drop off. When this strategy was first encountered in pilot testing, the Experimenters kept repeating the item to make sure the child had understood. The child would continue to select the more polite of two requests, and then describe his choice as *Because this one said 'Gimme some candy'*. It became clear that this was the child's approach to regenerating the requests he had heard, and not an error due to inattention. The same type of response was found among both the American and the Italian pilot samples, and was confirmed with the larger experimental sample.

Explanations that add or substitute polite elements ("plus polite") within the stimulus sentence increase until age 4½ to 5, and then drop off. Within this response category there are answers that substitute a completely different polite form for the one correctly discriminated, so that it is not simply a matter of mistaking similar surface forms for one another. For example, one child correctly selected the more polite of two forms, and then explained her choice by saying *Because he gave a kiss*. Since the puppet did nothing of the sort, this response has obviously substituted for the given polite form a behavior that is equally "nice" from the child's point of view. The plus and minus polite strategies are illustrated by age groups in Figure 9, together with the developmental curve for correct explanations. The significance level of the developmental "trade off" between minus and plus polite strategies was measured with a t-test comparing the proportion of plus polite to both plus and minus polite responses in 4–4½-year-olds versus 4½–5-year-olds. This relationship was significant at the $p < .01$ level, with a t-statistic of 3.98.

These findings suggest four stages in the child's ability to regenerate or explain his passive choice of polite forms. First, children respond with an absolute linguistic judgment, e.g., *He talked nice,* recalling only that their

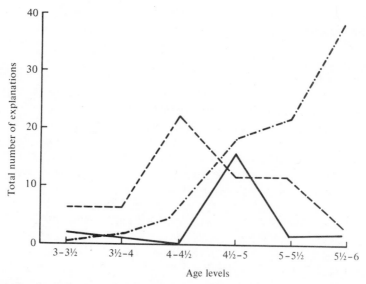

Figure 9. Strategies in pragmatic reasoning: "Plus" and "minus" politeness versus correct explanations as a function of age. Correct explanations: –·–·–; "plus polite" responses: ——; "minus polite" responses: – – –.

choice was based on something linguistic, without recalling specific content. Second, in the "minus-polite" period, the children can correctly discriminate one polite form over another, but can only regenerate the portion IMPERATIVE, e.g., *Because he said 'Gimme'*. Third, in the plus polite stage children make a correct discrimination, and then regenerate their choice from the description IMPERATIVE + POLITE, substituting whatever polite devices they control best. Finally, when correct choices and explanations are both possible, the children not only regenerate IMPERATIVE + POLITE, but also include a description of the particular devices that actually appeared in the stimulus sentence. Later in this chapter, we will discuss the implications these findings may have for a theory of pragmatic processing and memory in adults as well as children.

Overall, the ability to explain pragmatic judgments was related to the difficulty of the item in question. Table 18 presents the incidence of correct explanations for each type of item, and the percentage of correct choices that children could accurately explain. This difference in types of items was tested with a χ^2 statistic comparing easy items (please and intonation) with difficult items (conditional, formal address, interrogative) on the number of correct passive judgments that were or were not correctly explained by the child. This test yielded a χ^2 statistic of 9.73, significant at $p < .01$, indicating that the more difficult the item, the more difficult it is to regenerate the reason for choosing it.

This effect is based primarily on the explanations provided by the older children. It is a predictable result within that age group. But it is more interesting that most younger children who could make correct passive judgments still could not explain or reproduce that item actively. For example, 25 of the 30 younger subjects did choose *please* as more polite, yet only three of them could tell the experimenters why that item was "nicer." Hence, the results on active reasoning about pragmatic choices are not simply a direct function of the ability to make passive judgments. Recall that among the younger children, only 8% of correct passive judgments were also accurately explained by the child. Among younger children, 45% of their correct passive judgments were explained correctly. IT SEEMS FAIR TO CONCLUDE THAT THE ABILITY TO REASON ACTIVELY ABOUT PRAGMATIC CHOICES IS A SEPARATE AND LATER DEVELOPMENT, DISTINCT FROM PASSIVE PRAGMATIC COMPETENCE.

Finally, there were a few explanations that did not fit into any of the above categories. One boy tested in the Italian pilot sample, age around 5;3, was asked why he had chosen *tu* as more polite than *Lei* in one of the formal address items. He responded

Be', mica è sera!   'Well, it's hardly evening!'

This child seemed to have derived a unique rule to generate the dif-

Table 18   Difference between Types of Politeness Items on Correct Explanations for Choices

Item type	Total number of items that were correctly discriminated		Total number of correct explanations		Percent of correct choices that were correctly explained
	Total	Average per item	Total	Average per item	
Please (1 item)	54		21		38
Intonation (1 item)	48		21		43
Interrogative versus imperative (1 item)	38		10		26
Conditionals (3 items)	106	35.33	23	7.28	21
Formal versus informal address (2 items)	66	33	16	8	24
Total	312	36	92	11.5	29.5

ferences between pronouns of address in Italian. Based undoubtedly upon his own observations of his environment, he has concluded that *tu* is said in the mornings and *Lei* is said in the evenings. Since we had questioned him in the morning at the preschool, where the *tu* form is invariably used, the *Lei* request form clearly could not be the nicer of the two. This kind of result demonstrates the value of probing for the reasons underlying pragmatic judgments, rather than simply observing the use of a particular form. It is reminiscent of Quine's warning that the rules of language are like the arrangement of branches in hedges clipped to look alike. The external form may conform to conventional standards, but the inward network of rules for producing that form may differ greatly from one individual to another.

Subjects' Own Requests

One last type of information drawn from the experiment relates to the request produced by the children themselves when they were asking for candy. Table 19 divides the children's requests according to the kinds of syntactic devices used, on the first try and on subsequent attempts to be "nicer."

Older versus younger children were compared on the total proportion of polite requests (i.e., requests with at least one identifiable polite element, as opposed to simple statements of desire or imperatives) among the total number of requests elicited from each group. This comparison yielded a *t*-statistic of 3.47, significant at the $p < .01$ level. Hence, older children are producing a significantly greater proportion of polite requests than

Table 19 Types of Spontaneous Requests by Children

Subjects	Refusal to respond	Statement or simple imperative	Inter-rogative	Please	Conditional	Modal	Formal
All children:							
First attempt	4	26	26	10	2	3	3
Second attempt	12	8	35	16	2	5	5
Total	16	34	61	26	4	8	8
Younger subjects:							
First attempt	3	17	7	5	0	0	1
Second attempt	7	6	12	6	0	1	2
Total	10	23	19	11	0	1	3
Older subjects:							
First attempt	1	9	19	5	2	3	2
Second attempt	5	2	23	10	2	4	3
Total	6	11	42	15	4	7	5

younger children. Since the data on passive judgments indicate that the discrimination of polite forms increases developmentally, it is not surprising that the older children should also produce more polite requests than younger children.

Recall that in the longitudinal transcripts, Francesco and Claudia used interrogative requests as early as 1½ years of age. We suggested in the last chapter that, although the interrogative functions as a stronger or more efficient command for these children, it may not necessarily be the case that they view the interrogative as "nicer." One answer to this question would be to determine whether younger children produced interrogative requests when asked to be "nicer." It is indeed the case that the 3 to 4½-year-olds did produce interrogative requests. However, a χ^2 statistic comparing younger versus older children who did or did not produce interrogative requests is significant at the $p < .01$ level, with a χ^2 statistic of 7.99.

Using no interrogatives	Using interrogatives	
12	17	Younger subjects (3 to 4½)[1]
2	28	Older subjects (4½ to 6)

[1] One subject in the younger group was not administered from the elicitation task.

Hence, there are children in the younger group that do not in any way demonstrate productive mastery of the interrogative as a "nicer" form.

Nevertheless, for many of the younger children and all of the older children, the request *Mi dai?* 'Give me?' was a frequent form. Also, there was a tendency for both younger and older children to use the interrogative more often in their second and third requests, when they were told to be "nicer." A χ^2 comparing requests with and without interrogatives, for the first request versus subsequent requests, is significant at the $p < .05$ level ($\chi^2 = 4.4231$) for younger children, and at the $p < .01$ level ($\chi^2 = 8.7753$) for the older children.

In sum, the data do indicate that older children control more devices for improving the politeness of requests. Hence, the level of sophistication of polite requests improves over time. However, if we ignore the particular devices used, and simply look at the ability somehow to improve a request when asked, it is clear that the younger children are equally able to "tune up" their pleas with some type of surface change. Overall, there is a contrast between the use of simple statements versus polite forms on the first versus subsequent requests ($\chi^2 = 11.52$, $p < .001$). But this effect is significant within both the younger and the older halves of the subjects. A χ^2 comparing statements versus polite requests on first versus subsequent attempts is significant at $p < .02$ for younger children ($\chi^2 = 5.64$) and $p < .02$ for older children ($\chi^2 = 4.46$).

This last point becomes clearer if we open the class of possible "improvements" to include not only polite devices by adult standards, but any idiosyncratic improvements that the child may temporarily adopt. For example, there was a use of diminutives or quantifiers to reduce the dimensions of a request, e.g., *You give me a little one?* or *You give me a pretty caramel?* Another child encoded the politeness literally in his second request with the sentence

> *Molto gentilmente quella*   'Very nicely that caramel.'
> *caramella.*

Several children repeated their first request word for word but said the second with a pronounced "nice" intonation or else whispered the second request in the puppet's ear. In another example, the child put both of the Italian words for *please* in the second request, thereby doubling its polite value:

> *Mi dai per favore per piacere*   'You give me please[1] please[2]
> *una caramella?*   that caramel?'

All of these devices are represented among the earliest polite forms for Claudia and Francesco, with the element *please* and the reduced request rule.

If we regard all these devices as improvements in the politeness of an utterance, together with the standard devices of conditional, interrogative, *please,* etc., it is possible to measure the increase in politeness from one request to another in the "Ask even nicer" task. Giving one point to each type of device added to the subsequent requests, we obtain a range of zero to four points among the 60 subjects. A one-way analysis of variance for younger versus older children on total increments from one request to another yields a nonsignificant F-ratio of 1.205.

Another measure of the same effect is obtained by comparing the number of older versus younger children who could or could not increase the politeness of subsequent requests:

Younger subjects	Older subjects	
15	9	No increase
14	21	Some increase

Although there is a tendency for a larger number of older children to tune up their requests in some way, this difference does not reach significance ($\chi^2 = 2.05$).

The conclusion drawn from these comparisons is that, while the number and complexity of polite devices available to children does increase between three to six years of age, a dimensional concept of politeness has already been acquired by the younger children. Within their limited repertoire, including several idiosyncratic devices, younger children can operate on their own requests to move them up or down a gradient of politeness.

Postscript—An Adult Datum

As a control on the order of complexity or politeness assumed in constructing test items, nine requests for candy were presented to 12 Italian adult subjects. Each request was typed on a separate index card. The cards were given to the subjects in random order, and they were asked to rank the cards from most to least polite request. A rank of nine was given to the most polite, down to a rank of one for the least polite. Table 20 presents the nine requests in order from the least to most polite as chosen by adult subjects.

The simple command *Give me* and the wish statement *I want* are clearly the least polite, followed by *Give me please*. The compound conditional/modal/interrogative requests (8) and (9) (see Table 20) are clearly the most polite. Within the middle range, a simple wish in the conditional is less polite than an interrogative request with the conditional (items 4 and 7 respectively, Table 20). The choice of you-formal over you-informal made a slight difference in degree of politeness, but only within items that were equivalent in terms of other polite devices. Hence, *potrebbe* ('Could you-formal') is ranked slightly higher than *potresti* ('Could you-informal'), and *Mi da?* ('You-formal give?') is slightly higher than *Mi dai?* ('You-informal give?'). Some adult subjects had no trouble ranking formal address as more polite than informal. Others expressed frustration with the task, complaining that the formal–informal dimension was categorically different from the politeness dimension and could not be decided without a supporting context and a given listener. They could deduce politeness from formality in the abstract only in such a forced choice task.

Table 20   Adult Judgments of Relative Politeness

Request		Total points
Italian	English	
1 *Dammi un dolce.*	'Give me a candy.'	18
2 *Voglio un dolce.*	'I want a candy.'	19
3 *Dammi un dolce per favore.*	'Give me a candy please.'	44
4 *Vorrei un dolce.*	'I would like a candy.'	53
5 *Mi dai un dolce?*	'You-informal give me a candy?'	56
6 *Mi da un dolce?*	'You-formal give me a candy?'	67
7 *Mi daresti un dolce?*	'You-informal would give me a candy?'	80
8 *Mi potresti dare un dolce?*	'Could you-informal give me a candy?'	101
9 *Mi potrebbe dare un dolce?*	'Could you-informal give me a candy?'	104

These results do correspond roughly to the order of acquisition of polite devices by Italian children. Simple statements and commands are lowest, followed by Imperative + Please. Conditionals and formal address are ranked highest. Interrogative requests are ranked overall as higher in politeness than a declarative version of the same request. While the ranking of interrogative items does not correspond to the order of production by Italian children, as drawn from the longitudinal records, it does correspond to the order in which children judged the interrogative as more polite.

Hence, complexity and number of pragmatic devices parallels both the degree of politeness as judged by adults, and the order of acquisition as observed in Italian children.

Summary and Discussion

The results from the politeness experiment can be briefly summarized as follows:

1. PASSIVE JUDGMENTS OF POLITENESS. The order in which polite forms were discriminated correctly parallels the order in which those forms are acquired in the longitudinal records. *Please* and intonation items are recognized by four years of age, while conditional and formal address items are not discriminated correctly until 5½ years of age. The one exception is the interrogative request. Even though this form is used by children as young as 1½, it is apparently not recognized as a polite form by the younger children.

2. REASONING ABOUT POLITENESS. The kinds of explanations offered by children when they are asked why the form they chose was "nicer" fall into six categories: no response, absolute judgments such as *'cause I like him,* absolute linguistic judgments such as *Because he talked better,* "minus polite" responses in which a correctly discriminated form is reproduced as a straight imperative (e.g., *'Cause he said 'Gimme some candy'*), "plus polite" responses in which the child correctly discriminates a polite form but reproduces a different type of polite request, and correct explanations. These response types occur developmentally in the above order. It appears that children first cannot actively reproduce their choice at all. Then they reproduce IMPERATIVE only, followed by IMPERATIVE + POLITE substituting any polite form. Finally, they can reproduce the correct polite device in the original stimulus sentence.

The ability to reason actively about passive judgments also appears to be an ability that develops separately from passive pragmatic competence. Younger children who CAN make correct passive judgments CANNOT explain the reason for their judgments.

3. SPONTANEOUS REQUESTS BY CHILDREN. When asked to produce requests for candy themselves, younger children have fewer polite devices available to them than the older children. However, when told to ask again "even nicer," children at all age levels studied were able to increase the politeness of their original request with some kind of device. Apparently a dimensional concept of politeness is already well-established by age 3. All further increases in pragmatic skill involve the acquisition of more sophisticated forms and an improved ability to reason about their own pragmatic knowledge.

4. ADULT JUDGMENTS. Overall, the order of acquisition for various polite forms parallels adult judgments of relative politeness, as measured in a rank-ordering task for all the request forms studied in the politeness task.

It remains for us to characterize the psychological nature of the politeness dimension itself, to understand better how this dimension is acquired by children. Then we can examine in more detail the reasons why different polite forms are acquired in the above developmental order.

Politeness as a General Concept

Robin Lakoff (1973), in a discussion of the concept of politeness, places it among the rules of general pragmatic competence. The two major pragmatic rules are

1. Be clear.
2. Be polite.

Rule (1) includes Grice's conversational postulates, all of which are based on efficiency, or economy and informativeness:

(A)	Quantity:	Be as informative as required.
		Be no more informative than required.
(B)	Quality:	Say only what you believe to be true.
(C)	Relevance:	Be relevant.
(D)	Manner:	Be perspicuous.
		Don't be ambiguous.
		Don't be obscure.
		Be succinct.

These rules have been challenged on a number of grounds. For example, Larkin and O'Malley (1973) offer a long list of noninformative declaratives that are used for emphasis or "put downs," e.g.,

> As I recall, Dr. Smith, you are not yet a member of
> the tenured faculty.

Lakoff also concedes that much of ordinary language violates the Rule (1) conversational postulates. However, she feels that most of the exceptions can be generated from Rule (2), "Be polite," which in turn involves three principles:

(A) Don't impose.
(B) Give options.
(C) Make the listener feel good—Be friendly.

Lakoff stresses that being polite will often necessarily involve a violation of Rule (1) laws of efficiency, particularly the principles regulating quantity and ambiguity. For example, Brown and Gilman (1960) have noted that there is a significant positive correlation between the length of an utterance and its judged degree of politeness. If we examine the adult judgments of politeness presented earlier, it is clear that the same is true in many cases for Italian.

These politeness principles can be paraphrased with a single regulation—"Do not offend." The principle is not specific to human interaction. A great deal of animal communication (Hinde, 1966) involves agonistic displays, signals regulating aggression, submission, and appeasement. Among humans, the smile has been related to the set of innate signals that regulate aggression (Freedman, 1972; Eibl-Eibesfeldt, 1970), and smiling is purportedly derived phylogenetically from the submissive gesture of teeth baring that has been observed in many primates. According to such an ethological approach, signals that obey the rule "Don't offend" are generated automatically by children and by nonhuman species. Why should the manifestation of the same rule in speech be delayed until one or two years after speech begins?

The answer may lie in two factors. First, the ability to encode aggression-appeasement with a conventional signal system rather than an innate display may require a more conscious, reflective control of one's own emotions and the potential emotions of others. Insofar as all speech requires planning in advance, polite speech also requires control of speaker-hearer emotions as symbol structures that can be projected into sound.

Second, as Lakoff states, politeness rules tend to run counter to the rules of conversational clarity. The conflict between efficiency and politeness may be one of the main factors in the delay of acquisition of polite forms. As was pointed out in previous chapters, from the gestural communication of Marta and Carlotta through the early speech records for Claudia and Francesco, the choice and alternation of signals seems to depend on the efficiency of those signals within a given situation. Recall again the purse sequence with Marta. These children are apparently preoccupied during early language acquisition with scanning the linguistic environment to select signals that serve to increase efficiency. This sort of learning strategy would automatically select against the longer or less economical polite forms, at least until such a point when the repertoire of more economical signals have been tried and found wanting.

Although the principles of economy and politeness may be in conflict, efficiency and politeness are not mutually exclusive. A command is by definition more efficient if it gets things done. Presumably imperative signals will be tried and discarded depending on their success in achieving the child's goal. Hence, a more primitive notion of efficiency—e.g., getting cookies—may lead the child gradually into a discovery of politeness, as a better way of convincing adults to dispense cookies. The problem will rest in part on the child's ability to predict the listener's willingness to comply.

This last development will in turn depend to some degree upon a general role-taking capacity, the ability to reverse one's own perspective and to take viewpoints different from one's own. But some predictions about listener reactions could also be based on a less sophisticated kind of reasoning. On the basis of past experience, children should be able to classify some listeners and situations into cookie and non-cookie-producing contexts. There is a great deal of evidence from lower species of behaviors linked to different listeners or partners in different situations. Most domestic animals recognize which humans are most likely to feed them, and respond accordingly. In fact, Pavlov's original discovery of the conditioned response was based on just such an observation in his laboratories. Dogs that he had kept for a separate, physiological study began salivating at the sound of footsteps in the corridor, around the time when keepers brought food to them. Hence, it should not surprise us that human children show skill in predicting the likelihood of compliance from various listeners, before they can understand the listener's reasons for complying. Even when some minimal understanding of politeness does begin, it may also be the case that children will extend these forms to one class of listeners and not to another. Volterra and Taeschner (1975), for example, describe the speech of a German–Italian bilingual child who used extremely polite, German speech with her father, and straight imperative, Italian speech with her mother. Lawson (cited in Ervin–Tripp, 1975) has noted a similar phenomenon in a monolingual English-speaking child, who used polite and somewhat indirect speech with her father but did not extend the same forms to her mother.

There are other examples of an ability to predict differences between listeners with respect to classes of signals. Gardner and Gardner (personal communication) report that Washoe the chimpanzee distinguishes one listener from another when she signs. If the listener is a visitor or a new laboratory assistant, she will sign slowly and deliberately. If the listener is a familiar old friend, she will sign more rapidly, with less articulated movements. As for human children, Halliday (1975) reports that his 1-year-old son uses an interrogative intonation to point out objects or to recount events to someone who has just entered the room. To someone who was there during the event, or has been present during play, he will use something closer to a declarative intonation. Finally, in addition to the Volterra and Taeschner example cited above, the literature on bilingual children is filled with examples in which children distinguish quite early the setting in which one language is more appropriate than another.

Therefore, an ability to generate different signals for different occasions or listeners is a discovery that can be derived from regular experience with the results of communicating. It need not necessarily require creative reflection, reversals of perspective between speaker and listener; nor would it necessarily require a general politeness principle of the kind described by Lakoff. For the purposes of this chapter, we are interested in the point at which the child generates polite speech from a principle, rather than matching memorized routines to remembered contexts.

How Politeness Is Acquired

If early polite speech (from the adult point of view) were restricted only to the use of the word *please* in requests, we would not be justified in inferring the existence of a general principle of politeness. However, at the same time in the transcripts for both Claudia and Francesco, we find a more creative set of polite requests. Both children begin to reduce the dimensions of their requests. They modify a demand by asking for less, or asking for the objects for a shorter period of time. Claudia starts to use diminutives (e.g., *biscottino* 'little cookie') when the original request fails (e.g., *biscotto* 'cookie'). These same devices appear in the experimental sample, when the youngest children are told to ask "even nicer." There is no information in the longitudinal transcripts about intonation. However, in the spontaneous requests produced by younger children in the experimental setting, there was a tendency to whisper or change to a markedly "nicer" tone of voice for the second or third request attempt. The younger children in the sample, like Claudia and Francesco in the early stages of politeness, seem to follow a sort of aesthetic–pragmatic principle that "less is more." Hence, the whisper or reduction in intonation can be viewed as a vocal icon to the reduced quantity in the request. By asking for less, or reducing the force of the request in any available way, the likelihood of compliance by the listener should increase.

Note the difference between this principle and the earlier principle of message efficiency. As far back as the gestural sequences of Marta, when a message failed the child would either issue a new signal, or repeat-augment the first signal. The earliest rule for judging the pragmatic effect of signals is probably something such as:

1. Listener is not responding.   (goal failure)
2. Signal is insufficient.   (reject means)
3. Select new signal.   (new means)

But when children begin to reduce requests to increase compliance, the above rule has branched into two possible alternatives:

EFFICIENCY RULE
1. Listener is not responding.   (goal failure)
2. Signal is insufficient.   (reject means)
3. Change or augment signal.   (new means)

POLITENESS RULE
1. Listener is not responding.   (goal failure)
2. Signal is offensive.   (reject means)
3. Change or reduce signal.   (new means)

The second alternative will probably be adopted when the first alternative has failed, when it is clearly established that the listener has indeed understood but is still unwilling. Gradually the child will develop a good set of cues for determining a priori if the listener will be offended or otherwise unconvinced, but in the early stages the politeness rule will probably be a last resort.

According to this interpretation, the politeness rule is indeed learned instrumentally, as a means of increasing signal efficiency. But it requires means that differ categorically from earlier strategies of augmenting the informativeness of the original signal. Polite devices do not render requests more informative, at least not with respect to the speaker's goal and/or the course of action recommended to the listener. Instead, they render requests less offensive.

There are two possible types of learning that can lead the child from the concept of efficiency to the concept of politeness. TYPE 1 learning will involve explicit sociolinguistic training, in which the adult listener ties politeness to efficiency by withholding the goal, e.g., *I won't give you a cookie until you say 'please'*. The longitudinal transcripts for Claudia and Francesco indicate that the ritual term *please* is learned in this fashion, since the first uses of the word by both children follows an adult admonishment. TYPE 2 learning requires a creative deduction based on knowledge of the power relations involved, and the fact that some speech acts leave options open for the listener. It is possible that some polite devices require a manipulation of several rules, and cannot be learned through explicit sociolinguistic training alone. Hence, the developmental differences underlying these two types of learning may account for the order of acquisition observed in both the experimental and longitudinal data.

Like the ritual word *please,* the rule REDUCE REQUEST may also be learned in part through sociolinguistic training. This rule may be induced from considerable experience indicating that the more one wants, the less one gets. Once this rule is derived, it is apparently applied iconically, so that not only the amount requested, but the manner and tone of voice in requesting something are also reduced. However, it is interesting that both *please* and the reduction rule are discovered around 2 to 2½ years, when both children were undergoing toilet training. According to psychoanalytic interpretations, this period marks the beginning of a concept of morality. If this is in fact the period in which children learn to classify behaviors as "good" and "bad" or "unacceptable," then it is not surprising that they also begin to understand that some types of utterances are also bad or unacceptable. Hence, politeness would be a subset within new schemes for moral judgment.

What is responsible for the later stage in polite requests, if there is already a concept of politeness at 2½? In the longitudinal records for Francesco, several late developments enter simultaneously around 3½ to 4 years of age. While no conditional verbs appear, there are uses of the imperfect past tense during requests (e.g., *I wanted to see that!*), together with implicit warnings and promises (*If you aren't good . . .*) and indirect request questions (*Why aren't you drinking your coffee?*). Also, we find Francesco using intentional rudeness in the expression of desires (*I'm gonna eat them all up myself, I don't care*), and formal address in play situations (*Tenga, Signorina Alessandra*).

Conditional verbs and formal address are also among the last developments in the politeness experiment. And while interrogative requests appear in the earliest speech records, they are not judged as more polite until much later in development. Finally, the ability to explain why some utterances are more polite than others, i.e., to reason actively about politeness, begins around 4 to 4½.

One possible explanation for the late development of these polite forms as opposed to forms such as *please* and reduced requests is that they require deductions not only from specific contexts, but from the Gricean principles of conversation. A wide variety of original, very indirect requests could be generated, in an infinite set of situations, by following the steps that Gordon and Lakoff suggest, based upon Gricean postulates. The process is illustrated roughly in the following example.

1. SPEAKER RULES (ENCODING)
   A. All speakers abide by cooperative principles of relevance, quantity, etc.
   B. Speaker wants to know what time it is.
   C. Listener may be offended by a straightforward command (see rules for context–listener interaction).
   D. Select a conversational form that violates principles of relevance in situation X, but contains information about the speaker's goal. Samples are as follows:
      Do you know what time it is?
      Gee, I forgot my watch.
   E. Decision: Encode *Do you know what time it is?*

2. LISTENER RULES (DECODING)

A. Message violates principles of relevance. Speaker would not sincerely request information about my knowledge of the time.

B. If Speaker is being conversationally cooperative, then he must intend some further meaning.

C. Construct alternative interpretation *Speaker wants to know the time.*

D. Accept or reject speaker's goal.

E. Decision: Tell speaker what time it is.

While these steps look quite elaborate when outlined, they are no more elaborate than a good deal of verbal banter, humor, puns, sarcasm, etc., that are common currency in adult conversation. At what age should children be capable of executing these steps? Francesco's speech acts in the last transcripts contain a variety of indirect threats and promises that seem to require a deduction on the listener's part. This is also a period in which Francesco organizes games of "School," "Mechanic," "Going skiing with David," "Little Red Riding Hood," "Doctor." During these games he assigns roles to various adults and small cousins, and cues their entrances and exits. It is also in this period that he uses formal address to increase the weight of a request to his parents, and argues the pros and cons of why he should be granted a favor. It is therefore not unlikely that he is also capable of exercising the series of steps involved in a Gricean deduction of power relations, probability of compliance, knowledge of conversational rules, and selection of camouflaged illocutionary force for an utterance.

The interrogative would take on the new connotation of a polite form, long after its use to increase efficiency, because the child can now deduce that a question leaves a yes or no option to a listener. By the same token, commands or statements can be tuned down to be intentionally rude or emphatic by decreasing the options of the listener, e.g., *I'm eating them all up myself, I don't care.*

This is also the period in which pseudoconditionals with alternative verbs appear, as discussed in Chapter VI. According to the analysis presented earlier, all conditionals involve an assertion IF X, THEN Y, coupled with an instruction not to assume that the speaker assumes the truth of the antecedent. When a conditional appears in a polite request, without an "if" clause, e.g.,

I would like some candy.

it carries out a double function of automatically calling up an empty IF condition, which can be filled with something such as *If you don't mind,* plus signalling that the IF condition may not necessarily hold in this situation. Thus a conditional also serves to leave the listener's options open, by implying that the wish or request is contingent on something other than the speaker's will. Therefore, it is not surprising that requests with conditional verbs are not judged as more polite until later, and that this development coincides with other constructions that depend on listener deductions from conversational postulates.

The above developments, if they have the internal structure that we have described, could not be acquired by Type 1 learning only, i.e., through explicit parental training and withholding of favors. These polite forms will require an ability to coordinate several principles, and to produce a complex and often original speech act. A few conditionals or modals could perhaps be learned by simply adding them to a finite list of utterance types that belong in certain situations. Ervin–Tripp (1974) suggests that English children learn *Can I have . . .* as just such a memorized routine, prior to a more productive use of modal verbs. But the ability to construct a potentially infinite set of creative polite combinations will require more abstract knowledge of how speech acts work, and the desirability of general conditions such as leaving the listener's options open.

To summarize, the early polite forms (please, intonation, reduced requests) may depend in part on Type 1 learning, plus a general notion that some speech acts are bad or offensive in certain situations. It may be for this reason that they are learned around 2½. Psychoanalytic findings indicate that this same period, toward the end of toilet training, marks the beginning of a concept of morality, or behavior that is good or bad in the eyes of others. Also, this is the stage discussed in Chapter V, when children become capable of talking about speech acts. A concept of morality, and a metapragmatic capacity, will allow children to derive a rule that some speech acts are better than others, regardless of their relative economy or informativeness.

The late polite forms will of course necessarily be based on these earlier developments. But the conditional forms, the various indirect speech acts observed in Francesco's last transcripts, and the delayed realization that interrogatives are more polite than imperatives, all may be pragmatic devices that require something approaching concrete operational reasoning. All these forms require an ability to predict the listener's knowledge of conversational rules, in order to insure that the listener will derive second-order meanings from camouflaged surface forms.

In the Italian sample, formal address was acquired together with the indirect, complex speech acts that are apparently based on conversational rules. There is, however, no a priori reason why some uses of formal address could not be learned earlier, through Type 1 learning, from sociolinguistic training in specific situations.

To take an extreme case, imagine a society in which children were electroshocked every time they used the informal pronoun or verb form when addressing a grey-haired person. Chances are good that these children would find other available verb inflections (if they do not cease talking altogether), and would soon generalize these inflections to all encounters with grey-haired people. There is no deep-seated structural reason why such learning could not occur, as soon as children had any control over inflections at all.

Would this type of learning explain, however, Francesco's use of formal address in playing tea party with his 4-year-old cousin? How would the child learn to pair formal address with appropriate cooccurring forms, such as the title *Signora,* unless of course such titles were reinforced in a similar way to associate the two. Could this kind of conditioning explain Francesco's use of the formal pronoun to emphasize an important request made to someone who is usually addressed as *tu*? Francesco's mastery of formal address seems to be based on a flexible rule of "formality," a rule that can be used creatively in a variety of situations. It is perhaps for this reason that formal address is acquired together with other pragmatically creative speech forms. However, since formal address does not have Gricean reasoning as a necessary part of its underlying structure, there is no reason why certain aspects of formal address could not be learned through Type 1 learning, matching surface forms with a catalogue of situations.

The electroshock situation is fortunately an unlikely one. However, it is not unreasonable to expect that some forms of respect language could be enculturated much earlier than 3½ to 5 years of age in a culture that places high value on such behavior. The prediction is made here that in such cultures, very early manifestations of respect language will be bound to concrete situations and specific listeners, or to classes of situations and listeners that are divided according to observable characteristics—e.g., all grey-haired people are called "(X)-san." It should be possible within such cultures, to design an experiment that will require the child to deduce an appropriate address form in situations that vary along abstract dimensions, to test whether the child has mastered address through Type 1 cataloguing, or through Type 2 reasoning from principles.

More specifically, Brown and Gilman (1960) suggest that all systems of respect language, from binary systems like Italian and French, through to systems with multiple levels of address, are based on location along two orthogonal dimensions: power or status, and solidarity or intimacy. Native speakers make decisions regarding the appropriate address form in a given situation by locating himself and the addressee along both dimensions, and calculating the choice of address based on the pairs of coefficients. If this is the system underlying native competence in respect language, then we would expect mastery of the system to be delayed until the child is capable of coordinating two dimensions and placing himself and the listener along those dimensions. This should occur around the same period when other complex pragmatic forms are mastered. (See Friedrich (1966) for a multidimensional analysis of the same system.)

Obviously a thorough test of this hypothesis would require detailed ethnographic information about the adult system of honorifics to which the child is exposed. However, with such information, organized along dimensions such as power and solidarity, it should be possible to assess the level of competence of children at various stages of cognitive development, to determine precisely what kinds of logical operations are necessary to resolve a question of address—locating the participants in discourse along abstract dimensions, or simply generalizing from concrete situations.

Within the Italian community, a child's acquisition of respect language is treated with a great deal of tolerance. Throughout the preschool era, the *tu* form is universally permitted. In elementary school the requirements apparently vary according to the teacher. In a study currently underway by Bates and Benigni (1975), an adaptation of Brown and Gilman's questionnaire is being used to assess social class and age differences in the use of address forms in the Rome area. In our adaptation, we have included several items regarding the appropriate ages for giving and receiving formal *Lei.* Preliminary results indicate that Italian adults experience a great deal of embarrassment when asked when a child should begin to use *Lei.* Answers include statements such as *When they are old enough, that's all, When they feel like it,* or more often *I just don't know.* The prevailing sentiment seems to be that children are permitted to discover the system for themselves. The example of the child who invented the morning/evening rule for formal address (page 309) is an illustration of sociolinguistic learning in a system that permits the child to decode adult rules in his own good time, without explicit pressures.

In a tolerant system, which does not withhold rewards on the basis of level of address in speech, children will probably wait to apply Type 2 rather than Type 1 learning in the use of formal address. Hence, Italian children seem to discover honorifics via abstract rules based on dimensions of importance, status, and/or intimacy. They master the system together with other complex deductions about speech acts. However, a careful ethnography of children in other cultures may produce very different results.

In short, formal address need not necessarily require concrete operational reasoning. We must examine the kind of logic children use in deriving address forms before we know what sort of rule system is being used.

Finally, the results of the pragmatics experiment also yield information about the form in which pragmatic material is analyzed and stored for recall. There were several stages in the development of an ability to reason about politeness. Around 4 to 4½, children could regenerate only the stem

IMPERATIVE, even though they had passively discriminated the more polite of two request forms. Then, from 4½ to 5, they seem to generate their responses from the description IMPERATIVE + POLITE, substituting whatever polite devices they have available. Finally, they reproduce the entire relevant portion of the original stimulus sentences. This developmental progression suggests that the memory for complex pragmatic forms may involve a separate record for (1) function (e.g., imperative) and (2) manner (e.g., polite), without necessarily storing the precise form that was used. This is what we might expect if certain polite forms are decoded by referring to conversational postulates and unraveling the underlying intention, as Gordon and Lakoff suggest. In fact, the IMPERATIVE + POLITE reconstructions do occur in the period in which children begin to discriminate the more difficult and indirect polite forms. While these stages are visible here during the gradual build up of a complex pragmatic system by children, they may also reflect processes that adults use in storing pragmatic information during an interaction.

This hypothesis leads to several possible experiments on adult processing of pragmatics. Bransford, Barclay, and Franks (1972), Fillenbaum (1973), Sachs (1967), and others have recently investigated semantic memory with techniques that involve recognition of a stimulus sentence from paraphrases of that sentence. They have discovered that subjects often claim to recognize a sentence that they have not actually seen before, when that sentence is deducible from the previous stimulus sentences. For example, Fillenbaum finds that subjects who had been asked to read a stimulus sentence such as *If the man had been in time, he wouldn't have missed the train* will later claim that the sentence *The man missed the train because he was late* had been on the original stimulus list. These authors claim that there is no memory for specific sentences. Rather, subjects store information derived from sentences, and often combine the information in such a way that the original form is no longer available for reconstruction.

The same techniques that have been applied to the study of semantic memory could be applied to variations in the pragmatic value of sentences. For example, subjects might falsely recognize paraphrases of requests that are equivalent in degree of politeness to the original stimulus sentence. It would be possible to control the sentence paraphrases to contain different components of a hypothesized pragmatic structure, to determine whether they are recalled or recombined in predictable ways.

In conclusion, it appears that the acquisition of polite forms begins as early as 2½, but is not completed until children have acquired a flexible, concrete operational system that enables them to construct indirect speech acts from abstract principles concerning conversational postulates, listener options, and so forth. In addition, the results indicate that pragmatic material is processed by dividing input into meaning and function. The original form is then recalled by regenerating an utterance from these separate stems.

Three issues raised in this chapter will be discussed in more detail in the final chapter. One is the notion of dimensional, nondiscrete concepts such as "degree of politeness," and that problem that dimensional constructs pose for linguistic representation. The other two issues pertain more to cognitive theory. First, it appears as though "role-taking," or performing operations on a model of the listener and taking the listener's perspective, is not a unidimensional capacity. There are different cognitive operations involved in different kinds of role-taking, for different kinds of problems. Second, the age boundaries that we have called "concrete operational" are one to two years earlier than the age norms quoted by the researchers at the Institute for Genetic Epistemology. It will be necessary to examine in more detail the kinds of "prestructures" leading to full concrete operations, particularly with regard to language acquisition.

CHAPTER X

Conclusion

In the series of studies just presented, I have tried to provide a broad ontogenetic view of the acquisition of pragmatics. An effort has been made to relate each level of pragmatic development to a corresponding level of cognitive development, using Piaget's model of genetic epistemology. Not surprisingly, this broad-gauged effort has raised a great many questions, but furnished few definitive answers. Furthermore, so many kinds of data were employed in this heterogeneous work that the reader may have experienced some difficulty in sorting out the findings. In this final chapter, we will proceed by first summarizing the findings in sequence, recalling the various types of data used in constructing a tentative model of pragmatic development. Then, I will propose some lines for future research on cognition and pragmatics in child language. Finally, we will turn to some last, nagging questions about the nature of this whole enterprise.

Summary

1. Pragmatics in the Sensorimotor Period

In the section on pragmatics in the sensorimotor period, our primary source of data was a longitudinal, videotaped study of three infant girls (Serena, Carlotta, and Marta), from 2 months of age to 18 months (see Bates, Camaioni, and Volterra, 1973, 1975). A number of studies by other authors were also used at various points in these three chapters.

First, in the chapter on sensorimotor performatives, we traced the development of intentional communication, concentrating on the period between 6 to 12 months. During a period in which independent cognitive measures classify two subjects at sensorimotor Stage 5, we also find the first evidence of intentional communication (or illocutions), with protoforms for both the imperative (using the adult as means to an object) and the declarative (using an object as means to an adult). These communicative developments seem to be one more manifestation of the cognitive capacity to invent new means to familiar ends, a capacity most markedly displayed in the use of tools and supports—e.g., using an object to obtain another object. Hence, the so-called "protoperformative" can be seen as a kind of sensorimotor tool use, in this case the use of phonetic or gestural signals.

In the next chapter, on the growth of reference and propositions, we traced the passage from preverbal performatives into the use of words in the same performative frames. Our two older subjects began to use words in both imperative and declarative sequences between 12 to 16 months of age. In this same period, both children showed the beginning of what Piaget calls the "symbolic capacity," manifested in nonverbal behaviors such as ludic or "pretend" play, memory for absent objects, etc. This led us to the conclusion that referential speech (the locutionary aspect of illocutionary schemes) is one of several manifestations of a Stage 6 symbolic capacity. However, this conclusion must be qualified by two major points. First, the passage into referential speech was a gradual one, with many in-between cases of words that were part sensorimotor procedure and part symbol. Second, even though a minimal symbolic capacity can be inferred, it is not necessary to conclude that all the meaning underlying a one- or two-word proposition is constructed at the symbolic level. In fact, the lengthy one- and two-word stages in language development could be explained by limits on a more general, cognitive capacity for internal representation. Part of the meaning underlying the use of a proposition may be constructed at the symbolic level, while the implicit portions of a message may be controlled by the child only at the sensorimotor level. Finally, in the chapter on the growth of reference we also tried to emphasize the dynamic, causal aspect of the symbolic function, as opposed to the traditional view that symbols grow out of primarily imitative, accommodative schemes. The suggestion was made that means–end analysis and tool use precede the development of symbols because they are integrally involved in the structural system that permits the child to create symbols.

In the chapter on sensorimotor presupposing, we returned to the division of messages into said and unsaid portions, suggesting that this same division underlies the proposition/presupposition relationship. Even one-word messages seem to obey certain rules of informativeness and appropriateness in a given context (Greenfield and Smith, 1976; Veneziano, 1973; Snyder, 1975). But it is not necessarily the case that the child constructs both his proposition and his presupposition at the symbolic level. Rather, "presupposing" can be seen as a communicative procedure, the act of selecting one element for overt phonetic encoding to the exclusion of others. This capacity could be a linguistic manifestation of basic orienting and figure–ground mechanisms over which the child has little or no reflective control. In short, the child simply encodes those elements of a structured situation that most attract his attention. He has no choice but to presuppose, or take information for granted. It would be far more difficult for him to do otherwise, encoding less interesting information in order to help the listener locate the topic for a subsequent comment. Hence, much of the course of pragmatic development will involve learning when NOT to presuppose.

2. Pragmatics in The Preoperational Period

Most of the analyses presented in this section were carried out on longitudinal speech transcripts collected at CNR, for Claudia (from 15 to 33 months) and Francesco (from 16 to 45 months of age). In addition, the chapter on word order and presuppositions included reports of several related experiments by this writer and by other researchers.

In the preoperational period (from $1\frac{1}{2}$ to 4 years) the child elaborates his capacity for internal representation (figurative knowledge) and operations on that representation (operative knowledge). The whole process of assimilation and accommodation that characterized sensorimotor adaptation to an object world is now repeated on a new and more flexible world of symbols. There is evidence that during the preoperational period, the child also gains representational control over performatives and presuppositions. The communicative acts or procedures of an earlier stage—performing and presupposing—are turned into symbolic objects, which can in turn be marked or signalled explicitly in the surface form of an utterance.

With regard to performatives, around two years of age in our subjects we find an ability to refer explicitly or talk about the speech act itself. The clearest evidence that children can think about their own performative procedures is an ability to talk about those procedures, to make metapragmatic statements such as *he said* (x) or *You can't say* (x). This kind of utterance appears around 24 months for both children. At the same time, there is a broad set of changes in the overall structure of discourse, including

1. A dimensional concept of time, reflected in both temporal adverbs (tomorrow, Saturday), and imperfect past and future tense verbs.
2. The use of conjunctions such as *but* and *or else* which relate or link an utterance to previous discourse in fairly complex ways.

3. Mastery of the person pronoun system, including reference to the shifting contextual roles of speaker and hearer.

4. Explicit sentence embedding.

In terms of syntactic structure, this is a very heterogeneous set of developments. The ability to make metapragmatic statements seems to be one thread within a larger structure that is built around 24 months, as is indicated by the nonpragmatic development of sentence embedding in the same period. In very abstract terms, we can view all the above developments as dimensional and/or nested relations requiring coordination of at least three mental "chunks," one of which is related to the other two by some common dimension. Around the same time in development that these children can coordinate two nested propositions, they can also explicitly control both a proposition and a presupposition, or a proposition and a performative. The changes in discourse structure also involve seriating sequential events in time, including a sequence of speech acts. All these diverse developments are brought together by the two children in a new effort to narrate long stories. However lacking those stories may be in internal logic, they do at least reflect a new ability to handle larger units in discourse within a single communicative scheme. We have attributed these diverse developments not to a formal, specifically linguistic acquisition, but to a broad increment in the child's cognitive system, an ability to control several procedures as objects subordinated to a higher organizing principle.

The control and explicit encoding of certain simple presuppositions is also an achievement of the early preoperational period. We stated above that the presupposition–proposition relationship is derived from a basic sensorimotor procedure for selecting new information out of a background of old or given information. In examining the development of word order in Italian children, we witnessed a transition from a sensorimotor presupposing scheme—in which the children simply extended the automatic attention rule of the one-word period by blurting out interesting or new information first and less interesting information second—to a reflective, preoperational control of the procedure for presupposing. In the latter period, the children acquire standard SVO ordering, and use the subject-final orders (which they initially preferred for most purposes) only to express strong topicalization on the object or focusing on the subject. Insofar as a rule for placing focused material last requires suppressing the tendency to blurt out focused or interesting material first, we can view this transition in word order preferences as a passage from sensorimotor to preoperational use of the proposition–presupposition and topic–comment relationship. This capacity to reflect on sensorimotor procedures for presupposing occurs in roughly the same developmental period as the capacity to reflect upon and encode performatives explicitly in messages.

As such, it may be yet another manifestation of a postulated shift or increase in the child's general cognitive capacity for coordinating several mental "chunks" or events.

3. Pragmatics in the Concrete Operational Period

In this section, the data on polite forms and counterfactual conditional verbs come from two sources: an analysis of the longitudinal transcripts for Claudia and Francesco, and experiments with 60 Italian preschool children from 2;10 to 6;2 years of age. Hence, in this section we came closest to the optimal combination of in-depth longitudinal views and large-scale cross-sectional views of the same developmental phenomena.

Although children do explicitly mark performatives and presuppositions during the preoperational period (hence, indicating a control over both as symbol structures), there are several pragmatic developments that apparently do not occur until late in the preoperational period, at a point corresponding to the transition into concrete operational thought. The two developments examined in this section are counterfactual conditional verbs and indirect, polite speech acts. I have suggested that these are late pragmatic developments because they require reversible transformations and coordination of several internal structures, including certain relations between the speaker's and the hearer's point of view. While we have no independent cognitive data classifying our subjects at the concrete operational stage, on purely theoretical grounds the operations required for counterfactuals and polite forms seem to be related to the operations that Piaget describes for the concrete operational stage. This interpretation is supported by the age levels at which our subjects mastered these pragmatic devices.

Counterfactual conditional verbs, for example, are not mastered by Italian children until around 5 years of age on the average. Prior to this time, from 3½ to 5 years, subjects approximate the truth conditions of a counterfactual with other kinds of verbs, e.g., imperfect past (*I was eating a banana*), future (*I will eat a banana*). And before 3½ years of age, responses to counterfactual questions are in the present indicative, as if the counterfactual presupposition were not processed at all. This sequence is compatible with cognitive theory insofar as the counterfactual presupposition is simply not motivated unless the speaker knows what sort of inferences a listener MIGHT make unless otherwise warned. In the second phase, the children have begun to grasp the purpose of the counterfactual in suspending truth. Hence, they do realize that the listener must be warned not to assume that the speaker believes the antecedent (as opposed to assuming the falsity of the antecedent, page 222). But they can only approximate the counterfactual suspension of truth with irreversible operations from an egocentric position in time. The verifiability of the antecedent is displaced from "now" to some other, indefinite time period removed from the speaker. A true counterfactual suspends verifiability at all points on a time continuum regardless of the time of utterance, while these "pseudoconditionals" hold in only one direction on the time continuum. The ability to coordinate the truth of an event with time in such a way that the relationship is equivalent at all points in the time series, apparently requires a reversible, transitive operation that is not available to children until concrete operations.

Certain types of polite forms are also late acquisitions, coinciding with the end of the preoperational period. These include requests with conditional verbs (predictable from the above data), formal address, and nonidiomatic, implicit speech acts. Certain types of implicit request forms—i.e., requests that make no explicit mention of either the goal of the speaker or the action required of the listener—never appear at all in the records for Claudia and Francesco (e.g., the statement *Golly, it's noon already* as a request for lunch). Indirect requests which do at least refer obliquely to the desired end state appear in Francesco's records (e.g., *If you're not good, we'll use the wolf*), but toward the end of data collection, near his fourth birthday. Some current proposals for both types of polite forms involve the creation of contrasts to Gricean conversational postulates. According to such an analysis, the speaker knows how conversation is supposed to work, and he knows that the listener shares that knowledge. So he creates utterances which violate the rules in such a manner that the listener is forced to derive alternative, second-order meanings. The polite forms appearing late in the development of Italian children are, in fact, forms which are analyzable within the Gricean proposal (see Gordon and Lakoff, 1971).

However, certain kinds of polite forms appear much earlier, e.g., *please*, reduced intonation, and reduced quantity in requests. There is a crossover from efficiency in communication (expanding messages which fail) to politeness (diminishing the force of messages which fail), a shift that must involve the knowledge that some speech forms are unacceptable, and an ability to predict the likelihood of cooperation from the listener. Such an understanding seems to have been established by age 3, while the more complex Gricean manipulations of the same system do not appear until later. Evidence for a sequence of developments WITHIN the politeness dimension points to the need for a more elaborate theory of role-taking, with sequences or steps in the build up of a model of the listener and the kinds of operations that can be performed on that model. Finally, while an ability to recognize politeness and tune up an utterance to make it more polite is apparently developed by age 3 to 3½, the ability to reason about why one item is more polite than another, or to identify actively which element in an item makes it more polite, does not appear until 4½ to 5 years.

Pragmatics and Cognition:
Suggestions for Future Research

In this section, we will first examine some general issues regarding the relationship between cognition and social-communicative developments. Then we will go through the three Piagetian stages once again, exploring lines of future research on pragmatics and cognition.

The issue of "cognitive prerequisites" for communication is clearly related to the old philosophical question of language–thought relations. Does language depend on thought? Does thought depend on language? Or are the two essentially independent though interacting systems? In adopting a Piagetian model of cognitive development, we have accepted the position that language depends on thought, as one manifestation of a broad capacity for symbolic representation that begins at the end of the sensorimotor period.

This position is not established entirely by fiat. Considerable research by various Piagetian psychologists has indicated that (1) deaf children can develop at least as far as concrete operations without having acquired a functioning language system (Furth, 1966), and (2) training in language does not have any measurable effect on the acquisition of logical structures (e.g., Sinclair, 1969). Even Eric Lenneberg (1967), who has put forth the strongest position to date on the innate, biological basis of language, has concluded that

> There is evidence . . . that cognitive function is a more basic and primary process than language, and that the dependence relationship of language upon cognition is incomparably stronger than vice-versa . . . [page 374]

Persuaded by the evidence that language depends on cognitive development, we have tried to extend that position to the acquisition of pragmatics. But the problem of providing evidence for such a position (or, for that matter, for its converse) is exceedingly difficult. We are arguing about the existence of underlying processes, and the dependence of various surface (i.e., observable) events on such underlying processes. This generally involves observing some kind of coincidence between two or more surface events, and attributing that coincidence to some common structure. However, since the postulated structure may be several steps removed from its various surface manifestations, such "coincidences" provide at best weak support for our elaborate theories.

The same problems are encountered in the more general area of social cognition (e.g., Kohlberg, 1969; Shantz, 1975). Research on the cognitive bases for various social developments includes work by Bell (1970) on the relation between object permanence and mother–child attachment, studies by Flavell and associates (1968) on the relation between concrete operations and social perspective taking, and research by Kohlberg (1969) on cognition and the development of moral reasoning. Insofar as pragmatics involves knowledge of the social use of language, this volume could also be considered a contribution to the area of social cognition. As such, we also inherit all the problems of social–cognitive research. The largest of these problems involves establishing a dependence between social behaviors and cognitive structures.

There is one very straightforward position on social cognitive development, implicit in the work of several authors including Selman (1971). According to this position, at any given stage children should demonstrate a capacity for physical cognition before they apply the same structures to the social realm. This position yields simple ordinal predictions that are easily tested and easily disconfirmed. But it also involves the indefensible claim that the child's interactions with physical objects permit direct observation of "pure" cognition, while interactions with social objects yield mixed observations of presumably "impure" cognition. There is absolutely no logical reason, within anything like a Piagetian model, why this should be the case. According to Piaget, ANY act of knowing—whether social or nonsocial—involves both operative and figurative aspects. Stages are defined primarily in terms of operative logic. But operative structures can only be inferred as they are applied to some kind of figurative content. Since figurative and operative knowing are inseparable, we can never observe "pure cognition." Object permanence tasks with physical objects involve as much figurative content as object permanence tasks with mother disappearing behind a screen. In both cases, we observe the application of a postulated underlying structure to some kind of content area. There are no OPERATIVE reasons why one content area should precede another. The horizontal decalage between two content areas is a function of the figurative knowing involved in the respective domains. The operative knowing—which defines developmental stages—is at least in principle the same for both.

There is, then, no reason why a development in the physical domain should ALWAYS precede the application of the same operative scheme to the social domain. However, it should be possible to predict a sequence of developments between these two content areas in certain cases. Some social developments (e.g., imputing causality to human agents) may almost invariably appear later than nonsocial versions, simply because they involve inherently difficult, "resistant," or unpredictable material. This is another way of saying that human beings may be harder to figure out than blocks, balls, and chairs. On the other hand, there are undoubtedly cases in which adult caretakers prove to be more malleable and predictable objects of study than other, more remote events. Furthermore, the child's motivation to master or understand social content may be higher than his motivation with nonsocial objects. Thus a child with a stable, warm relationship with his mother may develop "mother permanence" before he develops standard object permanence. Both the inherent difficulty of the material and the individual experience of the child may determine the order in which a given operative structure appears in different figurative domains. If the notion of horizontal decalage is to be more than a sort of "fudge factor" for defining away varied age norm data, then we should be able to build positive predictions about horizontal decalage into our developmental theory.

On the other hand, the figurative–operative distinction becomes an empty claim if the horizontal decalage between two manifestations of the same hypothetical structure becomes indefinitely wide. For example, if children demonstrate Stage 5 tool use several months before supposed Stage 5 communication begins, what right do we have to interpret these two developments as applications of the same operative structure? In the straightforward cognitive prerequisite model, where "pure cognition" is invariably supposed to precede social cognition, all claims are subject to disconfirmation. It is sufficient to show a case in which a social development comes before a nonsocial version of the same structure, and the cognitive prerequisite claim is defeated. In the more sophisticated cognitive model adopted here, the "prerequisite" for both social and nonsocial behaviors is an unobservable operative structure. Hence our claims are far more difficult either to confirm or disconfirm. We predict that social and nonsocial manifestations of the same purported underlying structure should appear in ROUGHLY the same age range. Furthermore, within each domain the sequence of developments should be parallel (e.g., "mother permanence" with one screen should precede "mother permanence" with two screens just as object permanence with one screen precedes object permanence with two). The ordinal relations WITHIN domains are easy enough to establish. But who is to determine the range beyond which a claim of interdependence in two domains is no longer useful? We must make an arbitrary decision that two weeks, or two months, or two years of decalage are enough to weaken the explanatory power of our figurative–operative interpretation. In other words, we can prove (or at least disprove) ordinal relations within domains, but we cannot incontrovertibly establish a dependence between domains.

There are ways of demonstrating at least some statistical support for a claim of social/nonsocial interdependence. According to the figurative–operative model, operative schemes develop from procedures carried out on various figurative objects. If a child can successfully understand a given relationship or operation on one set of materials, he should have greater success on the next set of materials. There should, then, be transfer from one domain to another, as the operative schemes become increasingly stable and active with each successful application. Therefore, a child who successfully completes a development in the social realm should arrive at the nonsocial version earlier than a child who has not yet worked the relationship through. Similarly, success in the nonsocial realm should contribute to success in interactions with social objects. We can, then, predict that across a sample of children there should be a correlation between age of onset for social versus nonsocial accomplishments in the same realm.

There are problems with this suggestion as well, however. How do we know that such a correlation is the product of a structural dependence? Suppose it is simply the case that precocious babies do everything earlier than nonprecocious babies? Insofar as this is true, about the only underlying structure we can talk about is a ephemeral Spearman's g, or general intelligence. One way out of this difficulty is to administer a battery of cognitive tests and social–communicative tasks. Presumably, by factoring out the contribution of "general precocity," we can derive a pattern of correlations in which some cognitive tasks are better predictors of social development than others. It is the pattern of relationships, and not the overall level of the correlations, that can tell us the most about structural interdependencies in social and nonsocial domains.

I am not advocating a "shotgun correlational approach" to social cognition. Presumably, our developmental theories tell us which tasks SHOULD be related on structural grounds, and which tasks should not. The various tasks that we include in our battery should be determined by predictions about the nature of social versus nonsocial development and the operative structures that should be shared by the two figurative realms.

To summarize thus far, we can support a theory of the cognitive basis for social-communicative events with four kinds of "coincidence":

1. Logical coincidence, i.e., structural analyses pointing out precisely why on theoretical grounds we should expect two behaviors to be related to a central structure (e.g., our analysis of tool use in Stage 5 communication in which the use of an object to obtain an object is structurally related to the use of an adult to obtain an object, and an object to obtain an adult).

2. The appearance of social and nonsocial manifestations of a postulated structure in roughly the same age range, regardless of the order between the two.

3. Demonstrations of transfer from one realm to another, through correlations between time of onset in one domain and time of onset in another, across a sample of children.

4. Patterns of intercorrelations in which, regardless of the general strength or level of various correlations, some tasks are better predictors of one another than others.

In addition, our theory of social and nonsocial manifestations of operative structures is strengthened if we can predict the order of acquisition of each in terms of either the inherent difficulty of the material, or of the motivation and experience of particular children.

Given this general statement of the problem, let us turn now to suggestions for research on the relationship between pragmatics and cognition in the sensorimotor, preoperational, and concrete operational stages.

1. Pragmatics in the Sensorimotor Period

At the sensorimotor stage, we tried to show how the acquisition of performative schemes (e.g. using an object to obtain adult attention, using an adult to obtain an object) is related to the Stage 5 capacity for tool use (e.g., using an object to obtain an object). Similarly, we pointed out (after Piaget, 1962) how the growth of reference is related on structural grounds to the development of the symbolic capacity. Finally, it was suggested that the early tendency to encode the most informative element in a situation (such that the encoded element "presupposes" uncoded meaning) can be explained in sensorimotor terms if that tendency is viewed as a linguistic manifestation of more general attention and figure–ground mechanisms.

In the longitudinal study cited throughout the sensorimotor section, we were able at the very least to point out structural reasons why communicative developments SHOULD be related to cognitive developments. Hence, the first of the above recommendations, the establishment of logical coincidence or correlation, seems to have been satisfied. Second, we demonstrated that Stage 5 and 6 cognitive developments tend to appear in roughly the same respective periods as Stage 5 and 6 communicative developments. In this respect, our longitudinal study has one definitive advantage over the studies used in the rest of the book. In the longitudinal project we have independent, nonlinguistic measures of cognition for the same children that were studied for communicative development. In the rest of the volume, however, when we note a rough coincidence in age of onset for pragmatic versus noncommunicative developments, we are referring almost entirely to work on cognitive development by other authors. For example, conditional verbs are acquired around 5 years of age. Because we can point out structural reasons why conditional verbs should require concrete operations, and because 5 to 7 happens to be the age range most often cited for the onset of concrete operations in various tasks, we have pointed out a coincidence in the range in which the two developments occur. But this coincidence is not derived from the same sample of children. Since our longitudinal project does yield both cognitive and communicative data for the same children, we can make somewhat stronger claims for a relationship between pragmatics and cognition in the sensorimotor period than in later developmental stages.

Nevertheless, although a coincidence within the same two subjects is preferable to a coincidence in age norms in two separate studies, our results are still questionable from a statistical point of view. Two subjects just aren't very many. It was for this reason that we began a larger, cross-sectional study of 25 infants, studied at monthly intervals between the ages of 9½ to 13 months. The sessions involved cognitive testing (using the Hunt and Uzgiris scales (1975), based on Piaget's developmental theory), interviews with the mother, videotaping of sequences designed to elicit communication, and a number of other measures. Data collection has just been completed at this writing, and a great many correlational and ordinal analyses remain to be done. However, preliminary analyses (see Bates, Benigni, Bretherton, Camaioni, and Volterra, 1975) do indicate strong support for the hypotheses derived from our original longitudinal study. The hypothesized Stage 5 developments in communication do occur in the same age range (within eight weeks) as noncommunicative Stage 5 behaviors (e.g., the use of the support relation). Also, toward the end of the period studied, several different manifestations of a Stage 5 capacity for symbolic representation began to appear in our infants, including referential speech, certain types of symbolic play, and Stage 6 object permanence (i.e., the ability to follow invisible displacements of a hidden object).

Within the fifth and sixth stage respectively, most children do show their first manifestations of the proposed operative structures in noncommunicative sequences. However, there were certainly cases in which social Stage 5 and Stage 6 (i.e., gestural communication, referential speech) appeared before nonsocial versions. Recall the Bell (1970) study in which children with a secure attachment relationship to their mothers demonstrated mother permanence before they attained Stage 4 object permanence for nonsocial objects; children with an insecure attachment bond were later overall in cognitive development, and when they do display object permanence they manifest it first with objects, and somewhat later in seeking mother behind a screen. In our cross-sectional study, we have also included a measure of mother–child attachment (Ainsworth, 1973) to determine whether the order in which children develop social and nonsocial tool use (and social and nonsocial Stage 6) can be predicted from the nature of the child's relationship to his mother. This represents our first effort to predict decalage in these domains, and it may well be the case that 25 infants are too few to determine such subtle individual differences (if, indeed, such individual differences exist at all). Nevertheless, even if our first efforts fail, we are convinced that such research will add important information about the nature of the relationship between cognition and social development.

From detailed correlational analyses, we also hope to determine whether children who develop early in one domain will also develop early in another. Furthermore, the pattern of correlations among the various subscales of the cognitive tests and the various communicative measures should add to our knowledge about social–cognitive relations. For example, from a preliminary round of correlations it does seem that cognitive developments in the area of causality (e.g., means–end relations) are better predictors of communicative development than such cognitive tasks as object permanence and space relations. This would be consistent with findings by Snyder (1975), that means–end tasks distinguish language-delayed versus normal children better than other scales from the Hunt and Uzgiris battery.

In all three of the areas in the sensorimotor section—propositions, performatives, and presuppositions—a great deal of research remains to be done. For example, what are the developmental precursors to the interrogative performative? Can we distinguish sensorimotor interrogatives that prepare the child for the interrogative function in speech? Regarding the development of propositions, are there nonlinguistic correlates to the passage from one- to two- to n-word speech? In the area of sensorimotor presupposing, what further evidence can we provide to implicate attention and figure–ground mechanisms in the child's decision to encode one element at the exclusion of others in his early utterances? Research in this area will depend in large measure on the development of sensitive experimental techniques for working with very young children. But in some ways, research on pragmatics and cognition in the sensorimotor period—when the child is far less capable of "internal," representational knowing—is much easier than research during the preoperational period, when significant developments are less amenable to direct observation. Furthermore, in the sensorimotor period we have a detailed set of heuristics from Piagetian theory regarding stages in cognitive development. In comparison with the range from 0 to 18 months, the preoperational period is virtually uncharted territory. This brings us to the second section, on pragmatics and cognition in the preoperational stage.

2. Pragmatics in the Preoperational Period

Theories of development from 2 to 4 years tend to concentrate primarily on the major event that takes place in that period: the acquisition of language. As a result, it is particularly difficult to discuss nonlinguistic correlates of language development in the preoperational period. In Piaget's theory of development, the preoperational stage (as indicated by the very name for that period) is defined primarily in terms of what it is not, i.e., as the absence of concrete operations. Piaget speaks in relatively vague terms of intuitive and transductive logic, without defining in positive terms the accomplishments of the period from 2–4. His major work on that age range is *The Language and Thought of the Child* (1926), an early work that concentrates primarily on the egocentric nature of child language prior to the onset of what he would later term concrete operations. Other major works by cognitive theorists dealing with this age range include those of Vygotsky (1962), Bruner (1964), and Werner and Kaplan (1963), all of which revolve around the acquisition of language, and the consequent socialization of thought.

This state of affairs is particularly frustrating, since the most interesting developments for psycholinguists do indeed take place in this uncharted stage. There has been a surge of interest in cognitive bases for language acquisition. And yet between the ages of 2 to 4, when most children acquire their native language, most theorists abandon efforts to characterize nonlinguistic developments in cognitive processing. In the section on pragmatics in the preoperational period, we suggested that a heterogeneous set of syntactic developments (e.g., nested propositions, dimensional time as expressed in verb tense and temporal adverbials, complex conjunctions, metapragmatic speech, and the switch from pragmatic to syntactic strategies in word order) may be rooted in some general shift in the capacity to coordinate symbol structures. After Pascual–Leone (1970), it was further suggested that this shift may involve a quantitative and qualitative shift in the kind of "chunks" that can be processed at a given moment. Pascual–Leone has referred to the "central processing space" to which such a chunking capacity is relevant as "operative memory." A related proposal has been put forth by Miller, Galanter, and Pribram (1960), with regard to "planning memory," a level of processing midway between short-term and long-term storage. Olson (1973) has also discussed the role of quantitative limits in perception and memory on the child's capacity to plan and execute various types of linguistic structures. It should be possible to design nonlinguistic memory and processing tasks that will determine whether the shifts in the linguistic capacity (from one- to two- to n-word speech, and from simple to nested propositions) are related to comparable shifts in the capacity to process nonlinguistic material.

Even if we do discover nonlinguistic correlates to shifts in language processing, we cannot be sure how or if these developments are causally related. Given the major role that language acquisition plays in the period from 2 to 4, it may well be that changes in nonlinguistic processing reflect a transfer from figurative experience in the linguistic realm to figurative experience in other areas. More precisely, changes in the child's short term memory and perceptual processing strategies during the preoperational period may be directly due to an increased capacity for linguistic encoding. Regardless of the causal direction, or the primary contribution of linguistic versus nonlinguistic experience, it would be interesting enough just to establish the existence of qualitative and quantitative developments during the preoperational period, beyond those that are expressly observed in language development. Indeed, if it can in the very least be established that language acquisition has repercussions beyond its own domain, the rich and easily accessible material of language development could be used to establish and/or enrich a theory of general cognitive development in the period from 2 to 4 years.

3. Pragmatics in the Concrete Operational Period

In this section, as in the section on preoperational pragmatics, all arguments regarding the relationship between pragmatics and cognition have been based on age norms from studies by other authors. An obvious line for future research would involve administering nonlinguistic concrete operational tasks to a single sample of subjects who are also tested for the pragmatic developments reported here. For example, a set of role-taking tasks, conservation tasks, seriation and classification tasks could be administered to children in the 4 to 7 age range, together with the experiments cited here on conditional verbs and polite forms. We suggested, for example, in Chapter VII that the stage in which children use alternative verb forms in conditional frames may be related to the tendency to construct partial, nonreversible orderings in seriation tasks. Therefore, we would predict that children who have not yet completed the acquisition of conditionals are also less proficient at seriating different length sticks from smallest to largest.

It might also be interesting to test the use of conditional presuppositions WITHIN Piagetian classification or conservation tasks. For example, I recently piloted some conditional questions in a drawing task with a 4½-year-old boy. He had drawn a series of squares and circles, and had counted all the squares first, and all the circles second, giving me the sum of each. I then asked *If all the circles were squares, how many squares would there be?* This exceptionally bright child immediately recounted all the geometric forms, both squares and circles, and gave me the overall total. However, apparently to make his point clear, he then volunteered *Now I'll tell you how many **real** squares there are* and counted the squares only. It should be possible to construct tasks similar to the above interaction, contrasting counterfactual conditional questions with present indicative conditional questions. Performance on these tasks could then be related to performance on classification tasks which do not invoke the "if/then" question.

In all the social–cognition literature, the one development that is consistently implicated in social–communicative progress is the capacity to role-take, or take the perspective of others even when that perspective contrasts with the child's own. As it was originally conceived in Piaget's work, role-taking supposedly required the operation of reversibility, and as such was considered to be a development of the concrete operational period. Several studies of communicative development between 5 to 8 years have invoked role-taking as an explanation for improved communicative competence, e.g., Wertsch (1974) and Krauss and Glucksberg (1969). However, in more recent research certain types of role-taking have been established as early as 2½ to 3 years of age (e.g., Devries, 1970; Maratsos, 1973a). Flavell's own research on role-taking has led him to make serious criticisms of stage theory in general (1971), stressing that a number of content areas for a particular structure (i.e., horizontal decalages) can take years to acquire, resulting in very unstagelike acquisition curves.

Since role-taking necessarily involves the child's construction of a model of the listener, it is not surprising that some kinds of role-taking appear long before others. Marvin (1972) uses some of Flavell's more recent tasks to establish a limited understanding of the listener's perspective around 2½ to 3 years of age. For example, the child is drawing a picture, and the Experimenter asks him to *Hold the picture up so I can see it.* Before 30 to 36 months, children will hold the picture so that only they can see it, with the back of the page presented to the Experimenter. Around 30 months, some children will begin to turn the picture around so that it is visible to the Experimenter. This ability is slightly delayed if the child must turn it around upside down. With each such increment in task complexity, role-taking is delayed. Another task involves less directly perceptible norms. When asked *What does Mommy want for her birthday, a dolly or a new dress?*, very young children will opt for the toy. Around 3 years of age, children will hesitate and choose the dress, and slightly older children will even scorn the Experimenter for posing such a stupid question.

Piaget's own role-taking tasks, the ones which predictably find acquisition occurring around 7 years of age, are far more complex than the above tasks. The child is seated before a plastic mountain with houses, people, etc. on its various sides. He is then asked to describe (or to draw) the array as seen by someone on the other side of the mountain. If one recalls the task of simply holding up a picture, a task which is increasingly difficult if the picture must be held upside down, etc., then it should be clear that Piaget's task requires several more recursions on the role-taking ability than the simpler tasks. It shouldn't surprise us that his results place acquisition later than do the more recent tests.

In fact, there is a tendency for most replications of Piaget's concrete operations tasks to establish age norms slightly below those reported by the Geneva group. This in no way violates the stage model, since precise age of onset is not evidence for or against the ORDER in which structures are acquired. However, it does suggest that there has been interference due to task complexity. In the present study, the period from 4½ to 5 years seems to be a pivotal moment in pragmatic development. It was at this point that children began to discriminate more complex requests (although correct discrimination on these items did not reach significance until 5½), and to reason about pragmatic choices that were already under passive control. It is around 3½ to 4 years of age that precocious Francesco begins using speech forms that correspond to Gricean principles. 4½ years is the age at which children approximate the truth conditions of the counterfactual with pseudoconditionals, indicating an understanding that the listener must be warned not to make inferences about the speaker's beliefs. While this ability may not be completely concrete operational, it at least demonstrates some minimal role-taking capacity, permitting the computation of something such as *I'd better warn him not to assume that I think X*. In one of his earliest works, *The Language and Thought of the Child*, written before he had investigated the concrete operational tasks of later works, Piaget notes that egocentric speech (e.g., the use of pronouns when the listener doesn't know the antecedent) declines between 4 to 5 years. It is this operational level, neglected in later studies with more complex tasks, to which the pragmatic developments of the present study most closely correspond. Again, these results point out the need for a more detailed stage model of preoperational thinking, defined in terms of what the child CAN do rather than what particular operations he cannot yet perform.

In the future, when role-taking is invoked as an explanatory principle, it will be necessary to specify what kind of role-taking, at what level of complexity, is required to perform a certain linguistic operation. For example, our study points to two levels of role-taking in acquisition of politeness. 3 to 3½-year-olds have at least a minimal concept of "talking nice." Early politeness seems to involve adding ritual words and reducing the dimensions of a request (through both intonation and quantity of content) so that the listener won't be offended, and compliance will be more likely. The next level of politeness also involves assuring that the listener won't be offended, in this case by selecting less direct speech acts which violate conversational postulates—hence assuring that the listener will seek alternative interpretations and arrive at the camouflaged meanings. Now, in terms of the role-taking required in the two periods, there are clear differences in the complexity and abstractness of the model of the listener used to build polite speech. The first level of politeness requires a prediction of concrete results—*If I ask for less, she'll give me a cookie*. The second level requires coordinating my own perspective with that of the listener in terms of a rule of conversation, a conceptual rather than a perceptual norm. Just as *Show me a picture* and *Show me a picture upside down* produce different results, these two kinds of role-taking reflect different levels of complexity.

Since there is no "one moment" when the child completes a model of the listener, there can also be no "one moment" when pragmatic structures involving listeners are mastered. Some presuppositions, as was stated in

Chapter VI, are available for encoding early in the preoperational period. Other presuppositions will require more abstract principles and more complex operations on the listener's point of view. Each pragmatic structure must be examined in terms of its complexity before we can predict its relation to cognitive development.

This last point is particularly relevant to the study of topicalization in child language. We stated in Chapter VI that topicalization competes for surface expression to the degree that the child is aware of the need to make the listener aware of information that the child speaker himself takes for granted. Obviously, the child's ability to predict the listener's needs and to topicalize needed information will depend in part on the nature of the information in question. Studies of egocentrism in child language have referred rather obliquely to this point, noting only that preschool children "take things for granted" that are not obvious to the listener. For example, in the Krauss and Glucksberg task (1969), two children are seated on opposite sides of a screen. Child A is asked to describe a two- or three-dimensional form to Child B, so that Child B will be able to select the correct form on the basis of that description. A measure of relative egocentrism of messages is obtained by taking the child's messages out of context, and administering them to an adult judge. Indeed, the adult judges generally find that the children's descriptions are "too egocentric" to permit correct identification of the object or form in question. However, Hoy (1975) and Sinclair (1975) have both found that despite the relative egocentricity of their utterances, children are surprisingly successful at identifying the poorly described referent when the messages occur in context. Apparently, children are using idiosyncratic conventions and aspects of the temporal sequence of messages to permit them to disambiguate messages which, when taken out of context, are virtually impossible to decode. In the Bates and MacWhinney project mentioned in Chapter VI, we plan to analyze child utterances in supposedly "egocentric" conditions from the point of view of particular pragmatic structures (e.g., pronominalization, contrastive stress, ellipsis, etc.), in their appropriate order (i.e., in the sequence in which the message actually occurred) to determine what linguistic forms the child has chosen to express the relationship between topicalized and focused information. Hopefully, such research will yield a more precise characterization of egocentric speech, and of substages in the transition from egocentric to decentered communications, than have been obtained from the less precise method of subjective adult judgments as employed by Krauss and Glucksberg.

The various suggestions presented above represent just a few possible lines of research on language and cognitive development. At a recent conference on child language in London (The Third International Child Language Symposium, London, 1975), a great deal of interest was expressed, by researchers from many countries, on the cognitive bases of language acquisition. However, since there are so few heuristics from cognitive theory concerning nonlinguistic developments between 2 to 6 years of age, many researchers are uncertain as to precisely how to proceed to establish relationships between linguistic and nonlinguistic events. For example, Greenfield and Smith (1976) and Bloom (1973) recommend research on the kinds of cognitive developments that prepare the linguistic changes noted in their respective monographs. And yet guidelines for precisely how to carry out such research are few (as they are in this volume as well). Sinclair (1973) has been one of the strongest advocates of a theory that derives language from cognitive structure. She has observed, for example, that the major constituents of syntax, and the operations involved in the transformational process, are structurally similar to the syntax of action described by Piaget for the sensorimotor period. She suggests that the child in fact derives his syntactic operations from his sensorimotor operations—e.g., the conjoining of sentences comes from an ability to conjoin two activities in play; the embedding of propositions comes from an ability to embed objects in one another, or to interrupt action patterns to insert another action. However, there is a curious anomaly in Sinclair's own research with respect to these same theoretical concepts. Although she discusses the parallels between Chomskian syntactic operations and Piagetian mental operations, her studies invariably test children between the ages of 3 and 8. Some of the structures she studies—word order (Sinclair and Bronckardt, 1972), verb tense (Bronckardt and Sinclair, 1974)—have been used productively by children long before they perform adequately on the experimental tasks. For example, the authors conclude that the imperfect past is not mastered by French children until concrete operations. Yet Claudia and Francesco mastered the Italian imperfect past in spontaneous production data around 2 years of age. The Geneva group is wary of using free speech data because they claim that some syntactic forms may appear as "pseudostructures" well before the child actually understands them. This is true in many cases, such as Francesco's use of quantifiers as commands (*Uno ... Tanti!* ...) or temporal adverbs as refusals (*oggi no ... domani*). But it is often possible to distinguish pseudostructures from adultlike uses of a syntactic form within the free speech data itself. In the case of imperfect past verb, Claudia's sentence (page 144) *But at moments I was going onto the ground* to indicate an uncompleted act, seems to be irrefutable evidence that she understands both the temporal and the aspectual components of the Italian imperfect past. How do we explain the enormous decalage between production data and experimental data? In part, there may be interference due to the testing situation itself, creating shyness in some children, difficulty with the instructions, and so forth. However, another possibility is that the experimental tasks used by the

Geneva group involve a metalinguistic component that is not required for free production of the same forms. In short, perhaps the tasks for eliciting imperfect verbs and word order strategies do not actually tap the strategies used by the children for speaking, but rather involve strategies for thinking about time, aspect, or word order. This would explain a delay until after 4 years of age for forms that are productive at 2 to 2½. Recall that in Chapter IX, children could not actively reproduce the pragmatic forms that they discriminated passively, until around 4½ years. DeVilliers and deVilliers (1974) have also noted that grammaticality judgments in young children become proficient around four years (with certain more passive judgments operating prior to that time).

The essential challenge, as Sinclair herself suggests, is to characterize linguistic transformations in themselves, the operations that are actually used by children to produce and understand speech. It is the cognitive structure of these latter operations that is of greatest interest within a cognitive theory of language acquisition. But such an effort will require a better understanding of cognitive development in the preoperational period.

In published work (e.g., Greenfield et al., 1972; Dodson and Greenfield, 1975) and in research in progress, Greenfield has illustrated a particularly exciting new line for research on the structural relations between cognitive and linguistic development. The clearest example is her 1972 study of strategies in nesting cups between 11 and 36 months of age. She found a sequence of strategies, starting with the primitive use of one cup to touch all the others one at a time, through to the final strategy of nesting each cup within the next largest until the series is complete. Greenfield relates these successive structures to parallel strategies in the acquisition of language, starting with simple topic–comment structures through to nested propositions. The parallel developments in the two domains are established entirely on logical grounds. No effort is made to correlate, for example, stages in nesting cup strategies with stages in linguistic development within individual children. Greenfield is primarily interested in establishing what we referred to earlier as logical coincidence between domains, and in ordinal parallels within domains. Nevertheless, she has put forth perhaps the strongest position to date on structural similarities between linguistic and nonlinguistic development.

As we noted in Chapter I, recent proposals in linguistic semantics provide a rich source of hypotheses concerning parallels between linguistic structure and cognitive development. But we must be careful not to take various formal linguistic models too literally when we apply them to psychological functioning. In the next section, we will discuss some limits in the applicability of various formal modals to the representation of psychological events.

On Pragmatics and Linguistic Representation

Dimensions

In examining issues of politeness, emphasis, and suspension of assertion, it seems evident that native speakers can rank order discrete devices for each of the categories, permitting them to move an utterance up and down dimensions of politeness and strength. 3 to 3½ year old children can increase the politeness of a request when asked to do so, and evidence from the longitudinal records of Claudia and Francesco indicates that there is at least a minimal control of degrees of politeness by age 2½. Different types of linguistic devices—adverbs, intonation, word order, pronouns, verb inflections—can be used interchangeably or in combination to increase a particular pragmatic effect. However, when we look at the various proposals for representing politeness and/or emphasis in deep structure, all that is available are discrete, proposition-like descriptions for each of the particular devices used.

If a grammar is a description of native competence, and if native speakers can control politeness or emphasis by adding and subtracting discrete elements, then we need some means of representing the DEGREE of a given pragmatic dimension that the speaker wishes to convey. Particularly in the case of topicalization and emphasis, the only function that such a proliferation of discrete devices can serve is to permit the speaker to induce in the listener a CONTOUR, an analogue of his own feelings about the relative informativeness and importance of elements within a given message. A complete pragmatic construction with a propositional content is like a black and white sketch with the shading and highlighting added. The speaker formulates the major constituents in relation to one another, and then tunes the constituent structures from "outside" until it conveys the feelings he has in mind. It is, as was mentioned in Chapter V, noteworthy that emphasis and politeness both employ intonation, the only analogue aspect of the speech channel, as a conventional part of pragmatic rules. The spontaneous requests of younger children in the politeness task involved literal reduction in tone of voice and in quantity terms, and the item involving difference in intonation was among the first to be described by children as "nicer."

The pragmatic component of a grammar will require a means of representing continuous ideas or meanings that play a part in the choice of necessarily discrete elements. The tree structures used by both generative semantics and interpretive semantics do not lend themselves easily to representation of continuous meanings. However, there are some recent efforts to include nondiscrete knowledge within a grammar of English. Lakoff has presented several proposals (e.g., 1972) for the representation of "hedges" and "fuzzy ideas." In general, his proposal is an extended version of Zadeh's concept of fuzzy logic. Zadeh (1975) offers a formalism for representing the probability that a given token or instance belongs within a particular category. For example, instead of true–false statements that P is an instance of Q—with values of either zero or one—it is possible to state that P is an instance of Q by a probability of .6. The truth value of P $\neq$ Q is then calculated to be (1 to .6), or .4. The system reduces back to ordinary propositional logic if we simply arbitrarily assign all values greater than .5 the value (1.0), and all values less than .5 the value (0). Hence "sort of true" becomes either true or false. These probability statements can be used to compute rank orders among given members of a class. For example, in a study by Eleanor Rosch (1973), subjects were asked to rank order several species along a dimension of "birdiness." Robins receive a high rating as members of the class of birds, penguins receive a lower rating, and bats a still lower one. Lakoff uses Rosch's results to generate the following set of sentences:

The robin is a bird.	**The robin is a sort of bird.*
The penguin is a bird.	*?The penguin is a sort of bird.*
*The bat is a bird.	*The bat is a sort of bird.*

Hedges such as *sort of, a little bit,* or *you might say* are triggered when the match or lack of match of one member to a given class reaches a given threshold (a threshold that may in turn have idiolectic variants). Lakoff goes on to extend the same system to the computation of truth values in relation to presuppositions. Thus a statement that only partially violates its own presuppositions is only partially false—yielding a nonsense ratio that can be corrected by invoking one or more hedge mechanisms.

Ross (1972) has recently extended the notion of nondiscrete meanings to the assignment of syntactic categories, the "squishy" categories that cover many of the border cases in grammaticality judgments. For example, there is a scalar relationship holding among the following syntactic categories:

$$\text{Verb} < \frac{\text{Present}}{\text{Participle}} < \frac{\text{Perfect}}{\text{Participle}} < \frac{\text{Passive}}{\text{Participle}} < \text{Adjective}$$

such that a given lexical item may sometimes behave as a verb, sometimes as an adjective, and often somewhere in between depending on a given context. The decision to treat the item according to one of these syntactic categories apparently depends on more than arbitrary, discrete category membership.

In the case of politeness and emphasis, the native speaker may possess some type of rank order listing among available, discrete linguistic devices. In constructing an utterance, he may be forced to choose a discrete device that ranks slightly below his own analogue "feeling" of anger, powerlessness, warmth, politeness, etc. If this occurs, he can "fine tune" the utterance up the emotional gradient by increasing intonation or non-verbal gestural devices that carry the same emotional message as the discrete linguistic element. Or if he chooses a linguistic element that exceeds the intended degree of emphasis, politeness, etc., he can use intonation and gesture to decrease the pragmatic effect back down to his "feeling" along that dimension. This proposal would provide a heuristic for relating verbal and nonverbal conventions in social interaction, and for describing the verbal art or style that characterize much of casual speech. In studying the acquisition of politeness by children, this sort of descriptive system would enable us to capture the beginning of a new function as it makes a transition from nonverbal to verbal means of expression (or vice-versa). There are means of testing these relations empirically, in experiments controlling the choice of discrete categories while specifying a given gradient of politeness, status, assertiveness, emphasis, warmth, etc. For example, the subject is instructed to say verbatim the sentence *I want that article* as he would direct it to his superior at work, his wife, etc. There are also several natural experiments that reflect that same conditions. During second language learning, a speaker is often faced with a limited set of discrete linguistic devices. We can predict certain nonverbal compensations to take place when the speaker faces realistic social situations in the second language. Furthermore, if it is the case that these pragmatic meanings have a nondiscrete component in deep structure, then we can predict that speakers using a less discrete channel of communication—for example, deaf speakers of American Sign Language—will express those pragmatic meanings with the analogue components in the manual-visual channel, e.g., duration, speed of gesture, spatial encompassment, etc. A description of ASL by Stokoe (1972) indicates that this may in fact be the case. Finally, there are also natural languages with greater restrictions on the analogue aspects of the speech channel, e.g., tone languages in which a pragmatic variation of stress might be ambiguous with a semantic-syntactic marking. If it is true that pragmatic meanings contain DEGREES of emphasis, politeness, etc., then we would expect to find other devices in these tone languages to substitute for the strict categorization on intonation.[1] There are a few developmental observations to support this contention. In certain middle-class areas, it is considered better to speak French with a fairly flat intonation, holding intonational color to a minimum. French informants tell me that children brought up in such families are continually corrected for using expressive intonation, and yet intonation is a persistent "error" in the speech of these

---

[1] This suggestion comes from a discussion with F. Antinucci on devices for indicating emphasis in certain African languages.

children. This would be predicted if the children are using the analogue channel to encode pragmatic effects that they cannot yet encode with discrete devices.

It is also the case (Duncan, 1969; Birdwhistell, 1970) that there are discrete choices to be made in nonverbal channels as well, such as a decision to interrupt the speaker at a given segment in conversational turn taking. If nonverbal conventions must be violated for some reason, we might expect a compensatory shift in the choice of discrete verbal means of expression, e.g., the employment of polite expressions at a well-considered point of interrupting the speaker.

The advantage of a formalism for dimensional constructs is its usefulness in equating forms with a different "discrete" tree structure, so as to predict the alternation and cooccurrence rules holding among them (Ervin-Tripp, 1972). Also, if such formalisms permit a more natural generation of conversational interaction, they could be incorporated within artificial intelligence models of natural language to enhance the capacity for disambiguation. Finally, an adequate account of pragmatic dimensions will be useful in examining the acquisition of unrelated syntactic elements as they are used within a shared function slot.

On the Nature of Pragmatic "Trees"

A more central issue with regard to the relations between language and cognitive structure revolves around the appropriateness of propositional trees to describe mental operations, particularly operations associated with rules of use.

It is recognized by many linguists and mathematicians (e.g., Maxwell, 1973) that trees are only one kind of formalism out of an array of possible structures. The neat hierarchical arrangement of tree structures can be contrasted with heterarchical structures (Bobrow and Raphael, 1973) in which the lowest subordinate node also dominates or calls up the higher nodes. Greenfield (personal communication) and Maxwell are among researchers investigating the uses of graph theory as a source of diverse formalisms for diverse psychological structures. Graph theory permits a broad set of hierarchical relations, heterarchical relations, loops and partial orderings, etc. There is no a priori reason why all these formalisms might not describe mental operations, including the operations underlying language (see Tyler (1969) for a discussion of alternatives to the usual formalisms for cultural structures as well, e.g., kinship). Research in this area may challenge the current convention of using rigid, hierarchical tree structures to describe all propositions, and all the organization underlying complex lexical meanings.

If it is true that trees may not be universally appropriate for describing semantic content, then it is equally likely that trees may not be the only formalism for describing pragmatic intentions. This introduces a second question: should semantic content and pragmatic rules of use ever be described with the same notational system? Does this violate the essential psychological differences separating the two kinds of operations? Or are there advantages in using the same kind of formalisms to describe both?

In the present study, I have also adapted the generative semantic convention of describing pragmatic intentions—both performatives and presuppositions—with propositional notation. This was done not because pragmatic operations are in themselves propositions, but on the contrary because propositions are also mental operations. Insofar as pragmatic and semantic constructions are both based on PROCEDURES, they can both be described with whatever notation is most appropriate to a description of procedures. Hence, the propositional structures cited here could all just as easily have been described with a set of action flow charts, e.g., DO (X) TO CAUSE (Y) or USE (X) TO COMMENT ON (Y).

However, there is another reason why pragmatic and semantic structures have been described with similar notational systems. In the present study, I have suggested that pragmatic development proceeds like the rest of cognitive development, with lower-order procedures being constructed as the objects or elements for higher-order procedures. This means that a scheme which the child DOES at the sensorimotor level—e.g., using a signal so that the listener will do X—later becomes a symbolic object which the child HAS. By reflecting on his own action patterns, the child can derive the propositional content for metapragmatic comments, e.g., *I told you to do (X)*. He can reflect upon an earlier selection procedure, which had involved choosing one item to encode to the exclusion of others, and turn that procedure into a presuppositional object describing the relation between old and new information. Later on, in even more complex recursions on his own action patterns, he can reflect upon his own ability to encode pragmatic information and hence camouflage his pragmatic intentions with polite or hedged utterances. Insofar as pragmatic procedures can be converted into the semantic content of other procedures, it is advantageous to store procedures in a form that lends itself to both roles, as actions and as content. The use of propositional notation to describe propositions, performatives and presuppositions, acknowledges this translatibility of cognitive status between pragmatic procedures and symbolic content. However, the use of pragmatic structures as symbolic objects is always relative to a given moment in processing. To determine which role a pragmatic procedure is serving, i.e., act or object, we must examine the way that it is being exercised in a particular utterance.

On Cognitive Levels in Linguistic Representation

At several points in the preceding chapters, we have suggested that children construct propositions, performatives and presuppositions at different cognitive levels. For example, in Chapter III we claimed that the meaning underlying one-word utterances is constructed almost entirely at the perceptual–motor level. At the level of symbolic representation, the child constructs only that portion of his meaning that will be projected into sound.

It is possible, indeed likely, that adults operate in a similar fashion during spontaneous, natural discourse. Recall the example in Chapter VI, from Rommetveit (1974), in which one football fan communicates to another his evaluation of a brilliant touchdown. That same meaning can be conveyed with an approving look, with a one-word comment (*Magnificent!*), with a full sentence, or indeed with a lengthy discussion of the history of football, depending on how much topicalization needs to be provided for the comment to work. Any message—from highly implicit to highly explicit utterances—has long and tangled roots into vast stores of related information, both presuppositions and entailments (see Chapter I). How much of that information needs to be represented at the level of so-called semantic deep structure? There is evidence that even weakly related information is "called up" (see Chapter I on demons and open files) every time a message is produced or received. Therefore, the long roots of an utterance, regarding both preceding material and material called up during a particular message, are in some way psychologically present during the production and/or understanding of that utterance. And yet surely such information is less "centrally" present when compared with the information that is explicitly encoded.

If linguistic representations are to correspond to anything that is psychologically real, then it would be useful to include in those representations information about levels of consciousness and/or accessibility at which various aspects of meaning are found. There is a growing literature on levels of processing and memory for explicit versus implicit information (Kintsch, 1974; J. Keenan, 1975; P. Baggett, 1975; Bransford, Barclay, and Franks, 1972). Most of these studies have dealt with information presented to the subject in paragraphs. Another interesting line of research might involve memory for information presented in natural conversations between two or more interlocutors. For example, are there differences in recall for information that is presented explicitly in conversation vs. information that is presented via anaphora, ellipsis, pronominalization, and so forth? The research cited by Kintsch, J. Keenan, and Baggett suggests that the difference in recognition memory for implicit versus explicit material is time limited. The subject eventually loses the ability to recognize explicitly presented information, and apparently recalls only an integrated structure in which implicit and explicit material are indistinguishable. Presumably, a similar process is going on in natural discourse, in which much of our ongoing analysis of meaning depends on reference to the situation in which meaning is used. There may also be differences in processing and memory depending on the TYPE of implicit material. For example, presupposed material that is crucial to an understanding of the explicit message may be processed differently than entailed or otherwise related material that is "called up" by a message but not necessarily used in decoding that message. Also, our data on children's memory for polite forms suggests that speech acts may be stored in terms of their illocutionary force rather than their explicit surface expression. It would be interesting to determine whether the same phenomena occurs in adult memory for requests and other indirect performatives.

We are far from a complete or even an adequate psychological theory of levels of meaning. A great deal of psycholinguistic research needs to be done to confirm and elaborate a theory of levels of semantic-pragmatic processing and memory. Hence we are not yet ready to propose a formal model for linguistic representation of such levels. Nevertheless, the point at least deserves consideration by psychologists and linguists interested in the relation between formal models and the actual processing of utterances.

A Final Comment

The purpose of this study was to examine the acquisition of pragmatic structures by children, as it relates to general cognitive development. In the process of relating pragmatics to cognition, it may seem that we have clouded the very distinctions that made pragmatics an area of study. Pragmatics was defined as the study of rules for using language, as distinguished from the propositional or semantic content of language. Yet the epistemological model used here derives all linguistic knowledge—pragmatic, semantic, and syntactic—from a cognition-action system. Can pragmatics still be considered a separate area of language science? I think it can.

First, the translation of pragmatic and semantic structures into their cognitive equivalents does not change the fact that these are distinct functional modes during transactions BETWEEN individuals. A description of the linguistic system itself, the set of conventions that exist in a community as a whole, will still require careful attention to the difference between propositions with corresponding truth values, and rules for using statements in different contexts. One can describe the relation between content and objective context (e.g., sociological investigations of language use) without examining the psychological processes that enable individuals to master these rules. In short, the description of conventions, even pragmatic conventions, is a separate enterprise from psychological explanations of how people acquire and use these conventions.

Second, although in the model presented here both pragmatic and semantic structures are made of similar cognitive material, they still constitute separate functional processes at any given moment in speaking. The speaker can simply use a pragmatic procedure to generate a communicative act. Or he can take his own pragmatic procedure as the object or content of a higher procedure. But when he does use procedures as objects, he has changed the function of that procedure at the moment of use. He has shifted cognitive levels. The translatability of rules of use into content greatly enhances the communicative capacity of the system, permitting verbal play and artful shifting between levels. But the distinction between use and content has not disappeared. The speaker has simply decided to assign procedures a different role, at a given moment.

Finally, the epistemological system presented here in a sense establishes pragmatics as the first and primary structure in the ontogenesis of language. Recent psycholinguistic research (e.g., Brown, 1973; Bowerman, 1973) has suggested that syntax might be derived ontogenetically from semantics. We are carrying that suggestion a step farther, proposing that semantics is derived ontogenetically from pragmatics. Austin (1962) notes that "To say something is to do something." Insofar as the content of early utterances is built out of the child's early procedures or action schemes, semantics is derived from efforts to do things with words. Language is a powerful and complex tool, an artificial system that is created by the child in the same way that it evolved historically—in an effort to make meaningful things happen.

References

Ainsworth, M. The development of infant-mother attachment. In B. M. Caldwell and H. Ricciutti (Eds.), *Review of child development research*. Chicago: University of Chicago Press, 1973.

Aksu, A. Request forms used by Turkish children. Unpublished manuscript, University of California at Berkeley, 1973.

Amidon, A., and Carey, P. Why five year olds cannot understand before and after. *Journal of Verbal Learning and Verbal Behavior*, 1972, **11**, 417–423.

Antinucci, F. I presupposti teorici della linguistica di F. Bopp. Rome: Consiglio Nazionale delle Ricerche, Istituto di Psicologia, 1973a.

Antinucci, F. Sulla deissi. Rome: Consiglio Nazionale delle Ricerche, Istituto di Psicologia, 1973b.

Antinucci, F., and Miller, R. How children talk about what happened. Manuscript, Berkeley, 1975.

Antinucci, F., and Parisi, D. Early language acquisition: a second stage. Paper presented at the Conference on Present Problems in Psycholinguistics, Paris, 1972.

Antinucci, F., and Parisi, D. Early language acquisition: a model and some data. In C. Ferguson and D. Slobin (Eds.), *Studies in child language development*. New York: Holt, 1973.

Antinucci, F., and Volterra, V. Lo sviluppo della negazione nel linguaggio infantile: uno studio pragmatico. In *Studi per un Modello del Linguaggio: Quaderni della Ricerca Scientifica*. Rome: Consiglio Nazionale delle Ricerche, Istituto di Psicologia, 1973.

Austin, J. L. *How to do things with words*. New York: Oxford University Press, 1962.

Baggett, P. Memory for explicit and implicit information in picture stories. *Journal of Verbal Learning and Verbal Behavior*, 1975, **14**, 538–548.

Barclay, J. R., and Reid, M. Semantic integration in children's recall of discourse. *Developmental Psychology*, 1974, **10**(2), 277–281.

Baroni, A., Fava, E., and Tirondola, C. L'ordine delle parole nel linguaggio infantile. Unpublished manuscript, University of Padova, 1973.

Bartlett, F. C. *Remembering*. Cambridge: Cambridge University Press, 1932.

Bates, E. The development of conversational skill in 2, 3 and 4 year olds. Unpublished masters thesis, University of Chicago, 1971 (Reprinted in *Pragmatics Microfiche*, 1975, **1**(2), Cambridge University).

355

Bates, E., and Benigni, L. Rules of address in Italy: a sociological survey. *Language in Society,* 1975, **4**, 271–288.

Bates, E., Benigni, L., Bretherton, I., Camaioni, L., and Volterra, V. From gesture to the first word: on cognitive and social prerequisites. Paper presented to the Third International Child Language Symposium, London, 1975. Also to appear in M. Lewis and L. Rosenblum (Eds.), *Origins of behavior: language and communication.* New York: Wiley, 1976.

Bates, E., Camaioni, L., and Volterra, V. The acquisition of performatives prior to speech. Rome: Consiglio Nazionale delle Ricerche, Istituto di Psicologia, 1973. (Rev. ed.) *Merrill-Palmer Quarterly,* 1975, **21**(3).

Bell, S. The development of the concept of object as related to infant-mother attachment. *Child Development,* 1970, **41**, 291–313.

Bergson, H. *Oeuvres.* Paris: Presses Universitaires, 1970.

Birdwhistell, R. *Kinesics and context.* Philadelphia: University of Pennsylvania Press, 1970.

Bloom, L. *Language development: form and function in emerging grammar.* Cambridge, Massachusetts: M.I.T. Press, 1970.

Bloom, L. *One word at a time: the use of single word utterances before syntax.* The Hague: Mouton, 1973.

Bloom, L., Rocissano, L., and Hood, L. Adult-child discourse: developmental interaction between information processing and linguistic knowledge. Manuscript, Columbia University, 1975.

Bobrow, D. C., and Raphael, B. New programming languages for artificial intelligence research. Proceedings from the Third International Joint Conference on Artificial Intelligence, Stanford, 1973.

Bopp, F. *Vergleinchende Grammatik des Sanskrit, Zend, Griechischen, Lateinischen, Litthaunischen, Gothischen und Deutschen.* Berlin, 1833.

Bowerman, M. F. Structural relations in children's utterances: syntactic or semantic? In T. E. Moore (Ed.), *Cognitive development and the acquisition of language.* New York: Academic Press, 1973.

Bowerman, M. F. *Early syntactic development: a cross-linguistic study with special reference to Finnish.* Cambridge: Cambridge University Press, 1973.

Bowerman, M. F. Learning the structure of causative verbs: a study in the relationship of cognitive, semantic and syntactic development. *Papers and Reports on Child Language Development No. 8.* Committee on Linguistics: Stanford University, Stanford, California, 1974.

Bowlby, J. *Attachment and loss: volume I.* London: Hogarth Press, 1969.

Braine, M. D. S. The ontogeny of English phrase structure. In C. Ferguson and D. Slobin (Eds.), *Studies in child language development.* New York: Holt, 1973.

Bransford, J. D., Barclay, J. R., and Franks, J. J. Sentence memory: a constructive versus interpretive approach. *Cognitive Psychology,* 1972, **3**, 193–209.

Bronckardt, J. P., and Sinclair, H. Time, tense and aspect. *Cognition,* 1974.

Brown, A. L. The Development of memory: knowing, knowing about knowing, and knowing how to know. In H. W. Reese (Ed.), *Advances in child development and behavior,* Vol. 10. New York: Academic Press, 1975.

Brown, R. *A first language.* Cambridge, Massachusetts: Harvard University Press, 1973.

Brown, R., Cazden, C., and Bellugi, U. The child's grammar from I to III. In C. Ferguson and D. Slobin (Eds.), *Studies in child language development.* New York: Holt, 1973.

Brown, R., and Ford, M. Address in American English. *Journal of Abnormal and Social Psychology,* 1961, **62**, 375–385.

Brown, R., and Gilman, A. The pronouns of power and solidarity. In T. Sebeok (Ed), *Style in language.* Cambridge, Massachusetts: M.I.T. Press, 1960.

Brown, R., and Hanlon, C. Derivational complexity and the order of acquisition in child speech. In J. Hayes (Ed.), *Cognition and the development of language.* New York: Wiley, 1970.

Bruner, J. The course of cognitive growth. *American Psychologist,* 1964, **19,** 1–15.

Bruner, J. S. Organization of early skilled action. *Child Development,* 1973, **44,** 1–11.

Carter, A. Communication in the sensorimotor period. Unpublished doctoral dissertation, University of California at Berkeley, 1974.

Chafe, W. *Meaning and the structure of language.* Chicago: University of Chicago Press, 1970.

Chomsky, N. *Syntactic structures.* Cambridge, Massachusetts: M.I.T. Press, 1957.

Chomsky, N. *Aspects of a theory of syntax.* Cambridge, Massachusetts: M.I.T. Press, 1965.

Chomsky, N. *Language and mind.* New York: Harcourt, 1968.

Chomsky, N. Deep structure, surface structure, and semantic interpretation. In D. Steinberg and J. Jakobovitz (Eds.), *Semantics.* Cambridge: Cambridge University Press, 1972.

Clancy, P. The acquisition of conjunctions in Italian. Unpublished manuscript, University of California at Berkeley, 1974.

Clark, E. How children describe time and order. In C. Ferguson and D. Slobin (Eds.), *Studies in child language development.* New York: Holt, 1973.

Clark, H. Space, time, semantics, and the child. In T. E. Moore (Ed.), *Cognitive development and the acquisition of language.* New York: Academic Press, 1973.

DeLaguna, G. *Speech: its function and development.* Bloomington, Indiana: Indiana University Press, 1927.

DeVilliers, J., and DeVilliers, P. Competence and performance in child language: are children really competent to judge? *Journal of Child Language,* 1974, **1,** 11–22.

Devries, R. The development of role-taking as reflected by behavior of bright, average and retarded children in a social guessing game. *Child Development,* 1970, **41,** 759–770.

Dewey, J., and Bentley, A. F. *Knowing and the known.* Boston: Beacon Press, 1949.

Dezso, L. A gyermeknyelv mondattananak elvi-modszertani kerdesei. *Altalanos Nyelvestzeti Tanulmanyok,* 1970, **7,** 77–99.

Dore, J. On the development of speech acts. Unpublished doctoral dissertation, City University of New York, 1973.

Dowty, D. On the syntax and semantics of the atomic predicate CAUSE. *Papers from the Sixth Regional Meeting of the Chicago Linguistic Society,* 1972.

Drach, K. The language of the parent: a pilot study. In *The structure of linguistic input to the child,* Working Paper No. 14, University of California Language Behavior Research Laboratory, 1969.

Duncan, S. Non-verbal communication. *Psychological Bulletin,* 1969, **72,** 119–137.

Eibl-Eibesfeldt,I. *Ethology: the biology of behavior.* New York: Holt, 1970.

Ervin-Tripp, S. On sociolinguistic rules: alternation and cooccurence. In J. Gumperz and D. Hymes (Eds.), *Directions in sociolinguistics.* New York: Holt, 1972.

Ervin-Tripp, S. Children's understanding and production of requests. Paper presented at the Stanford Child Language Forum, Stanford, 1974.

Ervin-Tripp, S. Is Sybil there?—The structure of American directives. *Language in Society,* in press.

Fantz, R. L. Pattern discrimination and selective attention as determinants of perceptual development from birth. In A. J. Kidd and J. L. Rivoire (Eds.), *Perceptual development in children.* New York: International Universities Press, 1966.

Farris, D., and Bates, E. The development of coyness and greeting behavior in 2, 3 and 4 year olds. Unpublished paper, University of Chicago, 1971.

Feldman, C. Questions in meaning structure: what did you say? Unpublished paper, University of Chicago, 1971.

Feldman, C. The interaction of sentence characteristics and mode of presentation in recall. *Language and Speech,* 1971, **14,** 18–25.

Feldman, C., and Hass, W. *Sentence meaning: a psycholinguistic theory of communication.* In press.

Feldman, C., Lee, B., McLean, J. D., Pillemer, D. B., and Murray, J. R. *The development of adaptive intelligence.* San Francisco: Jossey Bass Publishers, 1974.

Ferguson, C., and Slobin, D. (Eds.).*Studies in child language development.*New York: Holt, 1973.

Fillenbaum, S. *Syntactic factors in memory?* The Hague: Mouton, 1973.

Fillmore, C. The case for case. In E. Bach and R. T. Harms (Eds.), *Universals in linguistic theory.* New York: Holt, 1968.

Fillmore, C. Types of lexical information. In D. Steinberg and J. Jakobovitz (Eds.), *Semantics.* Cambridge: Cambridge University Press, 1971.

Firbas, J. On defining the theme in functional sentence analysis. *Travaux Linguistique de Prague,* 1964, **1,** 267–280.

Flavell, J. Stage related properties of cognitive development. *Cognitive Psychology,* 1971, **2,** 421–453.

Flavell, J., Botkin, P. T., Fry, C. L., Wright, J. W., and Jarvis, P. E. *The development of role-taking and communication skills in children.* New York: Wiley, 1968.

Fodor, J. How to learn to talk: some simple ways. In F. Smith and G. A. Miller (Eds.), *The genesis of language.* Cambridge, Massachusetts: M.I.T. Press, 1966.

Fraser, B. An examination of the performative analysis. Mimeograph, Harvard University, 1971.

Freedman, D. G. The origins of social behavior. In U. Bronfenbrenner (Ed.), *Influences on human development.* Illinois: Dryden Press, 1972.

Frege, G. *Philosophical writings.* P. Geech and M. Black (Eds.). Oxford: Basil Blackwell, 1952.

Friedrich, P. Structural implications of Russian pronominal usage. In W. Bright (Ed.), *Sociolinguistics.* The Hague: Mouton, 1966.

Furth, H. *Thinking without language: Psychological implications of deafness.* New York: The Free Press, 1966.

Gardner, R. A., and Gardner, B. J. Teaching signs to a chimpanzee. *Science,* 1969, **165,** 664–672.

Garvey, C. Requests and responses in children's speech. *Journal of Child Language,* 1975, **2,** 41–64.

Geis, M., and Zwicky, A. M. On invited inferences. *Linguistic Inquiry,* 1971, **2,** 561–566.

Givon, T. Toward a discourse definition of syntax. Manuscript, Department of Linguistics, UCLA, 1974.

Givon, T. Topic, pronoun and grammatical agreement. Unpublished manuscript, Department of Linguistics, UCLA, 1974.

Goodall, J. A preliminary report on expressive movements and communication in the Gombe Stream chimpanzees. In P. Jay (Ed.), *Primates: studies in adaptation and variability.* New York: Holt, 1968.

Gordon, D. A developmental study of the semantics of factivity in the verbs "know," "think," and "remember." University of Michigan Phonetics Laboratory, *National Language Studies No. 15,* 1974.

Gordon, D., and Lakoff, G. Conversational postulates. *Papers from the Seventh Regional Meeting of the Chicago Linguistic Society,* 1971.

Greenfield, P., Nelson, K., and Saltzman, E. The development of rulebound strategies for manipulating seriated cups: a parallel between action and grammar. *Cognitive Psychology,* 1972, **3,** 291–311.

Greenfield, P., and Smith, J. *The structure of communication in early language development.* New York: Academic Press, 1976.

Grice, H. P. The logic of conversation. Unpublished paper, University of California at Berkeley, 1968.

Grice, H. P. Logic and conversation. In P. Cole and J. L. Morgan (Eds.), *Syntax and semantics, volume 3: Speech acts.* New York: Academic Press, 1975.

Gruber, J. Topicalization in child language. *Foundations of Language*, 1967, **3**, 37–65.

Gruber, J. Correlations between the syntactic constructions of the child and the adult. In D. I. Slobin and C. Ferguson (Eds.), *Studies in child language development.* New York: Holt, 1973.

Guzman, A. Computer recognition of 3-dimensional objects in a visual scene. *American Federation of Information Processing Conference Proceedings*, 1968, 33–291.

Gvozdev, A. N. *Voprosy izucheniya detskoy rechi.* Moscow: Aka. Edag. Nauk RSFSR, 1961.

Halliday, M. A. K. Notes on transitivity and theme in English, part 2. *Journal of Linguistics*, 1967, **3**, 199–244.

Halliday, M. A. K. Language structure and language function. In J. Lyons (Ed.), *New horizons in linguistics.* Baltimore: Pelican, 1970.

Halliday, M. A. K. Early language learning: a sociolinguistic approach. Paper prepared for the IXth International Congress of Anthropological and Ethnological Sciences, Chicago, 1973.

Halliday, M. A. K. *Learning how to mean: Explorations in the development of language.* London: Edward Arnold, 1975.

Harris, Z. Cooccurrence and transformation in linguistic structure. *Language*, 1957, **33**, 283–340.

Hatcher, A. G. Syntax and the sentence. *Word*, 1956, **12**, 234–239.

Haviland, S., and Clark, H. What's new? Acquiring new information as a process in comprehension. *Journal of Verbal Learning and Verbal Behavior*, 1974, **13**, 512–521.

Hewes, G. W. Primate communication and the gestural origin of language. *Current Anthropology*, 1973, **14**(1–2), 5–24.

Hewitt, C. Actor. Proceedings from the Third International Joint Conference on Artificial Intelligence, Stanford, 1973.

Hinde, R. *Animal behavior.* New York: McGraw-Hill, 1966.

Holzmann, H. The use of interrogative forms in the verbal interaction of three mothers and their children. *Journal of Psycholinguistic Research*, 1972, **1**, 211–236.

Hornby, P. The psychological subject and predicate. *Cognitive Psychology*, 1972, **3**, 632–643.

Hornby, P., and Hass, W. Use of contrastive stress by preschool children. *Journal of Speech and Hearing Research*, 1970, **13**, 395–399.

Hoy, E. The measurement of egocentrism in children's communication. *Developmental Psychology*, 1975, **11**(3), 392.

Huttenlocher, J. Origins of language comprehension. In R. Solso (Ed.), *Theories in cognitive psychology.* Hillsdale, New Jersey: Erlbaum Associates, 1974.

Ingram, D. Transitivity in child language. *Language*, 1971, **47**, 888–910.

Ingram, D. Stages in the development of one-word sentences. Paper presented at the Stanford Child Language Forum, Stanford, 1974.

Jackendoff, R. *Semantic interpretation in generative grammar.* Cambridge, Massachusetts: M.I.T. Press, 1972.

Jacobsen, T. On the order of emergence of conjunctions and notions of conjunctions in English-speaking children. Unpublished manuscript, University of California at Berkeley, 1974.

Karttunen, L. Counterfactual conditionals. *Linguistic Inquiry*, 1971, **2**, 566–569.

Keenan, E. Conversational competence in children. *Journal of Child Language*, 1974, **1**(2), 163–183.

Keenan, E. O. Topic as a discourse notion: a study in the conversations of children and adults. In Charles Li (Ed.), *Subject and topic.* New York: Academic Press, 1976.

Keenan, E. O., and Klein, E. Coherency in children's discourse. *Journal of Psycholinguistic Research*, 1975.

Keenan, J. M. The role of episodic information in the assessment of semantic memory representations for sentences. Unpublished doctoral dissertation, University of Colorado, 1975.

Kiefer, F. On presuppositions. In F. Kiefer and N. Ruwet (Eds.), *Generative grammar in Europe*. Dordrecht: Reidel, 1973.

Kintsch, W. *Representation of meaning in memory*. Hillsdale, New Jersey: Erlbaum Associates, 1974.

Kohlberg, L. Stage and sequence: the cognitive-developmental approach to socialization. In D. A. Goslin (Ed.), *Handbook of socialization theory and research*. New York: Rand McNally, 1969.

Kohler, W. *The mentality of apes*. New York: Harcourt, 1927.

Krauss, R., and Glucksberg, S. The development of communication: competence as a function of age. *Child Development*, 1969, **40**, 255–266.

Lakoff, G. Linguistics and natural logic. *Studies in generative semantics, No. 1*, Phonetics Laboratory, University of Michigan, 1970.

Lakoff, G. Hedges: a study in meaning criteria and the logic of fuzzy concepts. *Papers from the Eighth Regional Meeting of the Chicago Linguistic Society*, 1972.

Lakoff, G. The inseparability of semantics and pragmatics. Paper presented at the Texas Conference of Performances, Conversational Implicature, and Presuppositions, Austin, Texas, 1973.

Lakoff, G., and Ross, J. R. Is deep structure necessary? Mimeograph, Cambridge, Mass., 1967.

Lakoff, R. Ifs, ands and buts about conjunction. In C. Fillmore and T. Langendoen (Eds.), *Linguistic universals*. New York: Holt, 1971.

Lakoff, R. The logic of politeness: or minding your P's and Q's. *Papers from the Ninth Regional Meeting of the Chicago Linguistic Society*, 1973(a).

Lakoff, R. Language and woman's place. *Language and Society*, 1973(b), **2**, 45–80.

Larkin, D., and O'Malley, M. H. Declarative sentence and the rule-of-conversation hypothesis. *Papers from the Ninth Regional Meeting of the Chicago Linguistic Society*, 1973.

Lawson, C. Request patterns in a two-year-old. Unpublished manuscript, University of California at Berkeley, 1967.

Lenneberg, E. H. *The biological foundations of language*. New York: Wiley, 1967.

Lock, A. Acts not sentences. In W. von Raffler-Engel and Y. Lebrun (Eds.), *Baby talk and infant speech*. Holland: Swets and Zeitlinger B. V., in press. (First presented at the Second International Child Language Symposium, Florence, 1972. Original title: *From out of nowhere . . .*)

Lord, C. Variations in the patterns of acquisition of negation. Paper presented at the Stanford Child Language Forum, Stanford, 1974.

Lyons, J. The linguistic development of young children. Project reports. *Journal of Child Language*, 1974, **1**, 157–162.

Lyons, J., and Wales, R. J. (Eds.), *Psycholinguistic papers: proceedings from the 1966 Edinburgh Conference*. Edinburgh: Edinburgh University Press, 1966.

MacWhinney, B. How Hungarian children learn to speak. Unpublished doctoral dissertation, University of California at Berkeley, 1974.

MacWhinney, B. Pragmatic patterns in child syntax. *Papers and Reports on Child Language Development*, Stanford University, 1975(a), **10**.

MacWhinney, B. Psycholinguistic approach to pragmatic focusing. Unpublished manuscript, University of Denver, 1975(b).

MacWhinney, B., and Bates, E. A cross-cultural study of pragmatic processes. Paper presented at the Third International Child Language Symposium, London, September, 1975.

Maratsos, M. Non-egocentric communicative abilities in preschool children. *Child Development*, 1973(a), 697–700.

Maratsos, M. The effects of stress on the understanding of pronominal coreference in children. *Journal of psycholinguistic Research*, 1973(b), **2**, 1–8.

Maratsos, M. Preschool children's use of definite and indefinite articles. *Child Development,* 1974, **45,** 446–455.

Marvin, R. Attachment, role-taking and communicative behavior in 2, 3 and 4 year olds. Unpublished doctoral dissertation, University of Chicago, 1972.

Maxwell, E. Graphical representation of semantic fields. Mimeograph, Northeastern Illinois University, 1973.

McCawley, J. The role of semantics in a grammar. In E. Bach and R. T. Harms (Eds.), *Universals in linguistic theory.* New York: Holt, 1968.

McCawley, J. Tense and time reference in English. In C. Fillmore and T. Langendoen (Eds.), *Linguistic universals.* New York: Holt, 1971.

McCawley, J. Remarks on the lexicography of performative verbs. Paper presented at the Texas Conference on Performances, Conversational Implications, and Presuppositions, Austin, Texas, 1973.

MacClay, H. Overview. In D. Steinberg and J. Jakobivitz (Eds.), *Semantics.* Cambridge: Cambridge University Press, 1971.

MacNamara, J. The cognitive basis of language learning in infants. *Psychological Review,* 1972, **79,** 1–13.

McNeill, D. The creation of language by children. In J. Lyons and R. J. Wales (Eds.), *Psycholinguistic papers: proceedings from the 1966 Edinburgh Conference.* Edinburgh: Edinburgh University Press, 1966.

McNeill, D. *The acquisition of language.* New York: Harper and Row, 1970.

McNeill, D. Semiotic extension. Paper presented at the Loyola Symposium on Cognition, Chicago, 1974.

Mehler, J., and Savin, H. Memory process in the language user. In T. Bever and W. Weksel (Eds.), *The structure and psychology of language.* New York: Holt, 1969.

Menyuk, P. *Sentences children use.* Cambridge, Massachusetts: M.I.T. Press, 1969.

Michotte, A. *The perception of causality.* New York: Basic Books, 1963.

Miller, G. The magic number $7 + 2$. In G. Miller, *The psychology of communication.* New York: Penguin, 1970.

Miller, G., Galanter, E., and Pribram, K. *Plans and the structure of behavior.* New York: Holt, 1960.

Minsky, M., and Papert, S. Research at the laboratory in vision, language, and other problems of intelligence. *Artificial Intelligence Progress Report,* Memo No. 252. Cambridge, Massachusetts: M.I.T., 1972.

Moore, T. (Ed.). *Cognitive development and the acquisition of language.* New York: Academic Press, 1973.

Morris, C. *Signs, language and behavior.* Englewood Cliffs, New Jersey: Prentice-Hall, 1946.

Mueller, E. The maintenance of verbal exchanges between young children. *Child Development,* 1972, **43**(3), 930–938.

Neisser, U. *Cognitive psychology.* New York: Appleton-Century-Crofts, 1967.

Nelson, K. Structure and strategy in learning to talk. *Monographs of the Society for Research in Child Development,* 1973, **38,** 1–2, No. 149.

Olson, G. Developmental changes in memory and the acquisition of language. In T. Moore (Ed.), *Cognitive Development and the acquisition of language.* New York: Academic Press, 1973.

Paris, S. G. Integration and inference in children's comprehension and memory. In F. Restle, R. Shiffrin, J. Castellan, H. Lindman, and D. Pisoni (Eds.), *Cognitive theory: Volume I.* Hillsdale, New Jersey: Erlbaum Associates, 1975.

Parisi, D. What is behind child utterances? *Journal of Child Language,* 1974, **2,** 97–105.

Parisi, D., and Antinucci, F. *Elementi di grammatica.* Turino: Boringhieri, 1973. Published in English translation as *Essentials of grammar* (trans. Elizabeth Bates). New York: Academic Press, 1976.

Parisi, D., and Giannelli, W. Language and social environment at two years. CNR, Institute of Psychology, Rome, Italy, 1974.

Parisi, D., and Puglielli, A. Hopping adverbs. *Proceedings of the XIth International Congress of Linguists,* Bologna, 1972.

Park, T. Z. A study of German language development. Unpublished manuscript, Psychological Institute, Berne, Switzerland, 1974.

Pascual-Leone, J. A mathematical model for the transition rule in Piaget's developmental stages. *Acta Psychologica,* 1970, **32**, 301–345.

Peal, E., and Lambert, W. The relation of bilingualism to intelligence. *Psychology Monographs,* 1962, **76**, 1–23.

Peirce, C. *Collected papers.* C. Hartshorne and P. Weiss, (Eds.). Cambridge, Massachusetts: Harvard University Press, 1932.

Pfuderer, C., Drach, K., and Kobashigawa, B. *The structure of linguistic input to children.* Working Paper No. 14, Language Behavior Research Laboratory, University of California at Berkeley, 1969.

Piaget, J. *The language and thought of the child.* New York: Harcourt, 1926.

Piaget, J. *The construction of reality in the child.* New York: Ballantine, 1954.

Piaget, J. *Play, dreams and imitation in childhood.* New York: Norton, 1962.

Piaget, J. *Genetic epistemology.* New York: Norton, 1970.

Piaget, J. *La prise de conscience.* Paris: Presses Universitaires de France, 1974.

Piaget, J., and Inhelder, B. *The psychology of the child.* New York: Basic Books, 1969.

Piaget, J., and Inhelder, B. *Memory and intelligence.* New York: Basic Books, 1972.

Piaget, J., Inhelder, B., and Szeminska, A. *The child's conception of geometry.* New York: Basic Books, 1960.

Pittenger, R., Hockett, C., and Danehy, J. *The first five minutes.* New York: Martineau, 1960.

Postal, P. The best theory. In S. Peters (Ed.), *Goals in linguistic theory.* Englewood Cliffs, New Jersey: Prentice Hall, 1972.

Poulsen, D. P. The development of memory: a study of recall and recognition of information in narratives and pictorial sequences. Unpublished doctoral dissertation, University of Colorado, 1976.

Price-Williams, D. R. A study concerning concepts of conservation of quantities among primitive children. In D. R. Price-Williams (Ed.), *Cross-cultural studies.* Middlesex: Penguin, 1970.

Puglielli, A., and Ciliberti, A. Il condizionale. *Atti del VI Convegno Internazionale della Societa Linguistica Italiana.* Rome: Bulzoni, 1973.

Quine, W. *Word and object.* New York: Wiley, 1960.

Radulovij. Unpublished doctoral dissertation, University of California at Berkeley, 1975.

Roeper, T. Theoretical implications of word order, topicalization, and inflections in German language acquisition. In D. Slobin and C. Ferguson (Eds.), *Studies in child language development.* New York: Holt, 1973.(a)

Roeper, T. Connecting children's language and linguistic theory. In T. Moore (Ed.), *Cognitive development and the acquisition of language.* New York: Academic Press, 1973.(b)

Rommetveit, R. *On message structure.* New York: Wiley, 1974.

Rosch, E. On the internal structure of perceptual and cognitive categories. In T. Moore (Ed.), *Cognitive development and the acquisition of language.* New York: Academic Press, 1973.

Ross, J. R. On declarative sentences. In R. A. Jakobs and P. S. Rosenbana (Eds.), *Readings in English transformational grammar.* Waltham, Massachusetts: Ginn, 1970.

Ross, J. R. The category squish: endstation hauptwort. *Papers from the Eighth Regional Meeting of the Chicago Linguistic Society,* 1972.

Russell, B. On denoting. *Mind,* 1905, **14**, 479–493.

Sachs, J. Recognition memory for syntactic and semantic aspects of connected discourse. *Perception and Psychophysics*, 1967, **2**, 437–444.

Sadock, J. Speech act idioms. *Papers from the Eighth Regional Meeting of the Chicago Linguistic Society*, 1972.

Sadock, J. *Toward a linguistic theory of speech acts.* New York: Seminar Press, 1974.

Schlesinger, I. M. Relational concepts underlying language. Paper presented at the NICHD Conference on Language Intervention with the Mentally Retarded, Wisconsin Dells, Wisconsin, 1973. (Reprinted in R. Schiefelbusch and L. Lloyd (Eds.), *Language perspectives—acquisition, retardation and intervention.* Baltimore: University Park Press, 1974.)

Scollon, R. The acquisition of discourse. Unpublished doctoral dissertation, University of Hawaii, 1973.

Searle, J. What is a speech act? In M. Black (Ed.), *Philosophy in America.* Ithaca, N.Y.: Cornell University Press, 1965.

Sechehaye, M. A. *Essai sur la structure logique de la phrase.* Paris: Champion, 1926.

Selman, R. Taking another's perspective: role-taking development in early childhood. *Child Development*, 1971, **42**, 1721–1734.

Sgall, P., Hajicova, E., and Benesova, E. *Topic, focus and generative semantics.* Kronberg-Tanns: Scriptor Verlag, 1973.

Shantz, C. U. The development of social cognition. In E. M. Hetherington (Ed.), *Review of child development research: Volume 5.* Chicago: University of Chicago press, 1975.

Shatz, M. The comprehension of indirect directives: Can two-year-olds shut the door? Paper presented to the Linguistic Society of America, summer 1974.

Shatz, M. How young children respond to language: procedures for answering. Paper presented to the Stanford Child Language Forum, Stanford, 1975.

Shatz, M., and Gelman, R. The development of communication skills: modifications in the speech of young children as a function of the listener. *Society for Research of Child Development Monographs*, 1973, **5**, 1–38.

Silverstein, M. Hierarchy of features and ergativity. Paper presented to the Chicago Linguistic Society, January 1973.

Silverstein, M. *Shifters, linguistic categories and cultural description.* In preparation.

Sinclair, R. Communication competence in young children. Paper presented to the Third International Child Language Symposium, London, 1975.

Sinclair, H. Developmental psycholinguistics. In D. Elkind and J. Flavell (Eds.), *Studies in cognitive development.* New York: Oxford University Press, 1969.

Sinclair, H. The transition from sensorimotor behavior to symbolic activity. *Interchange*, 1970, **1**, 119–126.

Sinclair, H. Sensorimotor action patterns as a condition for the acquisition of syntax. In R. Huxley and E. Ingram (Eds.), *Language acquisition: models and methods.* New York: Academic Press, 1972.

Sinclair, H. Language acquisition and cognitive development. In T. Moore (Ed.), *Cognitive development and the acquisition of language.* New York: Academic Press, 1973.

Sinclair, H. Remarks addressed to the Stanford Child Language Forum, Stanford, 1974.

Sinclair, H., and Bronckardt, J. P. SVO a linguistic universal? *Journal of Experimental Child Psychology*, 1972, **14**, 329–346.

Sinclair, J., and Coulthard, R. M. *Towards an analysis of discourse: the English used by teachers and pupils.* London: Oxford University Press, 1974.

Slobin, D. The acquisition of Russian as a native language. In F. Smith and G. Miller (Eds.), *Genesis of language.* Cambridge, Massachusetts: M.I.T. Press, 1966.

Slobin, D. Cognitive prerequisites for grammar. In C. Ferguson and D. Slobin (Eds.), *Studies in child language development.* New York: Holt, 1973.

Slobin, D. On learning about language by watching it change through time . . . Invited address, Stanford University Child Language Forum, Stanford, 1975.

Slobin, D., and Welsh, C. Elicited imitation as a research tool in developmental psycholinguistics. In C. Ferguson and D. Slobin (Eds.), *Studies in child language development*. New York: Holt, 1973.

Slobin, D. (Ed.). *Field manual for the cross-cultural study of the acquisition of communicative competence*. University of California at Berkeley Bookstore, 1967.

Slobin, D. (Ed.). *Field manual for a study of the acquisition of language in four cultures*. Mimeograph, University of California at Berkeley, 1974.

Snow, C. Mother's speech to children learning language. *Child Development*, 1972, **43**, 549–565.

Snyder, L. Pragmatics in language-deficient children: prelinguistic and early verbal performatives and presuppositions. Unpublished doctoral dissertation, University of Colorado, 1975.

Sokolov, E. N. *Perception and the conditioned reflex*. Moscow: University of Moscow Press, 1958.

Spitz, R. *The first year of life*. New York: International Universities Press, 1965.

St. Anselm. *Proslogium*. London: Open Court Publishing Company, 1910.

Stokoe, W. *Semiotics and human sign language*. The Hague: Mouton, 1972.

Strawson, P. F. On referring. *Mind*, 1950, 59.

Sugarman, S. A description of communicative development in the prelanguage child. Honors thesis, Hampshire College, 1973.

Svachkin, N. The development of phonemic speech perception in early childhood. In C. Ferguson and D. Slobin (Eds.), *Studies in child language development*. New York: Holt, 1973.

Trubetskoy, N. S. Grundzuge der Phonologie. Travaux Linguistique de Circle de Prague, 1939, **7**.

Tyler, S. *Cognitive anthropology*. New York: Holt, 1969.

Uzgiris, I. C. Patterns of cognitive development in infancy. *Merrill-Palmer Quarterly*, 1973, **19**, 181–204.

Uzgiris, I. C., and Hunt, J. McV. *Toward ordinal scales of psychological development in infancy*. Champaign, Illinois: University of Illinois Press, 1975.

van Dijk, T. A. Text grammar and logic. In J. S. Petafi and H. Riser (Eds.), *Studies in text grammar*. Dordrecht: Riedel, 1973.

Veneziano, E. Analysis of wish sentences in the one-word stage of language acquisition: a cognitive approach. Unpublished Master's thesis, Tufts University, Medford, Massachusetts, 1973.

Vennemann, T. Topics, sentence accent, ellipsis: a proposal for their formal treatment. In E. L. Keenan (Ed.), *Formal semantics in natural language*. Cambridge University Press, in press.

Volterra, V. Nota in margine sul participio passato nel linguaggio infantile. Unpublished paper, 1974.

Volterra, V. Come viene vissuta nel linguaggio di un bambino di due anni l'attesa di una sorellina. Unpublished manuscript. Rome: Consiglio Nazionale delle Ricerche, Istituto di Psicologia, 1975.

Vygotsky, L. S. *Thought and language*. Cambridge, Massachusetts: M.I.T. Press, 1962.

Wales, R. J., and Marshall, J. C. Linguistic performance. In J. Lyons and R. J. Wales (Eds.), *Psycholinguistic papers: proceedings from the 1966 Edinburgh Conference*. Edinburgh: Edinburgh University Press, 1966.

Weiman, L. *Stress in child language*. Unpublished doctoral dissertation, University of Washington, 1974.

Weizenbaum, J. *Communications of the Association for Computing Machines*, 1966, **9**, 36–45.

Werner, H., and Kaplan, B. *Symbol formation: an organismic-developmental approach to language and the expression of thought*. New York: Wiley, 1963.

Wertsch, J. Simply. *Papers from the Tenth Regional Meeting of the Chicago Linguistic Society,* 1974.

Winograd, T. *Understanding natural language.* New York: Academic Press, 1972.

Winston, P. Learning structural designs from examples. In P. Winston (Ed.), *The psychology of computer vision.* New York: McGraw Hill, 1975.

Wittgenstein, L. *The blue and the brown books.* New York: Harper and Row, 1958.

Wittgenstein, L. *Philosophical investigations.* Oxford: Blackwell, 1972.

Wolff, P. The natural history of crying and other vocalizations in early infancy. In B. M. Foss (Ed.), *Determinants of infant behavior.* New York: Methuen, 1969.

Yngve, V. A model and an hypothesis for language structure. *Proceedings of the American Philosophical Society,* 1960, **104,** 444–466.

Zadeh, L. A. Calculus of fuzzy restrictions. In L. A. Zadeh, K.-S. Fu, K. Tanaka, and M. Shimura (Eds.), *Fuzzy sets and their applications to cognitive and decision processes.* New York: Academic Press, 1975.

Author Index

Page numbers refer to citations within the text. Complete references are listed on pages 355–365.

A

Ainsworth, M. S., 338
Aksu, A., 290
Amidion, A., 115
Antinucci, F., 43, 47, 50, 80–82, 97, 99–101, 105–107, 115–116, 125–126, 128, 143, 150–153, 161, 182–183, 191, 204–205, 211, 224, 254, 349
Austin, J. L., 8, 14–15, 19, 22–23, 271, 354

B

Baggett, P., 352
Barclay, J. R., 115, 325, 352
Baroni, A., 168, 198–199, 210
Bartlett, F. C., 11
Bates, E., 44–47, 50, 62–63, 79, 89, 97, 205, 207, 293, 324, 327, 338, 344
Bell, S., 70, 333, 338
Benesova, E., 166
Benigni, L., 45, 63, 79, 89, 293, 324, 338
Bentley, A. F., 3
Bergson, H., 99
Birdwhistell, R., 46, 350
Bloom, L., 47, 80–83, 98, 115, 185, 345
Bobrow, D. C., 31–32, 350
Bopp, F., 106
Botkin, P. T., 333

B (continued)

Bowerman, M. F., 50, 80–81, 109, 119, 178–180, 185, 190, 199, 354
Bowlby, J., 46–47, 58–59
Braine, M. D. S., 126, 175, 187, 197
Bransford, J. D., 115, 325, 352
Bretherton, I., 63, 79, 89, 293, 338
Bronckardt, J. P., 115, 180, 345
Brown, A. L., 115
Brown, R., 4, 44–45, 68, 117, 162, 176, 178–180, 187, 194, 199, 224, 257–258, 290–291, 316, 323–324, 354
Bruner, J., 51–52, 340

C

Camaioni, L., 44–47, 63, 79, 89, 97, 293, 327, 338
Carey, P., 115
Carter, A., 69
Castelfranchi, 163, 166, 182–183, 191
Chafe, W., 168, 197, 199, 285, 291
Chomsky, N., 4–7, 43, 93, 161–162, 168, 175, 177, 179, 182, 345
Clancy, P., 115
Clark, E., 115
Clark, H., 168–169, 251
Coulthard, R., 115

367

Subject Index